NATIONAL
GEOGRAPHIC
TRAVELER

new zealand

new zealand

By Peter Turner
Photography by Colin Monteath

National Geographic
Washington, D.C.

CONTENTS

Pages 2–3: Mt. Adams, Westland National Park
Left: Oriental Bay graces Wellington's waterfront

TRAVELING WITH EYES OPEN

Alert travelers go with a purpose and leave with a benefit. If you travel responsibly, you can help support wildlife conservation, historic preservation, and cultural enrichment in the places you visit. You can enrich your own travel experience as well.

To be a geo-savvy traveler:

- Recognize that your presence has an impact on the places you visit.

- Spend your time and money in ways that sustain local character. (Besides, it's more interesting that way.)

- Value the destination's natural and cultural heritage.

- Respect the local customs and traditions.

- Express appreciation to local people about things you find interesting and unique to the place: its nature, scenery, music or food, historic villages, and buildings.

- Vote with your wallet: Support the people who support the place, patronizing businesses that make an effort to celebrate and protect what's special about the place. Seek out shops, local restaurants, inns, and tour operators who love the place—who love taking care of it and showing it off. Avoid businesses that detract from the character of the place.

- Enrich yourself, taking home more memories and stories to tell, knowing that you have contributed to the preservation and en-hancement of the destination.

That is the type of travel now called geotourism, defined as "tourism that sustains or enhances the geographical character of a place—its environment, culture, aesthetics, heritage, and the well-being of its residents." To learn more, visit National Geographic's Center for Sustainable Destinations at *www .nationalgeographic.com/travel/sustainable.*

NATIONAL GEOGRAPHIC
TRAVELER

new zealand

ABOUT THE AUTHOR & THE PHOTOGRAPHER

Peter Turner

Drawn by family ties and a love of New Zealand's natural splendor, Peter Turner has been a regular visitor to the Land of the Long White Cloud for more than two decades, traveling the length and breadth of the country numerous times on writing assignments. Australian by birth, journalist by trade, and wanderer by nature, he has worked as an editor, publisher, and journalist in Australia and for newspapers in Indonesia, Thailand, and Brunei. As a travel writer and photographer specializing in Southeast Asia and the South Pacific, he has contributed to newspapers and magazines worldwide and to more than 20 guidebooks.

Colin Monteath

Based in Christchurch, New Zealand, Colin Monteath is a freelance photographer, writer, and mountaineer who has traveled widely in the polar and high mountain regions of the world. In 1983, he started Hedgehog House New Zealand, a photographic library that specializes in polar, mountain, natural history, and travel imagery.

Colin has spent 28 seasons working in Antarctica and has taken part in 20 Himalayan expeditions. His assignments have taken him to countries on nearly every continent, and his pictures and stories have appeared in *National Geographic, Time, New Zealand Geographic,* and many other publications around the world.

Charting Your Trip

Nature has blessed the big islands of the South Pacific with magnificent landscapes: peaks, deserts, volcanoes, seas, forests, and beaches. Here's how to make the most of your visit.

In addition to being a natural paradise, New Zealand is also a fascinating mix of cultures, its cities steeped in English heritage and its society shaped by Maori history. Welcoming, well-equipped, and easy to navigate, New Zealand offers a host of fresh-air activities, from outdoor adventures to wildlife viewing.

How to Visit

New Zealand is neatly divided into two similarly sized islands, both wonderfully scenic in their own way and with their own character. If you are on a short visit of a week or so, it's best to concentrate on one island, but it's also possible to get in all the highlights of both.

A one-week highlights tour would most likely include Auckland–Rotorua–Christchurch–Mount Cook–Queenstown–Milford Sound–glaciers and return to Christchurch/Auckland. That itinerary is action-packed, and is best arranged as a package tour with internal flights and arranged bus transportation. However, if you have the time to travel at a more leisurely pace, you can easily get around independently by car; buses and flights are also readily available.

Two or three weeks will allow you to really appreciate New Zealand without busting your spleen. In two weeks, you can savor all the highlights of the North and South Islands listed above, while three weeks or more give you access to a host of other wonderful places.

Starting in the North

The main attractions of the North Island can be summed up as Maori culture, volcanoes, and beaches. More intensively farmed and populated, the North Island provides more settled, rural vistas, but natural wonders also abound. A North Island one-week tour might be: Auckland–Bay of Islands–Rotorua–Lake Taupo–Tongariro National Park–Wellington. With a rental car you could also make a few side trips. Bus tours include a number of points of interest

Maori carving

between the main sights.

The first stop for most visitors, the country's main metropolis of Auckland lies on a wonderful harbor. This is a great Pacific Rim city, with a host of cultural attractions, fantastic scenery, and the country's best restaurants, nightlife, and shopping.

Maori, the indigenous peoples, always favored the warmer North Island and, for the visitor, Maori culture is at its most accessible in Rotorua, a three-hour drive south of Auckland. The country's main tourist destination, Rotorua is also famed for its geysers and bubbling mud pools.

Two other North Island standouts are also within easy reach of Auckland: The superb seascapes and rich history of the Bay of Islands await about four hours north, and the impossibly scenic volcanoes of Tongariro National Park near Lake Taupo stand a five-hour drive south.

The nation's capital, Wellington, a five-hour drive south of Tongariro, is much smaller than Auckland but no less scenic, with a fine harbor of its own. At the southern tip of the North Island, Wellington is the place to get ferries to the South Island.

Moving South

The main attractions of the South Island are the Southern Alps, the fjords, and the glaciers. For most visitors, the South Island encapsulates New Zealand's magnificent wilderness and, for this reason, many favor the South over the North.

Christchurch, the South Island's main town and a delightful English garden city, is easily accessed by air from Auckland, Rotorua, or Wellington. From here, you can head across the plains to the foothills of the mighty Southern Alps—these brooding, rugged mountains reach their peak at Aoraki/Mount Cook. Or, you can take a short plane ride or a scenic eight-hour drive southwest from Christchurch to Queenstown, a buzzing alpine resort on a superb lake ringed by mountains. In addition to wonderful scenery, this is the country's adventure capital with

---

NOT TO BE MISSED:

Currency

The unit of currency is the New Zealand dollar, made up of 100 cents, which replaced pounds, shillings, and pence in 1967. Notes come in $5, $10, $20, $50, and $100 denominations and are made of polymer propylene, a tough, colorful, and difficult-to-forge plastic alternative to the old paper notes. Coins in circulation since 2006 are the bronze-colored 10¢ piece, silver-colored 20¢ and 50¢ pieces, and gold-colored $1 and $2 coins. Currently, one New Zealand dollar is worth about 80 U.S. cents.

Best Times to Visit

The favored time to visit New Zealand is in the summer months from December through February, when the days are warm to mild, the beaches are at their best, and the alpine national parks are accessible. That said, from around Christmas to mid-March the main tourist areas can be jam-packed and accommodations and rental cars difficult to find.

Reservations should be made as far in advance as possible at these peak times. The shoulder seasons of October/November and April/May are slightly cooler but much less crowded and noticeably cheaper. June through September is the off-season, but ski slopes come alive in the Southern Alps and on Mount Ruapehu on the North Island.

outdoor activities and tours galore.

Next stop, about five hours west of Queenstown by car, should be Milford Sound for a cruise on this famous fjord surrounded by vast, snow-flecked mountains. This wilderness wonderland rates as one of the most stunning sights in a country packed with them. (For the more adventurous, the famous five-day Milford Track walk is a must.)

The South Island's other main attractions lie on the other side of the Alps, a picturesque six-hour drive north of Queenstown. On the remote West Coast, Franz Josef and Fox Glaciers are among the world's most accessible glaciers, lying close to the sea in temperate rain forest.

You can see all of the South's main highlights by rental car in a week. To save a day or two, you could skip Milford or the glaciers, or even Christchurch by flying straight into Queenstown.

If You Have More Time: North Island

Northland, the "winterless north" a few hours by car above Auckland, is recommended for its fine beaches and superb seascapes along the east coast. A loop through Northland from the Bay of Islands can include the mighty kauri forests of the Kauri Coast, and those with no time budget can head past giant sand dunes to Cape Reinga, the country's most northerly point.

For a fine two-day excursion, visit the Coromandel Peninsula, an hour and a half east of Auckland, with perhaps the best beaches in the country and a fine mix of scenery. Continuing south along the east coast of the North Island, the sunny Bay of Plenty has more good

Tipping Tips

Tipping is optional in New Zealand. Once upon a time it was considered a foreign custom, if not an outright insult, to tip, but those days have long since passed, and the practice is becoming much more common. While it is by no means considered mandatory, a 5 to 10 percent tip is appreciated for good service in the country's fancier restaurants. (But don't tip if the service is subpar.) Tip taxi drivers for good service by rounding up the fare, up to 10 percent. In top hotels, it's customary to give porters NZ$1 to $2 for carrying your bags.

beaches, while an expedition to smoking White Island 30 miles (48 km) off the coast of Whakatane is a must for volcano hounds. The East Cape is a remote Maori area, off the main tourist circuit, which makes it a fascinating rural detour for those with a car. Traveling south down the center of the North Island, the Waitomo Caves and their glow-worms are a required stop on the way to Rotorua. After absorbing the Maori culture and sulfurous geothermal activity in Rotorua, you can continue on to Lake Taupo, Tongariro National Park, and then Napier, the delightful art deco city on the east coast at the center of a prolific wine district, before heading back to Auckland.

The west coast of the North Island is a much less trammeled route, but it includes the awe-inspiring, Fujiesque volcano Mount Taranaki and the wilds of the Whanganui River.

If You Have More Time: South Island

On the South Island, the sunny northern districts of Marlborough and Nelson deserve serious exploration. Ferries from the North Island dock in the Marlborough Sounds, the most stunning waterways in the country, while Abel Tasman National Park a few hours west has wonderful beaches and coves, which can be explored on foot, by boat, or by kayak. Other attractions include the cheerful city of Nelson, fine wineries near Blenheim, and the whale-watching and other wildlife tours that abound in Kaikoura.

Once the country's main city, southerly Dunedin, five hours south of Christchurch, has gracious reminders of grander times. On Dunedin's doorstep, the Otago Peninsula is a major destination for those interested in marine wildlife, while the Catlins farther south teem with seals, sea lions, penguins, waterfalls, and forests.

At the very bottom of the South Island, 450 miles (725 km) from Christchurch, Stewart Island is a remote last stop, isolated but bountiful in nature and the best place in New Zealand to spot a kiwi, the elusive national bird.

Other South Island highlights include the former French town of Akaroa near Christchurch, the fine resort of Wanaka on the lake of the same name, and Doubtful Sound, the worthy rival to Milford.

Bear in mind that the national parks hold the country's greatest attractions, with plenty of opportunities to get up close to magnificent wilderness. But wherever you go, little gems can be found, often more rewarding for the lack of tourist hordes. ∎

How to Call Home

International calls can be made from public telephones, which take coins, credit cards, or prepaid phone cards. International phone cards available at newsstands and convenience stores offer the cheapest rates for landline calls overseas. A prepaid SIM card for your cell phone from Vodafone NZ makes a handy investment. For international calls, dial 00, then the country code, area code (minus any initial 0), and number. The country code for the U.S. is 1. (For more details, see p. 280.)

Resident of Canterbury

Two islands filled with spectacular scenery and two distinct, complementary, and sometimes competing cultures with Polynesian and British roots

A Tale of Two Islands

Body surfing in Cathedral Cove, Coromandel Peninsula

New Zealand Today

When the first Maori arrived in canoes from Polynesia, they found a land like nothing they had seen before, a prehistoric world, isolated and unique. They called it Aotearoa, "land of the long white cloud," for mist often shrouded the towering volcanoes, and snow-topped peaks stretched farther than the eye could see.

View of Auckland from the Sky Tower

Teeming, ancient forests of giant conifers and temperate ferns covered much of the land, while turquoise and deep blue seas lapped the many coves and beaches of these vast, untouched islands.

Maori tribes thrived, and fought each other, in this great southern land for nearly 500 years before the English arrived and established a colony that would flourish by tapping the islands' rich natural resources. Aotearoa became New Zealand and the settlers transformed the landscape, felling timber for export and turning hills and valleys into rich farmland and rolling green pastures dotted with sheep. The newcomers clashed with the Maori, who succumbed to disease, guns, and increasing waves of land-hungry migrants, but Aotearoa would never lose its Polynesian roots.

Therein lie the seeds of modern New Zealand, a land of spectacular beauty and natural wealth, with a fascinating overlay of cultures. It is an English-speaking, developed country dominated by European culture, but Polynesian blood runs forever in its veins.

Not only is resurgent Maori culture evident everywhere, but New Zealand is also a focus for the rest of the South Pacific, still drawing Polynesians in search of new opportunity from far-flung islands such as Samoa, the Cook Islands, Tonga, and Niue. Migrants from Asia, particularly China, are also increasingly attracted to New Zealand, while much of the large Indian community comes from the Pacific. But despite growing multiculturalism, New Zealand's population as well as its outlook remain overwhelmingly bicultural.

Two Peoples, One Country

Within a population of 4.2 million, around 15 percent identify as Maori and 80 percent European (or Pakeha, the Maori name for Europeans now widely used by both communities). This makes New Zealand a meeting ground of Maori and English cultures— an odd juxtaposition at times, but a fascinating one.

For a colonized nation, race relations began well with the Treaty of Waitangi in 1840, guaranteeing Maori rights and sovereignty over their land, but plummeted as the settler rush for land inevitably led to war. Maori were fierce fighters, but in the end no match for British military might. Colonists seized land in retribution, discarded the treaty, and consigned the tribes mostly to remote areas. The two societies lived largely separate lives until the 1950s, when Maori migrated to the cities in large numbers. Urban life delivered economic benefits, but many urban Maori lost contact with their language and culture.

In recent decades, a snowballing interest in *Maoritanga* (Maori culture) has seen increased interest in all things Maori and enriched New Zealand as a whole. Governments take Maori issues very seriously and are eager to redress social and economic injustices. The greatest change in Maori-Pakeha relations came with the establishment of the Waitangi Tribunal in 1975 to rule on breaches of the Treaty of Waitangi and make compensation payments to tribes. It signaled not just a desire to redress the past, but a new era in race relations. The process continues, and biculturalism has its critics, from Pakeha demanding "one New Zealand" to Maori demands for a separate state, but tolerance prevails and gives hope for the future.

For the visitor, Maori culture, especially in the North Island, offers a colorful insight into a rich tradition. Even though many Maori are urban and urbane, they are proud to showcase their culture, at its most accessible in tourist areas such as Rotorua.

Kiwi Heroes

Kiwi heroes range from atom-splitting scientist Ernest Rutherford to the first conqueror of Mount Everest, Edmund Hillary. Sport stars such as the all-conquering All Blacks, the national rugby team, are demigods, but the arts are also well represented, from writer Katherine Mansfield to Hollywood exports Sam Neill, Russell Crowe, and *Lord of the Rings* director Peter Jackson.

Most European New Zealanders trace their descent back to English, Scottish, or Irish settlers, and many regarded Britain as the homeland well into the 20th century. Today, the country has thrown off the shackles of Britain. It is equally keen to distance itself from Australia, its bigger, brasher, patronizing cousin across the Tasman Sea, with which it shares a similar relationship to that between Canada and the United States.

Fiercely proud and independent, New Zealanders call themselves (and New Zealand culture) Kiwi, after the flightless, nocturnal national bird. National pride swells when Kiwis make a splash on the world stage, and for such a small population, the country has produced an inordinate number of high achievers. Although New Zealanders may claim to have invented everything from powered flight to jogging, nationalist indulgences are kept in check by a wry sense of humor and distrust of authority. Kiwis like to see their society as iconoclastic, egalitarian, and a world leader in social reform, beginning in the 1890s when New Zealand became the first country to give women the national vote.

Enlightened environmental, racial, and social policies continue to define the country, and with a high standard of living and relatively low crime rates, New Zealand regularly tops livability indexes. As a small country, New Zealand hasn't completely thrown off the parochialism and conformity of the past, but the most obvious excesses tend to be extremes of political correctness, and the Kiwi way of life is an enviable one.

European Kiwis often define their national character in terms of the early settlers.

Three Maori boys on Waikanae Beach, Gisborne

Living harsh, isolated lives, the pioneers overcame adverse conditions through hard work, determination, and adaptability. Kiwis also pride themselves on their ingenuity and self-sufficiency, and you may hear they can do anything with "No. 8 fencing wire," a reference to the popular wire gauge used on farms.

Myth as much as fact plays a part in all national identities, and while the manly values personified by rugby are lauded, alternative lifestyles are also welcome. New Zealanders thrive not just in the big cities, but in small towns where artists and craftspeople abound. Women also drive much of the dynamic in modern New Zealand and are prominent in leadership positions, from the prime minister's office to the courts, political bureaucracy, and business.

Despite its farming background, New Zealand is an urban society, but most visitors will end up in the countryside as they seek out the country's glorious landscapes. Even in larger towns, New Zealand has a village atmosphere where everybody knows each other or acts like it. Strangers greet each other with a smile, a quick word, a hello. On back roads, drivers wave at one another like old friends.

Off the Sheep's Back

A shifting world economy has created dramatic changes in New Zealand over the past few decades. After years enjoying one of the world's highest standards of living in a generous welfare state, New Zealand has had to make readjustments in an age of falling farm incomes. Once an efficient offshore farm for Britain, riding on the sheep's back, New Zealand has had to seek new markets and reposition its economy as Britain has looked more toward Europe for its imports and economic ties.

Agriculture, particularly dairy products, meat, and plantation timber, still dominates exports, but service industries such as tourism have assumed growing importance. As you travel around New Zealand, you will see once-booming farming towns, old-fashioned and quaint, on a downhill road. In contrast, tourist towns hum with development, bustling cafés, and "No Vacancy" signs, their asphalt sidewalks now replaced with creative paving, a sure sign of new money in New Zealand.

Cafés mark a pedestrian area in Christchurch.

Since the 1980s, New Zealand has increasingly embraced the free market. This shift has undoubtedly brought new wealth and new opportunities. Smart entrepreneurs are finding new international opportunities for New Zealand, despite the difficulties faced by a small economy far removed from world markets. Two obvious candidates are the export-oriented wine industry and the thriving film industry. The world is increasingly savoring the fine wines from down under, and the success of the *Lord of the Rings* trilogy and *King Kong* is attracting new overseas investment to New Zealand's world-class production houses.

Growth tends to concentrate in the metropolises such as Auckland, the only big city in New Zealand, but coastal towns are also doing well, attracting baby boomers flush with real estate winnings. Retirees, along with tourists, seek sunny climes with fine beaches and yachting harbors, with which New Zealand is well endowed.

> **New Zealand is famed for its hikes, or tramps as they are called, such as the Milford Track, Routeburn, and Tongariro Crossing.**

Nature Nurtured

New Zealanders love their landscapes and the outdoors. The mountains hold a special place in their hearts—it is no accident that the first man to conquer Mount Everest, Sir Edmund Hillary (1919–2008), was a New Zealander—but the sea is equally revered. Kiwis are a fit and healthy bunch on the whole, eager to get out into nature and hike, climb, sail, swim, kayak, surf, or fish.

Despite the havoc wreaked by early settlers on the environment, or perhaps because of it, nature is worshipped in New Zealand. A superb system of national parks protects the country's national treasures. New Zealand's greatest attractions—the Southern Alps, glaciers, fjords, volcanoes, and the country's wonderful hikes—are in national parks administered by the Department of Conservation, known simply as the DOC.

DOC offices in the parks and/or nearby towns are a wonderful resource and can fill you in on hikes, the extensive system of huts throughout the parks, and weather. New Zealand is famed for its hikes, or tramps as they are called, such as the Milford Track, Routeburn, and Tongariro Crossing. The nine best are designated by the DOC as Great Walks: the country's premier trails through its best scenery, featuring higher-grade huts for overnighting. Most of these need to be reserved through the DOC's website *(www.doc.govt.nz)*. Even if you don't intend to do any long hikes, bring your hiking boots, for trails are everywhere, from posted strolls through city parks to short hikes in spectacular wilderness. Walking is free, and fabulous, in New Zealand.

Though New Zealand has no native land mammals apart from bats, it has unique and prolific bird life and an abundance of marine creatures. Seals, sea lions, and penguins come ashore at many beaches and bays, where you may also see dolphins frolicking. This abundance has inspired a whole wildlife-tourism industry, ranging from swimming with the dolphins to whale-watching at Kaikoura on the South Island.

New Zealand's Two Personalities

New Zealand is a country of two islands, two halves, two personalities.

Dominating the country, the North Island has three-quarters of the population. Noted for its thermal activity, volcanoes, and Maori culture, the North Island also

Hikers brave a swing bridge near Mount Sefton on the South Island.

has forested mountains and fine coastal scenery, though the enduring images are of pastureland and crumpled hills dotted with sheep.

The South Island is wilder, more spectacular, and the main destination for visitors. Home to mighty mountains, fjords, glaciers, and pristine lakes, wilderness is its greatest attraction. The Maori influence is less noticeable and its cities cling to British roots.

The North Island is dominated by Auckland, the big city of Polynesia with a population of 1.3 million, one-third of the country's total. The capital, however, is the smaller but cultured and scenic Wellington in the south of the North Island.

The North Island is the Maori heartland, particularly in the Far North and the east where *marae* (traditional meeting places) hold strong to Maori tradition. For the visitor, the most accessible glimpse of Maori culture can be seen at Rotorua, the country's biggest tourist destination. Here the Te Arawa tribe lived long before tourists came to see the famous bubbling mud pools and geysers.

Volcanic activity defines the North Island, and the towering volcanoes of Tongariro National Park in the center are a highlight of any visit. Nearby Lake Taupo, resembling an inland sea, makes a good base. But New Zealanders often look to the sea, and the North Island is rewarded with a stunning coastline. While the windswept west coast is pounded by surf, the sheltered east coast is a craggy loop of bays, beaches, and isles, at its most beautiful in the serene Bay of Islands in the Far North.

Separated by a swift and sometimes treacherous channel, the South Island is slightly larger than the North, more rugged, less populated, and even more scenic. The majestic Southern Alps run the length of the island—for a close-up view of the highest peaks, visit Aoraki/Mount Cook National Park. On the west side of the mountains, the stunning glaciers of Fox and Franz Josef are another must-see.

In the far south, ancient ice flows have carved the awe-inspiring landscapes of Fiordland. A string of spectacular fjords tatter this rugged remote coastline, a World Heritage wilderness that includes famous Milford Sound.

In the shadow of the alps, Queenstown on Lake Wakatipu is everyone's favorite resort town. It is also the adrenaline capital of New Zealand, home of the bungee jump and other thrills such as white-water rafting, jet boating, tandem skydiving, and parasailing.

The South Island's main city of Christchurch nestles on the Avon River, and its fine parks and neo-Gothic buildings attest to its English heritage. Second city Dunedin celebrates its Scottish roots, while the nearby Otago Peninsula is a haven for wildlife.

Blessed with unique natural wonders, it is fitting that the country counts tourism as a main industry. Where once nature was exploited, now it is treasured, and clean, green New Zealand is one of the world's most ecologically enlightened countries, keen to shares its blessings with visitors.

Though primal landscapes were forged over millions of years in isolation from the rest of the world, cultural evolution has been much more rapid. From Polynesian homeland to colonial outpost and then independent nation, New Zealand is a young but dynamic country. Though mindful of its British heritage, it has embraced its Polynesian roots to forge a unique national identity that continues to evolve as New Zealand confidently takes on the world. ∎

The Kiwi Accent

No discussion of New Zealanders is complete without commenting on the accent. Similar to the Australian accent, it has diverged over the last couple of generations and is linked to a growing sense of nationalism and pride in Kiwi culture. Its omission of the short vowels can floor the visitor at times, and is most noticeable in the short *i*, such that "fish and chips" becomes "fush and chups." Other vowels are also affected: For example, "Money's lift air looks bugger then her right" is Kiwi for "Minnie's left ear looks bigger than her right."

New Zealand History

The last major landmass to be inhabited, New Zealand is an isolated remnant of the great continent of Gondwana, which tore apart 80 million years ago to form India, Australia, Antarctica, South America, and Africa.

Cut off from the rest of the world, New Zealand developed unique flora and a rich bird life, but no mammals walked the land. The moa, the world's largest bird at 12 feet (3.7 m) high, roamed free of predators, except for the giant Haast eagle. Birds came to rule a fiery world born of upheaval and eruption.

Maori Migration

Exactly why or from where the Maori originally came is uncertain, but the Maori language is most closely related to the Polynesian languages of the Cook Islands and Tahiti, so it's presumed they ventured from those regions.

Some Maori oral traditions attribute the discovery of New Zealand to the great explorer Kupe, who set sail from the Polynesian homeland of Hawaiki and called the new land Aotearoa (Land of the Long White Cloud). This story, along with theories of a later single Great Fleet migration and a separate migration by Melanesians known as Moriori, was taught as fact in New Zealand schools for many years but has since been largely debunked.

Certainly, though, a number of *waka* (canoes) made the journey, and Maori tribes trace their lineage to the waka their ancestors arrived in. The date of their arrival has been hotly debated, some theorists claiming as early as A.D. 800, though recent opinion dates Maori settlement of New Zealand from the 13th century.

The newcomers found a land like nothing they had seen before. Stretching 1,000 miles (1,600 km), it was huge, mountainous, and fertile. The Polynesians from the tropics also found it cold. Not all of their crops would grow, and farther south the mountains were topped with *huka* (foam), as they called never-before-sighted snow.

Maori culture became defined by adaptation, which was made easy at first by the hunting of moa. The huge, easily caught birds were found in abundance, but within perhaps as little as a hundred years they were hunted to extinction. In northern areas, seals were a major food source, but their numbers also declined.

By the 14th and 15th centuries, agriculture became more important, and the Maori less nomadic. *Kumara* (sweet potatoes) were an important crop and, unlike in the tropics, their tubers had to be kept in storage pits, which also mitigated against travel.

Maori Ancestry

About 5,000 years ago, the Austronesian people of Southeast Asia developed sophisticated seafaring skills that allowed them to spread into the Pacific. By about 1000 B.C. they had reached Tonga and Samoa, becoming the ancestral Polynesians.

They stayed put in the new homeland for almost a thousand years before pushing on into the eastern Pacific. Using double-hulled canoes, they migrated east to the Marquesas, then south to Tahiti and north to Hawaii.

Maori *waka* (war canoe) at rest in Wairoa Bay, Northland

Distinct Maori styles of carving developed, as did the use of native resources such as flax for weaving and highly prized *pounamu* (greenstone) for carving.

As the population and competition for resources increased, so did conflict. Fortified villages, or *pa*, were built on hilltops and occupied at times of attack, and larger tribal groupings became more important for defense and for pooling labor for farming and fishing. Tribal war flared, but trade was also well established. A thriving greenstone trade existed between South Island Maori and the tribes of the north, and other areas similarly exported their minerals such as obsidian. By the time Europeans first visited Aotearoa in the 17th century, a Maori culture distinct from its eastern Polynesian antecedents had developed.

At the time of first European contact, it is estimated the country had a population of 100,000 Maori, the last major group of people not to have had contact with the wider world.

European Exploration

Dutch mariner Abel Janszoon Tasman (1603–1659) was the first European to sight New Zealand. Sailing from Batavia (modern-day Jakarta) in the Dutch East Indies, he sought the great Unknown Southern Continent (Terra Australis Incognita), which geographers surmised must exist to balance the northern landmasses. Crossing the sea that now bears his name, he spied the South Island, near Punakaiki, on December 13, 1642. Five days later he anchored in Golden Bay at the top of the South Island.

Kupe & Toi— The Great Explorers

Maori migration stories vary, but usually begin with Maui, the demigod who fished up the North Island from his canoe—the South Island—with Stewart Island as his anchor. Most tribes trace their ancestry to one of several *waka* (canoes) that brought their forefathers from the ancestral homeland, called Hawaiki, but many traditions also speak of Kupe and Toitehuatahi, the great pre-migration explorers. Kupe features strongly in mythologies along the west coast of the North Island—some tribes say he settled in Hokianga before returning to Hawaiki and passing on directions to the new land. On the east coast of the North Island, many tribes trace their ancestry to Toitehuatahi, or Toi. In some traditions, he was an early explorer from Hawaiki; in others, he is indigenous to New Zealand and founded the tribe Te Tini o Toi (Toi's Multitudes).

Maori trumpets greeted the Dutch, who replied in kind, not knowing they had accepted a challenge to battle. Four of Tasman's men were killed in an altercation, and the Dutch ships hastily pulled anchor. Tasman continued to chart the west coast of the North Island, but dared not land. Named Nieuw Zeeland, after the Dutch province, this new world was deemed hostile and lacking in commercial interest, and no Europeans visited for another 127 years.

In 1769, British explorer James Cook (1728–1779) spent six months circumnavigating New Zealand in the *Endeavour*, coming away with a very different view of the country. Thanks largely to Tahitian chief Tupaia, who accompanied Cook and acted as a translator, Cook met with Maori on many occasions. Together with scientists such as botanist Joseph Banks (1743–1820), Cook gathered a wealth of information on the land and its inhabitants. From New Zealand he sailed on to Australia and became the first European to chart the east coast of that country. On his return to England in 1771, he was hailed as a hero by the scientific community.

Cook found the Maori "brave, noble, open and benevolent," and he visited New Zealand on each of his three Pacific voyages. Cook proved to be an enlightened leader, if a little musket-happy, and his dealings with the Maori were mostly friendly and respectful, but not without incident. On his second voyage in 1773, ten of his men were killed and eaten by Maori in Queen Charlotte Sound. To his credit, Cook showed restraint, a virtue that deserted him in Hawaii in 1779 when he was killed by villagers after a dispute over a stolen dinghy.

The Pacific also attracted French explorers, and Jean de Surville (1717–1770) arrived in New Zealand hot on Cook's heels. Marion du Fresne (1724–1772) made the Bay of Islands his base in 1772 while repairing his ships. Two months of cordial relations with the Maori soured when du Fresne and 25 of his crew were killed after a fishing expedition. In retaliation, the French sacked a village, killing 250.

Seals, Whales, & Missionaries

Given the problems early Europeans experienced in New Zealand, the British decided to establish their first Pacific colony at Port Jackson (Sydney) in Australia in 1788, using convicts from Britain's overcrowded prisons to develop the colony. As the penal colony expanded, eyes looked across the Tasman for economic opportunities.

Cook had reported on New Zealand's abundance of seals, prized for their fur, and in 1792 sealers established a base in Dusky Sound at the bottom of the South Island. Despite the harsh conditions, many others followed, and hundreds of thousands of skins were taken. Within 20 years, seal populations declined dramatically, but whaling soon

Statue of Captain Cook in Victoria Square, Christchurch

became a major industry. In the Bay of Islands, the village of Kororareka (modern-day Russell) serviced dozens of British, French, and American whaling ships at any one time. This interaction signaled the first significant contact between Maori and Europeans, but taverns and prostitution flourished as well as trade. Kororareka was dubbed the "hellhole of the Pacific," but the missionaries soon brought a glimpse of their heaven. Samuel Marsden (1765–1838) set sail from Australia in 1814 to deliver the country's first sermon on Christmas Day in the Bay of Islands, and more soon followed.

The missionaries introduced more than religion. The Reverend Thomas Kendall (1778–1832), who compiled the first Maori dictionary, befriended the great Ngapuhi chief Hongi Hika (ca 1772–1828) and took him to London. On the return journey, Hika managed to acquire up to 500 muskets that allowed the Ngapuhi tribe to settle ancient scores with devastating effect during the so-called Musket Wars (see p. 110).

The signing of the Treaty of Waitangi, painted by Marcus King (1939)

British Annexation

Early European settlement was limited mostly to sealers and whalers, many of whom married local women. By 1830 the European population was only around 300, but with growing trade and increasing lawlessness in the Bay of Islands, the colony in Australia looked to bring some order to the settlement.

James Busby (1802–1871) was appointed British resident, and in 1833 he set up home at Waitangi, across the bay from Kororareka. Busby had no real power and no police force, and persistently petitioned his reluctant superiors for intervention, citing lawlessness and concern over Maori depopulation. The British finally acted, prompted by fears of annexation by the French and the private New Zealand Company, which was engaging in wholesale land grabs and looked to form its own government.

William Hobson (1792–1842) was appointed lieutenant-governor of the new colony. He arrived in the Bay of Islands in 1840 and set about convincing Maori chiefs

to transfer sovereignty to Britain, a transfer secured by the Treaty of Waitangi. The hastily prepared, well-intentioned treaty remains the most contentious document in New Zealand's history (see pp. 90–91). The northern chiefs met in Waitangi to debate and eventually sign the treaty on February 6, 1840. It granted sovereignty of the country to Queen Victoria, but gave Maori control of their land and the same rights as British subjects. The treaty toured the country for other chiefs to sign and on May 21, 1840, Hobson proclaimed New Zealand a British colony. The following year he shifted the capital south to Auckland.

Annexation paved the way for wholesale settlement, and as migrants flooded in, Maori disenchantment with the new order grew. Land sales were a major source of dispute, with communal Maori property often sold by those not authorized to do so.

In the South Island, fighting broke out in June 1843, when the New Zealand Company sought to establish a settlement in the Wairau Valley based on a suspect land deed. After Maori chief Te Rauparaha (ca 1760–1849) hindered attempts to survey the land, the company sent an armed party to arrest him. Twenty-two Europeans were taught a fatal lesson. In the Bay of Islands, Ngapuhi chief Hone Heke (ca 1810–1850), the first signatory of the Treaty of Waitangi, soon became disillusioned with British taxes and justice. After thrice felling the British flagpole in Kororareka, he attacked the town in 1845. Hundreds died in the following months as Heke, with his ally Kawiti, fought British troops backed by old tribal foes. After Heke and Kawiti made peace with Governor George Grey (1812–1898), war subsided, but Maori resentment simmered.

Settler Rush

From a European population of about 2,000 when the Treaty of Waitangi was signed, Pakeha numbers swelled to nearly 60,000, the same as Maori, by the late 1850s. By 1881 the number of European settlers had grown to 500,000.

Early settlement was driven by the New Zealand Company, founded by Edward Gibbon Wakefield, a former convict jailed for abducting a 15-year-old heiress (she was willing, her father not). Backed by influential patrons in London, a rehabilitated Wakefield pushed his vision of a better Britain in the Pacific, preserving British traditions, including the class system, but offering opportunities for the lower classes to advance through hard work. This approach boiled down to buying land cheaply from the Maori, selling it at a handsome profit to well-to-do capitalists, and attracting skilled labor to serve the colony and the new landed gentry.

Of all the major settlements, only Auckland grew unfettered by social or religious visions. It boomed despite losing its status as capital to more central Wellington in 1865. Half of the country's immigrants were English, followed in number by Scots, who made up one-quarter. The Irish, being mostly Catholic, were not encouraged to migrate, but their numbers swelled to nearly 20 percent of the European population during the

1860s. French settlers founded an early colony at Akaroa in 1840 and sought to claim the South Island for France, but arrived too late. By the time they reached New Zealand after months at sea, the Treaty of Waitangi had been signed.

The new migrants cleared, burned, and plowed at a ferocious rate. Sheep farming was the preferred pursuit, and by 1858 the country had 1.5 million sheep, a number that grew tenfold over the next three decades. On the South Island grasslands in particular, wool barons made fortunes, but the real economic and population boom had to wait for the discovery of gold.

New Zealand Wars

While settlement increased in the coastal areas, the hinterlands remained firmly Maori, but European agriculture soon threatened to gobble up the interior.

To counter Pakeha dominance, Maori united across tribal boundaries for the first time to stop land sales. The Kingitanga (King Movement) was formed, and its members elected a Maori king in 1856, a move seen as treasonous by most settlers. In 1860, after a Taranaki chief tried to stop the sale of land near New Plymouth, troops were sent in, sparking the Taranaki War. From their fortified pa, Maori forces inflicted heavy casualties and laid siege to New Plymouth before a truce was called in 1861.

In 1863, war broke out again and 20,000 troops were called on to crush the King Movement. Dozens of battles across the Waikato region left 1,000 Maori and 700 British troops dead; fighting spread to the Bay of Islands before the wars died down in 1864.

The King Movement was defeated and huge areas of Waikato land were seized, but guerrilla skirmishes continued for another eight years. The Hauhau, whose messianic movement combined missionary Christianity with Maori beliefs, terrorized parts of Taranaki and the east coast of the North Island before capture and exile in 1866.

This gave rise to Te Kooti (ca 1830–1893), a visionary who started his own faith and promptly led his followers to slaughter 54 people near Gisborne in 1868. Chased across the central North Island by troops and Maori forces, he battled for nearly four years before retreating into the remote King Country (see pp. 110–111).

Gold

Gold was mined on the Coromandel Peninsula in the 1850s, but the gold rush took off with the discovery of the alluvial goldfields in Otago on the South Island in 1860–1861. Miners flocked from all over the world and towns sprang up overnight. Great wealth flowed through Dunedin, which became the country's largest and grandest city. Though the gold began to peter out by the 1870s, the rush had doubled New Zealand's population and rapid growth pointed to a bright future for all—except the Maori.

Nation-Building

The New Zealand Wars did much to shore up Maori prestige, but only briefly slowed the advance of settlement in the North Island. More land was seized, and businessmen-turned-politicians made huge profits.

Julius Vogel (1835–1899) provided the most effective political leadership. As premier and treasurer in a number of civilian administrations, the former journalist presided

Christchurch's Victorian stone cathedral lords over Cathedral Square.

over an economic boom in the 1870s. Massive loans funded rail, road, and telegraph, and Vogel introduced assisted passage schemes to lure migrants. British women, mostly domestic workers, traveled free in an effort to redress the imbalance of the sexes. Gold, farming, and forestry had attracted hordes of single men, who often lived harsh, isolated lives, and New Zealand society developed a rugged male perspective.

Fortunes waned in the 1880s as the worldwide depression hit New Zealand. Wool prices dropped dramatically, but were partly offset by frozen meat exports to England made possible by new refrigeration technology. Another major export, the kauri trees of the Coromandel and Northland, provided durable, straight-grained wood prized in ship- and housebuilding. Kauri milling was hugely profitable, but reduced the mighty forests almost to extinction by the early 20th century.

As the depression dragged on into the 1890s, poverty stalked the streets of New Zealand cities. Cries for industrial and labor reforms brought the Liberal Party to governmental power in 1891. The Liberals introduced sweeping changes that made New Zealand the social laboratory of the world. Industrial legislation improved conditions for workers, and land reform helped break down large estates, resulting in wider land ownership. In 1893 New Zealand became the first country in the world to give women the national vote; it also introduced the aged pension in 1898 and poured money into public-health spending. Richard Seddon (1845–1906), prime minister from 1893 to 1906, acquired the moniker "King Dick" as the Liberal Party went on to dominate New Zealand politics for the next 21 years.

ANZAC troops in Gallipoli, Turkey, 1915

Political stability brought prosperity, and New Zealand's GDP per capita was the highest in the world in 1900. The North Island, no longer embroiled in conflict, overtook the South Island. Auckland grew dramatically and the country became increasingly urbanized. Maori, however, remained rural. Though improved health reversed the decline in their numbers, by 1900 they composed only 10 percent of the population.

In 1907, New Zealand went from colony to dominion, status which conferred greater independence from Britain. New Zealanders remained staunchly British, however, and were eager to follow the call of the empire to send troops to the Boer War in South Africa in 1899. But a new sense of national identity was forming, and patriotism sprang from the rugby field when the national team (the All Blacks) defeated England in 1905.

New Zealand also went from colony to colonizer, with Britain handing over control of the Cook Islands and Niue. New Zealand wanted Samoa as well, but had to wait for World War I to wrest control of the islands from Germany.

Independence

In 1947, New Zealand ratified the Statute of Westminster, which gave it complete autonomy from Britain in foreign as well as domestic affairs. Despite this independence, Britain remained the homeland for many, and an adoring public turned out to welcome their new queen, Elizabeth II, when she visited in 1952–1953.

World Wars

New Zealand again answered Britain's call to war in 1914, and 100,000 men, 10 percent of the population, joined the Australian and New Zealand Army Corps (ANZAC) to fight in Europe and Africa. Casualties were heavy, nowhere more so than at Gallipoli in Turkey, where thousands were cut down in an ill-advised attempt to storm the heavily fortified peninsula. Almost every town across the country has a memorial honoring the dead, which nation-wide totaled 17,000, a huge toll for such a small country.

The troops embodied the national self-image of ruggedness, comradeship, and resourcefulness against the odds. These qualities were not so well received when workers organized. The conservative Reform government, which succeeded the Liberals, sent in the police when gold miners at Waihi went on strike in 1912, and a striker was killed. Socialists then began to gain popularity and the Labour Party entered mainstream politics.

In the 1930s, the Great Depression hit hard, and New Zealand's agricultural exports to Britain plummeted. Nature, too, conspired against the country when an earthquake flattened Napier and Hastings in 1931. The Labour Party grew in strength but did not gain the top post until 1935, after it had ditched its more radical socialist policies.

Under Prime Minister Michael Joseph Savage (1872–1940), Labour led the recovery and laid the foundations of the welfare state with increased spending on pensions, education, and health. Labour policies particularly benefited the disadvantaged Maori, though Maori and Pakeha lived largely as two separate societies.

When Britain found itself at war again in 1939, New Zealand committed 200,000 troops. Casualties were high. New Zealanders, including a Maori battalion, fought with distinction, but this time the war was closer to home. After Japan stormed British positions in Asia, New Zealand looked for the first time to the United States for defense.

Prime Minister Helen Clark greets the public on Waitangi Day (February 6), 2008.

Boom & Bust

The end of the war brought a new dynamism to the economy, as well as greater conservatism as the Cold War intensified. New Zealand turned away from leftist Labour in 1949, and the free-enterprise National Party came to power. Fear of communism saw New Zealand send troops to Korea and form the ANZUS military pact with Australia and the United States, which would lead to New Zealand engagement in Vietnam.

Refugees from war-torn Europe sought a better life in affluent New Zealand, but migration remained overwhelmingly British. Society was conformist, if not puritanical. From a country that banned Marlon Brando in *The Wild One* and forced pubs to close at 6 p.m., New Zealand writers, scientists, academics, and other elites made a beeline for more liberal London and its greater opportunities.

The 1960s and 1970s ended New Zealand's isolation. Cheap air travel, satellite communication, and television helped bring in the world. Conservatism continued to dominate politics, but times were changing. Feminism challenged rugby machismo and white-oriented migration barriers fell. Demonstrations demanded troops out of Vietnam and an end to rugby with apartheid South Africa.

Above all, the Maori challenged the Pakeha belief that New Zealand was a model of race relations. The postwar boom had witnessed the mass migration of rural Maori to the cities, where unskilled jobs were plentiful. Assimilation was the order of the day, but by the 1970s Maori questioned not only the decline in Maori culture and language but also injustices past and present. Increasing radicalism, protest marches, and calls to uphold the Treaty of Waitangi unsettled many in the wider community.

Labour came to power on the winds of change in 1972, but lasted only three years as inflation spiraled along with oil prices. A National Party government under Robert Muldoon (1921–1992) tried to reverse the economic decline, rising unemployment, and social liberalism. Wage and price freezes and "Think Big" infrastructure projects only worsened New Zealand's economic woes as foreign debt skyrocketed.

New New Zealand

In 1984, voters brought in David Lange (1942–2005) and a new Labour government, which introduced sweeping reforms, including deregulation of financial markets and abolition of agricultural subsidies. Labour also forged a fiercely independent foreign policy and took a tough antinuclear stance, a popular move at home as well as in the neighboring Pacific, where France continued to test nuclear weapons. Reform of social policies—from local administration to drinking laws—was just as sweeping, and Labour set about redressing long-festering Maori grievances. The Waitangi Tribunal was given powers to rule on claims dating back to the treaty of 1840, resulting in hundreds of land claims. The treaty now became a guiding agreement for race relations. The government has made multimillion-dollar settlements with some tribes, but the process is far from over.

The rapid restructuring of society unsettled many, and policy differences saw the government fragment and Lange resign in 1989. New Zealand's two-party political system began to break up as new parties tapped voter resentment at radical policies that had been introduced without electoral support. The answer, in another twist of reform fever, was to overhaul the voting system in 1993 to bring in proportional representation (known as MMP), similar to that in Germany. This system encouraged minor parties and further fragmented New Zealand politics.

In December 1997, an internal power struggle led to the election of Jenny Shipley (b. 1952), New Zealand's first female prime minister, but she lost the 1999 election to another woman, Labour leader Helen Clark (b. 1950), who formed a coalition government with minor parties. Through strength of will and a political balancing act, Clark has brought some stability to a turbulent political scene, helped largely by a strengthening economy.

> New Zealand is a vastly different country than it was 30 years ago, as national pride looks to throw off the influence of Britain and neighboring Australia.

New Zealand is a vastly different country than it was 30 years ago, as national pride looks to throw off the influence of Britain and neighboring Australia. The country revels in its own heroes—from sports to literature and popular music—and is eager to define its own identity. Pacific Island and Asian migrants have broadened the country's outlook, though not without some backlash. The biggest change has been growing biculturalism. Maori culture and sensibilities percolate throughout society, and MMP electoral reforms have delivered more Maori members of parliament and political clout.

Change has not pleased or benefited all, but the new New Zealand faces the world with a confident and independent identity. ■

Visiting a *marae* on Lake Rotorua

Maori Culture

Maori have been in New Zealand since at least the 13th century and came from eastern Polynesia, their language being most closely related to that of Tahiti and the Cook Islands.

Some Maori oral traditions attribute the discovery of New Zealand to Kupe, who set sail from the ancestral homeland of Hawaiki. After exploring the islands he called Aotearoa ("Land of the Long White Cloud"), he returned to tell of his find, prompting a great fleet migration.

Scientific evidence points to a series of migrations, but Maori tribes still attribute their ancestry to one of seven canoes: Arawa, Aotea, Horouta, Mamari, Mataauta, Tainui, and Takitimu.

Social Organization

The main social grouping in Maori society is the *iwi* (tribe), usually comprising several

hapu (subtribes). Tribal names often have the prefix *ngati* or *ngai,* meaning "the people of" or "descendants of." For example, the Ngati Pikiao (Descendants of Chief Pikiao) is a hapu living around Lake Rotorua. Together with other subtribes from the Rotorua/Taupo region, they make up the Te Arawa iwi, which takes its name from the original canoe that brought them to Aotearoa.

In pre-European society, hapu were more important than iwi. Hapu would sometimes fight each other, though they would unite against other iwi. A hapu numbered up to several hundred members and was made of a number of *whanau* (extended family groups).

A whanau of 20 to 30 family members would occupy one or more sleeping houses and often had its own compound in a village. As a warrior society, Maori also built fortified villages, or *pa,* that they would occupy in times of war. Usually constructed on hills in strategic locations, they were terraced, with a series of concentric walls topped with stakes to repel invaders.

Whakapapa (ancestry) was an important determinant of status and tribal grouping in Maori society, and at *hui* (gatherings), speakers would often recite extensive genealogies to establish their credentials.

Power was held by the *rangatira,* or aristocratic families. The firstborn son of the senior family was the *ariki,* hereditary chief, who passed on power to his son. Below the rangatira were the *tutua* (commoners) and below them *taurekareka* (slaves) taken in battle or born into a slave family.

Another important class, the *tohunga* (priests) specialized in religious ritual and magic, but also in knowledge of agriculture, carving, genealogy, oral tradition, and tattooing.

The arrival of the Pakeha (Europeans) resulted in the dispersal of many tribes through war, appropriation of land, and missionary activity. To counter growing Pakeha influence, the tribes sought to unite in the middle of the 19th century, helping to make iwi more important than hapu.

After World War II, iwi became the dominant tribal determinant as the government set up trust boards, based on iwi, to represent Maori interests and handle compensation claims for breaches of the Treaty of Waitangi.

Urbanization in the latter half of the 20th century undermined Maori identity, and many lost contact with their tribal roots. Up to one-fifth now cannot name their iwi and more do not know their original hapu. However, many Maori are increasingly interested in retaining or rediscovering their tribal connections through the *marae,* the meeting place of the tribe.

EXPERIENCE: Inside a *Marae*

The marae, the sacred meeting place, is where Maori culture and language are promoted, tribal matters discussed, and weddings, funerals, and important ceremonies held.

A marae is usually found in the tribal homeland, and it serves as a focus for members of the tribe or subtribe who may be scattered across the country. There are also intertribal city marae, university marae, and church marae. Te Papa, Wellington's national museum, has a marae that you can visit (see p. 154).

Technically the marae itself is the gathering place in front of the meetinghouse (*wharenui* or big house), but the whole compound is commonly referred to as the marae. Other community buildings include the *wharekai* (dining hall) for group meals.

The outside area is for welcome ceremonies and formal speeches, while the meetinghouse is the location for important meetings, cultural activities, and entertaining or accommodating visitors.

The meetinghouse is the most important building. The house usually bears the name of an ancestor, and the building symbolically represents him with ornate carving. The *tekoteko* (carved figure) on the roof represents the ancestor's head, the *maihi* (barge boards) angling down represent the arms, the ridge pole the spine, and the rafters the ribs. Supporting the rafters inside are *poupou,* carved representations of other ancestors.

You can visit marae around the country, including Nga Hau E Wha in Christchurch (*www.library.christchurch.org.nz)* and Piritahi in Onerono (*www.piritahmarae.org.nz).*

Religion

Traditional Maori religion was based on nature and ancestor worship. All living things and natural elements possessed *mauri,* or life force, and a host of gods and demigods, usu-

A Maori woman at a cultural show in Rotorua

ally connected to nature, required respect and propitiation through rites overseen by the priests.

Two important aspects of Maori spiritual life are *mana* and *tapu.* Mana (spiritual power or respect) could be accumulated through warfare, wisdom, oratory, inheritance, or by eating an enemy, thereby consuming his mana. Great chiefs sought and possessed great mana.

Tapu (sacred, or taboo, as Captain Cook translated it) applied to a range of restricted activities, from hunting and fishing rules to

prohibitions regarding the dead or sacred places. Defying tapu could result in death, either imposed by the tribe or through sickness that would befall offenders. Some original tapu observations can still be seen in Maori funeral rites and marae protocol.

Maori underwent wholesale conversion by missionaries in the 19th century, with Christianity all but destroying their traditional religion, but the ensuing turmoil resulted in the rise of two prominent Maori Christian sects.

The Ratana movement, founded by an early 20th-century faith healer, still has a large following and considerable political influence. The smaller Ringatu or Upraised Hand faith was founded by the 19th-century guerrilla leader and prophet, Te Kooti. It still claims around 16,000 followers and influences others such as the Ngati Dread, a Maori Rastafarian sect.

Mythology

Maori society brought Polynesian mythology from the homeland but adapted it to the new surroundings. The demigod Maui is a popular figure throughout Polynesia, and Maori relate many of his exploits, such as when he fished up the North Island from his canoe, the South Island (in Hawaii he fished up the Hawaiian Islands).

Maori oral tradition also places great store on genealogy and migration traditions, and tribal histories were retold via amazing feats of memory.

Myths dealing with the gods and nature explained the world and formed the basis of religion. They varied from tribe to tribe, but most had a similar creation story that began with nothingness until the earth mother Papatuanuku and the sky father Ranginui came together.

Rangi and Papa had many male children, the gods of the Maori, who lived in a parental embrace so tight no light could penetrate. The gods, tired of eternal darkness, finally decided to separate their parents. One by one they tried but failed until Tanemahuta, the god of forests, slowly applied the strength of a growing kauri tree to part the sky from the earth.

Light flooded the world, which revealed a multitude of creatures. Tane then fashioned a woman from clay, and the human race was born (see sidebar p. 92).

Maori Arts

Of the rich Maori music and dance traditions, the *haka* is the most readily identified. A war dance designed to scare the heck out of enemies, the haka is most famously performed by the national rugby team (the All Blacks) to psych out the opposition. It is indeed a terrifying sight of stomping, body slapping, eye glaring, and tongue poking, accompanied by a booming guttural chorus guaranteed to raise the hair on the neck.

Visitors will see the haka performed at Maori concerts, where women also invariably perform the *poi* dance, a graceful performance based on the twirling of poi, (flax balls) on a string.

Maori were master carvers, unrivaled in the Pacific. Carving buildings and canoes was a privileged profession and was done with greenstone adzes before the introduction of metal tools in the early European era. Maori carving design is based primarily on human figures, such as ancestors. Spirals are also an important feature, and the *manaia* is a curious Maori motif seen variously as a bird, serpent, or human figure.

Carving included ornaments of bone and greenstone, as well as a variety of clubs for warfare. The most widely known ornament is the *tiki*, a pendant usually made of green-stone that depicts a distorted human figure with the head tilted to the side.

New Zealand's cold climate called for warm garments, and Maori women produced the best weaving in the Pacific. Plentiful flax made a fine thread woven into mats, cloaks, skirts, baskets, and other items. Most stunning are the cloaks adorned with feathers, though they are rarely produced these days and use imported feathers when they are.

Maori Language

Only about 4 percent of the population speaks Maori, but that figure is on the rise. Maori is an official language taught in schools. *Kohanga reo* (language nests)

provide total immersion in the language for Maori preschoolers in some areas. Maori words are increasingly used in everyday English, especially in the media, where presenters open with a "kia ora" ("hello"). Great care is made to pronounce Maori words correctly, despite some murderous accents. ∎

Arts & Literature

The enduring images of New Zealand are of the rugged outdoors, farming, and rugby. Against this backdrop, the arts have often been seen as a lightweight indulgence, but the search for identity and international acceptance have elevated cultural icons onto the same podium as sports stars.

Much of the turnaround can be attributed to the success of the film industry, but wherever you look, the arts are flourishing. The "cultural cringe," with which New Zealanders once embraced the international and disparaged anything homegrown, has long since passed. Kiwis want to read New Zealand writers, see New Zealand movies, and listen to local musicians, while theater and dance also thrive in the cities. In country towns, it often seems every second person is a potter or painter.

Literature

Katherine Mansfield (1888–1923) was the first New Zealand writer to garner international acclaim. She acquired her reputation as one of the finest short-story writers in English while an émigré in Europe, but much loved stories such as "The Doll's House" and "The Garden Party" are fine evocations of colonial New Zealand.

Outstanding New Zealand writers to emerge in the 20th century include John Mulgan (1924–2004), whose *Man Alone* illuminates early 20th-century New Zealand. Prolific novelist and Nobel nominee Janet Frame is best remembered for *An Angel at My Table,* part of her autobiographical trilogy touching on her battles with the mental health system.

National treasure Maurice Gee (b. 1933) is an elegant writer best known for his *Plumb* trilogy. Other contemporary novelists of note include Elizabeth Knox (b. 1959; *The Vintner's Luck),* Nigel Cox

(1951–2006; *Tarzan Presley*), and Emily Perkins (b. 1970; *Not Her Real Name*).

Maori writers provide much of the dynamism of modern New Zealand literature. The *Don Quixote* or *War and Peace* of New Zealand literature has to be *The Bone People*, Keri Hulme's (b. 1947) ambitious novel of violence, spiritualism, love, and death in the context of wider bicultural conflict. The book won the 1985 Booker Prize and remains Hulme's only novel.

Witi Ihimaera's (b. 1944) novel *Whanau* (1974) was the first by a Maori writer, and his body of Maori literature includes *The Whale Rider*, made into a popular film (see sidebar p. 43). Another seminal Maori writer, Patricia Grace (b. 1937; *Potiki*, among others) tackles relationships, displacement, mythology, and politics with equal aplomb.

Alan Duff (b. 1950) also focuses on cultural destruction, but his bleak, violent *Once*

Sculptures in the Giant's House garden, Akaroa

Were Warriors, later made into a hit film (see p. 42), offers no easy answers. His criticism of Maoridom for dwelling on past injustices at the expense of current responsibilities makes him the enfant terrible of Maori writers.

Music

A thriving popular music culture has produced a number of exports, most notably Split Enz, which had international success in the 1970s. Founders Neil and Tim Finn went on to lead a number of musical projects, including the widely successful band Crowded House.

The local recording industry came of age in the 1980s, when the Dunedin-based record company Flying Nun launched bands such as The Chills and The Clean. More recently, popular singer-songwriter Bic Runga (b. 1976) and groups such as The Mutton Birds and The Datsuns have reached large audiences. OMC had a huge international hit, "How Bizarre," in the mid-1990s, which propelled them to brief worldwide fame.

Hip hop music is popular in New Zealand, particularly among young Maori and Pacific Islanders. Important artists include Upper Hutt Posse and Che Fu.

New Zealand also has three symphony orchestras, including the acclaimed NZSO (New Zealand Symphony Orchestra), and is home to world-renowned opera diva Dame Kiri Te Kanawa (b. 1944).

Flight of the Conchords

In 1998, friends Jemaine Clement and Bret Mckenzie started Flight of the Conchords, the band that they would later describe as "New Zealand's fourth most popular guitar-based digi-bongo acapella-rap-funk-comedy folk duo." Their self-description is on the mark. The diverse music channels everything from Serge Gainsbourg to the Beastie Boys, but it's always about the comedy. The band has since met international acclaim, even creating a sitcom for HBO in 2007. The show, *Flight of the Conchords,* follows Jemaine and Bret as they experience the highs and lows of semi-stardom on the mean streets of New York City.

Painting

The Maori portraits of Charles Goldie (1870–1947) and Gottfried Lindauer (1839–1926) remain icons of early New Zealand art despite being pilloried in postcolonial New Zealand. Goldie's work, in particular, has been called racist for his melancholic depictions of Maori elders as the last of a dying race.

New Zealand's best-loved painters are those who embrace the country's vistas, from the pioneering works of Petrus Van der Velden (1837–1913) to the wonderful landscapes of Rita Angus (1908–1970), William Sutton (1917–2000), and Grahame Sydney (b. 1948).

One of New Zealand's most acclaimed artists, Frances Hodgkins (1869–1947) made her name in Britain, where she branched out from realist watercolors to become one of the leading artists of British modernism. The New Zealand art establishment staunchly resisted modernism for decades, as can be seen in the conservative collections of public galleries, but artists such as the highly influential Colin McCahon (1919–1987) broke new ground in his works, which are noted for their religious symbolism and the use of words.

For an overview of New Zealand art, the best galleries to visit are the Auckland City and Christchurch galleries, but the country has some good provincial galleries, such as the Govett-Brewster Art Gallery in New Plymouth.

Some of the leading lights of New Zealand's contemporary art scene include Bill Hammond, Julian Dashper, Robin White, Shane Cotton, Philippa Blair, Dick Frizzell, and Michael Smither.

Dance

Ballet relies on government funding to survive, but survive it has since 1953, when the Royal New Zealand Ballet was established. The troupe's dancers typically have looked to London for careers, and returning émigrés such as Russell Kerr (b. 1930) and Rowena Jackson (b. 1926) in the 1950s provided much impetus. Jon Trimmer (b. 1929), a veteran of the Royal Ballet School and Sadlers Wells, has been a leading artist since 1962 and continues to perform character roles. Though based in Wellington, this hardworking company tours all over the country and overseas. Long wedded to classical performances, it has performed more innovative works from local choreographers in recent years.

The pioneering Limbs Dance Company established modern dance in the 1970s, working with local composers including Don McGlashan (b. 1959) and Split Enz. Though it dissolved in 1989, the group had launched leading choreographers such as Douglas Wright (b. 1956) and Mark Balwin (b. 1959), artistic director the Rambert Dance Company.

One of New Zealand's leading contemporary companies, Auckland-based Black Grace is noted for its dynamism, fusing Pacific and contemporary dance in athletic performances.

Theater

Despite a long history of repertory theater, New Zealand had to wait until 1952 for professional theater to emerge with the New Zealand Players. Formed by Richard and Edith Campion, parents of film director Jane (b. 1954), the company lasted less than a decade but inspired a generation of thespians.

In 1964, Downstage Theatre Company in Wellington led the way, to be followed by the Mercury, Circa, and Court companies as the nascent arts scene increasingly examined New Zealand issues. Leading playwrights include British emigrant Roger Hall (b. 1939), whose social comedies were exported to the West End, and Greg McGee (b. 1950), whose landmark *Foreskin's Lament* (1980) has become a New Zealand classic. It revolves around the rugby locker rooms, questioning national identity and exploring conflict in a changing society.

Though the classics and recent overseas hits continue to be a staple of New Zealand theater, since the 1980s and '90s local plays have become the norm, and Maori theater has demanded recognition, particularly in the works of Hone Kouka (b. 1966; *Wairoa*) and Briar Grace-Smith (b. 1966; *Flat Out Brown*). The Bats Company in Wellington has led the way in innovative local productions, while Downstage and Circa continue to enhance Wellington's reputation as the center of theater in New Zealand.

INSIDER TIP:

Kiwi music has a laid-back, home-grown feeling. The Black Seeds and Fat Freddys Drop always put on a good show.

—CARRIE MILLER,
National Geographic Writer

The large Auckland Theatre Company has a wide-ranging commercial program and performs in theaters around the city, while Christchurch and Dunedin also have their own professional companies.

Cinema

New Zealand film is dominated by Kiwi *Lord of the Rings* director Peter Jackson (b. 1961), who has become the country's most influential cultural figure. Filmed in New Zealand, the *Rings* movies turned the whole country into a film set, provided a massive boost to the economy, and prompted worldwide interest in New Zealand film. Up next for Jackson: *The Hobbit,* also filming in New Zealand, set to release in 2011.

Lord of the Rings director Peter Jackson

New Zealand cinema began well before Middle Earth inspired visions. *Sleeping Dogs* (1977), an accomplished psychological thriller, kick-started the nascent film industry and launched the international careers of actor Sam Neill (b. 1947) and director Roger Donaldson (b. 1945), whose string of Hollywood credits include *Cocktail, Cadillac Man,* and *Dante's Peak.*

Kiwis flocked to locally made movies in the1980s. *Goodbye Pork Pie* (1980), an exuberant road movie, was one of many hits. *Bad Blood* (1981) provided social criticism of gun-toting psychosis in macho New Zealand, while *Smash Palace* (1981), about a failed marriage and custody chase, also tackled dark themes. Geoff Murphy's (b. 1938) *Utu* (1983) was a breakthrough Maori Western.

Vincent Ward's (b. 1956) *Vigil* (1984), a brooding coming-of-age film set in the country's rain-drenched backcountry, moved New Zealand film into the art house and impressed at Cannes, but international acclaim had to wait for director Jane Campion. Campion's masterpiece, *The Piano* (1994), garnered three Oscars and put New Zealand film on the map. About a mute woman and her daughter adapting to pioneering life, it used windswept beach locations outside Auckland to great effect.

Then came Lee Tamahori's (b. 1950) stunning *Once Were Warriors* (1994), a brutal tale of dysfunctional Maori family life. The international hit *Whale Rider* (2002), based on Maori legend, followed a much more spiritual path.

Peter Jackson's career dates back to early splatter movies such as *Meet the Feebles* (1989) before *Heavenly Creatures* (1994) attracted international attention. More recently, *King Kong* (2005) was produced at his Wellington-based Weta Workshop, which also did the special effects and postproduction work for *Lord of the Rings.*

New Zealand not only continues to produce fine homegrown features, but the expertise and relative affordability of its production facilities make it a magnet for U.S. film and television producers.

New Zealand Architecture

New Zealand's architecture has no great monuments, unlike Europe and America, but many buildings from early settlement to the 20th century survive to tell the tale of a European society developing in isolation in the Pacific.

The most notable indigenous architecture is that of the *wharenui* (meetinghouse) of the Maori. With a gabled roofed and front porch, the wharenui was increasingly decorated from the mid-19th century. It became the pinnacle of the wood-carver's art, with fine carvings on the gables and inside rafters, and has also influenced modern churches, such as the chapel in Arthur's Pass Village.

The first European architects employed the early Victorian styles of the era, most notably in the South Island cities of Dunedin and Christchurch, which boomed after the gold rush of the 1860s. Influential early architect Benjamin Mountford (1825–1898) specialized in the neo-Gothic style. His stone landmarks can be found all over Christchurch and include the Canterbury Provincial Council Buildings, Canterbury Museum, and the original University of Canterbury. He also supervised construction of ChristChurch Cathedral.

Great wealth flowed through Dunedin, which still has some fine reminders of its Victorian glory days. Robert Lawson (1833–1902) was responsible for the magnificent Gothic-style First Church and imposing Larnach Castle, as well as much of Oamaru's historic precinct, while George Troup (1863–1941) acquired the nickname "Gingerbread George" for his ornate Dunedin Railway Station.

On the North Island, plentiful wood, particularly kauri, was a ready resource and proved more resistant to earthquakes than stone. Early wooden buildings showed distinctive styles, ranging from Wellington's grand Government Buildings and Auckland's Old Government House to Gothic wooden churches such as the beautiful Old St. Paul's in Wellington. Known as Selwyn churches, after New Zealand's Anglican bishop from 1842 to 1868, many of these fine wooden churches can be found in Auckland. Above all, the superb Victorian wooden villas that dot the city suburbs show a unique New Zealand style, albeit one based on existing architectural traditions.

Later Italianate and Edwardian baroque public buildings can also be found in abundance, and the Napier earthquake resulted in some fine art deco buildings as the town rebuilt, the best example of whole streetscapes in the country.

After World War II, architects embraced modernism, while prefab construction came to define much of suburbia, a trend that continues. Architects such as William Toomath (b. 1925) in Wellington and Christchurch's Miles Warren (b. 1929) have led the way. Recent modernistic buildings of note are the Te Papa museum and Westpac Stadium in Wellington and Sky Tower in Auckland. ■

Whale Rider

The movie *Whale Rider* (2002), based on Witi Ihimaera's novel, was an international hit filmed in Whangara on the East Cape near Gisborne. Combining legend with contemporary Maori life, it tells the story of a 12-year-old girl's battle to gain acceptance from her grandfather, the village chief and descendant of Paikea, the ancestor of the Ngati Konohi people.

According to legend, Paikea was the favorite son of Chief Uenuku from Mangaia Island. His jealous brothers plotted to kill him on a fishing trip and tell their father he had drowned. Overhearing the plan the night before, Paikea sank the canoe when they were far out to sea, drowning his brothers. Paikea drifted on a plank, waiting for death, until Tohora the whale lifted him onto his back and took him south to Whangara, where he began his new life.

Food & Drink

New Zealand has a vibrant food culture, embracing a variety of cuisines and using a superb range of fresh produce, which is expanding as farmers, buoyed by the success of the kiwifruit industry, branch out into new areas. Though the country's British heritage is still evident on its tables, pan-Pacific flavors are now widely found on restaurant menus.

A visitor tries the wine at the French Festival in Akaroa.

Restaurants, wineries, cheesemakers, and a host of boutique food industries are burgeoning in a country whose culinary roots lie in British cooking—an uninspiring legacy. Though long blessed with quality lamb, beef, and seafood, for many years the staple was meat served without spice or variety, accompanied by boiled or roasted vegetables. "Meat and three veg" was the norm on the home dining table and in most restaurants. Spaghetti Bolognese was an exotic dish.

But from the 1980s, New Zealand increasingly turned its gaze away from Britain to embrace a wider global vision in many areas, which fortunately included food. Modern New Zealand cuisine is usually described as Pacific Rim, borrowing across a wide region from Asia to California, but Mediterranean and Middle Eastern influences also flourish on today's restaurant menus. The visitor will not be starved of choice, and wine lists are buoyed by a wonderful range of local vintages.

Maori cooking doesn't widely permeate the dining scene, though the *kumara* (sweet potato), brought from Polynesia, is a New Zealand favorite. On visits to Maori villages, the visitor might well sample a Maori feast, traditionally cooked in a *hangi* (earth oven), where meats and vegetables are put into baskets and cooked over hot rocks in a covered pit.

If the country had a national dish, it would probably be roast leg of lamb, for even though culinary horizons have expanded, green pastures still produce the prized meat. The country's sheep numbers may have declined in recent years along with world prices, but the lamb is just as succulent, while booming beef and dairy production add to the bounty. Pork, poultry, and venison are no less plentiful.

Straight from the Farm

The freshness of the produce is the key to New Zealand cuisine. Fine meats, fresh cream, and locally produced cheeses are available everywhere you turn, orchards supply a wide range of sun-ripened fruits, and the vegetables on your plate were probably grown just down the road. And though farming drives the country, the sea is equally productive, teeming not only with fish but with all manner of crustaceans.

A Maori *hangi,* or earth oven feast

Fresh Off the Boats

The ocean provided the Maori with a ready supply of gustatory treats. They dined on such shellfish as *paua* (abalone), *pipi,* cockles, *toheroa,* and *tuatua,* treats still consumed today, though numbers are controlled or declining. In good supply are the huge green-lipped mussels farmed in the Marlborough Sounds, while the fat oysters from Bluff in the far south are not to be missed in season. Delicious crayfish and scallops are also widely available.

Whitebait is another New Zealand delicacy, at its best on the West Coast of the South Island. Netted in river mouths, the tiny young fish are typically served as whitebait fritters in an omelet mix. Commercial fishing delivers flavorsome snapper, *tarakihi,* John Dory, *hapuka,* and other varieties, while many of the country's rivers teem with trout as well as salmon, which is also farmed.

Fish-and-chip shops, found everywhere, offer inexpensive seafood and rate as the country's favorite fast food emporiums, though New Zealand also does an excellent version of another traditional English import, the meat pie.

At the other end of the scale, fine-dining restaurants are readily available, particularly in the big cities. Even in the remoter regions of the country, wonderful dining experiences can be found, but that said, a lot of menus have a "me too" approach, all serving up the latest trend at similar prices, regardless of quality.

From the Local Vineyard

New Zealand wines rarely disappoint. Starting as an industry limited mostly to a few Dalmatian families producing cheap bulk wine, New Zealand wineries have exploded over the last 30 years. From the warm climes of Waiheke Island near Auckland to the barren extremes of Central Otago near Queenstown, New Zealand produces an exciting array of wines.

Cold winters and mild summers are particularly conducive to fine white wines, but lighter reds such as Pinot Noir and Merlot also do well. Marlborough province in the South Island is the country's best known and most productive wine region. The Wairau and other valleys here produce world-class Sauvignon Blanc, noted for its crisp floral tones, but many other varieties are grown. The same is true of the Hawke's Bay region around Napier in the North Island, noted for its Chardonnay and red varietals.

Other well-known wine areas include the Kumeu region west of Auckland, the Wairarapa near Wellington, and Waipara north of Christchurch. Many wine cellars are open to visitors, and you can book a wide variety of wine tours, including those with personalized itineraries and cycling tours. Quite a few wineries also have excellent restaurants, showcasing the best of New Zealand food and wine in delightful surroundings. ∎

> **Gustatory treats from the sea include paua, pipi, cockles, toheroa, and tuatua.**

EXPERIENCE: Maori Food Tours

For international visitors, Maori cuisine is usually represented by the traditional *hangi* or earth oven feast, a must on all Maori cultural tours from Rotorua. But the sea and forests hold a bounty of other foods and plants traditionally eaten by Maori.

Maori chef, raconteur, and television personality Charles Royal now shares his arcane knowledge of traditional foods on small group tours *(tel 07/345-3122, www.maorifood.com, $$$$$)*. Operating out of Rotorua, these trips start with hunting for plants and herbs in the outdoors, accompanied by commentary on Maori life and folklore, and end with a feast.

Foods introduced include *pikopiko* (fern fronds), *horopito* (bush pepper), *kawakawa* (bush basil), and *periperi*, a fiery seasoning. Flax, used for weaving, yields seeds that are toasted and made into a rich bread, or you may come across *huhu*, the fat grubs found in tree trunks and cooked with pikopiko to yield a traditional treat tasting like peanut butter.

Royal, who worked in some of New Zealand's top hotels and in the United States, then prepares traditional foods in a menu that may include salmon, chicken, and shellfish such as mussels, *paua* (abalone), or *kina* (sea urchin). Meals are accompanied by Maori wines and beer. Royal's food tours can also include *marae* visits, jet boating, and fishing. Tours are usually capped at a maximum of six people.

Land & Landscape

New Zealand is a jewel in the South Pacific, comprising large high islands, long isolated from the rest of the world and surrounded by vast stretches of ocean. Once covered in primeval forest, it is a land rich in biodiversity, and its geography is equally varied and stunning.

The country stretches more than 1,000 miles (1,600 km) from the sandy subtropical peninsula at the northern tip to the glacier-carved fjords of the far south. In between lie mighty snow-covered peaks, smoking volcanoes, vast lakes, dense forests, and fertile grasslands. Beaches, bays, and coves punctuate a convoluted, 9,400-mile (15,000 km) coastline.

With an area of about 104,000 square miles (270,000 square km), New Zealand is the same size as Colorado, or about 10 percent bigger than the United Kingdom. The South Island is slightly bigger than the North Island, which together make up the vast majority of the landmass, but significant smaller islands exist, most notably Stewart Island in the far south.

Lying on the boundary of the Australian and Pacific plates, New Zealand is geologically defined by the collision of these giant slabs of the Earth's crust. It is a highly active region of earthquakes, volcanoes, and geothermal activity, part of the Pacific Ring of Fire.

In the north, the Pacific plate subducts, or pushes underneath, the Australian plate, which carries the North Island. The enormous friction of this collision is responsible for the volcanoes and thermal activity of the north.

The Kermadec Trench to the east of the North Island marks the line where the plates meet, but around the center of the country the plates twist along multiple fault lines. In the South Island, the Australian plate pushes under the Pacific plate, forcing up the Southern Alps along the Alpine Fault, which runs the island's length.

Formation of New Zealand

According to the Maori, the demigod Maui, who dwelled in the ancestral homeland of Hawaiki, one day strayed far out to sea with his brothers. Using his magic fishhook, he felt a mighty tug on the line and called his brothers to help. After much straining, they hauled up the North Island, or Te Ika a Maui ("Maui's fish"). The head lies south around Wellington, while the tail stretches north to Cape Reinga.

Maui's canoe became the South Island, or Te Waka a Maui ("Maui's canoe"). However, most North Island tribes referred to the South Island as Te Wai Pounamu ("the greenstone waters"), for the South Island was the source of prized New Zealand jade.

North Island

Less mountainous than the South Island, the North Island makes up for it with volcanic display. All of the country's active volcanoes are found around the center

Giant Gate Falls on the Milford Track in Fiordland National Park

of the North Island, from smoking White Island just off the east coast, through the geothermal regions around Rotorua, to the trio of volcanoes—Tongariro, Ngauruhoe, and Ruapehu—in the high alpine desert of the Central Plateau.

Near the volcanoes, smack in the middle of the island, mighty Lake Taupo is the country's largest lake and itself the product of a massive volcanic explosion. From the lake, the Waikato River, the country's longest, surges north through fertile plains of rich volcanic soil. The farming heartland of the Waikato region is typical of the North Island, much of which is covered with green pasture dotted with sheep and cattle.

The Southern Alps trap the rains brought by the prevailing westerlies, making the West Coast of the South Island the wettest part of New Zealand.

Past the Waikato lies the city of Auckland, home to a third of the country's population, on a narrow isthmus that separates the Pacific Ocean and the Tasman Sea. The city sprawls for miles across old volcanic cones and is rent by harbors.

Northland, the region at the top of the North Island, is a long finger of land lashed by winds on the wild west coast, while the sheltered east coast has delightful coves and bays, such as the scenic Bay of Islands. Kauri forests once covered this area, but only a few small pockets of these massive conifers remain.

The east of the North Island extends from the attractive coastline of the Coromandel Peninsula along the Bay of Plenty, a sunny region noted for kiwifruit orchards, to the remote East Cape, a stronghold of Maori culture. Farther south, the east coast is backed by rugged forested mountains down to Hawke's Bay, a farming district noted for its wineries.

Where the west coast juts out into the Tasman Sea stands towering Mount Taranaki, a dormant volcano. The most stunning mountain in the country, Taranaki's sweeping white-tipped cone dominates the surrounding farmland for miles. Farther south along the west coast, the Wanganui District is named after New Zealand's longest navigable river, which flows from the mountains of the interior. The island tapers at the bottom, terminating at the country's capital, Wellington, which straddles fault lines that threaten earthquakes.

South Island

Scenic as the North Island is, nothing compares to the majestic landscapes of the South Island. The magnificent Southern Alps run the length of the island, flanking the highest peak of Aoraki/Mount Cook (12,316 feet/3,754 m) in the middle. They have another 18 peaks over 10,000 feet (3,048 m) permanently draped in snow and glacial ice, while most of the range is snow-covered in winter.

In the far south of the island around Fiordland, the alps are lower but no less awe-inspiring. In this region, ancient glaciers gouged out deep fjords as well as great inland lakes such as Te Anau and Manapouri. Much-visited Milford Sound is the most famous of the fjords, where sheer peaks rise from glassy waters, while low clouds threaten to drench the primeval forest.

The Southern Alps trap the rains brought by the prevailing westerlies, making the West Coast of the South Island the wettest part of New Zealand. The rain feeds a tangle of dense growth on the narrow strip of land between sea and mighty peaks, while up high, compacting snow creates the Fox and Franz Josef glaciers. These rivers of ice flow almost to the sea and are among the world's most accessible glaciers.

In complete contrast, the leeward side of the mountains is dry. Desert landscapes of craggy rock and scree are punctuated by turquoise, glacier-fed lakes. High plains of tussock grass give way to greenery lower down, but this beautiful world in the shadow of mountains is a harsh environment of freezing winters and baking summers.

Away from the alps, the east coast has rolling pasture around Southland, while the spreading Canterbury Plains around Christchurch are prime farming land. Smaller ranges and hills include the weathered volcanoes of the scenic Banks Peninsula, while in the north, the dramatic Kaikoura Ranges run next to the sea.

The far north of the island presents yet another face. Sheltered by forested mountains, Nelson and Marlborough are warm and sunny, the valleys and coastal land home to orchards and wineries. The seas are also sheltered, nowhere more so than in the stunning Marlborough Sounds, with sun-speckled waterways and forested islands just a ferry ride away from the North Island.

Climate

New Zealand has a temperate climate, and the main population centers rarely record temperatures below 32°F (0°C) or above 86°F (30°C). Climate patterns are highly variable, however, and range from subtropical in the far north to cool in the far south. The mountains experience severe alpine conditions and create a number of microclimates.

Surrounded by sea, the islands pull in a lot of rain, between 24 inches (60 cm) and 63 inches (160 cm) per year in most places. The prevailing westerly winds bring most of the precipitation, which is heaviest on the West Coast of the South Island, while the driest area is just 60 miles (100 km) away on the other side of the Southern Alps. Snow falls on the mountains of both islands, but is rare in coastal areas, though the south and

Other Islands

Stewart Island, found at the bottom of the country, is New Zealand's third largest island. Despite its southerly latitude, the island has an almost tropical appearance due to surrounding waters flowing in from warmer northern climes.

Great Barrier Island is the largest island in the north, lying close to Auckland in the Hauraki Gulf. Waiheke, another substantial island there, is virtually a suburb of the city.

New Zealand lays claim to a number of other remote islands, the only permanently inhabited group being the Chatham Islands, 500 miles (800 km) east of Christchurch. Chatham and much smaller Pitt are the main islands of this rugged, isolated group. They were settled by the Moriori, a Polynesian people who developed a different culture from the Maori. Debate still rages over whether they were originally Maori from the South Island or arrived directly from another part of Polynesia.

Other islands range from the subtropical Kermadec Islands, lying halfway between New Zealand and Tonga, to the sub-Antarctic Campbell Island and the Snares, Antipodes, Bounty, and Auckland island groups, all noted for their rich bird life.

east of the South Island may get snow in winter.

Winds are often gusty and bring sudden changes. Clouds can swirl in the sky, bringing rain, then sporadic sunshine, many times in one day. Areas sheltered from the westerlies have more sunshine; these include Nelson and Marlborough in the South Island and the Bay of Plenty and Hawke's Bay in the North Island. The lack of pollution and a thin ozone layer make for brilliant sunshine and high UV levels.

Flora & Fauna

Isolated from the rest of the world for 80 million years, New Zealand developed unique flora and fauna. Primitive forests flourished and flightless birds evolved free of warm-blooded predators, for the country had no land mammals except for two rare species of bat. Unique species include the long-beaked, flightless kiwi, the world's largest flightless parrot (kakapo), an ancient species of reptile (tuatara), the heaviest insect (weta), and the world's largest tree by volume (kauri).

The sea is teeming with warm-blooded wildlife, including whales, dolphins, seals, sea lions, and penguins.

Forests in New Zealand are dominated by podocarps, which are ancient Southern Hemisphere conifers, while in cooler areas, southern beeches are most common. Thick forests harbor a great array of ferns, including giant tree ferns. In subalpine areas, tussock grass and small shrubs dominate. In lowland regions, flax is common, the long leaves producing fiber used in Maori weaving.

The prolific birdlife once included the giant moa, a flightless cousin of the kiwi that stood up to 12 feet (3.7 m) high, but Maori hunters wiped out this ready source of food. Other flightless birds facing extinction today include the takahe, with brilliant blue and green plumage and a thick red bill, and the kakapo, a giant parrot weighing up to 6.5 pounds (3 kg).

Other, more prolific parrots include the kaka and the cheeky kea, found in alpine regions and in parking lots, where it likes to peck at rubber windshield seals. Native fowl include the weka and colorful pukeko, while seabirds are prolific and include the royal albatross, which nests on the Otago Peninsula near Dunedin and sports a 10-foot (3 m) wingspan.

New Zealand amphibians feature four primitive species of frog. Reptiles include the tuatara, dating back 200 million years to the age of the dinosaurs. The country has no snakes and only one poisonous spider, the rare katipo.

Despite a lack of land mammals, the sea is teeming with warm-blooded wildlife, including whales, dolphins, seals, sea lions, and many species of penguins (see pp. 180–181).

Loss of habitat threatens many species in New Zealand, and introduced animals such as rats and the Australian possum cause widespread damage. The Department of Conservation has an active program of island restoration, clearing offshore islands of introduced pests and reintroducing native species, particularly endangered birds. ■

The south face of Aoraki/Mount Cook, star of the Southern Alps

Sophisticated and attraction-packed, the country's biggest city sits on a glorious harbor near dozens of bays and beaches.

Auckland & Around

Auckland skyline and harbor, seen from Devonport

Auckland & Around

Draped over a string of volcanic cones and washed by the waters of two harbors, Auckland has been blessed by geography. The city's craggy coastline holds dozens of bays and beaches, ensuring that residents are never far from the sea, and yachts cram its marinas, earning Auckland the moniker City of Sails.

Add to this maritime scene a mild climate, a robust economy, and all the attractions of a major city, and it is little wonder that almost one-third of all New Zealanders have chosen to live here. Though political power officially resides in Wellington, the city of Auckland is the engine that drives the economy and the country with New Zealand's greatest concentration of wealth, education, and industry.

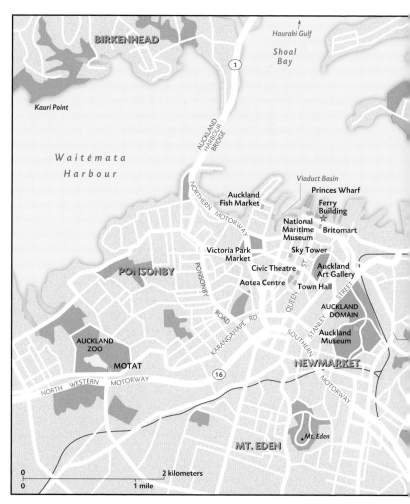

Auckland is also the world's largest Polynesian city. In addition to Maori, Pacific Islanders from Samoa, the Cook Islands, Tonga, Niue, and elsewhere have flocked to Auckland. Add in a growing migration from Asia, and Auckland is legitimately cosmopolitan, despite its relatively small population of 1.3 million.

The city lies on an isthmus barely 1 mile (1.6 km) across at its narrowest between the Pacific Ocean and the Tasman Sea. It is here that the Maori would haul their canoes

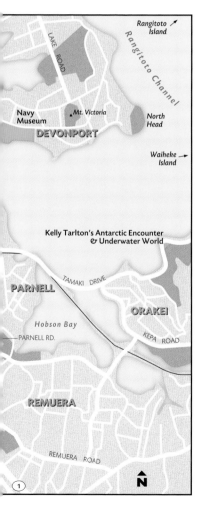

overland to travel between the coasts. Briefly the colonial capital in the mid-19th century, it lost that status to Wellington in 1865, but laissez-faire growth continued.

Urban sprawl defines Auckland. It now spreads over 25 miles (40 km) from the Bombay Hills in the south to Orewa in the north. Greater Auckland includes four main cities: Auckland City on the southern shores of Waitemata Harbour, North Shore City to the north over the bridge, Manukau around Manukau Harbour to the south, and Waitakere to the west. Forest and sea surround the city, providing interesting day trips west to the Waitakere Ranges and east to the islands of the Hauraki Gulf.

Most visitors pass quickly through Auckland, but this city of water and hills has plenty of attractions. Exploration will reveal much of the soul of modern New Zealand. ■

Auckland

On a glorious harbor with a mild climate, Auckland attracts growing numbers of residents and visitors alike. By far New Zealand's biggest city, it is also the country's cultural hub, mingling English and Polynesian influences, while offering a host of activities, diverse dining spots, and lively nightlife. Its Victorian heritage, happening inner suburbs, dormant volcanoes, and dynamic waterfront make the City of Sails one of the great Pacific Rim ports.

Yachting is a passion in the city of Auckland.

City Center

The Auckland central business district is a story of two cities. The traditional heart of the city is **Queen Street,** running from the ferry terminal up the hill to Karangahape Road. Dubbed the Golden Mile, Queen Street is more like the Olden Mile, with many of the once grand buildings now housing dog-eared fast-food and retail outlets.

Nonetheless, the old part of the city has interesting pockets and shopping opportunities, particularly in the side streets such as **High Street.**

The waterfront showcases the new face of Auckland. The City of Sails owes its revamp to yachting, for the Auckland waterfront underwent huge redevelopment after New Zealand won the prestigious America's Cup race in 1995.

INSIDER TIP:
Many of Auckland's less well-known volcanoes provide great solitude, impressive views of Auckland, and appealing picnic spots.

—JOHN BANKS, *Mayor of Auckland*

Amid national jubilation, plans were hatched to remodel the city before the cup defense in 2000.

Viaduct Basin, on the waterfront west of the downtown ferry terminal, housed the competing superyachts and has been transformed into a restaurant and nightlife hub, the city's liveliest. Fashionable new apartments continue to spread farther west into the old dock and market areas. At the other end of the waterfront near the old railway station, cheaply built apartment buildings are a debit on the town planners' ledger, but the city again looks to the water for inspiration.

National Maritime Museum

The National Maritime Museum at Viaduct Basin celebrates New Zealand's sea-bound heritage, from early Polynesian explorers to America's Cup heroes. A host of galleries and vessels provide an extensive display, and for a few extra dollars you can cruise the harbor on the *Ted Ashby*, a traditional-style scow, or on a steam launch.

The **Ferry Building,** where Queen Street meets the water,

is the gateway to Waitemata Harbour for the yachtless visitor. Numerous cruises operate from here, though the cheapest way to get out onto the water is to catch a ferry to Devonport (see p. 66), a delightful excursion and a must for any visitor to Auckland.

Heading south up Queen Street, landmarks include **Britomart** (*12 Queen St.*), once the gracious chief post office, now the city's transportation hub just up from the ferry terminal. Britomart includes the relocated train station, an attempt to improve Auckland's still limited rail network.

Halfway up Queen Street, the **Town Hall** hosts highbrow entertainment since its refurbishment and conversion to an arts venue. It imperiously guards the entrance to **Aotea Square,** a welcome city space that hosts everything from political rallies to festivals and a

---

Battle for Auckland

Maori legend tells of a great battle between the tribes of the Waitakere and Hunua Ranges, west and east of Auckland, respectively. A Hunua priest called on the sun to rise early, blinding the opposition, who fled. The Hunua warriors gave chase, but a Waitakere priest brought forth explosions from the earth, forming Auckland's volcanoes. The lava stopped the enemy's advance.

Auckland

⚠ Map pp. 56–57

Visitor information

✉ Arrivals hall, Auckland International Airport

☎ 09/275-6467

✉ Atrium, SkyCity, Victoria & Federal Sts.

☎ 09/363-7182

✉ 137 Quay St., Princes Wharf

☎ 09/307-0612

www.aucklandnz.com

DOC Information Centre

✉ Ferry Building, Quay St.

☎ 09/379-6476

National Maritime Museum

✉ Quay & Hobson Sts.

☎ 09/373-0800

💲 $$–$$$

www.nzmaritime.org

A Walk through Auckland

The best place to start a walking tour of the City of Sails is at the waterfront, heading inland to where the city's heritage unfolds. You'll finish at the Old Government House, a relic of Auckland's days as a capital city.

Start at the **Ferry Building ❶**, built in 1912, where ferries ply suburban routes to the north shore and the Hauraki Gulf islands, including Rangitoto and Waiheke. The Ferry Building also houses a couple of Auckland's best waterfront restaurants.

Styled after an ocean liner, the **Princes Wharf** redevelopment farther west includes exclusive apartments, the Hilton Hotel, restaurants, and bars. It is worth a wander along the wharf to see whose luxury liner or private cruiser is in town this week.

Viaduct Basin ❷ (see p. 59) is the grand-daddy of recent waterfront redevelopments. Though the America's Cup may have been lost, developers and Auckland nightlife continue to be big winners, for Viaduct Basin is ringed with bars, restaurants, and million-dollar waterfront views.

Continue around Viaduct Basin to **Market Square,** where the city markets once stood. Farther west, development continues with new apartments and expensive yachts moored in front. Turn left at Customs Street West, which passes the delightfully old-fashioned **Tepid Baths,** built in 1914. Originally saltwater baths divided into male and female pools, the facility has been redeveloped and now has freshwater pools, a spa, and sauna.

Farther along Customs Street West, on the corner of Albert Street opposite the Downtown Shopping Centre, the grand French Renaissance **Old Customs House ❸** was built in 1888 and converted into shops in 1997. It once housed a variety of government bodies, including the Native Land Court and the Office of the Sheep Inspector.

One block east, turn right up Queen Street. At No. 34–40, **Queens Arcade ❹**, an old-fashioned Victorian shopping arcade and Auckland icon, has craft, gift, and other shops to explore, including Marbecks music store, an Auckland institution since it opened here in 1934. At the next corner, Fort Street was originally Fore Street, for the shoreline once lapped here. Dinghies unloaded cargo from larger boats and Maori traded fruit and vegetables at shore-front markets.

Historic buildings on Queen Street include the neoclassical **Bank of New Zealand Building ❺** at No. 125, considered Auckland's finest building when it opened in 1867, now the Tower Shopping Centre.

Just off Queen Street, **Vulcan Lane** got its name from the blacksmith forges that once operated here. It is home to popular watering holes, including the wonderfully ornate Occidental Pub, dating from 1884. From Vulcan Lane, turn right onto **High Street,** lined with interesting fashion stores and other retail outlets. At No. 19, Unity Books is one of Auckland's best independent bookstores and always worth a browse.

After Your Walk...

Fun stops in the evening include:

Loaded Hog (204 Quay St., Viaduct Harbour) This well-patronized pub on the waterfront attracts yachties and a friendly, casual crowd.

Minus 5° (201 Quay St., Princes Wharf) Everything is made of ice here, included the glasses. Arctic gear is supplied.

Occidental (6 Vulcan Ln.) After a few drinks, you might think you're in Brussels at this fine Belgian beer bar.

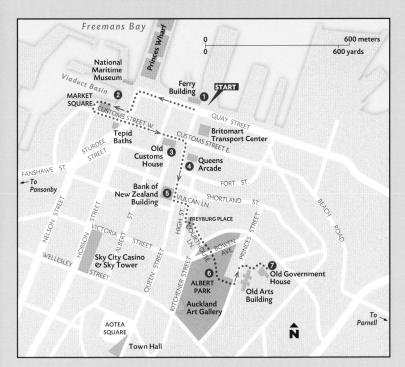

Freemans Bay

Princes Wharf

National
Maritime
Museum

0   600 meters
0   600 yards

Viaduct Basin

Ferry
Building

START

MARKET
SQUARE

②

CUSTOMS STREET W.

QUAY STREET

Tepid
Baths

CUSTOMS STREET E.

Britomart
Transport Center

STURDEE
STREET

Old
Customs
House

③

Queens
Arcade

④

FANSHAWE ST.

←To
Ponsonby

Bank of
New Zealand
Building

⑤

FORT ST.

SHORTLAND ST.

VULCAN LN.

NELSON STREET

HOBSON STREET

VICTORIA ST.

ALBERT STREET

HIGH ST.

COURTHOUSE LN.

FREYBURG PLACE

BEACH ROAD

WELLESLEY

QUEEN STREET

Sky City Casino
& Sky Tower

STREET

KITCHENER STREET

ALBERT
PARK

⑥

BOWEN AVE.

PRINCES STREET

⑦

Old Government
House

Old Arts
Building

AOTEA
SQUARE

Auckland
Art Gallery

To
Parnell →

N

Town Hall

Cross over High Street into Freyberg Place, named for Lord Freyberg, distinguished soldier and governor-general from 1946 to 1952, and head up to **Courthouse Lane,** a delightful paved piazza reminiscent of Rome. This popular al fresco dining spot once faced Auckland's first courthouse and police station. Veer right at the cafés, take the steps up to Kitchener Street, and cross to charming **Albert Park ⑥,** straddling Bowen Avenue and sandwiched between the city and the university. Despite the name, a statue of Queen Victoria stands in the center. A statue of Sir George Grey honors the career administrator who served as governor of New Zealand and superintendent of Auckland.

The **Auckland Art Gallery** (see p. 62) is on the southwest corner of the park, and on the eastern side, the imposing **Old Arts Building** (1926) is the university's most striking edifice, with a Gaudí-goes-to-Camelot clock tower. Behind the Old Arts Building is **Old Government House ⑦,** a stately wooden mansion with

✛ Also see area map p. 56
► Ferry Building
⟷ 1.4 miles (2.5 km)
⊙ 2 hours
► Old Government House

NOT TO BE MISSED:

Ferry Building • Viaduct Basin • Queens Arcade • Albert Park • Old Arts Building • Old Government House

---

faux stone facade and lacework portico. Built in 1856, it served as the governor's residence when Auckland was the capital. George Grey planted the massive flame tree in the garden. The mansion continued to serve as a vice-regal summer residence after the capital moved to Wellington in 1865, and visiting English royalty stayed here. It became part of the university in 1969. ∎

Sky Tower
- Map p. 56
- Victoria & Federal Sts.
- 09/363-6000
- $$–$$$$$

www.skycity.co.nz

weekend market. It is flanked by the modern **Aotea Centre** (*Mayoral Dr., tel 09/309-2677*), the country's preeminent performing arts center, part of the Edge public arts enterprise that also includes the **Civic Theatre,** nearby on the corner of Queen and Wellesley Streets. The Civic is an ornate art deco masterpiece, the grand dame of the city's theaters, famous for its painted ceiling of stars

---

EXPERIENCE:
Auckland Bridge Climb

For amazing views of the city and harbor, take the exhilarating climb up and over the **Auckland Harbour Bridge** on maintenance paths.

Guides share the secrets of the bridge. Built in 1959, within a decade the bridge lacked the capacity to carry the increasing traffic to the North Shore. In 1969 extra lanes were added, thanks to the box girder clip-ons manufactured by a Japanese company: hence the nickname Nippon Clip-ons.

The climb, easily negotiated by those of all fitness levels, takes around 1.5 hours. If you find the climb too tame, you can also bungee jump off the bridge. Book the climb and jumps through **A. J. Hackett** (*Westhaven Reserve, tel 09/361-2000, www.aucklandbridgeclimb.co.nz*).

---

representing the southern sky at 10 p.m. on an April evening.

It seems no Pacific city is complete without an incongruous needle-shaped tower to top all other buildings, and Auckland's version is **Sky Tower.** At 1,076 feet (328 m), it dominates the skyline by day and night, and an elevator

will whisk you almost to the top for dramatic views of the city. Thrill seekers can take it a step further and plummet downward on the sky jump, a wired adrenaline version of that New Zealand invention, the bungee jump. The tower is part of Sky City, a casino, hotel, and entertainment complex.

Culture Galore

Culture also prevails in the center city, and the **Auckland Art Gallery** (*closed for renovations until 2010*) has a diverse if modest collection of Western art from Renaissance and Dutch painting to cubism, with 18th- and 19th-century English painting heavily represented. The highlight is undoubtedly the Maori portraits by Auckland-born Charles Goldie and Gottfried Lindauer. The collection includes Goldie's 1898 "The Arrival of the Maoris in New Zealand," a portrayal of the first canoes that has been roundly criticized by Maori as a Pakeha (European) denigration. Divided into two buildings, the **Main Gallery** houses most of the permanent collection, while across the road the **New Gallery** focuses on contemporary art and visiting exhibitions.

K Road & Beyond

Queen Street ends at K Road, as locals abbreviate **Karangahape Road,** which winds along the ridge above the city center. Always worth a wander, K Road's shops mix sordid charm with history. The street has gone through many changes, from early settlement when churches

The IMAX Centre, Queen Street, Auckland

vied for position, to its heyday as a Pacific enclave in the 1960s and '70s. Asian restaurants now add to the mix, and though many of the adult stores are gone, K Road still clings to its red-light roots.

K Road ends at **Ponsonby Road,** one of Auckland's most popular restaurant and café strips. The historic suburb of Ponsonby threw off the slum tag back in the 1970s when students and artistic types moved in. Now firmly well-to-do, Ponsonby has restored Victorian villas that cost a small fortune and streets that are a joy to wander on a sunny day.

Of the close-in suburbs, **Newmarket,** just beyond Parnell, is a thriving shopping area and fashion outlet center. Commuter trains run there from the Britomart cen-

ter downtown. East of Newmarket, elevated **Remuera** is arguably Auckland's most prestigious suburb. Its boutiques and specialty outlets along Remuera Road offer quality, if expensive, shopping.

Parnell

To the east of the city center, Parnell is Auckland's oldest suburb, and its historic wooden villas are sought-after real estate. Chic restaurants, bars, and stores line the main drag, **Parnell Road,** one of Auckland's most popular dining spots. **Parnell Village** in the middle of the strip is a maze of boutiques, galleries, and restaurants along wooden boardwalks draped over the gorge behind.

Of the many historic buildings in Parnell, **St. Mary's Church** *(420–432 Parnell Rd.),* built in Gothic style between 1886 and 1897, is considered one of the finest wooden churches in New Zealand—its lofty interior is particularly impressive. It sits next to the Holy Trinity Cathedral.

Around Parnell

Kinder House *(2 Ayr St., closed Sun.)* was built as the home of the Church of England Grammar School's headmaster. Named after its first occupant, Dr. John Kinder, this two-story stone museum displays his watercolors and pioneering photographs.

A few doors down, charming **Ewelme Cottage** *(14 Ayr St., closed Mon.–Thurs.)* is a fine example of a colonial wooden cottage, built in 1863 for the salaciously named vicar, Vicesimus Lush, whose family lived there until 1968.

Auckland Art Gallery

🅰 Map p. 56

✉ Main Gallery: Wellesley & Kitchener Sts.

✉ New Gallery: Wellesley & Lorne Sts.

☎ 09/379-1349

$ $$

www.auckland artgallery.govt.nz

Auckland Museum

⚠ Map p. 56
✉ Auckland Domain
☎ 09/309-0443
💲 $

www.auckland
museum.com

Kelly Tarlton's Antarctic Encounter & Underwater World

⚠ Map p. 57
✉ 23 Tamaki Dr., Orakei
☎ 09/528-0603
💲 $$$–$$$$

www.kellytarltons
.co.nz

Off Parnell Road, Maunsell Road leads to the **Auckland Domain** (20 Park Rd.), a 185-acre (75 ha) expanse of greenery on the edge of the city. Among the gardens and cricket grounds, the **Wintergarden** comprises two

---

America's Cup Legend

In front of the National Maritime Museum, at the entrance to Viaduct Basin, *KZ1* is a gigantic 90-foot (27 m) sloop that challenged for the 1988 America's Cup, only to be trounced by U.S. champ Dennis Connor in a catamaran. The contest spent more time in court than on the water, but it helped spur New Zealand on to win the cup in 1995 with *Black Magic*. The Team New Zealand syndicate successfully defended the cup in 2000, only to lose it in 2003 to a Swiss challenger.

---

domed greenhouses crammed with exotics around a Victorian formal garden. The attached fernery walk provides a wonderful introduction to the ferns of New Zealand, and in front, the Wintergarden Pavilion café is the spot to take tea.

High on the hill in the Domain, the **Auckland Museum** is a major city attraction. Though Wellington's Te Papa Museum (see p. 154) in its impressive modern space is lauded as the country's best, it seems almost empty in comparison to this wonderful museum crammed with artifacts. Auckland's museum also has a fine new home since it moved into the solidly neoclassical Auckland War Memorial Museum building. Maori treasures, Pacific exhibits, and the Auckland 1866 streetscape are just some of the highlights of the extensive displays. **Maori cultural performances** (11 a.m., noon, & 1:30 p.m., $$–$$$) featuring song, dance, and storytelling are a popular addition.

Tamaki Drive

This scenic waterfront drive through some of Auckland's prime real estate shows the City of Sails at its best. The sandy beaches and calm bays facing Rangitoto Island teem with beachgoers in summer, but whenever the sun shines, yachts tack in Waitemata Harbour and kayakers, windsurfers, bicyclists, and anglers flock to the shore.

From the city center, take Quay Street, which runs in front of the ferry building, and head east. Tamaki Drive crosses Hobson Bay, lined with motorboats, before reaching exclusive Orakei. One street back from Tamaki Drive, **Parakai Drive** is millionaire's row, with fine views and the most expensive houses in New Zealand.

Orakei is also home to **Kelly Tarlton's Antarctic Encounter & Underwater World.** If you go to only one aquarium in New Zealand, this is it. An impressive array of big fish such as stingrays and sharks swim over you in a glass tunnel, but the pièce de

EXPERIENCE: Nation of Sails

From the Olympics to the America's Cup, New Zealanders have earned a reputation as the world's best sailors. Auckland, with its marinas crammed with sailing craft, is known as the City of Sails, but New Zealand should be called the Nation of Sails, for sheltered harbors and bays dotted with picturesque islands offer fine sailing right around the country.

If you've always wanted to experience this exhilarating sport, sailing operators offer cruises with a skipper and crew, ranging from afternoon-tea sightseeing trips to weeklong ocean-going voyages on maxi-yachts. Alternately, you can charter a vessel to sail yourself.

Premier destinations are Auckland's Hauraki Gulf, the Bay of Islands, and the Marlborough Sounds, though you can also set sail from Nelson, Akaroa near Christchurch, and even Queenstown on Lake Wakatipu.

In Auckland, many operators, such as the **Pride of Auckland** (tel 09/373-4557, www.prideofauckland.com) offer sailing, from lunch trips to all-day cruises. For something more adventurous, the heritage tallship **Soren Larsen** (tel 09/817-8799, www.sorenlarsen.co.nz) runs three to five-day trips to the Bay of Islands in summer and South Pacific cruises in winter.

Sail NZ (tel 09/359-5987, www.sailnz.co.nz) at Auckland's Viaduct Basin offers sailing on an America's Cup yacht, as well as sailing in the Bay of Islands from Pahia (tel 09/402-8234). Other Bay of Islands operators include **FairWind Charters** (tel 09/402-7821, www

.fairwind.co.nz) in Opua, which charters 28- to 45-foot (8.5–14 m) yachts for bareboat (sail-yourself) or skippered sailing trips.

The calm waters of the delightful Marlborough Sounds (see pp. 171–172) are also popular for sail-yourself or skippered explorations,

lasting from a day to a week. Operators in Picton include **Compass Charters** (tel 03/573-8332, www.compass-charters.co.nz) and **Charterlink** (tel 03/573-6591, www.charterlink south.co.nz), which also runs sailing and power-boat courses.

Sunbathers on a yacht in Waitemata Harbour

Devonport

◭ Map p. 57

Visitor information

✉ 3 Victoria Rd., Devonport

☎ 09/446-0677

www.devonport
.co.nz

résistance is the Antarctic experience, complete with colonies of king and gentoo penguins, a snowmobile ride, and displays on Antarctic exploration. Great for children and informative for adults, Kelly Tarlton's also runs a free shuttle bus.

Behind Kelly Tarlton's on the hill, **Bastion Point** was the site of a fort built in 1885 to fight off a Russian invasion that never happened. Ownership of the land, taken from the Ngati Whatua

Tropical plants fill the Auckland Regional Botanic Gardens.

people, was always disputed. In 1977 and 1978, Maori protestors occupied the site, an event that forever changed race relations in New Zealand. The Ngati Whatua eventually won title to their land, and their *marae* stands at the southern end of the parkland. To the north, an obelisk honors Labour Party prime minister Michael Joseph Savage, regarded as one of the country's greatest leaders.

Tamaki Drive continues to fashionable **Mission Bay**, with its gentle beach, seaside park, and lively restaurant strip. The road ends at smaller but even prettier **St. Helliers Bay.** Take Cliff Road from St. Helliers Bay to **Achilles Point Lookout** for dramatic views of the city, harbor, and Hauraki Gulf. Just below Achilles Point, stairs lead to delightful **Lady's Bay,** a popular nude beach.

Devonport & North Shore

A trip to Devonport, only a ten-minute ferry ride from central Auckland and a must on every itinerary, combines a cheap harbor cruise with a visit to a Victorian seaside village. Though a suburb, Devonport maintains its village atmosphere and its main-street stores and cafés are popular on weekends. Alternatively, Devonport's B&Bs make a good base to explore the city, just across the harbor.

The town's historic streets are a delight to wander, and the visitor center has a good walking-tour brochure. From the ferry wharf, head up Victoria Road to browse the shops or have lunch in one of the many cafés. At the end of the shops, continue up the road to **Mount Victoria.** A ten-minute hike (or easy drive) to the top of this volcanic cone is rewarded with fabulous views of the Auckland and its waters. Settled by the Kawerau people, the northern and eastern slopes show terracing and pits. Like Bastion Point, Mount Victoria once housed a fort built to defend Auckland from purported Russian attack.

Fear of the Russian threat also saw colossal fortifications built at **North Head,** 0.75 miles (1 km) farther east. The fort held three battery guns to pound any invaders entering Waitemata Harbour. On an old volcano with stunning views, North Head's military installations can be toured; a video plays in the historic stone kitchen.

Devonport also has a few small museums, the pick of which is the **Navy Museum** (Spring St., tel 09/445-5186), the museum of the Royal New Zealand Navy.

Devonport is part of North Shore City, which takes in the mostly affluent suburbs across the Harbour Bridge from Auckland. Ferries also run to **Birkenhead,** which oozes Victorian charm but is quieter than Devonport. At the heart of North Shore City, **Takapuna** has a thriving shopping center lying between a small volcanic lake and a good city beach overlooking Rangitoto Island.

Farther north, the suburban sprawls pushes inexorably on. **Orewa,** 22 miles (35 km) north of Auckland at the end of the freeway, was once a seaside village but now lies on the edge of Auckland suburbia. It has a pretty, shallow beach and a range of accommodations if you are traveling to or from the north and want to avoid rush-hour traffic.

Volcanoes

Auckland sprawls across 49 volcanoes, and though the Auckland volcanic field last erupted 600 years ago, it is by no means extinct. Most of the volcanoes are small cones less than 500 feet (150 m) high and the result of the material ejected in a single eruption. Unlike the much more active central plateau of the

Woolen Goods

With 40 million sheep, New Zealand is a major producer of wool and sheepskin products. Sheepskin jackets and coats are good buys, and cozy sheepskin boots are an antipodean specialty.

Hand-knit sweaters are a popular cottage industry here, along with knit cloaks, vests, gloves, and scarves. High-fashion items use factory-woven woolen cloth, which is often combined with mohair or possum fur to produce a beautifully soft and warm fabric.

Local artists produce woolen weavings, and rug producers such as Dilana (www.dilana.co.nz) create stunning modern designs. There is a workshop and gallery at 40 George St. in the Mount Eden section of Auckland.

North Island, volcanic activity here is not caused by the collision of tectonic plates, but by an isolated hot spot or plume 60 miles (100 km) beneath the city.

Rangitoto Island (see pp. 70–71) is by far the largest volcano in the field, and the most recent one to erupt, but if

Auckland does blow again, it is likely to be from a different spot in the earth's surface, meaning a new volcano could erupt anywhere in the city—a scenario that adds a new dimension to Auckland's overheated property market.

The volcanoes provided rich soils and their steep sides natural protection for the Maori tribes who settled the region from the

---

EXPERIENCE:
Cook Fish!

Auckland Fish Market is world famous for its fresh fish (though it offers fruit, vegetables, and premium ground coffees as well). But few people realize that, just upstairs, awaits Auckland's only dedicated seafood-cooking school, the **Auckland Seafood School** (22–32 Jellicoe St., Freemans Bay, tel 09/379-1497, www.afm.co.nz). The different class choices reflect the Pacific city's multicultural fabric. Among the most popular are "Seafood BBQ," "Sushi & Tempura," "A Taste of Thai," and "Summer Dining." Classes typically last a couple of hours.

14th century. Maori *pa* (fortified villages) dotted the cones, and extensive terracing can still be seen at Mount Eden (Maungawhau in Maori) and One Tree Hill (Maungakiekie), and across the harbor in Devonport at Mount Victoria (Takarunga) and North Head (Takapuna).

Mount Eden lies just 2 miles (3 km) south of the city center and is the highest of the mainland cones at 643 feet (196 m). Sky Tower now claims the city's highest viewpoint, but Mount Eden still provides magnificent (and free) views around Auckland. Farther south, off Manakau Road, **One Tree Hill** (600 feet/183 m) is surrounded by extensive parkland and offers superb views. It was the largest of the Maori pa and got its name from the lone tree at the top. That tree was cut down by a white settler in 1852, but replaced by a pine, which in turn was attacked by Maori protestors in the 1990s. Now dubbed None Tree Hill, it is topped by an obelisk.

Auckland's Markets

Auckland has a number of interesting markets. On the western edge of the central business district, **Victoria Park Market** (Victoria St. W. & Union St.) occupies the renovated premises of what was once the city's garbage processor. Though small, the market is worth a browse for bric-a-brac and cheap eats.

Nearby, close to the docks, **Auckland Fish Market** (Jellicoe & Daldy Sts.) has a great selection of freshly caught fish and lunchtime seafood cafés, as well as a program of cooking and seafood lessons.

Auckland's claim as the big city of the South Pacific can be glimpsed every Saturday morning at the **Otara Market** (Newbury St., Otara). Though not exclusively Polynesian, the Pacific Island influence is strong here and Pacific arts and crafts are a good buy at Auckland's biggest street market.

More Sights

South Auckland belies New Zealand's claim to racial equality and inclusion. The suburbs of

Fresh-picked produce at the Otara Market

Manukau City are predominately Pacific Islander, Maori, and poor. Manukau has a few tourist attrac-

INSIDER TIP:

Auckland's Botanic Gardens are a haven for anyone who needs a peaceful break from sightseeing in the big bustling city. Don't miss the hothouses.

—COLIN MONTEATH,
National Geographic Photographer

tions signposted off SH1, including **Rainbow's End,** the country's biggest amusement park with such eyeball-jolting rides such as Corkscrew Coaster and Fear Fall, as well as other more sedate attractions to amuse the kids. At the next highway exit south, the **Auckland Regional Botanic Gardens** (*tel 09/267-1457*), on

Hill Road, Manurewa, are relatively new gardens dating from 1973, but they have extensive plantings, with excellent native displays and a good visitor center.

Just off the western highway, 3 miles (5 km) from the city center, the **Museum of Transport & Technology** (MOTAT) is a sprawling collection of vintage vehicles from farm machinery to trains to military hardware. MOTAT has its own Victorian village re-creating early Auckland and a wonderful collection of vintage aircraft, including a huge Solent flying boat from the bygone days of luxury air travel and a reproduction of the plane Kiwi pioneer aviator Richard Pearse (1877–1953) flew in 1903.

A tram ride or walk around the lake from MOTAT, **Auckland Zoo** is home to the usual exotics, but the main attractions are the native animal enclosures. They include the kiwi and tuatara house, New Zealand aviary, and sea lion and penguin areas. ∎

Rainbow's End

✉ Great South
   & Wiri Station
   Rds., Manukau
☎ 09/262-2080
💲 $$$–$$$$$

**www.rainbowsend
.co.nz.**

Museum of Transport & Technology

🄰 Map p. 56
✉ 805 Great North
   Rd., Western
   Springs
☎ 09/815-5800
💲 $$

www.motat.org.nz

Auckland Zoo

🄰 Map p. 56
✉ Motions Rd.,
   Western Springs
☎ 09/360-3800
💲 $$–$$$

**www.aucklandzoo
.co.nz**

Around Auckland

Auckland's harbor opens out into the Hauraki Gulf, a sailing paradise dotted with islands reached by ferry. Rangitoto Island, a dormant volcano, makes an interesting day trip for walkers. Farther afield, Waiheke Island has fashionable B&Bs, beaches, wineries, and an artistic bent.

The Mansion House on Kawau Island is the former home of Governor Sir George Grey.

Visitors traveling farther will find remote Great Barrier Island a scenic retreat from the modern world. To the west, the Waitakere Ranges encompass a wilderness of regenerating forest, leading to wild, windswept beaches, rolling farmland, and wineries.

Hauraki Gulf Islands

Beyond Waitemata Harbour, more than 50 islands dot the sheltered waters of the Hauraki Gulf. The main islands can be reached by ferry from central Auckland and make an interesting day or overnight trip.

Rangitoto Island, visible from many parts of Auckland, is the youngest of the islands, born of a major eruption some 600 years ago. This symmetrical volcano rises 853 feet (260 m) from the sea, resembling a flattened Mount Fuji. From the Auckland Ferry Building, the journey takes less than half an hour. From the island's wharf, a one-hour walk leads to the top of the mountain for expansive views of Auckland and the gulf, as well as down into the forested crater. (The ferry company also runs trolley tours of the island.) Allow at least three hours including a side trip to the lava caves—rock tubes through which lava once flowed.

INSIDER TIP:

Grab a ferry to Waiheke Island for a great day of café hopping and wine tasting.

—REBEKAH MAWSON,
*Embassy of New Zealand,
Washington, D.C.*

Though the island is forested with pohutukawa trees, volcanic scoria covers the ground, so good footwear is recommended. A causeway connects Rangitoto to farmed Motutapu Island.

Virtually a suburb of Auckland, with 8,000 people living around its fine bays and beaches, **Waiheke Island** has long been a popular escape for city dwellers and visitors. Most of the population lives on the west end of the island, spreading out from the main settlement of increasingly chic **Oneroa,** which straddles a beautiful bay. The east half of the island is rural and picturesque. A haven for artists and craftspeople, the island abounds in galleries. Its wineries can be visited, and a host of accommodations cater to overnight stays. Tours run around the island, or you can rent bicycles, motor scooters, or cars from the Matiatia ferry wharf.

The largest of the islands, **Great Barrier Island** seems decades away from Auckland, despite being only two hours by ferry or 30 minutes by air. This rugged 25-mile-long (40 km) island attracts those seeking isolation. It has unpaved roads and no banks or ATMs. Electricity comes from generators and water from rain tanks. The Barrier, as locals call it, has scenic coves and beaches, fine walks, kauri forests, hot springs, and rugged mountains along its spine.

Bloody Sky

"Bloody sky" is the literal translation of Rangitoto, which seems to refer to the dramatic creation of the volcanically formed island. However, the island's name is actually taken from "Te Rangi i totongia a Tametekapua" or "the day the blood of Tametekapua was shed." Tametekapua was a Maori chief who died in battle at Islington Bay in the 14th century.

Tryphena, the main town in the south of the island, and nearby **Medlands Beach,** on a beautiful sandy bay, have most of the accommodations on the island, and they fill up in the height of summer, but at other times Great Barrier is simply serene. **Great Barrier Forest** in the center of the island has most of the popular walking trails, including those to the

The All Blacks perform the intimidating *haka* before a match.

The All-conquering All Blacks

For such a small country, New Zealand has produced an inordinate number of champions in sports as diverse as cricket, golf, cycling, auto racing, rowing, squash, and yachting. But in a sports-mad nation keen to flex national muscle on a much larger world stage, rugby rules. Above all, rugby stirs national passions, and the all-conquering national team, the All Blacks, are treated as demigods.

From muddy fields in rural towns to the gladiatorial arenas of the cities, winter weekends are devoted to the national obsession. Rugby's strong link to the national identity began with the New Zealand overseas rugby tour of 1905–1906, when the upstart colonials defeated Northern Hemisphere powerhouses of the games, including England, where the game originated at Rugby School and went on to spawn variants such as American football.

Since then, the All Blacks have been the team to beat in world rugby. They have won an astonishing 75 percent of all their international games, but have inexplicably disappointed at the Rugby World Cup. Apart from winning the

first cup in 1987, they have failed to live up to their status as favorites against the main rugby-playing nations such as England, Australia, South Africa, and France.

When the All Blacks lose, the country mourns and recriminations flow, but outside the World Cup their success rate remains high, particularly in annual competitions played against Australia and South Africa, the other two dominant nations in world rugby.

The national team takes its name from their jerseys, which traditionally are all black except for the silver fern logo. At the start of each match, the team famously performs the *haka*, the Maori war dance, a frightening sight and no

INSIDER TIP:

Don't accidentally wear your new "Australia" cap if you go to a rugby match, or you may have some quick and serious explaining to do to appease the local fans.

—LARRY PORGES,
National Geographic Editor

doubt a contributing factor in their wins.

Despite the legendary status of the All Blacks, rugby has its critics, including feminist groups and parents worried by the neck-crunching violence of the game, but tackle-free touch rugby has become very popular.

New Zealand rugby faced its biggest crisis in 1981, when the Springbok team from apartheid South Africa toured New Zealand despite world condemnation and massive street demonstrations by Kiwis. Public opinion was torn and the tour was marred by violence.

Despite turning a blind eye to apartheid in the past, New Zealand rugby owes much of its success to Maori and Pacific Islander players such as Jonah Lomu (b. 1975), born in Auckland to Tongan parents and one of the greats of the modern era.

The All Blacks play rugby union, the dominant form of rugby in New Zealand, but that is increasingly under threat from rugby league, a breakaway variant of the game popular in England and Australia. Though rugby purists scorn league, it has grown in popularity in New Zealand with the inclusion of the Auckland Warriors in the professional Australian league, which also poaches union players for its teams. Another variant, rugby sevens, is a faster game with only seven players instead of the usual fifteen.

The national competition representing New Zealand's regions is fiercely contested and can attract big crowds. It is well worth catching a game in winter at one of the country's major arenas such as Eden Park in Auckland, AMI Stadium in Christchurch, or the Westpac Stadium in Wellington, aptly called the Cake Tin. ∎

EXPERIENCE: Practice Your *Haka*

The Maori dance known as the haka is accompanied by shouting, stamping, club-wielding, and ferocious grimacing. Though not always a war dance, the haka was often performed to summon the god of war and frighten the enemy before going into battle. Today, the best-known haka, the Te Rauparaha haka or "Ka Mate," is performed by New Zealand's national rugby team, the All Blacks, before each match.

The Te Rauparaha haka is attributed to the great warrior Te Rauparaha, who when pursued by his enemies was given protection by a local chief, Te Whareangi (the "hairy man" of the verse). Te Whareangi concealed Te Rauparaha in his *kumara* (sweet potato) pit, where Te Rauparaha hid and composed his celebration of life over death until he emerged into the sunlight again. Give it a go, but remember to look fierce:

Ka mate. Ka mate. Ka ora. Ka ora.	I may die. I may die. I may live. I may live.
Ka mate. Ka mate. Ka ora. Ka ora.	I may die. I may die. I may live. I may live.
Tenei te tangata puhuru huru	This is the hairy man
Nana nei i tiki mai, Whakawhiti te ra	Who causes the sun to shine again
A upane. ka upane.	A step upward. Another step
A upane. ka upane.	upward.
Whiti te ra. Hi.	The sun shines.

Kaitoke Hot Springs and the historic kauri dams, built by loggers to float kauri logs downstream. The island's natural resources were ruthlessly exploited until the 1940s, but extensive reforestation since then has resulted in lush kauri and mixed forest.

EXPERIENCE:
Windsurfing

With hundreds of bays, consistent northeast sea breezes, and plenty of dedicated stores, Auckland is famed for its windsurfing. Ask longboard sailors and Olympic medalists Bruce and Barbara Kendall, who make Auckland their home. You can stop by any shop for information on where to go, on-the-spot lessons, and equipment. For beginners, **Dive Bomb** on Tern Lane (*tel 09/333-3322, www.divebomb.com*) is a good place to start. Advanced windsurfers will want to go to **Flying Forward** on Seagull Alley (*tel 09/223-5322, www .seagullalley.com*), where the best of the best hang out after a day on the water. Before even stepping foot in Auckland, visit *www.windsurf.co.nz* for more insights.

Kawau Island
⚠ Map p. 79

Kawau Island

Kawau Island can also be reached by regular ferry from Sandspit (see p. 81), 50 miles (80 km) north of Auckland. Kawau has long attracted yachts seeking refuge in idyllic **Bon Accord Harbour,** which bisects this small island, some 5 miles (8 km) long. Most of the island is privately owned, and accommodations can be arranged at mainland tourist offices or via the internet.

Kawau was home to a copper mine before one of New Zealand's founding fathers, Governor-General Sir George Grey, bought it in 1862. Sir George spent a fortune building the imposing **Mansion House** (*tel 09/422-8882, $*) and introducing a host of exotic trees and animals, including monkeys, zebras, and Australian wallabies. Until recently, the latter hopped around in abundance, but the Department of Conservation is doing its best to wipe out this non-native species. Now a museum, Mansion House and its gardens can be visited, and good short walks lead out from the house.

West of Auckland

The rugged **Waitakere Ranges,** a green haven on the city's doorstep, lie between Auckland and the windswept Tasman coast. A popular weekend day trip for residents, it can also be visited as a scenic detour skirting the city on the way to Northland. Fern-draped forest and long wild beaches give way to rolling farmland and vineyards farther north.

Access is normally through **Titirangi,** a fashionable Auckland suburb bordering Manukau Harbour and the foothills. From Titirangi, take winding **Scenic Drive** up to the impressive **Arataki Visitor Centre** (*tel 09/817-0077*). The spectacular views alone are worth the stop, but this is also the place for information on the **Waitakere Ranges Regional Park,** a vast area of regenerating rain forest and wild coastline.

Continue along Scenic Drive to Waiatarua and turn off to

Piha, a renowned surf beach dominated by towering Lion Rock. The often unruly weather gives the black-sand beaches of the west coast a brooding

INSIDER TIP:

Head west to Titirangi and explore the art galleries there—then drive through native forests to the wild west beach coast at Piha.

—ANGELA GORE,
*Embassy of New Zealand,
Washington, D.C.*

atmosphere, beautifully captured in *The Piano,* the 1994 Academy Award–winning film. The opening scenes were filmed at Karekare just south of Piha, where you'll find fine coastal walks.

Back at Waiatarua, take Scenic Drive north along the mountain ridge. A number of worthwhile, if poorly signposted, stops lie along this road. About a ten-minute drive from the Piha turnoff, Parkinson Lookout has harbor and city views, and farther on, Pukemateko Hill boasts a fabulous 360-degree panorama. From Scenic Drive you can also hike 45 minutes steeply downhill to Fairy Falls (signposted from the road), or take an easier walk there from Mountain Road, which turns off farther north.

The main road then descends to the lowlands around Kumeu, home to a number of good wineries. At Kumeu, turn left to Helensville on SH16, part of the Twin Coast Discovery tourist route to Northland. Coopers Creek Vineyard *(tel 09/412-8560)* on SH16 at Hupaia has landscaped gardens and wine tastings. One of New Zealand's largest wine makers, Nobilo *(tel 09/412-6666)* is nearby on Station Road. Another well-known winery, Matua Valley Wines *(tel 09/411-8301)* is north of the highway on Waikoukou Valley Road at Waimauku.

Also at Waimauku, turn off to Muriwai, another surf-pounded beach where viewing platforms on the cliff allow close-up views of a teeming gannet colony. ■

Rainbow Warrior

On July 10, 1985, the *Rainbow Warrior,* a ship owned by Greenpeace, was bombed and sunk by a team of French intelligence agents while it was docked in Auckland's Waitemata Harbour. The environmental organization had been protesting French nuclear testing in the South Pacific. Two of the agents, disguised as husband and wife tourists, were caught by New Zealand police. Convicted of manslaughter for the death of a Portuguese crew member, they were sentenced to ten years imprisonment, but served less than three in French custody. Although the French government initially denied responsibility for the attack, it eventually accepted blame. Soon afterward, "You can't sink a rainbow" became a global catchphrase among environmentalists.

A rich history, strong Maori roots, a "winterless" climate, and the most stunning coastline in the country

Northland

Cape Maria Van Dieman, Northland

Northland

The sea defines the long peninsula of Northland. It pounds the sand dunes of the west coast and caresses the sheltered bays and beaches of the east. Little wonder that the early seafarers, Maori and European, headed east. Here the Bay of Islands takes top billing for its historical import as well as its superb coastal scenery.

An angler pulls in kahawai along Ninety Mile Beach.

Many visitors to the north focus solely on the Bay of Islands, only four hours by road from Auckland, but a loop through Northland offers diverse scenery, from mighty kauri forests to the windswept splendor of Cape Reinga. Aquatic delights range from sailing and diving to swimming with dolphins. Venture off the beaten track in Northland for the best chance to find a beach all to yourself.

Northland is the birthplace of modern New Zealand. One of the first sites to be settled by the Maori, Northland was home to 25 percent of all Maori by the 18th century. One-third of the population is still Maori in this rural region. Europeans also settled in

Northland. Whalers and traders, followed by missionaries, came in the early 19th century, bringing disease and muskets. Led by Hongi Hika, the Ngapuhi tribe used the new weapons to devastating effect, and a series of tribal wars erupted from 1821 until the 1830s.

Early European settlement was limited mostly to the Bay of Islands, where inhabitants of the main town of Kororareka (Russell) acquired a reputation for drunkenness and vice. The British resident, James Busby, predicted decimation of the Maori population and urged Britain to intervene. The contentious Treaty of Waitangi in 1840 ostensibly secured Maori rights and regulated dubious land sales, but in effect it signaled the beginning of colonization.

European focus and trade soon moved south to the new capital of Auckland, but in the latter half of the 19th century logging of Northland's kauri forests became a major industry, centered around the sawmills of Dargaville. Migrants from what is now Croatia flocked here to dig for kauri gum. By the 1920s, most of the mighty kauri forests were gone and Northland fell into a rural slumber. Lacking industry and isolated by poor roads, it was a forgotten backwater for much of the 20th century, particularly in the far north, one of few regions that remained largely Maori-speaking until the 1970s.

Northland is often described as subtropical, perhaps wishfully, but certainly it is warmer than the rest of the country. The area can be explored by the Twin

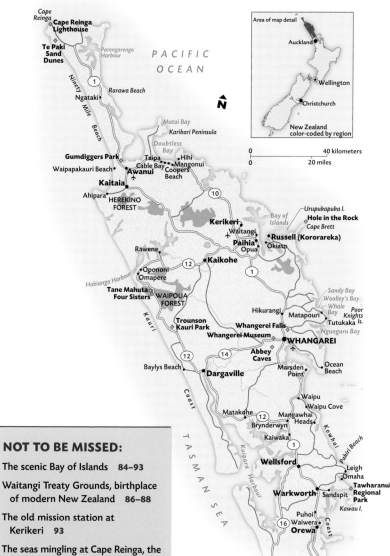

PACIFIC
OCEAN

Cape
Reinga
Cape Reinga
Lighthouse
Te Paki
Sand
Dunes

Parengarenga
Harbour

Ninety Mile Beach

Rarawa Beach

Ngataki

Matai Bay
Karikari Peninsula
Doubtless
Bay

Gumdiggers Park
Waipapakauri Beach
Awanui
Kaitaia
Ahipara
HEREKINO
FOREST

Taipa
Cable Bay Mangonui
Coopers
Beach
Hihi

Kerikeri
Waitangi
Paihia
Opua

Rawene
Kaikohe
Opononi
Omapere
Tane Mahuta
Four Sisters
WAIPOUA
FOREST

Hokianga Harbour

Kauri

Trounson
Kauri Park
Whangerei Falls
Whangerei Museum
Abbey
Caves

Baylys Beach
Dargaville

Coast

Matakohe
Bryinderwyn
Kaiwaka

Wellsford

Warkworth

Puhoi
Waiwera
Orewa

Urupukapuka I.
Hole in the Rock
Cape Brett
Bay of
Islands
Russell (Kororareka)
Okiato

Sandy Bay
Woolley's Bay
Whale
Bay
Hikurangi
Matapouri
Tutukaka
Poor
Knights
Is.
Ngunguru Bay

WHANGAREI

Marsden
Point
Ocean
Beach

Waipu
Waipu Cove
Mangawhai
Heads

Leigh
Omaha
Tawharanui
Regional
Park
Sandspit
Kawau I.

Pohiri Beach

Kowhai

TASMAN SEA

Kaipara
Harbour

Coast

Area of map detail

Auckland

Wellington

Christchurch

New Zealand
color-coded by region

0   40 kilometers
0   20 miles

N

NOT TO BE MISSED:

The scenic Bay of Islands 84–93

Waitangi Treaty Grounds, birthplace
of modern New Zealand 86–88

The old mission station at
Kerikeri 93

The seas mingling at Cape Reinga, the
country's northernmost tip 95

A tour along the sand highway of
Ninety Mile Beach 96

The giant kauri Tane Mahuta, lord
of Waipoua Forest 99–100

The jam-packed Kauri Museum
in Matakohe 101

Coast Discovery Road, a tourist route marked
by a dolphin logo, which takes in both coasts.
If time is limited, a short loop can include
the Bay of Islands and the Kauri Coast. A
longer time frame allows exploration of the
Far North and Hokianga; the East Coast has
many opportunities for beachcombing. ∎

Auckland to the Bay of Islands

Most visitors traveling north of Auckland head straight to the Bay of Islands, with little more than a lunch stop at Whangarei, the main city of Northland. Those with more time can explore the wonderful coastline east of the main highway, visiting hot springs, historic villages, fine beaches, islands, and diving spots. Past Whangarei, another coastal detour leads to the game-fishing, diving, and yachting port of Tutukaka and more beautiful beaches.

Mangawhai Heads beach

Kowhai Coast

Heading north out of Auckland on SH1, as you leave the suburbs behind, the vista opens out to the rolling hills and convoluted coastline of the Kowhai Coast between Auckland and Whangarei.

The first stop of interest is the pretty seaside village of **Waiwera,** at the mouth of the Waiwera River. Long noted for its hot springs, the **Waiwera Infinity Spa Resort** (tel 09/ 427-8800, www.waiwera.co.nz,

$–$$$$$) has thermal pools, a spa, a sauna, a fitness center, and water slides for family fun.

Picturesque **Puhoi,** just off SH1, was settled in the 1860s by Bohemian immigrants. The Puhoi Pub (Ahuroa & Puhoi Rds., tel 09/422-0812) is lined with artifacts and historical displays and is a favorite stop for a meal or drink on the journey north.

Nestled on the Mahurangi River, 39 miles (63 km) north of Auckland, is **Warkworth,** where steamboats and scows once docked. The town clings to its river traditions, though cafés and craft shops now command river frontage. Warkworth is the gateway to a scenic coastline punctuated by coves, bays, and beaches popular in summer.

On the southern outskirts of town, the **Warkworth & District Museum** (tel 09/425-7093, $–$$) has well-presented colonial exhibits, but of most interest is the kauri park opposite. The park holds the massive 800-year-old McKinney kauri, and you can take a delightful half-hour walk

INSIDER TIP:

Exploring the Abbey Caves Reserve, just west of Whangerai, is a cool way to spend a warm summer afternoon.

—BRENT OPELL,
National Geographic Field Scientist

through a grove of kauri trees, palms, and ferns.

Sheepworld (tel 09/425-7444, *www.sheepworldfarm.co.nz,* $$–$$$$) just north of Warkworth on SH1, is a theme park dedicated to New Zealand's most prolific export. Shearing and sheepdog shows (11 a.m. & 2 p.m.) are the highlights.

From Warkworth, SH1 continues north through Wellsford to Whangarei, or you can turn off SH1 to visit the Kauri Coast. An alternate route to Wellsford goes via Leigh and hugs the coastline, passing small beach resorts and

remote communities. This slower route is unpaved in parts, but makes a scenic excursion.

This alternate route heads east of Warkworth off SH1 to **Sandspit,** a tranquil harbor town and the departure point for ferries to Kawau Island (see p. 74). From Sandspit, the road north passes in-

Pakiri Beach Rides

Horseback riding is offered all over New Zealand, but for a ride with a difference, **Pakiri Beach Horse Rides** *(Taurere Park, Rahuikiri Rd., Pakiri Beach, tel 09/422-6275, www.horseride-nz. co.nz)* offers exhilarating gallops on an untouched stretch of white-sand surf beach with descendants of Maori chief Te Kiri of the Ngati Wai tribe.

Rides range from one hour on the beach for beginners to two-hour, half-day, and all-day rides through the dunes and forest. Overnight and multiday rides include warrior trails and stays in a converted woolshed or on a *marae.*

lets, small communities, and turn-offs to some fine beaches such as those in the **Tawharanui Regional Park** and at **Omaha.** Farther on, the fishing town of **Leigh** owes its existence to the snapper that once teemed on the nearby reefs, but tourism is taking over now as more visitors discover nearby **Goat Island Marine Reserve.**

Abbey Caves Reserve

▲ Map p. 79

✉ Abbey Caves Road 0175 Whangarei

☎ 09 430 6562

Whangarei
Map p. 79

Visitor information

✉ 92 Otaika Rd.

☎ 09/438-1079

**www.whangareinz
.org.nz**

Just offshore, tiny Goat Island is surrounded by waters swarming with fish. The best way to explore the marine reserve is by diving or snorkeling or on the glass-bottom-boat tours that operate in summer. Leigh has dive operators; just before you enter the reserve,

another scenic coastal detour to **Mangawhai Heads,** a small summer resort with a few stores and accommodation options. Boats moor in the estuary and a beautiful beach can be found near the point. The road then goes over the headland to **Waipu Cove,**

Sheepworld allows visitors hands-on experiences.

a café/aquarium rents snorkeling gear. Even if you don't enter the water, explore the rocky shore at low tide, an ecosystem in itself.

Continuing over the hills from Goat Island, you'll find **Pakiri Beach,** a wild stretch of golden sand with views of the islands. The beach is home to the rare fairy tern. Only 40 birds survive—observe all conservation signs. From here the road to Wellsford is gravel for about 6 miles (10 km) until it hits tarseal (Kiwi for "asphalt") again.

North of Wellsford on SH1, turn off at Kaiwaka onto the Kaiwaka-Mangawhai Road for

which has a couple of RV camps on a stunning stretch of beach. Farther on, the town of Waipu lies just off SH1, from where it is 25 miles (40 km) to Whangarei.

Whangarei

A diversion rather than a must-see destination, Whangarei is Northland's biggest city with a population of 48,000. It puts on its best face at the renovated **Town Wharf,** overlooking the yachts on the river in the center of town. Well worth a stop and a great spot for lunch, it has craft shops, cafés, and restaurants. **Clapham Clocks Museum** (tel 09/438-3993, $–$$), right by the big clock on Town Wharf, showcases all manner of timepieces and is best visited on the hour to hear the many weird and wonderful chimes. Four miles (6 km) west of town, the main **Whangarei Museum** *(tel 09/438-9630, $)* on SH14 has a restored homestead with colonial exhibits and a fine collection of Maori artifacts, including some wonderful feather cloaks.

Few cities can boast a waterfall as impressive as **Whangarei Falls,** on the northern outskirts of town just off Ngunguru Road to Tutukaka. The river plunges over a basalt cliff into a deep green pool; walks lead along the river.

Whangarei also has a superb beach, accessed by Whangarei Heads Road, which wends along the harbor past the port. Pounded by the Pacific, **Ocean Beach,** 21 miles (36 km) east of town, is a fine sweep of pristine sand stretching north for miles. During the week, you might just have it to yourself.

Tutukaka Coast

A loop road out of Whangerei takes in the fine seascapes of the Tutukaka Coast, noted for yachting, game fishing, diving, and surfing. The road meets the sea at the beautiful aqua-and-green estuary of Ngunguru and then winds over the headland to **Tutukaka.** On a fine harbor, Tutukaka's marina fills with expensive yachts from around the world. As well as being a noted game-fishing center, Tutukaka is the place to organize some of the best diving in New Zealand

around **Poor Knights Islands.**

Past Tutukaka, the road snakes through the hills to the peaceful estuary of **Matapouri Bay,** where

---

EXPERIENCE: Diving Poor Knights Islands

About 15 miles (24 km) offshore, Poor Knights Islands are part of a marine reserve washed by unusually warm sub-tropical currents that promote abundant and varied marine life, including sponges, manta rays, and tropical fish. Exceptionally clear water and a reef that plummets 328 feet (100 m) make this a world-class diver's paradise and New Zealand's top dive destination.

Underwater caves, archways, and fissures can be explored year-round with one of several dive operators in Tutukaka. Dive! Tutukaka *(Marina Rd., Tutukaka, tel 09/434-3867, www.diving.co.nz)* **is one of the main operators and also offers PADI courses. At the Tutukaka Marina, Ocean Blue Adventures** *(tel 0274 880-459, www .oceanblue.co.nz)* **and Pacific Hideaway Charters** *(tel 09/434-3762, www.divenz .co.nz)* **both have dive charters to the islands, including equipment.**

Whangarei dive companies that specialize in Poor Knights charters include Dive HQ Whangarei *(41 Clyde St., tel 09/438-1075, www.divenow.co.nz)* **and Dive Connection** *(135 Lower Cameron St., tel 09/430-0818, www.diveconnection.co.nz).*

---

an excellent coastal walk *(20 mins. one way)* leads to the stunning beach at **Whale Bay.** Adjoining **Woolley's Bay** is no less beautiful, and **Sandy Bay,** popular with surfers, offers one last glorious arc of sand just before the road heads back inland to SH1. ∎

The Bay of Islands

Sunny and sheltered by picturesque hills, some 150 islands dot the blue-and-turquoise waters of the Bay of Islands. Of all the coastlines in a country blessed with stunning seascapes, that of the Bay of Islands is by far the most renowned. The bay's lazy resort lifestyle in one of the country's premier tourist destinations belies a more turbulent past as the cradle of modern New Zealand.

The Paihia wharf is the gateway to the Bay of Islands.

Paihia

🗺 Map p. 79

Visitor information

✉ The Wharf, Marsden Rd.

☎ 09/402-7345

History

The bay's geography is that of a drowned river system. The rising sea flooded valleys over millions of years, stranding the ridges and peaks of ancient mountains. These islands—many just clumps of rock, but others more substantial—have long provided shelter for seafarers. The first Maori canoes may have arrived around a thousand years ago, and Maori villages once thrived on the islands and coves along the picturesque coast.

Captain Cook was the first European to arrive, in 1769, and he gave the bay its name. Despite firing muskets in warning and, when that failed, letting loose cannon shot "to try what Effect a Great Gun would have," Cook found the locals friendly, and he engaged in trade and entertained chiefs. French explorer Marion du Fresne was not so lucky in 1772 when he and 25 crew members were killed.

Europeans then stayed away until whalers began calling in for some early 19th-century R&R. Kororareka (modern-day Russell) became the favored village in which to fraternize with Maori "ship girls" and drink rum.

Kororareka's sordid reputation saw it dubbed the "hellhole of the Pacific," but the missionaries soon arrived to stamp out vice. Samuel Marsden delivered the country's first sermon on Christmas Day, 1814, at Rangihoua, on the northern shore of the Bay of Islands.

The glorious bay can be explored via a host of activities, from swimming with dolphins to fishing charters, but most popular are the cruises.

An Anglican mission station was set up at Kerikeri, while the Catholics under Bishop Pompallier settled at Kororareka. Some of the missionaries lapsed, however. Thomas Kendall took a Maori lover and helped the Ngapuhi chief Hongi Hika acquire muskets.

In the 1830s, James Busby was appointed resident to bring British order to the Bay of Islands. From his home at Waitangi, in the present-day Treaty House, Busby pushed for greater British intervention. In 1840, Maori chiefs were convinced to transfer sovereignty to the crown by signing the Treaty of Waitangi (see pp. 90–91) and William Hobson was appointed lieutenant-governor of the new colony.

The following year, Hobson moved the administration from Kororareka to Auckland, and the Bay of Islands went from capital to backwater. Hone Heke, the first chief to sign the Treaty of Waitangi, became increasingly disenchanted with colonial rule and laid siege to Kororareka in 1845, forcing the town to be evacuated. The sacked town was rebuilt and renamed Russell.

The Bay of Islands made it onto the tourist map in 1926 when U.S. writer Zane Grey came to fish for marlin and told the world. International game-fishing competitions helped spur international tourism, and the Bay of Islands is now a premier destination.

Visiting the Bay

Paihia is the tourist center of the Bay of Islands and adjoins the Waitangi Treaty Grounds, a must-see on every itinerary. The glorious bay can be explored via a host of activities, from swimming with dolphins to fishing charters, but most popular are the cruises. At the very least, catch a ferry to the charming historic village of Russell, which also makes an excellent base for exploring the bay.

Kerikeri is the primary service town of the Bay of Islands region and lies inland away from the main attractions. Just outside the town, the original mission station is a major tourist area.

Waitangi

△ Map p. 79

Waitangi Treaty Grounds

✉ Waitangi
National
Reserve,
1 Tau Henare
Dr., Paihia

☎ 09/402-7437

$ $$$

www.waitangi.net.nz

Visiting Maori Sites

Some Maori sites are *tapu* ("sacred" or "forbidden"), particularly burial grounds, and must not be entered. Before you can visit a marae (the tribe's compound), you must be invited and receive permission from the community or elders.

Maori greet guests there with a *powhiri* (formal welcome) that begins with a chant from the women. On formal occasions, a warrior performs the *wero* (challenge), wielding a club before laying it down for guests to pick up, signifying that they come in peace.

Remove your footwear before entering the *wharenui* (meetinghouse). After the *hongi* greeting (traditional touching of noses), guests present a *koha* (gift) to the hosts. Do not eat inside the meetinghouse.

Paihia

Paihia is the first port of call and overnight stop for most visitors to the Bay of Islands. Crammed with hotels, restaurants, and tour operators, Paihia has lost some charm to development, but this likeable resort town serves visitors well. It hums with vacationers in summer, when the "No Vacancy" signs go up, and you can walk from here to the **Waitangi Treaty Grounds,** one of the bay's principal attractions.

Two cruise operators at the town wharf, **Fullers** (*Maritime Building, The Wharf, Marsden Rd., tel 09/402-7421, www.fboi .co.nz, $$$$$*) and **Kings** (*Maritime Building, The Wharf, Marsden Rd., tel 09/402-8288, www.kings-tours.co.nz, $$$$$*) handle most of the voyages out to the islands past the Russell Peninsula. Popular tours include one to the **Hole in the Rock** at Motukokako Island, which involves a stopover at Urupukapuka Island. The Cream Trip takes in many major sights and is based on the original 1920s service around the bay that picked up produce from dairy farms and delivered mail.

Waitangi Treaty Grounds

Across the Waitangi River, 1.2 miles (2 km) north of the Paihia wharf, the Waitangi Treaty Grounds is the birthplace of the nation, where the Maori chiefs signed the Treaty of Waitangi and William Hobson proclaimed British sovereignty over the country.

Racial sensitivities are reflected at the treaty grounds, where Maori and Pakeha (European) styles come together. Surrounded by English lawns, the **Treaty House,** built in 1833–1834, was the original residence of the first British administrator, James Busby. This museum re-creates a colonial house and displays a copy of the treaty. Adjoining the Treaty House, **Te Whare Runanga** meetinghouse was built in 1940 to celebrate Maori involvement in nation-building. Designed as a meetinghouse for all the Maori tribes, the superb carvings inside

EXPERIENCE: Maori Culture

Traditional Maori culture is at its strongest on the *marae,* the meeting place of the tribe, usually found in the countryside. However, Maori culture also thrives in the cities, and most Maori are urban dwellers. Resurgent Maori traditions are celebrated, and the Maori influence permeates New Zealand society.

Don't miss an opportunity to visit a marae if you are lucky enough to get invited, but the most accessible glimpse into Maori culture is provided by cultural tours out of Rotorua. Many hotels and tour operators include cultural performances of Maori song and dance followed by a *hangi* (earth oven) feast.

As you would expect, performances are touristy, but the Maori involved are proud of their culture and keen to enlighten as much as to entertain. Rotorua's main Maori centers, Te Puia and Whakarewarewa (see p. 126) both offer cultural performances and hangi. Tamaki Maori Village *(1220 Hinemaru St., tel 07/349-2999, www.maoriculture. co.nz)* picks up visitors at hotels and takes them to their re-created Maori village in the forest for evening performances. Mitai Maori Village *(196 Fairy Springs Rd., tel 07/343-9132, www.mitai .co.nz)* is another good Rotorua operator. In Taupo, the equivalent can be found at Wairakei Terraces *(tel 07/378-0913, www.wairakei terraces.co.nz).*

Maori artists are famed for their wood carving.

Performances

Polished Maori song and dance performances (or *kapa haka*) at the Auckland Museum (see p. 64) are worth catching, and keep an eye out for festivals that include Maori performances, such as the Pasifika Festival, showcasing Pacific cultures every March in Auckland. The national kapa haka competition, Te Matatini, held every two years, highlights the best young Maori performers. In Auckland, Potiki Adventures *(tel 09/845-5932, www. potikiadventures.com)* puts together tours that include meeting artists and visiting Maori historical sites.

Immersion

For a deeper insight into Maori culture, look for rural experiences. Though limited, guides and tours can be found. Northland is a Maori stronghold. The Waitangi Treaty Grounds in the Bay of Islands is New Zealand's most historic site. Te Whare Runanga, on the grounds, is a national meetinghouse for all Maori tribes, and its superb carvings shouldn't be missed. Guides from the Ngapuhi tribe offer insights, and local Maori tour companies such as Culture North *(SH1, Okaihau, tel 09/402-5990, www.culturenorth. co.nz)* and Fernz EcoTours *(Kingfisher Rd., Jack's Bay, Russell, tel 09/403-7887, www .fernzecotours.co.nz)* have tours including canoe trips and marae visits.

Footprints Waipoua *(tel 09/405-8207, www.footprints waipoua.com)* in Opononi has tours explaining the legends of Waipoua Forest (see pp. 99–100) and of Hokianga Harbour, where the explorer Kupe is said to have landed. ∎

Russell

◪ Map p. 79

Visitor information

✉ Russell Wharf

☎ 09/403-8020

DOC Visitor Centre

✉ The Strand

☎ 09/403-9005

depict the ancestors and artistic styles of the main tribes.

At Hobsons Beach, the mighty 114-foot-long (35 m) war canoe *Ngatokimatawhaorua* is named for the craft that legendary explorer Kupe sailed to Aotearoa. The largest Maori canoe ever built, it is launched by 80 or more rowers every few years to celebrate Waitangi Day on February 6, when the prime minister and other dignitaries gather at Waitangi.

Allow at least a couple of hours to explore the reserve, which includes a video and exhibits at the visitor center, an excellent café,

The Strand in the historic town of Russell

and pleasant walks through the grounds. Guided tours and cultural performances are also offered. A good 3-mile (5 km) round-trip walk goes to the **Haruru Falls.**

Russell

When Charles Darwin visited Russell (then called Kororareka) in the *Beagle* in 1835, he described the English inhabitants as the "very refuse of society" and the Maori houses as "filthy hovels." Lawlessness, drunkenness, and prostitution were rampant.

Today, the town has gone from hellhole to historic. Old wooden villas line the waterfront and the lightly trafficked streets are a delight to wander. Russell has the feel of an island, for it is usually reached by passenger ferry from Paihia or by car ferry from Opua to Okiato, 6 miles (9 km) south of Russell. The alternative, the long and twisting Russell Road to Whangarei, is scenic but suitable only for those with time to burn.

From the ferry dock, turn left along the waterfront to the **Duke of Marlborough Hotel,** one of the oldest inns in the country. Farther along The Strand is the historic **police station** (1870), once the courthouse. At the end of the road, head up Wellington Street for the 30-minute walk to **Flagstaff Hill,** also reached by car along Tapeka Road. On this hill in 1844, Ngapuhi chief Hone Heke felled the flagstaff that flew the Union Jack, a symbol of oppression just four years after the signing of the Treaty of Waitangi. The flagpole was replaced and eventually defended by a garrison after Heke axed it twice more, the last time beginning a battle for Kororareka that resulted in the sacking of the town.

In the center of town, **Russell Museum** (*2 York St., tel 09/403-7701, $*) is well worth a look. It has a one-fifth scale model of Captain Cook's *Endeavour*, an interesting DVD on the history of Russell, and colonial and Maori artifacts.

EXPERIENCE: Swim with the Dolphins

Dolphins are a common sight in New Zealand waters and have long interacted with humans. Two of the most famous dolphins are Pelorus Jack, who regularly escorted ships across the Cook Strait between 1888 and 1912, and Opo, who played in the shallows at Opononi with vacationers and became a national celebrity in the 1950s.

It seems only natural that swimming with wild dolphins would become a commercial venture, beginning in the late '80s. Though now common in locations around the world, New Zealand remains one of the world's most popular dolphin-swimming destinations. Operators are regulated and closely monitored; the activity is said to have minimal impact on wild dolphin behavior.

One of the most popular destinations for dolphin swimming is the Bay of Islands, where **Dolphin Discoveries** (tel 09/402-8234, www.dolphinz.co.nz, $$$$$), **Dolphin Adventures** (tel 09/402-6985, www.awesomenz.com, $$$$$), and **Kings Cruises** (tel 09/402-8288, www.kingstours.co.nz, $$$$$) run trips out of Paihia to see and swim with bottlenose and common dolphins in a stunning natural setting.

Huge pods of dusky and other dolphins come close to shore in Kaikoura as well. **Dolphin Encounter** (tel 03/319-6777, www.dolphin.co.nz, $$$$$) runs the only dolphin-swimming trips there.

Other places to swim with the dolphins include Tauranga and Whakatane on the east coast of the North Island and at Akaroa near Christchurch, where rare Hectors dolphins frolic.

Book tours in advance in summer (Nov.–April) and check with operators regarding weather and other restrictions.

From the museum, head up Robertson Road to **Christ Church** on the corner of Church Street. Built in 1836, it is the oldest church in the country. Four seamen from the HMS *Hazard* were killed near the church during Hone Heke's 1845 attack on the town, and the original marker from their grave is inside the church. The graveyard outside tells a poignant tale of early settlement and includes the graves of Ngapuhi chief Tamati Waka Nene (who fought against Hone Heke), the Clendon family (James R. Clendon was the first U.S. consul), and many American whalers.

At the southern end of the waterfront, **Pompallier House** (The Strand, tel 09/403-9015, $–$$) formed part of the Catholic mission founded by Bishop Jean Baptiste François Pompallier (ca. 1801–1871) in 1838. This French provincial building housed printing presses to produce religious booklets in Maori. After the mission moved to Auckland, the building became a tannery. Stop in at the Department of Conservation office near Pompallier Mission for a rundown on the area's natural attractions, including the overnight **Cape Brett Track,** a superb coastal hike to the lighthouse.

Near the wharf, the **Bay of Islands Swordfish Club** on The Strand welcomes visitors wishing to view the fishing memorabilia, which includes a gigantic blue marlin on the wall, photos, and

Treaty of Waitangi

For a short treaty paved with good intentions, the Treaty of Waitangi continues to be the most bitterly contested document in New Zealand history.

Though the 19th-century treaty would signal annexation of New Zealand, Britain was at first a reluctant colonizer, following the debacle in the American colonies. But as lawlessness grew in New Zealand and the private New Zealand Company began wholesale settlement, even wanting to establish its own government, Britain decided to act.

British naval officer Capt. William Hobson arrived in the Bay of Islands on January 29, 1840, to establish a colony. The Colonial Office at that time was headed by men of deep religious beliefs who had fought against slavery, and they insisted that Maori agreement be obtained. Hobson drafted a treaty in four days and set about convincing Maori tribes to transfer sovereignty to the British crown.

The Maori Question

Missionaries translated the treaty into Maori, and on February 5 it was put before a gathering of northern chiefs on the lawns of the British resident's house at Waitangi. The chiefs debated the treaty into the night, and the following day 45 of them signed. The treaty then toured the North Island; by the end of the year, 500 chiefs had signed.

The Treaty of Waitangi consists of only three articles. The first grants the Brisitish monarch (then Victoria) sovereignty over New Zealand. The second gives the chiefs full "exclusive and undisturbed possession of their Lands and Estates Forests Fisheries and other properties." It also says that if the Maori wish to sell land, they can do it only through the Crown. The third article grants Maoris "all the Right and Privileges of British Subjects."

Debate has raged over the differences between the English and Maori versions of the treaty, but undoubtedly the chiefs signed believing Britain would protect their interests. As settlers flooded in, however, Maori rights were pushed aside. When Maori chiefs united to restrict the sale of land in the 1860s, the New Zealand Wars ensued, and in the aftermath the settlers seized huge tracts of Maori land. In 1877, the courts declared the treaty a "simple nullity," and it was all but dead for a hundred years.

Recent Disputes

Though the treaty was dishonored, New Zealand politicians trumpeted it as an example of the equality given to Maori. In the 1970s, Maori activists put to rest the "happy native" myth. Land protests became a focus for resurgent Maoridom, and in 1975 the government set up the Waitangi Tribunal to investigate treaty breaches from that date.

In 1985, the reformist Labour government extended Waitangi Tribunal powers back to 1840, and the number of claims burgeoned. Compensation of NZ$170 million was paid to the Tainui tribe for land seized in Waikato, and other claims included not just land but also forests, fisheries, and even FM transmission rights.

The backlog of claims continues, and while the country sees a need to redress past injustices, there is also a backlash against the "grievance industry." Only time will tell if the process will be one of reconciliation. ■

Opposite: James Ingram McDonald's 1913 portrait of Capt. William Hobson.
Above: Waitangi Day celebrations, February 6, 2008

Kerikeri

Map p. 79

www.kerikeriguide
.co.nk

the original 1920s catch boards that feature Zane Grey.

Urupukapuka Island

Most of the bay's islands are tiny outcrops, and only a handful have ever been inhabited or farmed. The main islands are now mostly recreation areas that are reached by yacht or chartered water taxi. The exception is Urupukapuka Island, which is a stop on some of the regular cruises. Walking trails traverse the grassy hills and regenerating forest and take in archaeological sites of the Maori villages that once dotted the island.

Zane Grey camped on the island at Otehei Bay, where a fishing club resort was established in 1927. The **Zane Grey** (tel 09/403-7009, www.zanegrey.co.nz) continues to lease the site and has a restaurant, simple cabins, and the finest position in the Bay of Islands.

Kerikeri

With a warm climate and surrounded by rich orchards and the delights of the Bay of Islands, the town of Kerikeri attracts growing numbers of residents. Though the town is well supplied with amenities, for the visitor the real attraction lies just to the north.

Maori Creation

In the beginning was nothingness, but then came Papatuanuku, the earth mother, and Ranginui, the sky father, who had many male children, the gods of the Maori.

Held in their parents' embrace so tight no light could penetrate, the gods tired of the continual darkness. They decided to separate their parents and break into the light.

For a long time they debated the best way to part Papatuanuku and Ranginui. The god of war, Tumatauenga, said "Let us kill our parents." But Tanemahuta, god of the forest, urged for separation, saying Ranginui should be forced up to the sky.

All the gods finally agreed except for Tawhirimatea, god of winds and storms. He held his breath as, one by one, the gods set about separating earth and sky.

Rongomatane, the god of cultivated foods, tried but failed, as did Tangaroa, god of the sea. The god of wild foods, Haumiatiketike, was also unable to part the heavens from the earth.

Tumatauenga the warrior hacked at the bonds between earth and sky, but he could not sever them. Finally, Tanemahuta stepped up. With the strength and patience of a slowly growing kauri tree, he strained and pushed, his shoulders against his mother Papatuanuku, his feet against his father Ranginui, until finally they parted and light flooded the world.

Tawhirimatea fled to be with his father, and to this day vents his stormy revenge upon the world.

A multitude of creatures were revealed by the light, but humans were missing, so Tanemahuta fashioned a woman, Hineahuone, from clay.

Tanemahuta and Hineahuone had a daughter called Hinetitama, whom Tanemahuta also took as his wife. They in turn had children, ensuring that humans would flourish, but when Hinetitama found out that Tanemahuta was her father, she fled in shame to the underworld where she became Hinenuiitepo, goddess of the night.

Kerikeri Mission Station is one of the country's oldest settlements and one of its most significant historical sites. In a picturesque basin where the Kerikeri River enters the estuary, the mission was established in 1819 next to the Kororiko Pa. Picturesque **St James Church** (1878) replaced the original church on the site.

The imposing **Stone Store** was built in 1832–1836 as a storehouse for the mission and is the country's oldest stone

Kerikeri's Stone Store is the country's oldest stone building.

Don't miss Kororiko Pa, a short walk uphill behind the wharf. All that remains of this fortress village is a series of terraces and ditches, but this evocative site is where the great Ngapuhi chief Hongi Hika assembled his war parties.

building. The Kemp family took it over after the mission's closure in 1848 and it was run as a shop for many years. Tickets to the shop, now decked out as a colonial store and museum, include entry to the Mission House behind.

The **Mission House** is New Zealand's oldest surviving European building. Now a museum with some original furnishings, this elegant wooden house was built in 1821–1822 for the Reverend John

Butler. James and Charlotte Kemp and their descendants lived in it from 1831 until 1974.

From the wharf in front of the Stone Store, cruises and kayaking tours depart in summer. Don't miss **Kororiko Pa,** a short walk uphill behind the wharf. All that remains of this fortress village is a series of terraces and ditches, but this evocative site is where the great Ngapuhi chief Hongi Hika assembled his war parties. Across the river, **Rewa's Village** (tel 09/407-6454, $) replicates a Maori village with huts built by traditional means.

For a good hike, take the **Kerikeri River Track** from the parking lot to Rainbow Falls (1 hour one-way) via Wharepuke Falls and the Fairy Pools. ■

Stone Store and Mission House

✉ 246 Kerikeri Rd., Kerikeri Basin

☎ 09/407-9236

$ $

Far North

Beyond the Bay of Islands, the Far North is the warmest region of the country and home to remote bays, beaches, and Maori towns.

The Cape Reinga lighthouse marks New Zealand's northernmost point.

Its highlights are Doubtless Bay, which includes charming Mangonui and fine beaches, and Cape Reinga, the country's most northerly point at the end of a long peninsula of sand dunes. Exhilarating tours along Ninety Mile Beach to Cape Reinga can be arranged in Kaitaia, the main town.

Doubtless Bay

The bay's name comes from Captain Cook, who sailed past the entrance in 1769 and noted it was "doubtless a bay" in his journals.

Whaling and later kauri attracted settlers, and the sleepy fishing port of **Mangonui** has a good heritage walk taking in historic buildings such as the Mangonui Hotel and the courthouse. The highlight for many is the self-proclaimed world-famous Mangonui Fish Shop *(Beach Rd.),* an ideal lunch spot perched over the water with tables on a deck. **Butler Point** *(tel 09/406-0006, $),* a privately owned property at Hihi on the other side of the harbor, has a whaling museum and the 1847 house of whaler William

INSIDER TIP:

Coopers Beach's north end is surrounded by pohutukawa trees, also called New Zealand Christmas Trees for their bright red flowers in summer.

—ANGELA GORE,
Embassy of New Zealand,
Washington, D.C.

Butler, which can be visited by appointment.

West of Mangonui on SH1, **Coopers Beach** is a sprawling collection of baches (New Zealandese for vacation houses) merging into **Cable Bay,** an arc of golden sand before a pretty headland, once linked to Australia by telegraph cable. The road then crosses the causeway to **Taipa,** the last part of this trio of small beach resorts, said to be the landing place of the great Polynesian explorer Kupe.

The **Karikari Peninsula,** a crooked finger of remote unspoiled beaches, forms the western flank of Doubtless Bay. The peninsula's most renowned beach, **Matai Bay,** has two perfect bays, ideal for swimming. Dolphins also frolic here. Summer vacationers flock to the simple Department of Conservation campground, but at other times you may have this idyllic beach to yourself.

Cape Reinga & Ninety Mile Beach

The country's main highway, SH1, snakes through the middle of the long Aupouri Peninsula to **Cape Reinga,** the last gasp of New Zealand at the top of the North Island. A lonely lighthouse looks out over the cliffs to the Columbia Bank where the Pacific Ocean meets the Tasman Sea, a swirling maelstrom in stormy weather. An obligatory signpost to other lands across the vast ocean only serves to confirm that this is the end of the world.

The Maori called the wind-

Speed Demon

On January 26, 1932, Australian daredevil Norm "Wizard" Smith attempted to set the world land speed record on Ninety Mile Beach. His car, the *Enterprise,* was built around a massive Napier Lion airplane engine, ice-cooled and supercharged to produce 1,450 horsepower. Although hindered by the tides, Smith set a new world 10-mile speed record of 164.08 miles per hour (264.06 kph).

swept and remote peninsula Te Hiku o te Ika a Maui, the "tail of the fish of Maui." From his canoe, the South Island, Maui dragged a giant fish out of the sea to form the North Island. Wellington is at the head of the fish, and Te Rerenga Wairua (Cape Reinga) lies at the tip of the tail. Te Rerenga Wairua translates as "departure place of the spirit," for the spirits of the dead make the long journey here to depart Aotearoa for Hawaiki, the spiritual homeland.

Captain Cook called this the Desert Coast, for the west coast along **Ninety Mile Beach** (in fact

---

EXPERIENCE:
Beach Bashing to Cape Reinga

By far the best way to reach Cape Reinga is to take the beach highway along the sands of Ninety Mile Beach at low tide. Given that insurance policies forbid rental vehicles traveling on the sand, a tour is the way to go. Buses and 4WD vehicles make the trip from Kaitaia and also from the Bay of Islands (a much longer day trip). Tours take in the Te Paki sand dunes, Cape Reinga lighthouse, the Ancient Kauri Kingdom woodcraft center, sand dune tobogganing, and possibly Gumdiggers Park, Rarawa Beach, and other points of interest. Kaitaia operators include Harrisons Cape Runner (tel 09/408-1033, www.90milebeach.co.nz), **Sand Safaris** (tel 09/408-1778, www.sandsafaris.co.nz), and **Cape Reinga Adventures** (tel 09/409-8445, www.capereingaadventures.co.nz). From Paihia, **Dune-Rider** (tel 09/402-8681, www.dunerider.co.nz) offers tours in a funky 4WD vehicle.

---

only 60 miles/100 km long) is a desolate landscape of surf-pounded sand and giant dunes. Vehicles can drive along the hard sands of the beach, which was once the default highway before SH1 was built, but all rental car agreements ban beach use, not without good reason. Travel can only occur around low tide or else soft sands will swallow vehicles whole. Tours

by 4WD vehicles and funky beach buggies operate out of Kaitaia. These are the most exhilarating ways to explore the peninsula and allow you to get up close to the giant **Te Paki sand dunes,** a spectacular sight. The dunes can also be approached along the Te Paki Stream Road, a turnoff from SH1 just before Cape Reinga.

The inland highway goes mostly through farmland and is not so stunning, but points of interest lie off it. If you are coming from the south at the start of the peninsula, wide and wild **Waipapakauri Beach** provides the easiest access to Ninety Mile Beach. About 10 miles (16 km) farther north on SH1, a signposted road leads east to **Gumdiggers Park** (Heath Rd., tel 09/406-7166, $–$$), where paths lead around the old swamp kauri forests. Gumdiggers once flocked here looking for fossilized kauri gum, the tree sap prized for varnish and linoleum. They dug holes all over this area and one of their huts remains. Halfway along the peninsula past Ngataki, turn off to **Rarawa Beach** and its white silica sands used in glassmaking. The beaches along the east coast here are a brilliant white, and culminate farther north at a giant white sandbar at the entrance to remote **Parengarenga Harbour.**

On the northern outskirts of Awanui, on SH1 just before the peninsula, the **Ancient Kauri Kingdom** (229 SH1) is well worth a stop. This large souvenir shop specializes in knickknacks and furniture made from ancient kauri dug up out of the swamps, some of it 45,000 years old. Don't miss

Sand tobogganing on the Te Paki sand dunes

the staircase carved out of a huge kauri stump and the massive lumps of salvaged wood outside.

Kaitaia

"Haere Mai, Dobro Dosli" ("Welcome" in Maori and Dalmatian) greets visitors entering Kaitaia, for this largely Maori town also celebrates its Dalmatian roots. Dalmatians from Yugoslavia settled here in droves in the 19th century to dig for kauri gum.

....

The Ancient Kauri Kingdom souvenir shop specializes in knickknacks and furniture made from ancient kauri dug up out of the swamps, some of it 45,000 years old.

....

Primarily a place to arrange trips to Cape Reinga, the Far North's main town has all the services a visitor could want, but few reasons to stay. The small **Far North Regional Museum** *(6 South Rd., tel 09/408-1403, $)* has an odd collection if you have time to kill.

Just a ten-minute drive west from Kaitaia, **Ahipara** lies at the southern end of Ninety Mile Beach. This small settlement has places to stay, and not much else, but the ocean aspect makes it a pleasant alternative to Kaitaia. The giant sand dunes of the Ahipara gumfields in the hills above the beach are popular for sand tobogganing, and the beach is ideal for long walks at sunset.

Heading to Hokianga, the scenic road from Ahipara to Rawene goes through the stunted but beautiful **Herekino Forest** and continues through a delightfully dilapidated world of one-horse towns forgotten by time. ∎

Kaitaia

🏔 Map p. 79

Visitor information

✉ Jaycee Park, South Rd.

☎ 09/408-0879

Kauri Coast

Mighty kauri trees grow only above the 38th parallel and once covered much of Northland. Now only a few pockets remain, mostly notably on Northland's west coast in the Waipoua Forest.

Matakohe's Kauri Museum is filled with the beautiful golden wood.

Hokianga Harbour

▲ Map p. 79

Visitor information

✉ SH12, Omapere

☎ 09/405-8869

The Kauri Coast follows SH12 from the Hokianga region, on the scenic harbor of the same name, south to the mighty trees of Waipoua Forest, then on to the smaller Trounson Kauri Park and the fascinating Kauri Museum at Matakohe.

Hokianga Harbour

Hokianga Harbour takes its name from Hokianga-nui-a-Kupe—the "departing place of Kupe"—for legend has it that after discovering and exploring New Zealand, Kupe made his last stop here and grew *kumara* (sweet potatoes) for the return voyage to Hawaiki.

French explorer Jean de Surville first sighted Hokianga in 1769, just before Captain Cook, but neither crossed the shallow sandbars into the harbor. The area relied on the kauri trade until the forests were ravaged in the early 20th century.

Today Hokianga rests in scenic slumber, its seaside towns graced with colonial homesteads and wooden churches on the backwater route between the

Kauri Coast and the Far North. Make sure to take the car ferry *(tel 09/405-2602)* that runs every hour between Rawene and the Narrows, a delightfully relaxed journey that cuts off a long drive around the harbor.

The town of **Rawene** awakens with a brief flurry of activity when the ferry docks. Otherwise the streets are quiet and a delight to wander, littered with historic buildings, including **Clendon House** *(tel 09/405-7874, Nov.–April, $).* You can also catch a bite to eat at one the town's cafés, such as the Boatshed next to the water.

Legend lingers at **Opononi,**

Dolphin Mania

The young bottlenose dolphin Opo has been immortalized by statues, books, and folk songs (most famously Crombie Murdoch's 1956 chart topper, "Opo the Friendly Dolphin"). After she died, possibly as a result of an explosive blast, the entire country mourned.

---

where a statue commemorates Opo, a wild dolphin that became a national celebrity in 1955 when it socialized with vacationers. The adjoining town of **Omapere** has a quirky museum showing a wonderful 1950s film on the "gay dolphin," who died before her prime, some say at the hands of dynamite fishermen. The museum also highlights the 1970s hippie commune that the council did its

INSIDER TIP:

Be sure to visit Tane Mahuta (Lord of the Forest), the largest tree in New Zealand and surely one of the largest you'll see anywhere in the world.

—BRENT STEPHENSON, *National Geographic Field Scientist*

best to close, but the area still taps its foot to an different beat.

Just west of Omapere above the heads of the harbor, turn off the highway and take the short **lookout point walkway** from the end of Signal Station Road for a superb panorama: beautiful beaches, the pounding surf of the west coast, and the bald, ravaged hills and giant sand dunes opposite Omapere.

Waipoua Forest

The Waipoua Forest, 12 miles (20 km) from Hokianga, is the most significant kauri reserve in the country, containing three-quarters of all remaining kauri trees. Bought from the Maori in 1876, the forest escaped logging because of its remoteness. After the State Forest Service began cutting some of the trees in the 1940s, a massive petition was launched and Waipoua became a forest sanctuary in 1952.

This beautiful rain forest also contains giant tree ferns and hardwoods as impressive as the kauri in many places, but nothing compares to **Tane Mahuta** (Lord

Dargaville

⬛ Map p. 79

Visitor information

✉ 69 Normanby St.

☎ 09/439-8360

www.dargaville.co.nz

of the Forest). The first stop if coming from the north, this giant kauri towers 168 feet (51.5 m) and has a girth of 45 feet (14 m). Believed to be 2,000 years old, it is the largest living tree in New Zealand, though by no means the largest kauri ever recorded—one specimen, named the Kairaru, was three times the volume. Only a five-minute walk from the road, Tane Mahuta is the park's number-one attraction.

A couple of miles south, a 20-minute walk leads from the parking lot to **Te Matua Ngahere** (Father of the Forest), the second largest tree in the forest. Just off this trail, the **Four Sisters** is a group of four graceful trees.

Farther south at the junction with the Waipoua River Road, **Rickers Walk** is a ten-minute round-trip through a copse of kauri to a lookout over the river. "Ricker" is the name given to a young kauri tree by the early foresters.

The Waipoua River Road leads to the Department of Conservation **Waipoua Visitors Centre** (tel 09/439-3011), which has informative displays on the kauri and the forest.

Waipoua to Auckland

Though much smaller than Waipoua, the 1,112-acre (450 ha) forest restoration reserve of the **Trounson Kauri Park** from Waipoua has an impressively dense stand of kauri that can be explored by an easy half-hour loop walk. The reserve is also home to such threatened species as kukupa

(pigeons), pekapeka (bats), kauri snails, and North Island brown kiwi. The nearby **Kauri Coast Holiday Park** (Trounson Park Rd.) offers guided night walks (tel 09/439-0621, $$–$$$) through the forest with a good chance of spotting kiwi—a rare experience.

The northern turnoff from

The giant kauri tree Tane Mahuta in the Waipoua Forest

SH12 to Trounson is 10 miles (16 km) south of Waipoua, but this access road is mostly unpaved. From the southern turnoff, 25 miles (40 km) north of Dargaville, it is only 4 miles (7 km) along a paved road.

Dargaville, on Kaipara Harbour, grew up on the kauri trade. Dozens of sawmills operated around the harbor, and in its heyday, a hundred million board feet of kauri was exported every year,

Kauri Trees

Kauri trees have taken on an almost mystical significance for New Zealanders now that most of them have been wiped out by logging. Though the sequoia may be taller and older, for sheer wooden bulk the kauri has no equal. Growing for up to 2,000 years, the trunks can reach a diameter of 16 feet (5 m) and soar over 160 feet (49 m) high. Moreover, the trunks don't taper until the first branches, sometimes over 65 feet (20 m) up, providing huge cylinders of straight-grained wood.

Kauri became the backbone of the country's timber industry and was at one stage New Zealand's greatest export.

Mills proliferated along the west coast in the 19th century and ports such as Dargaville on Kaipara Harbour boomed. The trade was so voracious that by 1900 only 10 percent of the forests remained. Now less than 4 percent are left.

A member of the Araucariaceae family, the kauri is high in resin, which the trees leak when damaged. The Maori prized this sap, or kauri gum, for burning in torches, and it was harvested in the 19th century for varnishes and linoleum. Sometimes harvesters bled the trees for the sap, but mostly it was dug up from ancient buried forests, which yielded great clumps of semifossilized gum.

---

the equivalent of 37,000 mature kauri trees, each about a thousand years old.

Dargaville grew rich on the kauri trade, but much of that wealth has drifted away and today Dargaville is noted for kumara production. On a hill with panoramic views across the town and river, the large **Dargaville Museum** (Harding Park, tel 09/439-7555, $–$$) has good exhibits on the kauri industry and a huge canoe from pre-European times, but most visitors save their energy for the more impressive Matakohe Kauri Museum down the highway.

For a taste of the wild west coast, **Baylys Beach**, 8 miles (13 km) west of town on Baylys Coast Road, has basic accommodations as well as a couple of good cafés on a 60-mile-long (100 km) beach.

For a complete education on all things kauri, the **Kauri Museum** (Church Rd., tel 09/431-7417, $–$$$) in the small town of **Matakohe** is a must-see on the Kauri Coast route, possibly the best museum in the country outside the main cities. As well as detailed kauri exhibits, this sprawling museum contains a reproduction of a sawmill, an old boardinghouse made of kauri, old machinery, and a host of pioneer exhibits. Pride of place goes to a huge vertical slice from the middle of a felled kauri that not only illustrates the size of the trees but the exquisite beauty of the wood.

From Matakohe, SH12 continues to Brynderwyn and joins SH1 south to Auckland. For an alternate route into Auckland, turn off at Wellsford, 17 miles (28 km) south of Brynderwyn, and follow the Kaipara Harbour on SH16 to Helensville and on to the west coast and Waitakere Ranges (see pp. 74–75). ■

Maori culture and geysers plus volcanoes, lakes, mountains, caves, beaches, and historic towns

Central North Island

Mount Taranaki looms over the central North Island.

Central North Island

The central North Island, stretching from Auckland to the lower south around Wellington, takes in volcanoes, geysers, lakes, craggy coastlines, sweeping beaches, the Maori heartland, and green pastures that nurtured a nation.

Cutting a fiery swathe from the east coast to the center of the North Island, the Taupo Volcanic Zone holds all of New Zealand's active volcanoes, from offshore White Island to the snowy peaks of the Tongariro National Park. Along this belt, geysers, mud pools, boiling ponds, and steam vent the landscape, especially around Rotorua, the biggest tourist magnet in the country.

Not only is Rotorua famous for its geothermal activity, but it also features Maori culture at its most accessible. The entire region is rich in Maori history. In the Waikato area, the tribes united to form the Maori King Movement and battle for their land. So, too, did the Maori in Taranaki on the west coast and at the Bay of Plenty in the east, while the remote East Cape remains a Maori stronghold.

While Rotorua is the tourist destination par excellence, the visitor has many options for interesting routes and diversions. From Auckland, the main highway leads to the rich farmland of the Waikato around Hamilton, then south to the King Country and the Waitomo Caves, a magical area riddled with caverns and glowworms.

Continuing down the less traveled west coast, the Taranaki region is dominated by the towering cone of Mount Taranaki, a snowcapped dormant volcano, one of New Zealand's most awesome sights. This rural route then leads south around to Wanganui, an old river port, where jet boats have replaced paddle steamers venturing upstream into the wilderness.

Alternatively, you can head east from Auckland to the Coromandel Peninsula, which has one of the country's most scenic coastlines, as well as fine beaches and historic old gold towns.

The Coromandel leads on to the Bay of Plenty, a sunny coast with some fine beaches and the possibility of trips to see the smoking volcano at White Island. Inland of the Bay of Plenty is a scenic lake district around Rotorua, where old volcanoes have filled with waters teeming with trout.

TASMAN SEA

NEW PLYMOUTH
Egmont Village
EGMONT N.P.
Mt. Taranaki
Dawson Falls
Stratford
45

The country's biggest lake, Taupo, lies at the very center of the North Island and is so large it resembles an inland sea. To its south are the volcanoes of Tongariro, Ngauruhoe, and Ruapehu—the mighty peaks of the Tongariro National Park—offering some of the best hikes in the country in the summer and good skiing in the winter.

South of Lake Taupo, Napier on the east coast is a delightful art deco city and seaside retreat. Wineries dot the countryside of surrounding Hawke's Bay, and farther north, Gisborne can be the starting point for an off-the-beaten-track adventure around the East Cape or into the virgin forests and lakes of Te Urewera National Park. ■

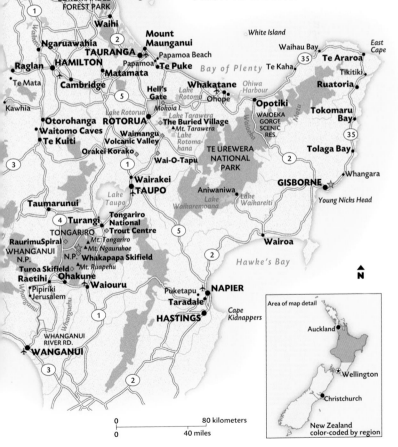

Waikato

The Waikato region was once a Maori stronghold and birthplace of the King Movement, which tried to unite the tribes against the colonial land grab. Now noted for its rich agricultural land and horse farms, the Waikato is also famous for the Waitomo Caves and the Otorohanga Kiwi House. You can also take a number of interesting side trips in the region.

The historic *Waipa Delta* paddle wheeler makes its way down the Waikato River.

Hamilton

Hamilton

⬛ Map p. 105

Visitor information

✉ Hamilton Transport Centre, Bryce & Anglesea Sts.

☎ 07/839-3580

www.visithamilton.co.nz

Hamilton (pop. 130,000) is New Zealand's fourth largest city, lying 81 miles (130 km) south of Auckland on the Waikato River, the country's longest waterway. It is the main city of the Waikato region.

Hamilton was founded on land confiscated after the New Zealand Wars, and in 1864 the gunboat *Rangiriri* established the first redoubt at Memorial Park near the town center.

The river was the town's vital link with the outside world until the railroad was built. The paddle wheeler **MV Waipa Delta** (tel 07/854-7813, $$$–$$$$) still plies the river, running popular tours from Memorial Park.

Nearby on the river, the town's main attraction is the **Waikato Museum** (1 Grantham St., tel 07/838-6606, www.waikatomuseum.co.nz), which has a wonderful collection of *taonga* (treasures) of the Tainui, the main Waikato tribe, including the impressive *Te Winika* war canoe.

About 1 mile (1.6 km) south of the city center on SH1, avid gardeners will appreciate the **Hamilton Gardens** (*Cobham Dr., tel 07/838-6782, www.hamilton gardens.co.nz*), an expansive collection of themed plantings, including Japanese, American, Italian renaissance, Victorian, and permaculture gardens.

Around Hamilton

On SH1, 12 miles (19 km) north of Hamilton, **Ngaruawahia** is the seat of the Kingitanga (Maori King Movement), formed when some of the Maori tribes united to counter British dominance.

INSIDER TIP:

BYOB (bring your own board) or try a surfing lesson at Raglan, New Zealand's most iconic surf beach, made famous by the classic cult film *Endless Summer*.

—CARRIE MILLER,
National Geographic Writer

They elected the Waikato chief Te Wherowhero (ca 1800–1860) as the first king in 1856. He took the name Potatau and ruled from Ngaruawahia. Though the ceremonial position holds no legal power, it confers great prestige, and Potatau's descendents continue to rule from here. Tuheitia Paki (b. 1955) ascended to the throne in 2006, following 40 years

---

Riff Raff

Where the old Embassy Theatre once stood on Victoria Street in Hamilton you will find a bronze statue of Riff Raff, the hunchback from *The Rocky Horror Picture Show*. Richard O'Brien, the show's creator, worked in a Hamilton barbershop as a young man. It is rumored that his life of cutting hair and watching the Embassy's late-night double features inspired the 1975 cult classic film.

---

of rule by his mother Dame Te Atairangikaahu.

On the northern side of town, the **Turangawaewae Marae** contains the king's residence and a traditionally carved meetinghouse, but is open to the public only on special occasions.

Thirty miles (48 km) west of Hamilton via SH23 is New Zealand's premier surfing destination, **Raglan**, a delightful seaside village on a sheltered inlet ideal for kayaking and swimming. The historic Harbour View Hotel (*14 Bow St., tel 07/825-8010*) dominates a main street lined with cafés. A pleasant stroll over a pedestrian bridge leads to the spit and the ocean, but Raglan's famous surf beaches are farther out along the Wainui Road.

Wainui Beach, 3 miles (5 km) southwest of Raglan on a large bay, has a gray-sand beach and surf lifesaving club that operates in summer. Surfing lessons are offered if catching a wave has been

---

Turangawaewae Marae

 29 River Road Ngaruawahia

 (07) 824 5273

🕐 Only open to visitors during the Annual Regatta, which is held in March

a lifelong dream. Farther west, **Manu Bay** has a famous left-hand break and the **Indicators** have world-class surf.

To reach the spectacular, gushing **Bridal Veil Falls,** take the turnoff 8 miles (13 km) out of Raglan on SH23 to Hamilton. Just past the tiny town of Te Mata, turn left and head 2.5 miles (4 km) to the falls. A scenic but rough, hilly road *(subject to closure; ask in Te Mata)* leads on to sleepy **Kawhia** on the impressive harbor of the same name. Kawhia is sacred to the Tainui people as the landing place of the ancestral Tainui canoe.

Fifteen miles (24 km) south of Hamilton on SH1, the delightfully green and very English town of **Cambridge** has horse racing in its veins, and its stud farms have

Hamilton's Pirongia Clydesdales

> Matamata has achieved fame for Hobbiton village, built on a nearby farm for the filming of *The Lord of the Rings* trilogy.

produced many champions. New Zealand loves its racing, and Waikato thoroughbreds have excelled at home and across the Tasman in Australia, where many have won the prestigious Melbourne Cup. Historic buildings and antique shops grace the town, while plaques in the pavement commemorate local equine heroes.

The **Cambridge Thoroughbred Lodge** *(SH 1, Karapiro, tel 07/827-8118, www.cambridge thoroughbredlodge.co.nz, $–$$)* has guided tours of their impressive stud and unique horse shows *(reservations required)* featuring champion thoroughbreds and other breeds.

Another renowned horse breeding center, **Matamata,** 33 miles (53 km) east of Cambridge on SH27, has achieved fame for **Hobbiton** village, built on a nearby farm for the filming of *The Lord of the Rings* trilogy. **Rings Scenic Tours** *(tel 07/888-9913, www .hobbitontours.com, $–$$$$$)* runs enjoyable tours from Matamata to what is left of the Hobbit houses.

The small town of **Otorohanga,** 31 miles (50 km) south of Hamilton via SH3, has long been on the tourist map for its famous **Otorohanga Kiwi House** (Alex Telfer Dr., tel 07/873-7391, www .kiwihouse.org.nz, $–$$$). Though kiwi houses, featuring New Zealand's native birds, have sprung up everywhere, this is still the most popular, largely because of its proximity to the Waitomo Caves. Kiwi sightings are guaranteed and a wide selection of New Zealand's native birds is on display throughout the attractive grounds.

in them permanently, no doubt because of flooding. (Waitomo means "water cave.") A few early Europeans visited the caves, but it was not until the 1880s that the area was surveyed and the extent of the vast underground network became known. More than 300 caves riddle the area, with hundreds of miles of interconnecting passageways, underground springs, and rivers carving great caverns out of the karst.

Waitomo Caves

Map p. 105

Visitor information

21 Waitomo Caves Rd., Waitomo

07/878-7640

www.waitomo-museum.co.nz

The Kiwi

New Zealanders proudly call themselves and all things New Zealand "Kiwi," for this unique, flightless bird has become the national symbol. The shy, nocturnal kiwi, about the size of a large chicken, has been around for 70 million years and is the dwarf cousin of the ratite family, which includes emus and New Zealand's extinct moa, the largest bird to walk the Earth.

The kiwi is difficult to see—most New Zealanders have never spotted one in the wild. Though endangered, and though their habitat is threatened, kiwi populations total about 70,000. The most

common species are the North Island brown kiwi and the great spotted kiwi of the South Island. Other species include the rowi, tokoeka, and little spotted kiwi.

Kiwis have a highly developed sense of smell and use their long bills to forage in forest undergrowth for worms, insects, and spiders, as well as berries and seeds.

Kiwis lay enormous eggs for their size, about one-fifth of their body weight, and the incubation period is around 80 days. Kiwi pairs are monogamous and the male usually incubates the eggs.

Waitomo Caves

Riddled with caves, the limestone wonderland of Waitomo lies in the heart of the King Country, an area named for the Maori King Movement. Forced out of Waikato after the New Zealand Wars, King Tawhiao (1822–1894) retreated into these rugged hills between Lake Taupo and the coast, a no-go zone for Europeans until the king laid down his arms in 1881.

The Maori camped at the Waitomo Caves, but never lived

By the 1890s, tourists began trickling in, and in 1908 the classic Waitomo Caves Hotel (see p. 291) was built to cater to the growing crowds. One of New Zealand's premier attractions for a century, Waitomo remains a North Island must-see and a required stop for tour buses between Auckland and Rotorua. This being New Zealand, thrill seekers are also indulged with underground adventures.

The big lure is the **Waitomo Glowworm Caves,** an impressive

Waitomo Glowworm Caves

39 Waitomo Caves Rd.

07/878-8227

$$$ (two-cave combo)

www.waitomo.com

John Williams' 1845 watercolor, "HMS *North Star*, destroying Pomare's pa, Otiuhu, Bay of Islands"

Times of War

With the introduction of muskets, Maori tribal wars quickly escalated, and as European settlement increased in New Zealand from the 1840s, conflict over land was inevitable. A series of land wars, also known as the New Zealand Wars or the Maori Wars, erupted on the North Island.

Musket Wars

Even before the land wars began, Maori chiefs such as Hongi Hika and Te Rauparaha had acquired muskets and had used the new technology with devastating effect against their traditional Maori enemies. While a precursor to the Land Wars, the so-called Musket Wars were just as cataclysmic. Lasting from the early 1820s through the 1830s, the wars claimed up to 20,000 lives as the new European weapons of mass destruction turned tribal war into genocide. Hongi Hika, sporting armor given to him by King George IV, led his warriors south against old foes such as the Ngati Paoa around Auckland, wiping out whole villages and taking slaves as he went. Ritual cannibalism to ingest the

mana (spiritual power) of the conquered was common.

Other tribes, facing extermination, clamored to get their hands on the new weapons. In exchange for muskets, they traded pigs, agricultural produce, and even the smoked heads of slain enemies—macabre trophies for European cabinets.

Wars escalated across the North Island, and the southern warrior Te Rauparaha created havoc along the west coast after being driven out of the Waikato region. From his base on Kapiti Island he then crossed Cook Strait and waged a ferocious campaign against the tribes of the South Island.

By around 1836, the wars began to subside as the balance of muskets, and power, settled.

Missionaries also began to make inroads, but up to a third of the Maori population had been wiped out by warfare and the growing tide of European-introduced diseases. The battle-hardened warriors that remained then turned their attention to the British, sometimes uniting against the settlers, other times joining colonial troops against traditional enemies. While the Musket Wars resulted in many deaths, the conflicts acclimated Maori to the ways of modern warfare, preparing them in part for sustained fighting against the British colonists. Because of the tactics and weapons acquired during this period, Maori fared much better than other indigenous people in the Empire.

The King Movement

Early skirmishes included the 1843 massacre at Wairau (see sidebar p. 176) in the South Island, when Te Rauparaha slaughtered a British militia sent to arrest him for impeding an illegal land grab. More serious battles broke out in 1845 when Bay of Islands chief Hone Heke, disenchanted with British rule, fought foreign troops for months until a truce was declared.

In the 1850s, as settlers flooded in, the Maori united across tribal boundaries for the first time to form the Maori King Movement (Kingitanga) to stop land sales and elect their own king. The Waikato chief Te Wherowhero became the first king in 1856 and ruled from Ngaruawahia. The King Movement was intended to protect Maori land and traditions, but most colonists saw it as treachery and an affront to the rightful monarch, Queen Victoria.

In 1860, a local chief offered to sell land at Waitara, near New Plymouth, to the British, but the supreme chief of the area objected and occupied the area. British troops were sent in, sparking the Taranaki War. A series of bloody battles ensued, with imperial troops suffering heavy losses trying to storm fortified Maori pa (villages). Maori forces laid siege to New Plymouth before withdrawing, and the two sides called a truce in 1861.

When fighting broke out again in 1863, Governor George Grey marshaled up to 20,000 men to crush the King Movement. War broke out across the Waikato and Taranaki regions and spread to the Bay of Plenty before the final battles of 1864. Dozens of skirmishes left 1,000 Maori and 700 British troops dead, and huge tracts of Waikato land were seized in retribution.

The Saga of Te Kooti

As the Waikato Wars subsided, the messianic Pai Marire movement rose to prominence in Taranaki. Biblical teachings combined with Maori beliefs gave rise to the Hauhau warriors, who battled to regain Maori land and mana, convinced God had made them invincible. The core of the movement was eventually crushed in 1866 with the aid of opposing Maori tribes, but not before it had spread to the east coast of the North Island. After missionary Carl Volkner was killed at Opotiki in 1865, war escalated until Pai Marire supporters were rounded up and exiled to the Chatham Islands.

One of the exiles, Te Kooti, had fought for the government and protested his innocence, but was refused a trial. In the Chathams he received a series of visions and founded the Ringatu (Upraised Hand) faith. He and his followers staged a dramatic jail break in 1868, seized a boat, and set sail for the North Island.

Te Kooti got his revenge at Matawhero on the outskirts of Gisborne, slaughtering 54 Pakeha (Europeans) and Maori. Chased by colonial and Maori forces, he launched a series of guerrilla raids around Poverty Bay and into the Urewera Mountains before continuing on to Lake Taupo. He built a pa in the desert near the volcanoes, convinced he could defeat troops and tribes alike. His army was crushed, and he finally retreated into the wilds of the King Country in 1872, where he developed his religion, which still survives in New Zealand. Te Kooti, the last warrior of the New Zealand Wars, was eventually pardoned in 1883. ∎

collection of stalagmites and stalactites illuminated for effect. The caves include the great Cathedral cavern where New Zealand opera diva Kiri Te Kanawa once performed. A black river flows through the caves, and tour boats glide into the gloom of the glowworm grotto, where the ceiling twinkles with a Milky Way of lights. The 45-minute guided tour of the grotto is best taken in the morning or late afternoon to avoid the tour-bus crush.

Two miles (3 km) west of the Glowworm Caves on the main road, the **Aranui Cave** was discov-

ered in 1910 by a young Maori, Ruruku Aranui, when his dog disappeared into a hole chasing a wild pig. The high chambers of this riverless cave have stunning stalactite formations of pink, white, and pale brown.

Guided tours of the **Ruakari Cave** begin from the Long Black Café, 0.6 miles (1 km) before the township on the road coming into Waitomo. The 1-mile-long (1.6 km) path leads to stalactites, stalagmites, underground rivers, and glowworms.

Adrenaline junkies, hold on to your hard hats, for Waitomo is the home of black-water rafting—the sport of riding the underground rapids of the Ruakari Cave in an inner tube. If that fails to excite, a host of rock-climbing, rappelling, and caving adventures are also offered.

Waitomo village has a museum/information center, a general store, a tavern for meals, and not much more, though a handful of places to stay are scattered around, including the iconic Waitomo Caves Hotel. The **Waitomo Museum of Caves** ($) in the information center has useful displays on the caves.

Twelve miles (19 km) south of Waitomo is **Te Kuiti**, where charismatic Maori guerrilla Te Kooti found refuge and built its impressive *marae*. The town also has a "Big Shearer" statue attesting to its sheep-farming credentials, celebrated at the **Te Kuiti Muster** in April with fairground fun, shearing, and other sheep contests. ∎

Glowworms

The New Zealand glowworm *(Arachnocampa luminosa)* is a different species from the fireflies and glowworms of Europe and the Americas, which are beetles. The glowworms at Waitomo are the larvae of mosquitolike gnats that spin thin, dangling webs to catch insects. The glowworms attract prey with their luminescent green light—the hungrier they are, the brighter they glow. The larvae live for 6 to 12 months before entering the pupa stage, when they hang from the ceiling for one to two weeks. Finally, the gnats hatch, but their lives are short. They exist only to breed, and after the female lays her eggs, she dies.

Coromandel Peninsula

A popular summer vacation playground for Kiwis, the Coromandel Peninsula has stunning coastal scenery, glorious beaches, rugged mountains, and old gold towns, all less than two hours' drive from Auckland. From the main center of Thames, a scenic road wends along the shoreline of the sheltered west coast to charming Coromandel town, and then over the hills to the surf beaches and resort towns of the east coast. Driving is slow and winding. Allow at least two days to tour the peninsula.

Children sifting through seashells, Whitianga, Coromandel Peninsula

West Coast

European settlement on the Cormandel Peninsula began on the west coast with the discovery of gold near Coromandel in 1852, but the real boom began with the news of a strike at Thames in 1867. Thousands flocked to the goldfields, but in a decade, gold waned and kauri became the main industry. The kauri forests of the mountainous interior were milled almost to extinction by the 20th century, but preservation has made the forests green again.

Today the Coromandel thrives mostly on tourism and real estate. The laid-back lifestyle attracts wealthy retirees and alternative lifestylers alike.

Thames: At the bottom of the shallow Firth of Thames, Thames is the main town and gateway to the Coromandel Peninsula. Thames looks like a

Thames

⛰ Map p. 105

Visitor information

✉ 206 Pollen St.

☎ 07/868-7284

www.thamesinfo.co.nz

Miniature train from Driving Creek Railway & Pottery

Wild West town, its main street lined with verandahed wooden buildings from the gold rush of the 1860s and '70s. In its heyday, Thames had over a hundred hotels, including the **Brian Boru Hotel** (*Richmond & Pollen Sts.*). Though named after an Irish king, all it needs is saloon doors to complete the gold-rush look.

One of the most impressive public buildings, the **Thames School of Mines and Mineralogical Museum** (*101 Cochrane St., tel 07/868-6227, $*) houses an extensive collection of rocks, minerals, and fossils. For a rundown on the town's history, the **Thames Historical Museum** (*Pollen & Cochrane Sts., tel 07/868-8509, $*) has an interesting photo collection and pioneer relics.

The best thing to do in Thames is visit the **Goldmine Experience** (*tel 07/868-8514, www.goldmine-experience.co.nz, $*) on SH25 just north of town. Volunteers run informative tours of this former gold mine every day in summer, weekends in winter.

East of Thames, the scenic **Kauaeranga Valley** in the **Coromandel Forest Park** has waterfalls, mountain streams, thick forest, and kauri dams accessed by a host of good hikes, ranging from 20 minutes to the overnight hike to the spectacular, craggy outcroppings of the Pinnacles. The Department of Conservation–run **Kauaeranga Visitor Centre** (*tel 07/867-9080*), 7.5 miles (12 km) from Thames on Kauaeranga Valley Road, has full details.

Coromandel: A twisting, narrow, impossibly scenic road, SH25 winds right next to the sea for 34 miles (55 km) from Thames north to Coromandel. Bohemian Coromandel has long been home to artists, potters, holistic healers, and other rat-race escapees. The town's main street, **Pollen Street,** is lined with historic buildings–like Thames, the gold rush produced a Victorian building boom, which subsequent decline left intact.

The town and the peninsula were named after the British Royal Navy's HMS *Coromandel,* which called here in 1820 to cut kauri for ships' spars. It was Charles Ring's discovery of gold in 1852, however, that put Coromandel on the map.

The **Coromandel Gold Stamper Battery** *(410 Buffalo Rd., tel 07/866-7933, $$),* 2 miles (3 km) north of town, is driven by a huge waterwheel to crush rock for gold extraction. Informative tours explain the process, and you can pan for gold.

The town's most notable attraction, **Driving Creek Railway & Pottery** *(380 Driving Creek Rd., tel 07/866-8703, $$$–$$$$)* on the

INSIDER TIP:

Rent a shovel and dig yourself your own oceanside Jacuzzi when the tide goes out on Hot Water Beach. The best time to visit is December to March.

—CARRIE MILLER,
National Geographic Writer

northern outskirts, is an eccentric but impressive blend of a pottery factory and a miniature railway that runs through the forest.

The town of Coromandel is a crossroads for travelers. Most visitors head straight across to Whitianga on the east coast via one of two routes—the 309 Road or SH25. You can also leave the beaten track and head north to the remote tip of the peninsula.

The mountainous, unpaved 309 Road to Whitianga goes through some beautiful forest. Recommended stops on the way include excellent short walks to the **Waiau Falls** and a kauri grove. The main highway, SH25, is longer but has fine coastal scenery, and you can detour to isolated beaches such as beautiful **Opito Bay.**

North of Coromandel: The scenic, paved Coromandel-Colville road leads north to sleepy **Colville,** where a café and general store mark the edge of civilization. The unpaved Port Jackson Road passes **Mount Moehau,** the peninsula's highest peak, and Port Jackson before ending at **Fletchers Bay,** a serene inlet with untrammeled beaches. The Port Charles road, the alternate east coast road north of Colville, leads to **Port Charles** and its wonderful beach, then on to **Stony Bay,** where the **Coromandel Walkway** *(3 hours one-way)* provides a scenic hike to Fletchers Bay.

East Coast

Like many vacationers, Captain Cook preferred the east coast of the Coromandel and spent most of November 1769 in Mercury Bay, where he tracked the transit of Mercury, traded with the Maori, and feasted on seafood. Beautiful **Mercury Bay** remains the jewel of the Coromandel's east coast.

Over the mountainous spine of the peninsula from Coromandel town, **Whitianga,** Mercury Bay's main resort, has curving **Buffalo**

Coromandel

⚠ Map p. 105

Visitor information

✉ 355 Kapanga Rd.

☎ 07/866-8598

www.coromandel town.co.nz

Mercury Bay & Whitianga

⚠ Map p. 105

Visitor information

✉ Albert St., Whitianga

☎ 07/866-5555

www.whitiangaco.nz

Beach, a pretty harbor crammed with pleasure craft, and a good range of accommodations and restaurants. Whitianga has a small **museum** (11A The Esplanade, $), but the town is all about beaches and water sports, which range from windsurfing and fishing to glass-bottom-boat cruises.

For a cheap cruise, take the ferry across the harbor to **Ferry Landing,** where a pleasant coastal walk leads to the beautiful beach at **Flaxmill Bay,** and then on to the **Shakespeare Cliff lookout** above secluded **Lonely Beach.**

The Hairy Moehau

Some stories claim that lurking behind kauri trees in the Coromandel is the fabled Hairy Moehau. Like his elusive American cousin Bigfoot, the Hairy Moehau is described as a cross between a man and an ape. While Maori say he is a descendent of the mythical Maero people, others believe he is merely an escaped gorilla.

The lookout has superb views across the white sands of **Cook's Beach,** where Captain Cook first raised the British flag in 1769.

Cook's Beach is about 2 miles (3 km) on foot from Ferry Landing, much longer by car via the circuitous SH25 around Whitianga Harbour. This route will also take you to delightful **Hahei Beach,** 25 miles (40 km) from Whitianga, a must-see on the east coast. As

well as a superb beach, Hahei is the starting point for the walk to **Cathedral Cove,** a majestic rock outcropping, a 2.5-hour round-trip hike along the beach (1.5 hours from headland parking lot). This superb walk passes gorgeous bays.

To top off a trip around Mercury Bay, soak in the sands at **Hot Water Beach,** 5.5 miles (9 km) south of Hahei. At low tide, a hot spring percolates up through the sand, where you can dig your own spa bath, mingling hot water with seawater.

The SH25 south from Whitianga travels inland until it hits the coast again at **Tairua,** an old milling town and small resort. For wonderful views, head toward the ocean beach, take Paku Drive off the beach road, and then walk to the **Paku Summit,** a rock mountain that dominates the town.

A short ferry ride across the estuary from Tairua is the town of **Pauanui.** One of the Coromandel's best beaches is only a short walk from the ferry dock, but the town itself is a soulless suburbia.

Whangamata, 25 miles (40 km) south of Tairua, has a long beach that attracts surfers and families. This large resort has a fine beach and plenty of services but lacks the charm of Whitianga.

South of Whangamata, the inland town of **Waihi** boomed in 1878 when gold was discovered. The **Martha Mine** (tel 07/863-9880, $) was the richest in New Zealand and can be toured. The **Waihi Arts Centre & Museum** (54 Kenny St., tel 07/863-8386, Thurs.–Sun., $) also has good mining exhibits. ∎

Bay of Plenty

The Bay of Plenty is a gently curving coast of sun, beaches, kiwifruit, and real estate booms, for this is one of the country's fastest-growing regions. Farther east, the area's other major attraction is White Island, New Zealand's most active volcano, with tours operating from the pleasant coastal town of Whakatane.

Mount Maunganui waterfront resort

Western Bay of Plenty

Captain Cook named the Bay of Plenty in 1769 for the abundance of food local Maori brought to his ship to trade, a welcome contrast to the hostile reception at his previous stop in Poverty Bay.

The main center of the Bay of Plenty, the city of **Tauranga** (pop. 109,000) is growing rapidly. Its fine harbor (Tauranga means "sheltered anchorage") is a major port for the surrounding agricultural region.

Abundant sun and fine beaches attract retirees, but Tauranga has not always been so placid. The area has a long Maori history, though by the time Europeans began to settle in the 1830s, the Musket Wars had reduced the population to only 2,000. In the 1860s, the New Zealand Wars spread from the Waikato to the Bay of Plenty, which witnessed fierce fighting that lingered on through messianic movements such as the Hauhau warriors and Te Kooti (see pp. 110–111).

Tauranga
■ Map p. 105
Visitor information
✉ 12 Hamilton St.
☎ 07/577-6234

Whakatane

⛰ Map p. 105

Visitor information

✉ Quay St.

☎ 07/308-6058

In Tauranga, fierce fighting broke out at Gate Pa. The British established Monmouth Redoubt in Tauranga to cut off Maori reinforcements heading to the Waikato, and in 1864, 1,700 troops launched an assault on 230 Maori at Gate Pa. After artillery bombarded the walls, 300 troops stormed the *pa,* but 100 were slaughtered within ten minutes before the rest retreated. Maori forces evacuated the pa overnight, leaving behind the most devastating British defeat of the New Zealand Wars.

The remains of **Monmouth Redoubt** lie in downtown Robbins Park on Cliff Road, while the impressive Te Awanui war canoe is nearby at the northern end of The Strand, along Tauranga's redeveloped waterfront. One of the city's main attractions, **Elms Mission House** *(tel 07/577-9772, Sat.–Sun. 2–4 p.m., $),* near the Harbour Bridge on Mission Street, was built in 1847 by the Reverend A. N. Brown. This fine Georgian home has original furnishings.

Tauranga may be a popular place to live, but visitors are advised to stay in **Mount**

INSIDER TIP:

In town in April, Tauranga's Easter National Jazz Festival features the country's best jazz musicians performing in fantastic venues across the city.

—MARY HERMANSON,
Consultant, Whakatane District Council

Maunganui, 3 miles (5 km) away across the Harbour Bridge. Dominated by The Mount, a huge

Surfers preparing to paddle out into the Bay of Plenty

EXPERIENCE: Into the Volcano

The most accessible volcanoes in New Zealand are in the Tongariro National Park near Taupo (see pp. 131–132), but if you want bang for your volcanic sightseeing buck, then White Island (Whaakari) has no peer.

Lying 30 miles (48 km) offshore, White Island is expensive to visit, but tours do guarantee an up-close look at an active volcano, where steam and boiling water pour from the youngest crater. Tours land on the island unless the volcano is erupting or seas are too rough (helicopters may be able to land).

Whakatane is the usual place from which to arrange a trip to the island. **White Island Tours** (15 The Strand E., Whakatane, tel 07/308-9588, www.

whiteisland.co.nz, $$$$$) has six-hour boat tours, with a 1.5- to 2-hour tour on the island, visiting the crater and old sulfur mine. From Whakatane airport, **Vulcan Helicopters** (tel 07/308-4188, www.vulcanheli.co.nz, $$$$$) spends a little over an hour on the island and does the round trip in just 2.5 hours, but costs 2.5 times as much.

For those in a hurry, **Volcanic Air Safaris** (Rotorua City Lakefront, Memorial Dr., tel 07/348-9984, www.volcanicair.co.nz, $$$$$) has helicopter flights from the lakefront in Rotorua and also from Tauranga. Another Rotorua company, **Helipro** (tel 07/357 2512, www.helipro.co.nz, $$$$$) has flights departing from Te Puia, Agrodome Park, and Skyline Skyrides.

---

volcanic plug rising seemingly out of nowhere, this beach resort with big apartment buildings resembles a mini Waikiki, an almost brash resort in a country that typically likes its beaches back-to-nature, suburban, or located overseas.

Mount Maunganui has a sheltered bay beach on one side and, on the other, the wonderful white-sand **Ocean Beach** stretching 14 miles (22 km) to Papamoa and beyond. You can live it up in a beachfront apartment, but even the campground has a fabulous beach frontage right at the foot of The Mount. The area has good walking tracks and **hot saltwater pools** (tel 07/575-0868) at the base.

Te Puke, 17 miles (28 km) southeast of Tauranga on SH2, is the "kiwifruit capital of the world." The local kiwi industry made even small farmers overnight million-

aires in the 1980s. In a marvel of marketing, New Zealand horticulturalists took the humble Chinese gooseberry, renamed it, and sold it to the world. Though now grown everywhere, kiwifruit are still a billion-dollar-a-year industry around here. The latest version, the gold kiwifruit, is a trademark of the local Zespri company.

Te Puke's big attraction is **Kiwi360** (tel 07/573-6340, www.kiwi360.com, $$–$$$$), an orchard/themepark under the big kiwi on the outskirts of town where "kiwi karts" tour the orchards.

Eastern Bay of Plenty

Viewed from the waterfront, the delightful seaside town of **Whakatane** resembles an archetypal South Pacific port. Yachts shelter in the river harbor, backed by a ring of almost vertical forested hills. But away from this scene, jackhammers pound in a building boom driven by increasing numbers of residents and visitors. The town is spreading rapidly inland and out 4 miles (6 km) to upscale **Ohope Beach,** a growing resort area with a fine, long beach backed by Ohiwa Harbour.

Founding of Whakatane

The hills around Whakatane were once dotted with *pa,* for this area has a rich Maori heritage, beginning with the arrival of the canoe of early explorer Toi. The ancestral *Mataatua* canoe, voyaging possibly from Poverty Bay, arrived centuries later. Legend tells that on arrival, the men went ashore and the canoe began to drift. In defiance of tradition, the women jumped in the canoe and paddled it back, crying *"Ka whakatane au i ahau"* ("I will be a man"). The settlement henceforth became known as Whakatane ("to be manly").

Amid the jostle of shops in the center of town, it is easy to miss the drama of the landscape, but look up to see **Pohaturoa** rising from The Strand. This towering rock with a natural archway has long been a landmark for the town, and in 1920 it became a memorial for those who died in World War I. Just behind on Canning Place, the **Kohi Point**

Walkway leads up to Hillcrest Road, then Seaview Road, where a lookout affords fine views of the harbor. For the best views of all, take the steps next to the lookout up to the top of **Puketapu,** another huge rock outcropping and the ancient pa site of the Ngati Awa people.

Marine activities are popular in Whakatane, including swimming with the dolphins, but for many it is primarily the base for making trips to White Island by sea or air.

White Island: New Zealand's only active marine volcano, White Island, or Whaakari ("dramatic"), is one of the country's most spectacular sights. Luring scientists and tourists alike, the volcanic island

INSIDER TIP:

Don't miss the scenic Pacific Coast Highway from Manukau to Napier. Highlights include the mural art in Katikati and New Zealand's longest wharf in Tolaga Bay.

—MARY HERMANSON,
*Consultant, Whakatane
District Council*

lies 30 miles (48 km) offshore and was so-named by Captain Cook because it was shrouded in steam. Various attempts were made over the years to mine sulfur on the island, with tragic results in 1914 when the crater rim collapsed, burying ten workers under boiling mud. Only the camp cat survived.

The last major eruption, in 2000, covered the island with mud and scoria and created a new crater, which has a small turquoise lake. This is still a very active volcano,

is the gateway to the east coast, a strongly Maori area with a rich history, though it is famous mostly for the killing of the Reverend Carl Volkner by Hauhau warriors in 1865. The good reverend was thought to be a spy for the British during the New Zealand

Opotiki

Map p. 105

Visitor information

St. John & Elliot Sts.

07/315-3031

Kiwifruit looms large in Te Puke.

and great jets of steam mixed with hydrochloric acid and sulfur dioxide pour from the fumaroles.

Tours operating out of Whaka-tane land on the island, and you can walk right to the edge of the crater. Boat tours are a full-day trip, and it takes about 1.5 hours to get to the island. Dive tours also run. In a hurry? More expensive helicopter tours land on the island and sightseeing planes buzz overhead (see sidebar p. 119).

Opotiki: This old-fashioned rural town lies in sharp contrast to booming Whakatane, 34 miles (54 km) away via SH2—no condo developments here, despite good beaches just outside town. Opotiki

Wars, and he was hanged, be-headed, and his eyes gouged out and eaten.

Pretty, wooden **St. Stephens Church** (112 Ford St.) has a headstone inside dedicated to its martyred cleric. The church is usu-ally open in the morning—Kawhai Takeaways across the road has the key if the church is closed.

The other major attraction, **Hukutaia Domain,** about 4 miles (6 km) south of town at the end of Woodlands Road, has scenic walks through 5 acres (2 ha) of native plants from all over New Zealand, some rare or endangered. The Domain includes Taketakerau, a 2,000-year-old tree once used as a Maori burial site. ∎

Rotorua

The enduring images of New Zealand—geysers, mud pools, and the fearsome *haka* war dance—are the reality of Rotorua. The biggest tourism destination in the country, Rotorua is where volcanic activity meets Maori culture, all wrapped up in a neat hot springs, haka, and *hangi* (underground oven) package. Water also defines the Rotorua area, which is studded with forested mountain lakes and trout-filled streams.

Rotorua is noted for its Maori cultural shows.

Rotorua

🅜 Map p. 105

Visitor information

✉ 1167 Fenton St.

☎ 07/348-5179

**www.rotoruanz
.com**

History

The Rotorua region lies on the volcanic rift that stretches from the White Island to the towering volcanoes of Tongariro National Park. A long history of massive volcanic explosions has rent the countryside, leaving cooled craters filled with lakes, but boiling mud and steam everywhere point to the turmoil still threatening below.

In 1886, nearby Mount Tarawera suddenly blew apart, showering fire and mud that destroyed whole villages as well as the famous Pink and White Terraces. These spectacular silica terraces, washed by thermal waters, were dubbed a wonder of the natural world and first brought tourism to Rotorua, but overnight they were gone.

The local Maori take their name from the ancestral canoe, *Te Arawa,* which arrived around the 14th century. As the tribe thrived and split into *hapu* (subtribes), conflict was inevitable, but nothing compared to the havoc wreaked by rival Ngapuhi chief Hongi Hika in 1823. Armed with muskets, he slaughtered all before him, and when the Arawa sought refuge on Mokoia Island in Lake Rotorua, he got his men to drag canoes over the mountains and onto the lake to finish the job. Hika is still bad news in these parts. When his picture appeared in a Rotorua history exhibition recently, it caused an outrage and Hika was likened to Hitler.

More grief later befell the Arawa at the hands of the Waikato Maori, so when war broke out in the 1860s, they aligned themselves with the British against old foes, keeping east-coast support from getting through to their enemies.

....

The biggest tourism destination in the country, Rotorua is where volcanic activity meets Maori culture, all wrapped up in a neat hot springs, haka, and *hangi* package.

....

The end of the war bought peace and tourism to the area. The Tarawera eruption in 1886 momentarily slowed the flow of tourists, but the area's many attractions continue to lure over two million visitors a year.

Rotorua's Favorite Lovers

In the middle of Lake Rotorua, Mokoia Island is the setting for Rotorua's favorite love story, that of Hinemoa, who lived on shore, and her lover Tutanekai, who lived on the island. Their union was forbidden by family, but when lovelorn Tutanekai played his flute, the mournful sounds drifted across to Hinemoa. Determined to be with him, Hinemoa braved the freezing water and swam over. She recovered in the island's hot spring, known as Hinemoa's Pool, and was forever united with her love.

Rotorua City Center

A busy city of 66,000, Rotorua sits on an expansive lake and has a mind-boggling number of attractions. Almost every activity New Zealand has to offer can be found here, except for perhaps swimming with the dolphins (will swimming with the trout become a reality?).

Most attractions are on the outskirts or outside the city, but the town center has a few must-sees. One thing you cannot miss is the smell. Sulfur fumes emerge from vents like steam from New York City manholes, giving the city its distinctive rotten-egg odor.

The best place to start a tour is the gracious **Government Gardens,** one block east from the main street, Fenton Street,

Rotorua Museum

✉ Queens Dr., Government Gardens

☎ 07/349-4350

$ $–$$$

www.rotorua museum.co.nz

and leading down to the lake. In the gardens, the always innovative **Rotorua Museum** is housed in a grand Tudor-style bathhouse built in 1908 for visitors seeking to "take the cure." Tour the old baths and the pumping works below ground. The well-presented museum section highlights the history of tourism, the Pink and White Terraces, Tarawera's eruption, and local Maori history.

Next door, the restored art deco **Blue Baths** (tel 07/350-2119, www.bluebaths.co.nz, $$) have a museum highlighting the salacious joys of mixed swimming in times past, but the thermally heated swimming pool and soak pools are the main attractions.

At the southern end of the gardens, the **Polynesian Spa** (end of Hinemoa St., tel 07/348-1328, www.polynesianspa.co.nz, $$–$$$) has been popular since 1882, when a bathhouse was built over the hot spring. You can swim in private and public pools or indulge in massage and spa treatments.

Along Lakefront Drive, near the end of Fenton Street, the waterfront is a fine spot from which to take in the sunset. Booths sell tickets for jet boating, helicopter flights, and the *Lakeland Queen* (tel 07/348-0265, $$$–$$$$), an old paddle wheeler that cruises on Lake Rotorua and takes in Mokoia Island in the middle.

Farther west along the lake, the historic Maori village of **Ohinemutu** was once the main settlement. Communal buildings line the village square. On one side is the traditional **Tamateka-pua Meeting House,** and facing it is **St. Faith's Anglican Church,** noted for its fine Maori carvings and a stained-glass window showing Christ in a Maori cloak walking on the water of Lake Rotorua.

While in town, plan to attend a Maori concert and hangi. At a hangi, meat and vegetables are cooked on hot rocks in an underground oven. Concerts feature

Government Gardens

EXPERIENCE: Hot Springs

Hot springs punctuate the land all over New Zealand. In many places their therapeutic waters have been developed into resorts where visitors can soak, swim, or indulge in massage or beauty treatments.

The geothermal activity seething underground rises to the surface most readily in the Central Plateau region of the North Island around Rotorua and Taupo, but keep a towel and swimwear handy everywhere in New Zealand for wonderful hot-springs experiences.

Visitors have flocked to Rotorua for over a hundred years to "take the cure," particularly at the wonderfully grand **Government Bath House,** which has become the city museum. Today a host of resorts, motels, and campgrounds have soaking facilities (see opposite page).

In the center of Rotorua, the best known are the **Polynesian Spa,** featuring swimming pools, massage, and spa treatments, and the nearby **Blue Baths,** which have a large heated swimming pool and soak pools. Outside town, the **Hell's Gate** geothermal area has a mud spa and hot pools.

Taupo has a number of hot springs, including the large **DeBretts Spa Resort** (SH5, tel 07/378-8559), a well-maintained complex with hot pools, swimming pools, a slide, and spa treatments. In a similar vein, north of Auckland at Waiwera, the attractive **Waiwera Infinity Spa Resort** (see p. 80) has thermal pools, a spa, a sauna,

Natural hot springs at Hot Water Beach

a fitness center, and water slides for family fun.

Other small hot-spring resorts are dotted all around the North Island, as are dozens of natural springs where soaking is free, though water should be tested for scalding heat before entering. Two well-known natural hot springs are at **Hot Water Beach** (see p. 116) on the Coromandel Peninsula, where the spring bubbles up through the sand at low tide, and the **Hot Water Stream** in Taupo, on the Huka Falls walking trail (see p. 131), where the hot stream flows into the Waikato River.

The South Island has less

geothermal activity and fewer hot springs, but two excellent sites are at **Hanmer Springs** (see p. 203), a large, well-maintained resort with a variety of pools and a swimming pool, and **Maruia Springs** (see p. 203) at the Lewis Pass. Maruia Springs's Japanese bathhouse and outdoor pools are at their best in winter when it snows while you soak in the steaming hot water. Of the natural springs, hikers rate the **Welcome Flat Hot Pools** on the Copland Track in Westland Tai Poutini National Park as a New Zealand highlight, but it is a seven-hour walk off the road south of Fox Glacier. ∎

Whakarewarewa

✉ 9a Tukiterangi St.

☎ 07/349-3463

$ $$$$$

www.whakarewarewa.com

Te Puia

✉ Hemo Rd.

☎ 07/348-9047

$ $$$$$

www.tepuia.com

Maori dance and song, including the inevitable haka and audience participation. A half-dozen operators run tours to the events, which are sometimes cheesy, but often fun and educational.

Whakarewarewa Valley

After Tarawera's eruption, many nearby villagers relocated to Te Whakarewarewa thermal valley, 2 miles (3 km) south of town at the end of Fenton Street. Former guides at the Pink and White Terraces helped build what would become Rotorua's

The Fortress of Te Puia

Before Te Puia was a tourist attraction, it was a center of war for hundreds of years. Constructed in 1325, the fortress was one of the most formidable sites of Maori warfare and was passed down to many different *hapu* (subtribes) over the centuries. In battle, the fortress's location couldn't be beaten, protected as it was by an intricate system of terraces and natural obstacles such as geysers and mudpools.

greatest attraction. The village, called Whaka (pronounced fukka) for short, was an enclave of Maori culture in a setting of geysers and boiling mud. In 1997, the village split off from the Maori Arts & Crafts Institute, which became Te Puia, taking up the western half of the valley.

Whakarewarewa doesn't get the same crowds anymore, though the old village with its wooden buildings and superbly carved meetinghouse is the real deal, if somewhat distorted by tourism. The entry fee includes a guided tour, cultural performance, hot-pool cooking class, and a look at the geysers from a viewing platform. Unguided walks lead around the thermal area to mud pools, but the valley is not that active.

Te Puia offers much the same but is in another league, with a cultural gallery, carving and weaving schools, re-created Maori village, *marae*, and cultural performances. It also has thermal attractions and good views of the famous **Pohutu** (Big Splash) geyser, which shoots up 70 feet (21 m) or more every hour. The huge parking lot, gift shop, and café all attest to the popularity and professionalism of Te Puia.

North Rotorua

A number of themed and other attractions lie north of the city along SH5. Trout teem in the waters of **Rainbow Springs** (tel 07/350-0440, $$$–$$$$), 3 miles (5 km) from town. The crystal-clear springs swarm with fish, but this mini-zoo has more than just trout ponds. Tuataras and other species are housed in a beautiful setting along with native bird enclosures and kiwi houses.

Nearby, the **Skyline Skyrides** *(tel 07/347-0027, $$–$$$$)* will whisk you to the top of Mount Ngongotaha for panoramic views. A restaurant, luge, and other amusements can be found at the top.

About 6 miles (10 km) north, just off SH5, the **Agrodome** *(Western Rd., tel 07/357-1050, $$$–$$$$)* provides a look at farming life with a variety of livestock. The star attraction is the sheep shows, including shearing and sheepdog displays. Cashing in on the adventure market, bungee jumping and other adrenaline activities are offered next door.

On the same road, **Zorb Rotorua** *(tel 07/357-5100, $$$$$)* is a surreal sight. Thrillseekers jump in giant plastic balls that roll, bounce, and hurtle down the long, grassy hillside.

Visitors watch the erupting Pohutu geyser in Te Puia.

East of Rotorua

Hell's Gate *(tel 07/345-3151, $$$, spa $$$$$)* is a small but action-packed thermal area 10 miles (16 km) northeast of Rotorua on the road to Whakatane (SH30). George Bernard Shaw gave it its name on a visit in 1934. A self-guided walk takes in attractions such as the mud-slapping **Devil's Cauldron** and the steaming hot **Kakahi Falls.** The attached spa (bring swimsuits) is a soothing bonus with mud and hot-water soaking pools. The highway, SH30, continues on to the beguiling, forested Lake Rotoiti and Lake Rotoma.

Southeast of Rotorua, take Tarawera Road off SH30 for a scenic drive through superb lake country. The road passes through the **Whakarewarewa Forest Park,** planted with Californian redwoods, before reaching Blue and Green Lakes. Just off the main road, on the narrow isthmus between the lakes, a fine walking trail goes around the **Blue Lake** *(1.5 hours round-trip).* The Blue Lake is a deep volcanic caldera, while the **Green Lake** is shallower with a sandy bottom, hence the color difference.

About 10 miles (16 km) past the lakes, the **Buried Village** *(Tarawera Rd., tel 07/362-8287, www.buriedvillage.co.nz, $$–$$$$$)*

is the site of Te Wairoa, the tourist village for the Pink and White Terraces before the eruption of Mount Tarawera. The eruption in 1886 killed more than 120 people and buried the village under rocks, ash, and boiling mud. The fascinating museum retells the story of the tragedy, while the grounds have building founda-

Lady Knox

In order to erupt, the Lady Knox Geyser must be coaxed with soap. The geyser contains two chambers, one with hotter water than the other. When soap is added to the top chamber, surface tension drops, the two pools mix, and the geyser erupts. This phenomenon was discovered in 1901 by startled convicts trying to do their laundry.

tions and some original Maori houses, as well as a waterfall.

Beyond the Buried Village, serene **Lake Tarawera** is flanked by jagged Mount Tarawera. Boats once took tourists across this lake to walk to the Pink and White Terraces. Cruises today retrace the route from Tarawera Landing, where the Landing Café makes an excellent spot for a meal.

South Thermal Areas

If you want bang for your thermal buck, then head to the thermal areas south of Rotorua, signposted off the SH5 highway to Taupo.

Waimangu Volcanic Valley

(tel 07/366-6137, www.waimangu .com, $$–$$$$$, cruise $$–$$$$$), 12 miles (19 km) from Rotorua, combines thermal activity with fine walks and a cruise on **Lake Rotomahana,** the site of the legendary Pink and White Terraces. Quieter than other thermal areas, it has fine panoramas and the best walks over a large area *(allow at least 2 hours plus 45 mins. for cruise)*. Waimangu ("black water") has no geysers, but vents steam and ponds boil throughout. Highlights are the pale blue **Inferno Crater Lake** and the multicolored **Warbrick Terrace.**

The most spectacular and extensive of the thermal areas, **Wai-O-Tapu** *(tel 07/366-6333, www.geyserland.co.nz, $$–$$$$$)*, 17 miles (28 km) from Rotorua, is a dramatic moonscape of collapsed craters, mud pools, silica terraces, many-hued lakes, boiling water, and steam. The number-one draw is the regular-as-clockwork **Lady Knox Geyser** that blows to 70 feet (21 m) every day at 10:15 a.m., when the crowds pack in. Blessed with such suitably demonic names as Devil's Ink Pots and Inferno Crater, the highlights of this feature-packed park also include the **Artist's Palette,** a large pool of changing colors, the adjoining **Champagne Pool** that bubbles at 165°F (74°C), and the **Devil's Bath** that can be green or yellow depending on the light. Don't miss the mud pools, just off the road, five minutes before the main entrance.

Farther south, the scenic **Orakei Korako** thermal area (see pp. 130–131) is 13 miles (21 km) off SH5, 41 miles (66 km) drive from Rotorua, but closer to Taupo. ■

Violent Nature

In the summer of A.D. 186, Roman historians recorded hazy skies and sunsets that "burst into flame," while in China, chronicles noted unusually blood-red sunsets.

These skies most likely resulted from the Lake Taupo eruption, the world's most violent in 5,000 years. The volcano sent great clouds of debris around the world and threw out 70 cubic miles (300 cu km) of rock and ash that buried all New Zealand at least a half inch (1 cm) deep. The huge crater left by the blast formed Lake Taupo, some 30 miles (48 km) across.

At Rotorua, other great lakes are the product of long-ago explosions, and the area is still far from inactive. In 1886, Mount Tarawera unexpectedly blew its top, burying villages and killing about 120 people.

Thermal activity seethes from Rotorua across to Lake Taupo and Tongariro National Park, a volcanic plain known as the Taupo Volcanic Zone. White Island volcano stands guard over its northern reaches. Smoldering 30 miles (48 km) offshore in the Bay of Plenty, White Island poses few threats to humans, but is highly active with a major eruption as recently as 2000.

At the southern end of the volcanic zone are the most dangerous volcanoes in New Zealand—Tongariro, Ngauruhoe, and Ruapehu. These towering stars of the Tongariro National Park are an awesome sight. Mount Tongariro last erupted from its red crater in 1926. Mount Ngauruhoe is the youngest vent, erupting 45 times in the last century, most recently in 1975.

Ruapehu is currently the most active of this destructive triumvirate. The tallest at 9,173 feet (2,796 m), it has erupted at least 60 times in the last 60 years, with major eruptions in 1895, 1945, and 1995–1996. On Christmas Eve 1953, Ruapehu caused 151 deaths when its crater wall gave way, sending water, mud, and boulders sweeping down the mountain into the Whangaehu River. The river washed away the rail bridge minutes before the Wellington-Auckland express plunged into the swirling waters.

The cause of all this turmoil lies far below, where the Pacific plate is pushing beneath the North Island, pressing against the overriding Australian-Indian plate on which New Zealand sits. As the plates grind against each other, the massive friction turns rock to magma, which

Eruption of Mount Ruapehu, Tongariro National Park

breaks through vents in the weakened crust.

The plates twist farther south around Wellington, and the northern Hikurangi Trench gives way to the Alpine Fault through the South Island. Tectonic plate collision in the South Island pushes up the Southern Alps, but produces no volcanoes.

Lying on a fault line, the Wellington area is prone to earthquakes, and in 1855, a powerful earthquake pushed up great tracts of land along the city's waterfront. Hundreds of earthquakes, usually very minor, occur throughout New Zealand every year, but the most destructive flattened Napier in 1931, killing 258 people.

Away from the main hot spots, majestic Mount Taranaki in the west of the North Island last erupted in 1755, but scientists warn it is overdue. The densely populated Auckland volcanic field last erupted 600 years ago, but it could erupt again, with devastating consequences. ∎

Central Plateau

The volcanic Central Plateau region hosts the volcanoes of the Tongariro National Park, a spectacular alpine desert region with fine walks, superb scenery, and skiing in winter. Near the park, expansive Lake Taupo is famed for trout fishing, and on its shores, Taupo town makes a fine base from which to explore the region.

Huka Falls near Taupo

Taupo

 Map p. 105

Visitor information

✉ Tongariro St.
☎ 07/376-0027

**www.laketauponz
.com**

Taupo

The resort town of Taupo sprawls around the northeast corner of **Lake Taupo,** New Zealand's largest lake. The product of a massive volcanic eruption (see p. 129), the lake resembles an inland sea, the Tongariro volcanoes making a stunning backdrop.

With magnificent vistas and nearby attractions, Taupo is a thriving resort, well stocked with accommodations, cafés, and a host of tour operators offering everything from bungee jumping to some of the world's best trout fishing. Taupo is also conveniently near Tongariro National Park and thermal areas.

Not the largest thermal area but crowd-free and in a glorious lake setting, **Orakei Korako** (tel 07/378-3131, $$–$$$$) is 23 miles (37 km) north of Taupo, off SH1. From the refreshingly low-key café/gift shop, a launch takes you across Lake Ohakuri to the park's many fine features. A one-hour scenic walk, uphill and down, takes in large silica terraces, the irregular **Diamond Geyser,** mud pools, boiling ponds, and **Ruatapu Cave,** a towering cavern holding an emerald green hot-water pool.

On the outskirts of Taupo, 4 miles (7 km) north of town, **Wairakei** is home to a massive geothermal power station *(SH5, tel 07/378-0913),* open for tours. Wairakei had one of the country's most active thermal areas until the 1958 power station siphoned off most of the action. Among the remaining steam vents and boiling ponds, **Wairakei Terraces** *(tel 07/378-0913, www.wairakeiterraces.co.nz, $$–$$$)* has man-made terraces that re-create and foster natural silica terraces. A re-created Maori village adds to the scene.

A little closer to town on Karapiti Road, steaming **Craters of the Moon park** *(donation)* has a walk passing numerous steam vents and boiling ponds.

Taupo is at the source of New Zealand's longest river, the Waikato, which flows out of the lake and surges through the impressive rapids of the **Huka Falls,** on the Huka Falls Road 2.5 miles (4 km) north of town. This road has a number of attractions—a honey center, a prawn farm, jet boating, helicopter flights, and the informative **Volcanic Activity Center** *(tel 07/374-8375, $–$$)* that monitors the region. **Huka Falls Walkway** is a lovely one-hour trail from the falls along the Waikato River. It comes out at Spa Road, near Taupo Bungy *(tel 07/377-1135,*

$$$$$), in a superb setting on a cliff over the river.

Tongariro National Park

A North Island highlight, Tongariro National Park houses the country's mightiest volcanoes—Mount Tongariro, Mount Ngauruhoe, and Mount Ruapehu.

Tongariro last erupted in 1926, and Ngauruhoe took over as the most active volcano for much of the 20th century. Ngauruhoe's 1954 lava flows were the largest in recorded history, but its last major show was in 1975.

Taniko **Weaving**

Taniko is a special type of Maori *raranga* (weaving) that does not require a loom. Also known as finger-weaving or twining, taniko is one of the strongest remaining Maori traditions. The term *taniko* also applies to the pattern, a hallmark of New Zealand. The vibrant repetition of triangles can be seen all over the islands.

In recent times, snowcapped Ruapehu has produced dozens of minor eruptions. Major eruptions in 1995–1996 had the region on alert as the volcano belched great clouds of steam, ash, and rock. In 1969, a nighttime lahar (volcanic mudflow) swept an area where 2,000 had skied that day. In 2007, advance warning systems averted any tragedy from another lahar.

This World Heritage area is a popular playground for visitors

Tongariro National Park

▲ Map p. 105

Visitor information

✉ Whakapapa Village, Mount Ruapehu

☎ 07/892-3729

year-round. In summer, day visitors, hikers, and volcano devotees crisscross the park. In winter, when the peaks are draped in snow, the Whakapapa and Turoa ski slopes on Ruapehu come alive.

Whakapapa Village, at the foot of Ruapehu, is the park headquarters where you'll find the historic Bayview Chateau Tongariro hotel (see p. 296) and the park's **visitor center.** The center has excellent displays on the park and can fill you in on its many walks, from easy one-hour strolls to the six-day hike around Ruapehu.

Serious hikers favor the three-day **Tongariro Northern Circuit,** but most popular of all is a one-day leg of this walk, the famous **Tongariro Crossing** (see pp. 134–135) taking in the peaks of Tongariro and Ngauruhoe.

Farther up the mountain, Whakapapa ski village is virtually deserted in summer. From here, experienced hikers can climb Ruapehu in a day, but as for all high-altitude hikes, you must be well equipped and prepared for alpine conditions and sudden savage changes in weather.

Around the Park

From Taupo, the highway south (SH1) hugs the lake all the way to **Turangi,** the biggest town close to the park. The Turangi visitor center (tel 07/386-8999) can fill you in on accommodations, the park, and hikers' transportation. The town is also a major trout-fishing center. The **Tongariro National Trout Center** (tel 07/386-8085), 2 miles (3 km) south of town on SH1, is a

---

EXPERIENCE: Trout Fishing

New Zealand has some of the world's best trout fishing, with beautiful lakes and crystal-clear rivers and streams teeming with large fish. Rainbow trout from California were introduced in the 1880s and typically average 3 to 4 pounds (1.5–2 kg), but can grow up to 15 pounds (7 kg) or more. English brown trout arrived 20 years earlier; those in rivers tend to be smaller than their lake cousins.

Good trout fishing can be found throughout the country, with popular destinations including Rotorua and the Lake Brunner region in the South Island. Lake Taupo and rivers that flow into it (especially the Tongariro) are the most famous and have long attracted anglers from around the world.

A license is required to fish inland waters (a separate license is required for the

Taupo area). Fish and Game New Zealand offices (www.fishandgame.org.nz) issue licenses and provide fishing information, as do local sports shops, where you can rent or buy gear.

Though it is not essential, many visiting anglers hire fishing guides, who are a great source of local information and can also provide lessons. Taupo has the most guides, but they can also be found in tourist centers such as Rotorua, Wanaka, and Queenstown. Tourist offices have details.

If trout fishing begins to pall, chinook salmon were introduced into east coast rivers in the South Island a century ago and the region has excellent salmon fishing in the Rakaia, Waimakariri, Rangitata, and Waitaki Rivers between November and March.

The New Zealand Army Museum in Waiouru

Department of Conservation–run trout hatchery with informative displays and an underwater viewing area.

SH1 heads south of Turangi to the desert plateau east of the park. Lying in the shadow of the mountains, this is a desolate area of tussock grass and stunted growth. The Desert Road that runs across the plateau is often closed in winter due to snow. This eerie road hits civilization again at **Waiouru,** home to the large **Army Museum** (*SH1 & Hassett Dr., tel 06/387-6911, www.army museum.co.nz, $–$$*).

The road from Turangi to Whakapapa (SH47) runs along the eastern side of the park and leads to the town of **National Park** on SH4. This utilitarian grid is scattered with accommodations. Though drab, it is handy to the park and lively in ski season.

Ohakune, on the southern flank of Mount Ruapehu, is the prettiest town near the park and is also a base for trips to Whanganui National Park (see p. 147). A host of chalets cater

to the ski crowds at **Turoa ski slope,** 11 miles (17 km) up the mountain. The main part of town buzzes with activity all year, while the northern edge around the old railway station is quiet in summer. The station area is at the southern entrance to the park, where the Ohakune Ranger Station has

INSIDER TIP:

Rent a bach (holiday home) on the lake at Acacia Bay in Taupo. You can roll out of bed, grab your line, and hook a trout for lunch.

—CMDR. MARK WORSFOLD,
*Asst. Naval Attaché, Embassy of
New Zealand, Washington, D.C.*

details on good walks and other activities; you can also try the **visitor information center** (*54 Clyde St., tel 06/385-8427*). The bus-up/bicycle-down service is a great way to experience Mount Ruapehu in summer. ∎

Walk: Tongariro Crossing

Dubbed the greatest one-day walk in the world, the spectacular Tongariro Crossing takes in volcanoes, crater lakes, alpine desert, forest, waterfalls, and hot springs all in seven to eight hours of walking. This glorious 10.6 mile (17 km) walk deserves all the accolades it gets, but appropriate clothing, equipment, fitness, and weather are essential for this high-altitude hike.

The aptly named Emerald Lakes, Mount Tongariro

The walk is usually done in summer, when the trail can sometimes look like a scene from *March of the Penguins*—an endless line of hikers stretching to the horizon. But it can be walked at most times of the year if the weather is good. Buses will drop you at the start of the trail and pick you up at the end. They are easily arranged through visitor centers or through your accommodations.

The walk starts from the **Mangatepopo car park ❶**, crossing a tussock-grass plain to the Mangatepopo Hut. Following the Mangatepopo Stream, the trail climbs gradually through the valley across old lava flows. After an hour or so, you reach the side trail to **Soda Springs ❷** *(10 mins. round-trip).*

From Soda Springs, it is a grinding climb up though volcanic rock, but after an hour you

reach the top with fabulous views back down to the valley. From here a poled route goes to towering **Mount Ngauruhoe** *(a demanding 3- to 4-hour round-trip),* but most walkers continue across the flat **South Crater ❸**. This high desert is flanked by the glorious red-tipped cone of Mount Ngauruhoe on the right and the craggy ridge of Mount Tongariro on the left.

After crossing South Crater, the trail climbs up to the ridge and then gets steeper between the two craters. The prevailing westerly is often bitterly cold at this altitude, the ground crunching with ice even in summer. Finally, the track levels out where the trail to **Mount Tongariro** *(1.5–2 hours round-trip)* leads off to the left, and on the right lies the magnificent **Red Crater ❹**. It is indeed red, and black, and menacing.

The trail traverses the lip of the Red Crater, the highest point of the walk at 5,970 feet (1,820 m), with views stretching forever. It then plunges down through loose scoria to the superb **Emerald Lakes ⑤**, which glisten and steam and make an ideal rest stop for lunch. The hard part of the walk is over, and the end is about 3.5 hours away.

The trail continues across the floor of the desertlike **Central Crater,** then up to the rim and the large **Blue Lake ⑥**, another stunning sight. Past the lake, it is all downhill on the sheltered side of the mountains, where mosses, shrubs, and other stunted plants begin to appear. The trail winds leisurely around the hillside, the panorama of far-off Lake Rotoaira and the lowlands a constant companion.

The trail then switchbacks down to **Ketetahi Hut ⑦**, a meeting place in the clouds to rest and chat. Another 20 minutes along the track, the billowing steam of the **Ketetahi Hot Springs** can be seen, but

unfortunately these are now off-limits.

Tussock grass waving in the wind then dominates the slopes, but as the trail continues its inexorable descent, more substantial plants appear until the trail enters forest, a lush surprise after the desert. Then the trail hits a gurgling stream and follows it, passing waterfalls, until finally it emerges at the **Ketetahi car park ⑧**, where tired but inspired walkers wait for their lift home. ∎

NOT TO BE MISSED:

Soda Springs • Red Crater • Emerald Lakes • Blue Lake • Ketetahi Hot Springs

---

✛ See area map p. 105
➤ Mangatepopo car park
↔ 10.6 miles (17 km)
🕑 7–8 hours
➤ Ketetahi car park

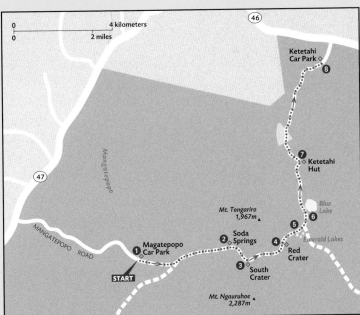

East Coast

The east coast comprises sunny Hawke's Bay, noted for wineries and the delightful art deco city of Napier, and the strongly Maori region of Gisborne and the East Cape. While Napier is the region's premier destination, a drive around the remote East Cape makes a fascinating diversion, and in the hinterland, Te Urewera National Park is a hiker's paradise.

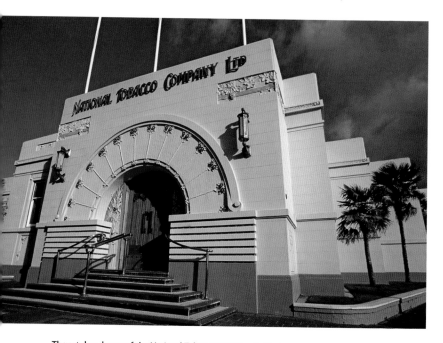

The art deco home of the National Tobacco Company in Napier

Napier

📍 Map p. 105

Visitor information

✉ 100 Marine Parade

☎ 06/834-1911

www.napierinthe city.co.nz

Napier

Washed by the Pacific, cheery Napier (pop. 55,000) basks in a sunny clime and is noted for its architecture. The central city's art deco streetscapes are a memorial to a disaster.

On February 3, 1931, a magnitude-7.9 earthquake flattened Napier and nearby Hastings, killing 258 people in what remains New Zealand's worst natural disaster. Most of Napier's brick buildings were destroyed and many wooden ones damaged. Some of the surrounding seabed was lifted more than 6.5 feet (2 m)—today's airport was once land under the Ahuriri Lagoon.

As fires swept the city, Napier had to be evacuated. New Zealand pitched in to rebuild. Remade in the fashion of the time, central Napier is an art deco delight, with almost all of its downtown buildings reflecting the style. Art deco tours and self-guided walks are the highlight of the city, with

Emerson and Tennyson Streets holding the pick of the buildings (see sidebar).

Napier also has seaside holiday attractions and a modern dynamic, with chic cafés, spas, and wineries to tour in the surrounding Hawke's Bay region.

Exploring the city: The delightfully old-fashioned seafront boulevard of **Marine Parade** is lined with majestic pines. It was rebuilt with art deco flourishes such as the **Veronica Sun Bay** near the tourist office, a memorial to the ship that helped survivors after the earthquake. Reminiscent of an English seaside resort, complete with pebble beach, the seafront has a sound shell, sunken gardens, and a host of family attractions.

At the northern end of Marine Parade, the **Ocean Spa** (42 Marine Parade, tel 06/835-8553, $–$$), a renovated swimming pool complex, has hot pools, spas, and massage—a welcome addition to the shorefront. A little south, the **statue of Pania of the Reef** is a city icon, based on an old Maori legend of how Pania was lured by the siren voices of the sea people and swam out to meet them, only to be turned into the reef.

On the opposite side of the road, the **Hawke's Bay Museum** (65 Marine Parade, tel 06/835-7781, $) has a wide range of exhibits with interesting Maori artifacts, but the main reason to visit is the earthquake displays, including a movie with eyewitness accounts.

Heading south on the waterfront, past the visitor information center and sunken gardens, you

---

EXPERIENCE:
Art Deco Napier

To explore Napier's art deco architecture, start on **Emerson Street** at the corner of Marine Parade, where the **A&B Building** with its dome clock tower was built in 1936 to house a nightclub. Farther down Emerson Street, the interior of the **ASB Bank** includes Maori carvings. Next, the **Criterion Hotel** has some wonderful leadlight work, and the **Napier Mall** is lined with art deco masterpieces.

Turn right at the Spanish mission-style **Provincial Hotel** on the corner of Clive Square and head one block to **Tennyson Street,** where at No. 163 you'll see the impressive **Deco Centre** (tel 06/835-0022). All things deco are sold in the center's shop, which also offers guided walks and self-guided tour brochures.

Heading down Tennyson Street to the waterfront, you see other fine buildings, including the **Municipal Theatre** and the superb **Daily Telegraph building.**

---

find **Marineland** (290 Marine Parade, tel 06/834-4027, $$–$$$), which has seal and dolphin shows and even offers swimming with the dolphins in the pool. Opposite Marineland, some fine Victorian wooden villas have survived the earthquake and ensuing years.

Much farther south, the **National Aquarium of New Zealand** (546 Marine Parade, tel 06/834-1404, $$–$$$) has marine and animal displays, including sharks, kiwis, and tuataras.

To see some of the city's pre-deco architecture, head up to massive **Bluff Hill,** which towers over the north of the city. Many of the Victorian wooden villas there survived, and the lookout on the hill has fantastic views over the bay.

Around Hawke's Bay

Art deco buffs will also appreciate **Hastings** (pop. 50,000), Napier's poorer cousin. While Napier prospers on tourism, inland Hastings is just another rural town, 13 miles (21 km) to the south on SH2.

The 1931 earthquake hit Hastings hard and also resulted in an art deco boom. A good place to start a tour is the **Westermans Building** (Heretaunga & Russell Sts., tel 06/873-5526), a former department store that also houses the visitor information center.

INSIDER TIP:

On the remote East Cape, you can stock up on necessities with one-stop shopping at the Hicks Bay general store, post office, and gas station.

—BRENT OPELL, *National Geographic Field Scientist*

The building has superb bronze-and-leadlight shop windows. The town's Spanish mission masterpiece is the **Hawke's Bay Opera House** (101 Hastings St. S.). Richly ornamented with imposing turrets, it was built in 1915 and repaired after the earthquake.

At the southern tip of Hawke's Bay, **Cape Kidnappers** acquired its unfortunate name from Captain Cook, after the servant of

his Tahitian translator was seized by Maori who had come to trade. "Obliged ... to fire upon them," Cook killed two or three Maori before the servant boy escaped.

Cape Kidnappers is noted for its gannet colony, where clouds of up to 20,000 of these graceful birds come to nest. The birds can be seen from September, when they build their nests, to early May. Seasonal tours (*check with visitor centers in Napier or Hastings*) run overland or along the beach from Clifton to the colony.

The other great attraction of Hawke's Bay is its wineries. The area is noted for its Chardonnay, but red varieties also do well. Pick up a *Hawke's Bay Winery Guide* brochure for details of over 30 wineries. Highlights include the historic **Church Road Winery** (150 Church Rd., tel 06/844-2053) in Taradale, on the outskirts of Napier, famous for its Cabernet Sauvignon, and **Sacred Hill Wines** (1033 Dartmoor Rd., tel 06/844-0138) in Puketapu, west of Napier, which has some superb Merlots.

Te Urewera National Park

This magnificent park protects the largest untouched native forest on the North Island, but most of the park's woodland, lakes, and mountains are accessible only by walking trails. The park **visitor center** (SH 38, tel 06/837-3900) at Aniwaniwa lies on the shore of the lake, 38 miles (61 km) north of the coastal river town of Wairoa. The park's crowning jewel is beautiful **Lake Waikaremoana,**

Apirana Ngata

Born in the East Cape village of Te Araroa, Sir Apirana Turupa Ngata (1874–1950) was one of New Zealand's most able politicians and an inspirational Maori leader. A lawyer and the first Maori university graduate, Ngata entered parliament in 1905 after winning the Eastern Maori seat. He was a skilled orator and political tactician, serving as a cabinet minister until he lost his seat in 1943.

Above all, he is noted for furthering Maori interests in education, health, and land reform, and he worked tirelessly to revive Maori language and traditions.

He was instrumental in setting up Maori arts-and-crafts schools, such as that in Rotorua, and encouraged the building of carved meetinghouses. He collected Maori songs and chants, studied the history of his Ngati Porou tribe, and worked on Maori dictionaries and translations of the Bible.

Ngata was a pivotal member of the Young Maori Party, which promoted Maori interests by working within Pakeha (European) institutions. Though later criticized by Maori activists, the party was the first effective modern organization run by European-educated Maori.

ringed by forest except for the cliffs of the spectacular Panekiri Bluff. One of the country's most popular hikes, the **Waikaremoana Track** leaves from the visitor center to circle the lake and can be walked in three to four days; reservations are required.

Shorter walks also fan out from the visitor center, including to the nearby **Aniwaniwa** and **Papakorito Falls,** or to **Lake Waikareiti** (2 hours round-trip).

Gisborne

The most easterly city in New Zealand and closest to the international date line, Gisborne had its 15 seconds of world fame as the first city to sight the new year during the 2000 millennium frenzy. Gisborne was also the first place Captain Cook set foot in New Zealand in 1769. After killing several Maori, Cook blighted the area with the name of Poverty Bay.

In a region where 45 percent of the population is Maori, Cook is still not highly regarded, judging by the dreary obelisk that marks **Cook's landing site,** behind the docks along The Esplanade. A plaque commemorating the first Maori landing gets equal billing. The steep walking trail over the road leads to the **Kaiti Hill lookout** for wonderful views across Gisborne and Poverty Bay.

The small but well-presented **Tairawhiti Museum** (18 Stout St., tel 06/867-3832) has a great position and café overlooking the river. Highlights include displays on messianic guerrilla Te Kooti (see p. 111) and a surfboard collection, for Gisborne has one of the country's top surfing spots in **Waikanae Beach** (end of Grey St.)

Gisborne has a flourishing wine industry and two wonderful wine cellars, including **The Works** (tel 06/863-1285), on The Esplanade near Cook's landing site, and **Lindauer Cellars** (11 Solander St., tel 06/868-2757) near the golf course. ■

Gisborne

🏕 Map p. 105

Visitor information

✉ 209 Grey St.

☎ 06/868-6139

Drive: The East Cape

The East Cape region has remained a remote Maori stronghold, showing the least European influence of any region in the North Island. This lightly populated, rural area is a detour from modern New Zealand along a stunning coastline dotted with small Maori towns, churches, and *marae*. It can be driven in one long day or two easy days.

Sunset behind the Ruakokore Anglican church

Begin at **Gisborne** and take SH35 north past fine surf beaches. After 13 miles (21 km), turn off to **Whangara ❶,** a picturesque Maori town with a finely carved meetinghouse on the bay where the film *Whale Rider* was shot.

The main highway again hits the coast at **Tolaga Bay ❷,** on a beautiful sweep of bay embraced by mudstone cliffs. Just before the town, turn off to the long Tolaga Bay Wharf. **Cook's Walkway** *(2.5 hours round-trip)* starts near the wharf and goes to the top of the cliff, then down to Captain Cook's landing place at Cook's Cove.

Dilapidated **Tokomaru Bay** comes next on another beautiful inlet surrounded by mountains. The old wharf and derelict freezing works are relics from better days.

The East Cape's largest town, **Ruatoria ❸,** lies inland off the main road. A center for the Ngati Porou people, this is also the home of the Ngati Dread, Maori Rastafarians who combine Rasta teachings with the Ringatu faith of Te Kooti, guerrilla leader of the New Zealand Wars (see p. 111). As well as dreadlocks, many Ngati Dread have full *moko* (face tattoos).

Another 12 miles (20 km) north, **Tikitiki ❹** is notable for beautiful **St. Mary's Church,** with its carved Maori entranceway and woven panels and carvings inside. About halfway along the East Cape drive, the small settlement of **Te Araroa ❺** lies on a scenic bay. In the schoolyard, the pohutukawa tree Te-Waha-O-Rerekohu is reputed to be the country's largest at 131 feet (40 m) around.

Te Araroa is also the turnoff to the **East Cape ❻,** 12 miles (20 km) along an unpaved road to the lighthouse, the most easterly such building in the world and the first to see the dawn. The climb to the top of the lighthouse is rewarded with expansive views.

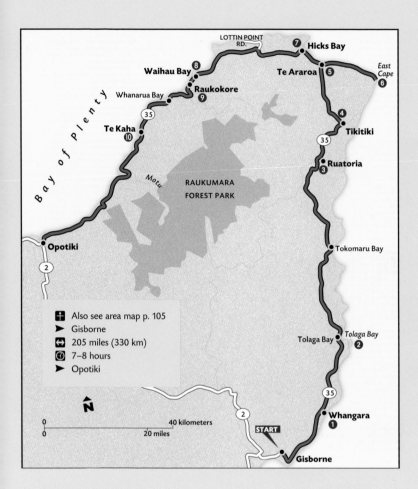

Also see area map p. 105
► Gisborne
↔ 205 miles (330 km)
⊘ 7–8 hours
► Opotiki

0   40 kilometers
0   20 miles

N

START

Past Te Araroa, **Hicks Bay** ⑦ has a great beach and farther on, **Lottin Point** lies 2.5 miles (4 km) from SH35 along a steep, narrow, and in parts unpaved road—but the views are spectacular. The road hits the coast again just before **Waihau Bay** ⑧; the settlement at **Oriti Point** has historic buildings.

From Waihau Bay, SH35 follows the coast through 65 miles (105 km) of glorious beach and bay scenery, the best of the journey. At **Raukokore** ⑨, the photogenic Anglican church with a carved entry stands out on a lonely promontory. The road then winds and dips through a number of pretty bays, such as

NOT TO BE MISSED:

Tolaga Bay • Tikitiki • East Cape lighthouse •Raukokore

Whanarua Bay, to the town of **Te Kaha** ⑩ with a beautifully carved meetinghouse.

Farther on, the road winds spectacularly along the **Motu River** with awe-inspiring views of mountain, river, and sea. SH35 then passes a number of tiny settlements and lonely beaches before finishing at Opotiki (see p. 121). ∎

Taranaki & Wanganui

The adjoining districts of Taranaki and Wanganui lie on the North Island's western bulge, well off the main tourist trail. These rural regions offer a glimpse into old New Zealand and contain two magnificent natural attractions: the towering volcanic cone of Mount Taranaki and the upstream wilderness on the Whanganui River.

A lone camper enjoys the view of Mount Taranaki, Egmont National Park.

New Plymouth
🗺 Map p. 104
Visitor information
✉ Puke Ariki,
   St. Aubyn St.
☎ 06/759-6060

New Plymouth

New Plymouth (pop. 69,000) is the main city of Taranaki, the district dominated by Fujiesque Mount Taranaki, which looms behind the city. With the only deepwater port on the country's west coast, the city serves the fertile rural interior and the country's offshore oil and gas installations.

The Ati Awa settled the area, but were driven out by musket-wielding Waikato tribesmen in the 1820s and '30s. In 1839, the New Zealand Company bought land

from the few remaining Maori, and the first boatload of settlers from Plymouth, England, landed in 1841.

As the traditional owners drifted back, land disputes were inevitable. In 1860, after Ati Awa chief Wiremu Kingi vetoed a land sale at Waitara, troops were sent in, sparking the Taranaki Wars (see pp. 110–111). Farmhouses burned and settlers fled to the safety of the New Plymouth stockade as Maori forces laid siege to the city. A truce was called in

1861, but conflict flared again from 1864 to 1866 and continued with Hauhau attacks in South Taranaki until 1869.

In the aftermath, settlers seized Maori land illegally and turned Taranaki into a green dairy farm. Well off the beaten tourist track, Taranaki remains a slice of old-fashioned rural New Zealand. That's where its charm lies, though New Plymouth does its best to put on a bright new face with an artistic bent.

Start a tour of the city at **Puke Ariki,** an impressive modern complex at the visitor information center that includes a library, galleries, cafés and museum. It also has a fine collection of Maori *taonga* (treasures). At the rear of Puke Ariki, charming **Richmond**

INSIDER TIP:

Grab your board and catch a wave at one of the beaches on Surf Highway 45 in Taranaki.

—ANGELA GORE,
*Embassy of New Zealand,
Washington, D.C.*

Cottage *(tel 06/753-2358, Sat.–Sun.)* on Ariki Street was built in 1853 and housed prominent early settler families.

The **Govett-Brewster Art Gallery** *(Queen St., tel 06/759-6060)* has interesting rotating exhibitions befitting its reputation as one of the country's best contemporary art galleries.

The permanent collection features the works of Len Lye (1901–1980), one of New Zealand's most renowned modern artists (see sidebar).

New Plymouth is noted for its beautiful gardens. Don't miss **Pukekura Park,** a ten-minute walk east of downtown, with its lakes, teahouse, fernery, hothouses, zoo, cricket ground, and more within 128 acres (52 ha) of rich greenery.

Len Lye

Len Lye (1901–1980), known primarily as a sculptor and filmmaker, was interested in how motion could be incorporated into art. He strove to collapse traditional boundaries between disciplines and cultures, making his films, for instance, by painting and scratching designs directly into the emulsion. His art, which blends Maori and European influences, is best summarized by his theory of life: "Individual Happiness Now."

Egmont National Park

One of New Zealand's most stunning sights, the towering volcano of **Mount Taranaki** is protected by Egmont National Park. Snow-capped for much of the year, Taranaki rises 8,261 feet (2,518 m) from the plains and dominates the horizon for hundreds of miles. A dormant volcano, it last erupted over 250 years ago. It is an almost perfect cone when viewed from

Tattooing

The Maori traditionally tattooed many parts of their bodies, but the facial tattoos, *moko,* that we are familiar with today were reserved for those of high rank. The painful moko were carved on the face, often over many years, with small bone adzes hit by a mallet and colored with charcoal and other pigments. High-ranking women also had moko, usually just on the chin.

the north, so reminiscent of Japan's Mount Fuji that it was used as a backdrop for the Tom Cruise movie *The Last Samurai.*

Dutch seafarer Abel Tasman was the first European to sight Mount Taranaki in 1642. James Cook was in awe of it in 1770,

naming it Mount Egmont after the Earl of Egmont, and the name stuck for 200 years. But to the Maori it was always Taranaki ("shining mountain"), and the name officially reverted to Mount Taranaki (Egmont) in the 1980s.

The park has three access points: North Egmont on the northern slopes *(take SH3 & turn off at Egmont Village),* East Egmont on the east, and Dawson Falls on the southeast *(both accessed from Stratford on SH3).*

North Egmont is the easiest to reach from New Plymouth. It has a Department of Conservation (DOC) **visitor center** *(2879 Egmont Rd., tel 06/756-0990)* with good displays, a café, and information on walks, ranging from 20-minute strolls to the three- to five-day **Mountain Circuit.** Be aware that the weather on the mountain is unpredictable and the highest reaches are suitable

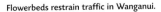

Flowerbeds restrain traffic in Wanganui.

EXPERIENCE: Canoeing the Whanganui

Another wonderful New Zealand wilderness experience is canoeing the Whanganui River. The 90-mile (145 km), five-day journey from Taumaranui to Pipiriki through the superb **Whanganui National Park** can be also done in three days (from Whakahoro to Pipiriki) or one day (Taumaranui to Ohinepane or variations).

From October 1 to April 30, huts and campsites along the way must be reserved through the Department of Conservation (*www.doc.govt.nz & search for Whanganui Journey*), which issues a Great Walk Pass for this popular trip.

The river has small rapids, but is easily negotiated; guided trips are also offered.

The journey is usually arranged in Taumaranui, to the north of the park, where operators provide canoes, all gear, and drop-off and pickup along the river. Taumarunui operators include **Taumarunui Canoe Hire** (*tel 07/896-6507, www.taumarunuicanoehire.co.nz*) and **Whanganui River Guides** (*tel 07/896-6727, www.whanganuiriverguides.co.nz*).

In Whakahoro, contact **Wades Landing Outdoors** (*tel 07/895 5995, www.whanganui.co.nz*), and in Raetihi, **Waka Tours** (*tel 06/385-4811, www.wakatours.net*) has Maori-focused canoeing trips staying at *marae*. Other operators can be found in Pipiriki, Ohakune, and Wanganui (*check with tourist offices*).

---

only for experienced climbers.

For an excellent 1.5- to 2-hour walk, the **Veronica Loop Track** climbs steeply for 30 minutes to the junction with the **Holly Track.** Take a ten-minute detour up the mountain on the Holly Track to the lookout for spectacular views. The Veronica Loop Track then gently curls back down the mountain through forest to the park headquarters.

The **East Egmont** access point is at the highest altitude. It leads to the Manganui ski slopes and the popular Stratford Mountain House (*tel 06/765-6100, www.mountainhouse.co.nz*), which has alpine lodge accommodations and a restaurant. The **East Egmont Lookout** is only a ten-minute walk from the top parking lot and provides panoramic views.

Dawson Falls has an alpine-style tourist lodge and a DOC visitor center (*tel 06/756-0990*).

Walks include the one-hour **Kapuni Loop Track** that takes in the cascading Dawson Falls.

Wanganui

The Whanganui River flows from its origins on Mount Tongariro though some of New Zealand's most diverse and beautiful countryside before disgorging its waters into the sea at the city of Wanganui ("expansive river mouth"). A faded river port, the city has enough historical charm to keep the visitor, but the river is the real lure for those with time to explore upstream.

The New Zealand Company settled Wanganui in 1840 based on contentious land sales. Skirmishes blighted the early years of the settlement, which became a major military base during the New Zealand Wars. Ironically, in 1864 the lower river tribes saved the city against marauding

Wanganui

🗺 Map p. 105

Visitor information

✉ 101 Guyton St.

☎ 06/349-0508

Hauhau warriors coming down the river. In the 1880s, the river became an artery to the remote interior, and riverboats thrived as much on tourism as on trade.

Today, the old heart of the city lies on the corner of the leafy main street, **Victoria Avenue,** and

Plague of Rabbits

First brought to New Zealand in the mid-19th century, rabbits provided meat, fur, and a friendly reminder of Britain for homesick colonists. But as the rabbit population sky-rocketed, so did damage to the ecosystem. Import-ed natural enemies such as ferrets and weasels proved just as disastrous to the environment. Finally, in 1947 the government set up the Rabbit Destruction Council, which decommer-cialized the rabbit meat and fur industries and instituted a "killer policy," advocating the year-round destruction of the animals. Rabbits have since been controlled.

Ridgeway Street, where fine his-toric buildings surround the **Watt Fountain,** topped by Victorian gas lamps.

Two blocks north in Queens Park, the **Whanganui Regional Museum** (Watt St., tel 06/349-1110, www.wanganui-museum.org.nz, $) is well worth a visit. Gottfried Lindauer's Maori portraits here

are national treasures and include a version of the famous "Ana Rupene with daughter Huria." Fine Maori artifacts include carvings, war canoes, and greenstone clubs. The history of Wanganui and the riverboats is also featured. Next door, the **Sarjeant Gallery** (tel 06/349-0506, www.sarjeant.org.nz) has rotating art exhibits in a fine neoclassical building.

Down on the river, the paddle wheeler Waimarie (Taupo Quay, tel 06/347-1863, daily Nov.–April, weekends May–Oct., $$$–$$$$) provides river cruises re-creating Wanganui's heyday. The small **museum** (www.riverboat.co.nz) on the waterfront showcases the boat's restoration and the river's history. Just along Taupo Quay, on the corner of Drews Avenue, a **tram restoration museum** is open on the weekends.

Across the river, **Drurie Hill** has panoramic views of the city and Whanganui River. Getting there is half the fun: You proceed along a tiled tunnel into the hillside, then take a 1918 elevator ($) that grinds the 216 feet (66 m) to the top. Perched on the hill, the **Memorial Tower,** dedicated to the dead of World War I, has unbeatable views from the top.

A great way to explore the river is with a rented canoe from the **Top 10 Holiday Park** (460 Somme Parade., tel 06/343-8402, $$$$$), located on the river bank 4 miles (7 km) northeast of the town.

Whanganui River

A highlight from Wanganui is the 50-mile (80 km) **Whanganui**

River Road drive to Pipiriki. The tiny settlements along the way relied on the river for transportation until the road was built in 1934, and this rugged area is still remote. The road is paved only half the way, but the slow twisting drive is rewarded with superb scenery. Bus tours also operate along this route.

The region's history is one of war and missionaries. The road passes old Maori fortresses high above the river and mission stations with classical names such as Atene (Athens) and Koriniti (Corinth) before reaching picturesque **Jerusalem.** French nun, Sister Mary Joseph Aubert established the Catholic mission in 1883 and worked with the sick and poor here until her death in 1926. Jerusalem was also home to poet James K. Baxter, who set up a commune in the 1960s that lasted until his death in 1972.

Pipiriki lies on the southern edge of the **Whanganui National Park,** a vast wilderness accessible only by river or on foot. **Bridge to Nowhere Jetboat Tours** *(tel 06/348-7122, $$$$$)* has wonderfully scenic four-hour trips on the river from Pipiriki to the **Bridge to Nowhere,** built for a settlement of returned World War I soldiers, and indeed in the middle of nowhere.

The park has some wonderful wilderness adventures, ranging from three-day hikes to three- to five-day canoeing trips along the river (see sidebar p. 145), with stays at campsites and huts. From Pipiriki it is 15 miles (24 km) to Raetihi and SH4, if heading

Canoeing the Whanganui River

north to Tongariro National Park and towns such as Ohakune (see pp. 131–133).

Taumaranui, west of Lake Taupo on SH4, is one of the best places to arrange kayaking trips (guided or independent) on the river. The visitor information center *(Hakiaha St., tel 07/895-7494)* and DOC office *(Orange Grove Rd., tel 07/895-8201)* are helpful. Railway buffs will appreciate the **Raurimu Spiral,** 23 miles (37 km) south of town. The track negotiates a steep incline with circles, horseshoe curves, and tunnels. ■

The nation's capital and most attractive and cultivated city, blending historical appeal with contemporary élan

Wellington & the South

The floating fern sculpture hangs over Wellington's Civic Square.

Wellington & the South

When the god Maui fished the North Island out of the sea, its tail fell to the north, while the head lay south around Wellington, at the bottom of North Island. Still the country's head, the capital city is a scenic metropolis draped across hills and precipitous gullies around a deep blue harbor.

Many visitors come to Wellington only to catch a ferry to the South Island, but the capital deserves exploration. A compact city easily explored on foot, its streets are a delight to wander. Historic buildings grace the downtown, while the rejuvenated waterfront buzzes with activity. Taking pride of place on the shorefront, the national museum, Te Papa, is not to be missed.

From downtown, take the cable car to the hills and see why Wellington is often compared to San Francisco. The panorama from the top takes in shimmering harbor, city towers, and hills speckled with wooden Victorian villas.

The New Zealand Company's first venture, Wellington was settled in 1840 on land hastily purchased from the Maori by William Wakefield (1801–1848). Land disputes and floods marred the early years of the colony, but Wellington grew and overcame the lack of flat land by reclaiming the shoreline, beginning in 1852.

Lying on a major fault line, the city is often shaken by tremors, none more ferocious than the 1855 earthquake that hit the fledgling settlement with a force of 8.2 on the Richter scale. However, the 1855 quake helped the shoreline reclamation process by pushing up large areas of land.

In 1865, the capital shifted from Auckland to Wellington, because of the latter city's central location and proximity to the South Island. Wellington expanded to suburbs such as historic Thorndon, built of earthquake-resistant wood, resulting in impressive structures such as the

Old Government Buildings (1876) in the Parliament District, where the country's lawmakers govern.

Though the population of 180,000 is small for a capital city, greater Wellington, including the adjoining cities of Lower Hutt, Upper Hutt, and Porirua, has a population of 456,000. The city belies its size with a thriving arts scene, lively nightlife, good shopping, and a parade of festivals, concerts, and exhibitions that make it the country's events center. The city is also a hub for New Zealand's vibrant film industry, thanks largely to *Lord of the Rings* director and Wellingtonian Peter Jackson.

Visible from the city's hilltops, the South Island lies just across Cook Strait, a

---

NOT TO BE MISSED:

Strolling and eating on the
   revamped waterfront   153–154

Te Papa, the impressive national
   museum   154

Views from the cable car to the
   Botanic Garden   156

Historic Parliament District   157–158

Lively nightlife of Courtenay
   Place and Cuba Street   158

A ferry across, or drive around,
   scenic Wellington Harbour   159

Fine wines of romantic
   Martinborough   160–161

Fauna of the Pukaha Mount Bruce
   National Wildlife Centre   161

swift and sometimes turbulent passage. Windy Wellington is noted for its howling gales, whipping around buildings, buffeting airplanes, and churning seas.

North of Wellington, the Kapiti Coast is something of a resort for the city. Good beaches and points of interest lie just off SH1, the country's main highway heading north. The alternative route, SH2 to Napier, lies over the ranges to the east and goes through the Wairarapa. This district is noted for wineries, historic towns, and the Pukaha Mount Bruce National Wildlife Centre. At the top of the "fish's head," the university city of Palmerston North is a crossroads between the two routes. ■

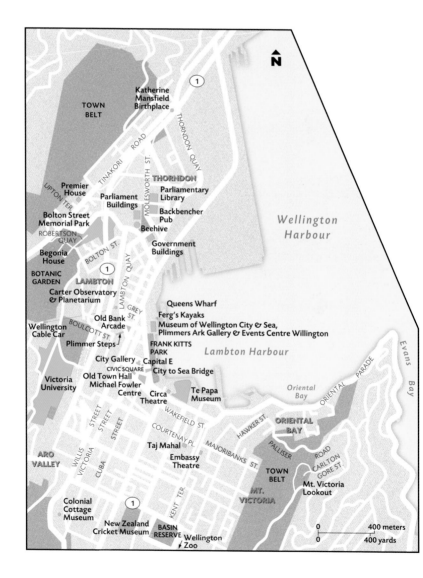

Wellington

Compact and easy to navigate, downtown Wellington is a delight to explore, taking in the city's heritage and the redeveloped waterfront, where the national museum, Te Papa, makes a statement. Make sure to take the cable car to the Botanic Garden for an overview of the fine harbor and hilly suburbs draped with Victorian villas.

Modern downtown Wellington

Civic Square

Civic Square
🅰 Map p. 151
Visitor information
✉ Victoria &
  Wakefield Sts.
☎ 04/802-4860
**www.wellingtonnz
.com**

Often busy with street performers and stalls, the Civic Square, behind the visitor information center, lies at the heart of the city's cultural precinct and is a good place to start a tour. Turned into a paved plaza in the 1990s, the square is lined with artwork, including stylized nikau palms and the striking "Ferns," a 385-pound (175 kg) globe suspended midair on wires, representing five different species of native ferns.

Buildings around the square include the imposing **Old Town Hall** (1904), which was saved from demolition in 1983 by a public campaign and now houses the New Zealand Symphony Orchestra. The futuristic **Michael Fowler Centre** stands next door and also has a fine auditorium, the city's preeminent concert venue. These two are the focus of the biennial **New Zealand Festival,** showcasing Wellington as the country's performing-arts capital.

The square is also home to the **Capital E** children's theater and events center, as well as the **City Gallery** in an impressive art deco edifice. Always worth a look, the gallery has rotating exhibitions highlighting New Zealand artists.

Waterfront

From Civic Square, take the art-lined City to Sea Bridge to the waterfront. Across the bridge, turn right and go past the **Circa Theatre** (1 Taranaki St., 04/801-7992), home to one of the city's liveliest theater companies. The theater's facade was transplanted from the old Westport Coal Company building, which once stood on the opposite side of Cable Street.

Dominating the waterfront is

INSIDER TIP:

A great time to visit Te Papa is on Thursday nights when the museum stays open until 9 p.m. You may well feel like you have the place all to yourself.

—KERRY PRENDERGAST,
Mayor of Wellington

the pride of the city, **Te Papa,** the Museum of New Zealand (see p. 154). Allow at least a couple of hours to take in its exhibits.

From Te Papa, walk back north around the waterfront, a lively open space where something is always happening. Dotted everywhere are artworks, such as in **Frank Kitts Park,** built

on reclaimed land and one of the few patches of green in the inner city.

Past the park, **Queens Wharf** is a dynamic hub of restaurants, bars, museums, and the **TSB Bank Arena,** which hosts concerts and other events. Queens Wharf was built on reclaimed shorefront land after the 1855 quake.

Colossal Squid

On February 22, 2007, the largest known colossal squid was pulled from the Ross Sea by a New Zealand fishing boat. It was 33 feet (10 m) long and weighed almost 1,100 pounds (495 kg). Its eyes, at 11 inches (28 cm) across, are the largest on record. The squid was frozen at Te Papa for over a year before scientists thawed and dissected it in April 2008. The museum plans to display the squid in a tub of formaldehyde.

This and other fascinating facts of the quake and early settlement can be found at the **Plimmers Ark Gallery** on the south side of Queens Wharf. The gallery houses the remains of the *Inconstant*, an immigrant ship wrecked in 1849 and bought by merchant John Plimmer for use as a bond store and shop, known as Plimmers Ark. The *Inconstant* was beached in the upheaval of the 1855 earthquake, and remains of the ship, now just lumps of blackened wood, were discovered in 1997 under the Old Bank Arcade on Lambton Quay.

City Gallery
- Map p. 151
- Civic Square
- 04/801-3021
www.citygallery .org.nz

Museum of Wellington City & Sea

▲ Map p. 151
✉ Queens Wharf
☎ 04/472-8904

www.museumof
wellington.co.nz

Te Papa

▲ Map p. 151
✉ Cable St.
☎ 04/381-7000

www.tepapa.govt.nz

The gallery forms part of the nearby **Museum of Wellington City & Sea,** housed in the old Harbour Trust and bond store offices (1892), one of the oldest buildings on the waterfront. Crammed with interesting tales of Wellington from its founding to recent times, the museum hosts exhibits covering everything from epic rugby matches to the *Wahine* disaster, which claimed 51 lives when the ferry sank in a furious storm crossing the Cook Strait on April 10, 1968.

Farther north along the waterfront, the historic harbor sheds now serve a variety of purposes from apartments to restaurants. **Ferg's Kayaks** *(tel 04/499-8898)* in Shed 6 has kayaks for rent to see the city from the water and is notable as the business of Ian Ferguson, New Zealand's great Olympian, winner of four kayaking gold medals.

Te Papa

The Museum of New Zealand Te Papa Tongarewa, universally known as Te Papa, houses the most important collection of national artistic treasures in the country. Opened in 1998 after 13 years of planning, the striking modern building on reclaimed waterfront land cost over NZ$300 million.

Among its architectural motifs, the gray wall that bisects the building symbolizes Wellington's fault lines. The building sits right on top of the Wellington fault, and state-of-the-art rubber-and-lead foundations are designed to dampen the effects of an earthquake.

Six floors of exhibition space highlight New Zealand's natural environment and Maori heritage, most poignantly at **Te Marae,** the meetinghouse and focal point for the Maori collection. **"Toi Te Papa: Art of the Nation"** features some of the museum's important art collection, once housed in the National Art Gallery.

Perhaps the only criticism of Te Papa is that, with all that space, more of its huge collection could be displayed, but rotating exhibits and innovative displays are designed to keep the masses coming back for more. Over a million visitors pour through the doors every year. Te Papa is open every day of the year and admission is free.

Lambton Quay

Now Wellington's premier shopping boulevard, Lambton Quay ran along the shoreline from the time of first European settlement in 1840. Its western flank rises steeply while the east traverses gently to the waterfront on reclaimed land. Lined with arcades and shops, the quay holds many historic buildings, none finer than the **Old Bank Arcade,** built in 1884. Once the headquarters of the Bank of New Zealand, it is now a hub for designer fashion boutiques.

Other points of interest include **Plimmer Steps,** leading up to Boulcott Street, named after prominent early businessman John Plimmer, the "father of Wellington." A statue of Plimmer

TE PAPA

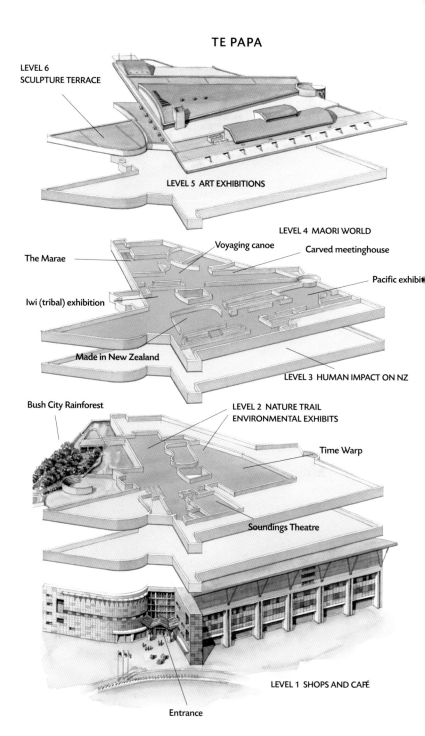

LEVEL 6
SCULPTURE TERRACE

LEVEL 5 ART EXHIBITIONS

LEVEL 4 MAORI WORLD

Voyaging canoe

Carved meetinghouse

The Marae

Pacific exhibit

Iwi (tribal) exhibition

Made in New Zealand

LEVEL 3 HUMAN IMPACT ON NZ

Bush City Rainforest

LEVEL 2 NATURE TRAIL
ENVIRONMENTAL EXHIBITS

Time Warp

Soundings Theatre

LEVEL 1 SHOPS AND CAFÉ

Entrance

and his dog Fritz stands at the entrance to the steps.

North on Lambton Quay, opposite Grey Street, lies the entrance to the **Wellington Cable Car** (04/472-2199, $), a must on every Wellington itinerary. Completed in 1902, it serviced the new suburb of Kelburn up in the hills as the city expanded beyond the limited flat lands. Cable cars

---

EXPERIENCE:
Eco-volunteering

Nature conservation projects across the country are attracting an increasing number of volunteers eager to learn about New Zealand's unique ecology and motivated to get out into that wonderful outdoors and make a difference.

The **Global Volunteering Network** (105 High St., Lower Hutt, tel 04/569-9081, www.volunteer.org.nz) has a program in the Wellington region that allows overseas visitors to preserve, monitor, and reestablish the natural environment. This might involve replanting of native forests, wildlife monitoring, pest control, trash collection, or park maintenance. Programs range from two weeks to six months and start at around US$1,000, which includes accommodations, food, and transportation to and from field projects.

---

carry thousands of residents and tourists daily until 10 p.m., passing Victoria University and terminating at the Botanic Gardens. At the top station, a small museum details the cable car's history.

If you want to return to Lambton Quay via cable car, you can head north from the quay to the Parliament District (see opposite).

Botanic Garden & Thorndon

At the top of the cable car route, Wellington's premier horticultural spot offers postcard panoramas of the city and harbor in 64 acres (26 ha) of superb gardens, exotic woodlands, and native forest. From the cable car station, walk past Carter Observatory and Planetarium to the garden's **Treehouse Visitor Center** (tel 04/499-1400) and down to the **Begonia House** and café, with the formal rose gardens at front.

From the Begonia House, you can continue on back to the city via **Bolton Street Memorial Park,** where many of the city's pioneers are buried. As you walk along Robertson Way through the Jewish section of the cemetery, you'll see the fine villas of Thorndon. Robertson Way comes out at The Terrace and leads back to the Parliament District and the railway station.

Alternatively, north of the Begonia House you can exit the gardens onto Tinakori Road in historic **Thorndon.** Head northeast along this road, which is lined with some of the city's finest houses. In 1865, the area was purchased for the new capital as part of the move from Auckland to Wellington. Behind Thorndon, the precipitous greenery of Tinakori Hill forms part of the Town Belt, a ring of parkland around the city set aside by early planners.

On Tinakori Road just past Upton Terrace, **Premier House** is the prime minister's official residence. The original cottage, built in 1843, underwent substantial additions

Katherine Mansfield

Born Kathleen Mansfield Beauchamp in a small house at 25 Tinakori Road in 1888, Katherine Mansfield went on to become New Zealand's most acclaimed writer. Her father, Harold Beauchamp, was a banker whose burgeoning career later saw the family move to a larger house at 75 Tinakori Road.

Educated at Wellington Girls High School and later Queens College in London, Mansfield moved permanently to Europe in 1908 and lived a bohemian life there, taking lovers of both sexes before marrying literary critic John Middleton Murry.

Though she published only three volumes of short stories, they garnered high critical acclaim and she mingled with the cream of Britain's literati, including D. H. Lawrence and Bloomsbury group

writers such as T. S. Eliot, Aldous Huxley, and Virginia Woolf. Mansfield died of tuberculosis in 1923 at the age of 34, not long after the publication of *The Garden Party* collection, considered the pinnacle of her short career.

over the years, but in 1935 Socialist prime minister Michael Joseph Savage thought it far too grand to live in and it became a children's dental clinic, dubbed the Murder House. The house was fully restored in 1990, when it once again became the prime minister's residence.

At 25 Tinakori Road, **Katherine Mansfield Birthplace** *(tel 04/473-7268, closed Mon., $)* was the childhood home of New Zealand's most famous writer. The beautifully restored house features a video portrait of the writer.

Parliament District

At the top end of Lambton Quay, the impressive **Government Buildings** (actually a single edifice) was built in 1876 as offices for public servants

and government ministers. The second largest wooden building in the world (the Todaiji Temple in Japan takes the number-one spot), it has a slab-style front designed to look like stone. It now houses Victoria University's law faculty.

Across the road, the distinctive and oft-maligned **Beehive** stands in modern contrast. The circular 1981 building houses the offices of the prime minister, cabinet, and other busy government bees. It is the national symbol of executive power. The parliament meets next door at the neoclassical **Parliament Buildings** *(free tours available),* built in 1922, a fine edifice though lopsided, for the southern wing that was planned to match the northern wing was never built. Next along, the delightful

Afternoon tea in Katherine Mansfield's dining room

Parliament Buildings

🅼 Map p. 151

✉ For tours, use Molesworth St. entrance

☎ 04/471-9503

www.ps.parliament .gov.nz

Parliamentary Library (1899) is a Gothic fantasy in pink-fringed stone, a survivor of the 1907 fire that destroyed the original wooden Parliament Buildings.

Facing the Parliament Buildings, the famous Backbencher Pub on Molesworth Street has beckoned politicians for decades. Drop in and share an ale with one of the

Effigies of politicians line the walls of the Backbencher Pub and Café.

nation's leaders, or at least with one of their sizable puppet effigies that line the walls in humorous and sometimes grotesque parody.

Courtenay & Cuba

South of Te Papa and the waterfront, Wellington's liveliest restaurant and nightlife district lies along Courtenay Place and the pedestrian Cuba Street running off it. A great area to dine, with a host of cuisines catering to all budgets, this buzzing locale really takes off on Friday and Saturday nights, when the bars stay open to the wee hours.

The area is also worth a wander during the day. Cuba Street has fine rows of Victorian merchant buildings and storefronts, as does Courtenay Place with its old theaters and oddities such as the **Taj Mahal,** a baroque public toilet built in 1928 and now converted into a restaurant.

At the end of Courtenay Place on Kent Terrace, the **Embassy Theatre** was restored in 2003 for the world premiere of *The Return of the King,* when the city turned out in force to celebrate the final installment of the *Lord of the Rings* trilogy.

From the Embassy Theatre, head to the waterfront, where Oriental Parade continues around to **Oriental Bay,** a chic area around a pretty swimming beach right on the edge of the city. Popular with runners, cyclists, and sunbathers, the beach strip also has a good selection of dining options.

Wellington Suburbs

Many of Wellington's suburbs are dotted with wooden villas clinging to green hills. The Aro Valley area, south of downtown, has kept many of its fine houses, thanks to resident action against urban renewal in the 1960s and '70s.

Rescued from the wrecker's ball, **Colonial Cottage** *(68 Nairn St., tel 04/384 9122, daily Jan.–Feb., Sat.–Sun. March–Dec., $)* is Aro Valley's oldest building, dating from 1858. The cottage is now a museum furnished in 19th-century style with an attractive garden. It can be reached on foot from the city center—head south on Willis Street, which ends at Nairn Street.

INSIDER TIP:

September's World of WearableArt is beyond a fashion show—it's a kaleidoscope performance of color, light, music, and crazy costume constructions.

—CARRIE MILLER,
National Geographic Writer

Just over half a mile (1 km) east of the cottage, the **Basin Reserve,** one of the country's prime cricket grounds, was originally a lake until the 1855 earthquake lifted it. The **New Zealand Cricket Museum** *(tel 04/385-6602, $)* in the Old Grandstand exhibits cricket memorabilia.

For the most stunning panorama of the city, reaching from the Cook Strait and the airport in the south to the full length of the harbor and the Hutt Valley in the north, head to the top of **Mount Victoria.** Though it can be reached on foot from the end of Courtenay Place, it is much easier to drive—take Majoribanks Street next to the Embassy Theatre, turn left at Hawker, then right at Palliser. Or, from Oriental Parade on the other side of the hill, take Carlton Gore Street.

The **Wellington Zoo** *(200 Daniel St., tel 04/381-6750, $$–$$$),* 2.5 miles (4 km) south of the city center, has a kiwi house in addition to tigers, chimps, and other animals in a green setting.

For a wonderful coastal drive around Wellington's eastern suburbs, take Oriental Parade east from downtown and follow the coast for 19 miles (30 km) around a series of pretty coves and beaches such as Evans Bay, pine-fringed Mahanga Bay, Breaker Bay where little blue penguins come to nest, and the surf beaches of Worser Bay and Lyall Bay near the airport. The road

Out On the Town

Choice Wellington nightspots include:

Bodega Bar *(101 Ghuznee St.).* This longrunning band venue highlights the best of New Zealand music, from rock to reggae.

Dockside *(Queens Wharf).* A mostly corporate crowd kicks in late at this restaurant-bar with outdoor areas overlooking the water.

Matterhorn *(106 Cuba St.).* A hip bar for the moneyed young, Matterhorn has cocktails, low lighting, and cool sounds at high volume.

changes name many times, but just keep following the coastline until Island Bay, where you head back to Wellington along The Parade/ Adelaide Road.

For a fine trip across the harbor, take the ferry *(tel 04/494-3339, www.eastbywest.co.nz, $–$$)* from downtown Queens Wharf to **Days Bay,** where you can swim, dine at the wharf café, or wander around the beach to the **Rimu Street shops** in Eastbourne. ∎

The South

The southern "head" of the North Island takes in two regions bordering Wellington: the beach strip of the Kapiti Coast to the north and the farmland, wineries, and remote coastline of the Wairarapa to the east. The university town of Palmerston North is the northern bridge between the two regions.

The gardens and main square of Palmerston North

Martinborough

M Map: inside back cover

Visitor information

✉ 18 Kitchener St.

☎ 06/306-5010

www.wairarapanz .com

Wairarapa

The lightly populated Wairarapa district northeast of Wellington lies across the rugged Rimutaka Range. The wilderness of the Tararua Ranges to the north also helps to isolate this undulating farming region of wineries, wildlife, deserted coastlines, and historic towns.

Heading out of the city, take SH2 through the sprawling suburban areas of Lower and Upper Hutt, major population centers of the greater Wellington area.

The Wairarapa takes its name from shallow Lake Wairarapa ("shimmering waters") outside of Featherston, where you turn off SH2 to reach **Martinborough.** Famed for the surrounding wineries, sleepy Martinborough comes alive on weekends when Wellington day visitors and wine sippers on romantic getaways fill the town's cafés and B&Bs. The grand **Martinborough Hotel** *(The Square, see p. 298),* built in

1882, is an icon in the center of town, offering fine dining as well as rooms, and you can sample local wines and produce at the **Martinborough Wine Centre** *(6 Kitchener St., tel 06/306-9040).* The visitor information center has the lowdown on the area's wineries and accommodations.

INSIDER TIP:

Stock up on local wine, pick up some food from the gourmet stores, and head to Cape Palliser for a decadent picnic and jaw-dropping scenery.

—KERRY PRENDERGAST,
Mayor of Wellington

From Martinborough, solitude seekers can head south to the scenic, windswept coast around **Cape Palliser.** Where the road hits the coast, a fine two-hour round-trip walk goes to the spectacular rock formations of the **Putangirua Pinnacles.** Past the isolated fishing village of Ngawi, a large seal colony sprawls on the rocks just before the **lighthouse** at the end of the road, at the most southerly tip of the North Island.

The Wairarapa's other well-known tourist town, **Greytown,** farther north on SH2, has historic wooden buildings, including the fine **St. Andrews Church,** and a host of antique and craft shops. A pleasing weekend getaway, Greytown has plenty of B&Bs and cottages for rent.

Heading north, you come to the Wairarapa's main town of Masterton, but keep going 19 miles (30 km) more on SH2 to the **Pukaha Mount Bruce National Wildlife Centre** *(tel 06/375-8004, www.mtbruce.org .nz, $–$$),* the country's most important and accessible wildlife center. This is the place to view New Zealand's fauna—mainly birds, but tuataras and other reptiles are also on display in native surroundings. This important breeding center has many rare species, including the South Island takahe.

Kapiti Coast

A beach retreat and growth corridor for Wellington, the Kapiti Coast runs northwest over the Ohariu fault line from the capital. The rugged Tararua Ranges line SH1 inland, while Kapiti Island dominates coastal views to the west.

Golden Shears

While no country wants to be known just for sheep farming, New Zealand does acknowledge the animal's importance. In celebration, Masterton in Wairarapa hosts the annual Golden Shears Shearing & Wool Handling Championships. Usually held at the end of February, the event has grown in scope and popularity. For tickets and information, contact the **Shear Discovery Centre** *(12 Dixon St., Masterton, www.sheardiscovery.co.nz).*

In Pursuit of the Rings

One of the biggest things to hit New Zealand in the last decade was the *Lord of the Rings* trilogy, the multimillion-dollar blockbuster filmed in New Zealand by Kiwi director Peter Jackson from the books by J. R. R. Tolkien.

The landscape of New Zealand makes an apt backdrop for a fantasy movie.

During the two years of filming, the country became Middle Earth, the filmmakers employing an army of digital and makeup artists, weapons and costumer designers, blacksmiths, stonemasons, carpenters, and over 20,000 extras. Almost every New Zealander knows someone who worked on the movies, many of whom dressed up in prosthetic feet and ears to become hobbits, orcs, or other creatures.

The boost to the economy and national pride was enormous. The government appointed a Minister for the Rings, Wellington (dubbed Wellywood) hosted the world premieres, and Peter Jackson, already a renowned director, became a cultural powerhouse leading a resurgent local film industry.

The Fellowship of the Ring (2001), *The Two Towers* (2002), and *The Return of the King* (2003) garnered a total of 17 Oscars, including best picture, best director, and best art direction.

The special effects of Weta Workshop, Jackson's Wellington-based production house, enhanced the country's magical scenery, but more than 150 stunning locations throughout New Zealand provided the perfect backdrop for Middle Earth.

Shooting Locations—North Island

Though the Rings frenzy has subsided from its dizzying heights, a host of tours take Tolkien fans to shooting locations, while restaurants and hotels that catered to the stars proudly display memorabilia.

The most immediately recognizable location is that of Hobbiton (see p. 108), filmed outside Matamata in the fertile Waikato region of the central North Island. The hobbit houses were

INSIDER TIP:

The Matterhorn bar on Cuba Street in Wellington was one of the preferred hangouts for the *Lord of the Rings* actors, especially Elijah.

—TRACY PELT,
National Geographic Manager

built into the green hills on a local farm, and though only the shells remain, the site is a very popular Rings tour destination.

Wellington and surroundings provided many of the filming sites, including those for the Middle Earth town of Bree, shot on the Miramar Peninsula and at an old army base in the suburb of Seatoun. The backdrop for Helms Deep was a quarry on Western Hutt Road, the main road from Wellington to Upper Hutt. A few miles on, Kaitoke Regional Park was the location for Rivendell and the Fords of Isen. Waitarere Forest, near Foxton on the Kapiti Coast north of Wellingon, was the backdrop for the Trollshaw Forest and Osgiliath Wood.

The striking volcanoes of the Tongariro National Park feature strongly in the movies. Whakapapa ski field on Mount Ruapehu was transformed into the desolate land of Mordor, the dwelling place of the evil lord Sauron. Nearby Mount Tongariro became Mount Doom with much computer transformation. The eerie landscapes along the Desert Road to the east of the park were a natural for the Plains of Gorgoroth.

Shooting Locations—South Island

Not surprisingly, the magnificent panoramas of the South Island also provided many filming locations. The Queenstown area was home to the massive main battle scenes in *Lord of the Rings,* with over a thousand people on set each day. The scene at Amon Hen, where the travelers battle orcs and the

fellowship breaks up, was filmed in a pine forest on the shores of Lake Wakatipu.

At the northern end of the lake near Glenorchy, the mountains of Mount Aspiring National Park were the location for the Misty Mountains. The Kawerau River, not far from the A. J. Hackett bungee-jumping site, was the backdrop for the scenes in which the fellowship paddles through the Pillars of the Kings, though the pillars themselves were computer generated.

Other South Island locations include Arrowtown (where the Arrow River was transformed into the Ford of Bruinen), Takaka Hill near Nelson (Chatwood Forest), Ida Valley near Alexandra (Rohan), and the landscape near Te Anau, where the Mararoa River was the location for the Silverlode River. ■

EXPERIENCE:
Lord of the Ring Tours

A number of major operators offer *Lord of the Rings* tours:

For a look at Hobbiton, contact **Rings Scenic Tours** *(101 Arawa St., Matamata, tel 07/888-9913, www.hobbitontours.com).*

From Queenstown or Wanaka, **Wanaka Sightseeing Tours** *(43 Kaiwara St., Hoon Hay, Christchurch, tel 03/338-0982, www.wanakasightseeing.co.nz)* visits over 20 filming locations.

Heliworks *(Queenstown International Airport, Tex Smith Ln., Queenstown, tel 03/441-4011, www.heliworks.co.nz)* offers aerial Rings tours.

In Wellington, **Wellington Rover Tours** *(tel 02/142-6211, www.wellingtonrover .co.nz)* has half- and full-day tours.

Wellington Movie Tours *(RD1, Porirua, tel 027/419-3077, www.adventuresafari .co.nz)* has a variety of *LOTR* tours.

Paekakariki, 25 miles (40 km) north of Wellington, is the first stop of note, a relaxed seaside town stretching back from the main road to a black-sand beach. Vast **Queen Elizabeth Park** on the northern edge of town includes the last area of natural dunes on the coast and

A little spotted kiwi (*Apteryx owenii*) chick with its father at the Karori Sanctuary near Wellington

offers swimming, fishing, walking, cycling, and horseback riding on the beach. Once home to many Maori villages, it housed 20,000 U.S. marines during World War II.

At MacKays Crossing, just off SH1, 3 miles (5 km) north of Paekakariki, the **Tramway Museum** (*tel 04/292-8361, wellingtontrams.org.nz, daily Dec. 26–Jan. 31, Sat.–Sun. Feb.–Dec. 24, $*) exhibits restored Wellington trams that run along a 1.3-mile (2 km) track to the beach.

The coast's largest town, **Paraparaumu,** sprawls down to a fine beach, preferable to the suburban jungle on the highway. The visitor information center (*Coastlands Parade, tel 04/298-8195*) has details on accommodations and activities. Paraparaumu has one of New Zealand's best golf courses as well as the **Southward Car Museum** (*Otaihanga Rd., www.southward.org.nz, tel 04/297-1221, $*).

The main attraction, especially for birders, is **Kapiti Island,** 3 miles (5 km) off the coast from Paraparaumu. Now a nature reserve, the island was once the base of Maori chief Te Rauparaha, whose well-armed raiding parties terrorized the west coast down to the South Island. The Department of Conservation has eradicated pests and made the island secure for breeding endangered birds, include a large colony of little spotted kiwis. You must obtain a permit well in advance through the DOC in Wellington (*tel 04/384-7770, wellingtonbookings@doc.govt.nz*) to visit the island. Kapiti Island has a lodge (*tel 03/363-6606, www.kapitiislandalive.co.nz*) for overnight stays; two ferries go there from Paraparaumu Beach.

In **Otaki,** Te Rauparaha helped build the Rangiatea Church, the finest Maori church in the country. Sadly, it burned down in 1995, but a reproduction now stands on the site. Otherwise, Otaki is the gateway for some fine Tararua Ranges walks accessed from **Otaki Forks,** 12 miles (19 km) east of town on Otaki Gorge Road.

Palmerston North

At the heart of the flat Manawatu farming district, Palmerston North (pop. 76,000) is a pleasant provincial city on the banks of the Manawatu River. Comedian John Cleese called it the suicide capital of New Zealand, saying if you lacked the courage to take your life then "Palmy" would do the trick. The council renamed its dump Mount Cleese in his honor.

Cleese must have visited when **Massey University** was on

INSIDER TIP:

Day trips to Kapiti Island, a birder's paradise, are limited to 50 people, and to only 16 for overnight stays—so book your trip well in advance.

—KERRY PRENDERGAST,
Mayor of Wellington

vacation, for the country's second largest university drives the city. Palmerston North's nightlife and cultural scene hums during term, but dies over the summer months.

European settlers arrived in 1866 and named the town Palmerston, later adding "North" to distinguish it from Palmerston in the South Island. They laid out the city around **The Square,** an expanse of lawn, gardens, and

lakes in the heart of the city.

Just west of the Square, **Te Manawa** is a combined museum/ art gallery/hands-on science center in an impressive complex. A few blocks northwest, Palmy's main attraction is the **New Zealand Rugby Museum.** Crammed with memorabilia, it is a mecca for rugby-mad Kiwis, but the non-initiated will also gain an insight into what makes the nation tick.

The much-loved **Victoria Esplanade Gardens,** 1 mile (1.6 km) south of the square on the river, are an oasis of rose gardens, lawns, walks, playgrounds, an aviary, and a miniature railway. The university is across the river, accessed by the bridge on Fitzherbert Avenue.

Heading east of the city toward Napier and the Wairarapa, SH3 passes through the impressive **Manawatu Gorge.** The popular hike through the gorge takes about three to four hours; you can also take a jet-boat tour along the river. ∎

EXPERIENCE:
Green Bikes

In Palmerston North, you can join the locals and get around by bicycle. Started in 1998, the Palmerston North Green Bike Trust has gathered thousands of old bikes, fixed them up, and given them back to the community. About 60 percent are "mufti" bikes—that is, bicycles permanently given to those in need. The rest are painted green and kept around town at one of the many public bike stands. You can pick one up and use it to tour the town. Just wear a helmet (also free) and return the bike when you're done.

Palmerston North
- 🗺 Map: inside back cover

Visitor information
- ✉ The Square
- ☎ 06/350-1922
- www.manawatunz.co.nz

Te Manawa
- ✉ 326 Main St.
- ☎ 06/355-5000
- www.temanawa.co.nz

New Zealand Rugby Museum
- ✉ 87 Cuba St.
- ☎ 06/358-6947
- 💲 $
- www.rugbymuseum.co.nz

Sun, sea, mountains, wine, and wildlife—delightful introductions to the scenic grandeur of the South Island

Marlborough & Nelson

Sea kayakers at Arch Point, Abel Tasman National Park

Marlborough & Nelson

The northernmost tip of the South Island encapsulates the country's attractions with craggy coastlines, mountains, beaches, wildlife watching, and wonderful hiking.

Sheltered by mountains, New Zealand's sunniest region (averaging up to 2,400 hours of sunshine per year) attracts hordes of Kiwi vacationers over the summer, but foreign visitors often miss its delights in the rush to reach the headline attractions farther south.

Marlborough district is the gateway to the South Island for visitors arriving on the ferry from Wellington. After the sometimes choppy voyage across Cook Strait, the Marlborough Sounds are a calmer haven of blue and green.

A glorious landscape of forested coves and islands greets seafarers on their journey through the convoluted waterways of the sounds. This stretch of coastline, one of New Zealand's finest, makes an ideal retreat. Certainly Captain Cook thought so, for he sheltered here for months on his Pacific voyages.

From the ferry town of Picton, the sounds can be explored or sampled on a wonderful drive to Nelson, the main city of the Nelson District. Those hurrying to the south will press on to the town of Blenheim.

Just a half-hour drive from Picton, Blenheim is the gateway to New Zealand's premier wine district. Vineyards crisscross the sunny Wairau Valley, where many delightful cellar doors offer

NOT TO BE MISSED:

of the park, a glorious meld of forest and sea. Kayaking trips or the park's coastal walking track make the most of nature, boat trips allow more leisurely exploration, and a cruise/walk combination delivers the best of both worlds.

Golden Bay lies barely 124 miles (200 km) from the nation's capital but is far removed from modern hustle. Separated from the rest of Nelson district by the towering Takaka Hill, it requires effort to reach, and once there demands leisurely exploration.

The sleepy town of Takaka moves to an alternative beat and provides access to the less-trammeled northern reaches of Abel Tasman National Park. Farther afield, Farewell Spit and the Kahurangi National Park are off-the-main-tourist-track destinations for those seeking quieter communion with nature.

From Nelson you can also head to the West Coast via Murchison or detour south to Nelson Lakes National Park, a lightly visited gem based on the twin lakes of Rotoiti and Rotoroa. ∎

fine dining and wine sampling. Allow a lazy day for touring the wineries, or two if you are a serious wine buff.

From Blenheim, the road and the rail line hug the rugged coast most of the way to Kaikoura. This fine scenic route combines sea and snow, for the towering Kaikoura Ranges lie just inland and are often snowcapped. The town of Kaikoura is New Zealand's number-one wildlife destination. Whales, dolphins, and seals flock to the nutrient-rich seas off Kaikoura, where a regular schedule of tours all but guarantees wildlife sightings.

Visitors who are not traveling from Picton to Kaikoura often move on to the city of Nelson, a good base for exploring the whole region. One of New Zealand's oldest settlements, and one of its most livable cities, Nelson's warm climate attracts retirees, artists, craftspeople, and others seeking the good life. Victorian villas dot the hilly suburbs nestled around a fine harbor.

Nelson is also the name of the northwestern district, and Abel Tasman National Park ranks as its premier attraction. Emerald bays and golden beaches ring the bulbous peninsula

World War I memorial, Blenheim

Marlborough

Visitors arriving on the ferry from Wellington are treated to some of the world's most picturesque waterways in the superb Marlborough Sounds. The waters can be explored from the pretty port of Picton, while to the south, Blenheim is the Marlborough district's main town, servicing the country's most prolific wine region. Farther south, Kaikoura is a major destination for whale and other marine mammal watching.

Boats moored in a Havelock marina, Marlborough Sounds

Picton

 Map p. 168

Visitor information

✉ The Foreshore, Picton (includes the DOC office)

☎ 03/520-3113

Picton

The first stop on the South Island for many visitors, Picton is an idyllic introduction to the scenic wonders of the south. Ferries from Wellington dock at this town on a reach of Queen Charlotte Sound, one of New Zealand's most beautiful bodies of water. Nestled at the foot of forested hills, Picton is the gateway to the Marlborough Sounds, which can be explored by cruises from town or with

kayaks rented at the wharf.

Picton was originally the Maori settlement of Waitohi. Little is known of early settlement before Capt. James Cook made Ships Cove, at the head of the sound, his home away from home. Cook spent a total of four months here between 1770 and 1777, trading with local Maori and releasing pigs and goats to breed. From here he claimed New Zealand for King George III and named the sound after George's queen, Charlotte.

The idyll was shattered in 1829 when the mighty chief Te Rauparaha crossed Cook Strait and launched a major assault on the Marlborough Sounds, annihilating most of the local tribes. The area was lightly populated when the New Zealand Company surveyed the site for a port in 1849.

After many name changes, in 1859 the town was named for Welsh general Sir Thomas Picton (1758–1815), who fell at the Battle of Waterloo. Picton was declared provincial capital, but soon lost that honor to the burgeoning farming center of Blenheim in 1865. It remains the main port of Marlborough, and though normally sleepy, the town buzzes when ferry and train arrive.

INSIDER TIP:

In Picton, take a kayaking trip in Kenepuru Sound— you'll share the water with a handful of boats and millions of beautiful jellyfish.

—DAVID LUNDQUIST,
National Geographic Field Scientist

For an insight into Picton's early Maori and European history, the **Picton Museum** on London Quay is staffed by knowledgeable volunteers. Exhibits on whaling and on Cook's visits are highlights.

The **Edwin Fox Maritime Museum,** near the ferry terminal, houses the *Edwin Fox,* built in

Pot-Bellied Sea Horse

New Zealand's waters teem with exotic creatures, among them a variety of sea horses. Boasting a (relatively) giant pouch and measuring 13 inches (33 cm) in length, the pot-bellied sea horse is one of the largest in the world. Like other sea horses, it is the males who carry the fertilized eggs. Brood size is normally around 300, although go-getters can hold up to 700 little ponies. While pot-bellied sea horses have few natural predators, they are dwindling in number because they are the principal ingredient in many traditional Chinese and Korean medicines.

Calcutta in 1853 of teak and said to the ninth oldest ship in the world. It looks it, but the deteriorating hull belies an interesting life that included transporting troops to the Crimean War, convicts to Australia, cargo to Asia, and immigrants to New Zealand.

Next door, in a modern space, the **EcoWorld Aquarium & Terrarium** specializes in sea horses but has other species, including sharks and stingrays, as well as touch pools for children.

Marlborough Sounds

The myriad of waterways, coves, bays, and islands of the Marlborough Sounds are the result of

Picton Museum
✉ 9 London Quay
☎ 03/573-8283
$ $

Edwin Fox Maritime Museum
✉ Dunbar Wharf
☎ 03/573-6868
$ $–$$

EcoWorld Aquarium & Terrarium
✉ Dunbar Wharf
☎ 03/573-6030
$ $–$$$$
www.ecoworldnz
.co.nz

the country's two main islands moving toward each other over millions of years. The South Island, resting on the Pacific plate, is gradually slipping under the Australian plate holding the North Island, drowning the valleys of the sounds and leaving only the mountaintops and ridges above the sea.

Governor's Bay in Queen Charlotte Sound

The Maori have a different but not dissimilar story about the sounds: When the god Aoraki crashed his canoe, the South Island, into the North Island, the debris of the shattered prow formed the sounds.

Whatever the origins, the outcome is divine. Captain Cook

thought so, and his descriptions of this refuge acted as a magnet for later seafarers. Whalers followed, hunting in the sounds and founding the first settlements.

Today the sounds are a haven for holiday homes and visitors looking to get away from it all. Peaceful lodgings are scattered throughout the region. A few twisting scenic roads make some of the many coves accessible by car, but boat is the most romantic means of transport. Mail is still delivered by boat in the sounds, and water taxis can drop you off at a B&B or hotel.

Queen Charlotte Drive: For a drive-through taste of the sounds, try the Queen Charlotte Drive from Picton to Havelock, a dramatic 25-mile (40 km) road winding through native forest. It hugs the coast of Queen Charlotte Sound before traversing a coastal plain to the lower reaches of Pelorus Sound. Of the many delightful coves on the way, **Governors Bay** is well worth a stop, and the ten-minute walk to **Cullen Point** has fine views across to Havelock. Craft shops and B&Bs are dotted along this road.

Halfway along Queen Charlotte Drive, a turnoff leads to the settlement of Anakiwa and the start of the **Queen Charlotte Track,** a spectacular walk through the Marlborough Sounds to historic Ship Cove. The trail goes through lush coastal forest and along ridges with unsurpassed views of Queen Charlotte and Kenepuru Sounds. The 45-mile (71 km) hike is a three- to five-day

EXPERIENCE: Wine Tours

While you can easily put together your own Wairau Valley winery tour, many tour operators offer informative excursions free of DUI concerns. Most are flexible, reasonably priced, and take small numbers. Lunch in a winery restaurant can be included, or breakfast for early starters.

Bubbly Grape Wine Tours

5 Landau Pl., Blenheim, tel 0800/228-2253, www .bubblygrape.co.nz. Small tours typically focusing on the region's prized Sauvignon Blanc.

Highlight Tours

15a Murphys Rd., Springlands, Blenheim, tel 03/577-9046, www .highlight-tours.co.nz Personalized tours take in five to eight wineries and last three to five hours.

Marlborough Tours

16a Admiralty Pl., Waikawa Bay, Picton 03/573-7122, www .marlboroughtours.co.nz Wine, food, and personalized tours, picking up in Picton or Blenheim.

Marlborough Wine Tours

24 Bythell St., Blenheim, tel 03/578-9515, www .marlboroughwinetours .co.nz Offers personalized half- and full-day tours, as well as luxury tours.

Molesworth Tours

29 Taylors Pass Rd., Blenheim, tel 03/577-9897, www.molesworthtours .co.nz A variety of tours including the main Wairau Valley wineries and the nearby Awatere Valley.

Wine Tours by Bike

191 Bells Rd., Blenheim, tel 03/577-6954, www. winetoursbybike.co.nz Provides pickup, touring bike, equipment, and winery map for a self-guided winery tour.

---

walk. It can also be mountainbiked in 13 hours, though part of the trail is closed to bikes from December through February.

Kenepuru Sound can also be explored by a paved road off Queen Charlotte Drive. The twisting, scenic drive passes farm, forest, and cove to the hamlet of Portage before reaching the resort at Kenepuru Head at the end of the sound. B&Bs and other options can be found throughout. The road is unpaved past the resort, but accesses a number of bays across to Pelorus Sound.

The sleepy port of **Havelock** is, along with Picton, a gateway to the sounds, and its harbor is packed with pleasure craft and fishing boats. The town is the green-lipped mussel capital of New Zealand, a status reflected on menus in the town's mainstreet restaurants, which are a good choice for lunch. Alternatively, dine by the water at the harbor, where cruises and water taxis depart, including the **Pelorus Mailboat**, which takes tourists along with the mail on an all-day trip to the far reaches of Pelorus Sound.

If gravel roads don't deter, to escape the tourist hordes take the road to the tiny seaside town of **French Pass** and nearby **D'Urville Island.** These communities offer fine scenery, fishing, wildlife watching, and accommodations. The spectacular road to French Pass begins at Rai Valley, along the road to Nelson about 16 miles (25 km) from Havelock.

Pelorus Mailboat

✉ Jetty 1, Havelock Marina

☎ 03/574-1088

$ $$$$$, children free

🕒 Tues., Thurs., & Fri.

Wairau Valley Drive

Marlborough is New Zealand's premier wine-growing district. The sun-drenched, sheltered plains of the Wairau Valley, with its long autumns and crisp winters, produce a unique grape and over 70 percent of New Zealand's wine. Famous for its crisp Sauvignon Blanc with intense fruit, the area also produces Riesling, Chardonnay, Pinot Noir, and other varieties.

Ripening grapes in a Blenheim vineyard

The small town of Renwick is the center of this prolific wine district, and a few accommodation options have sprung up in the town and among the wineries, but nearby Blenheim is the main base from which to explore the fine wines of Marlborough.

Dozens of wineries are an easy drive from Blenheim or Renwick for a sun-filled day, or two, of tasting. To avoid wining and driving, tours are available by bus or by bicycle (see sidebar p. 173), but the latter also has its hazards after a few drinks.

Wither Hills ❶ *(211 New Renwick Rd., tel 03/520-8270)* has one of the biggest and most impressive cellars. Sauvignon Blanc, Chardonnay, and Pinot Noir are the focus.

Villa Maria ❷ *(Paynters & New Renwick Rds., Fairhall, tel 03/577-9530)* has a wide selection from budget Sauvignon Blanc to Pinot Noir.

Matua ❸ *(New Renwick Rd., tel 03/572-8642)* is one of New Zealand's big wineries, famous for its Shingle Peak brand. Its Wairau winery serves up its Marlborough wines in a pleasant garden setting with a craft and furniture shop attached.

Cellier Le Brun ❹ *(Terrace Rd., Renwick, tel 03/572-8859)* is a friendly, family-run winery with sparkling wines, among others, and a café that serves good breakfasts and lunches.

Wairau River ❺ *(Rapaura Rd., tel 03/572-7950)* has a welcoming wine cellar and a fine, reasonably priced restaurant for lunch.

Clifford Bay 6 *(26 Rapaura Rd., tel 03/572-7148)* is another good choice for lunch in a cellar with a pleasant courtyard.

Domaine Georges Michel 7 *(Vintage Ln., tel 03/572-7230)* flies the *tricoleur*, and its graceful La Veranda café specializes in brunch.

Herzog 8 *(81 Jeffries Rd., tel 03/572-8770)* is the name dining spot in the valley at their pretty cottage wine cellar. The Swiss chef serves food with a Mediterranean bent. The winery produces a number of varieties and wines rarely seen in New Zealand.

Alan Scott 9 *(Jacksons Rd., tel 03/572-9054)* nearby is another well-established vintner with a fine selection and a café for lunch

Cloudy Bay 10 *(Jacksons Rd., tel 03/520-9140)*, more than any other winery, made Marlborough's Sauvignon Blanc famous. The winery has a new wine cellar, which can be overrun with tipplers, but it remains small.

A winery tour is as much about dining as wining. **Gibbs Restaurant 11** *(258 Jacksons Rd., tel 03/572-8048)* is down a lane off Jack-

sons Road, next to the Moa brewery. Run by a Swiss couple, it serves consistently excellent dinners in a delightful garden setting.

Hunter's 12 *(Rapaura Rd., tel 03/572-8489)* has an attractive cellar with an art gallery attached. Its restaurant, open for dinner, is one of the top dining options in the valley.

Last but by no means least, the big **Montana Brancott 13** *(SH1, tel 03/578-2099)* introduced wine to Marlborough. It has a big selection, a fine restaurant for lunch or dinner, winery tours, and even a playground. ∎

NOT TO BE MISSED:

Wither Hills • Matua
• Cloudy Bay • Alan Scott

▣ See also area map p. 168
➤ Blenheim
⬌ 26 miles (42 km)
◴ 1–2 days
➤ Montana Brancott

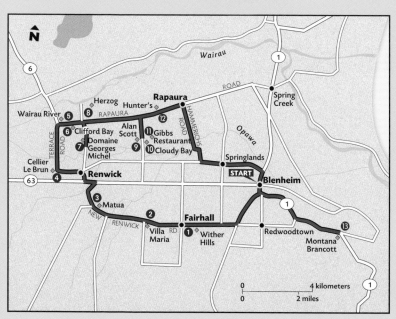

Kaikoura

🅰 Map p. 168

Visitor information

✉ Westend, Kaikoura

☎ 03/319-5641

www.kaikoura.co.nz

Fyffe House

✉ 62 Avoca St.

☎ 03/319-5835

🕐 Closed Tues. & Wed. in winter

Whale Watch Kaikoura

✉ Whaleway Station (old railway station)

☎ 03/319-6767

💲 $$$$$ (80% refund if no whales sighted)

www.whalewatch .co.nz

Wairau Affray

Colonial settlement around Blenheim was far from easy, and the Wairau Valley, now the country's premier wine district, saw proof of this in the infamous Wairau Affray. With the establishment of the colony at Nelson in 1842, the push was on for more arable land. The New Zealand Company began surveying the Wairau Valley based on its acquisition of a dubious land contract between whaling captain John Blenkinsop and Maori chief Te Rauparaha.

Despite opposition from the local Maori, surveying pushed ahead. When the surveyors' hut was burned down, the government at Nelson decided to step in and exert its authority. An armed party under the colony's leader, Capt. Arthur Wakefield, set out for Wairau in 1843 to arrest Te Rauparaha. Armed with muskets, the Maori had other ideas, and in the resulting battle 22 Europeans, including Wakefield, were killed.

Another little-explored but gloriously scenic route is the back road from Picton to Blenheim. Head north over the hill from Picton to its satellite sister Waikawa on a picturesque bay, then follow the **Port Underwood Road.** The road follows Queen Charlotte Sound before heading to the east coast at Opihi Bay, where the pavement runs out and the road dips and twists its way to Rarangi on sweeping Cloudy Bay.

Blenheim

Marlborough's largest town, Blenheim (pop. 27,000) sits on the flat, sun-drenched plains of the Wairau Valley. Just another farm town until grapes were introduced in the 1970s, Blenheim is now on the map thanks to the wine industry. In the second week of February, the town fills up for the popular **Wine Marlborough Festival,** featuring food, wine, and entertainment.

Wineries, rather than the town itself, are the attraction here, but the **Millennium Art Gallery** *(Seymour Sq., tel 03/579-2001)* in the city center is worth a browse to see works by local artists. The **Marlborough Provincial Museum** *(New Renwick Rd., tel 03/578-1712)* on the southern outskirts of town at Brayshaw Park provides a good insight into colonial life.

The **Awatere Valley** is a secondary wine-growing region just south of Blenheim. From here a rugged road heads up to the Inland Kaikoura Range and **Molesworth Station** *(tel 03/575-7043)*, the country's largest farm at 500,000 acres (180,500 ha). This cattle station can be visited in summer on 4WD tours from Blenheim or Hanmer Springs.

Kaikoura

Meaning "meal of crayfish," Kaikoura owes its existence to the abundance of the sea. Jutting out into the ocean on a peninsula, this is where Maui braced his foot when he fished up the North Island, according to Maori lore. In a stunning setting with the often snowcapped Kaikoura Ranges as a backdrop, Kaikoura today is a thriving tourism center based on wildlife watching.

Settled by the Ngati Mamoe and then the Ngai Tahu people, the area saw fierce battles at fortified hilltop villages around the

INSIDER TIP:

If you're swimming with the dolphins, take the 5:30 boat. It's their playtime after dinner; you'll get joyously dizzy trying to keep up with them.

—CHRISTY RIZZO,
Adventure Travel Expert

peninsula. In 1843, Capt. Robert Fyffe (d. 1854) established a whaling station and built **Fyffe House,** now a museum, on whalebone foundations. The whalers did such a good job that whale numbers plummeted in the 19th century.

Ironically, whales are again the town's main industry. Whalewatching and other ecoventures have made Kaikoura a tourist magnet. **Whale Watch Kaikoura** (see sidebar p. 181) has helped rejuvenate the town, and its tours are the town's main attraction. Other excursions include aerial tours, swimming with dolphins and seals, diving, sea kayaking,

and albatross viewing. In summer it is wise to book popular tours in advance, but note that bad weather can cause cancellations.

After all those high-price tours, the **Kaikoura District Museum** provides a welcome relief for the purse. It has marine, Maori, and colonial exhibits and the lowdown on the town's whaling industry. For even cheaper thrills, walk south along the shore past Fyffe House to the seal colony. Loop back to town on the peninsula via the clifftop or shoreline tracks, depending on the tide—a fine 2.5-hour walk in all. ■

Kaikoura District Museum

✉ 14 Ludstone Rd.
☎ 03/319-7440
$ $

Whale mural at Kaikoura's Adelphi Café

Nelson

Straddling the northwest tip of the South Island, Nelson district is a sunny, fertile region ringed by mountains and caressed by calm seas. From the pleasant city of Nelson, most visitors make a beeline for Abel Tasman National Park, but fine beaches and laid-back towns can be found right along the coast.

Nelson antique store

Nelson

 Map p. 168

Visitor information

✉ 77 Trafalgar St.

☎ 03/548-2304

www.nelsonnz.com

Nelson

Touted as one of the country's most livable cities, Nelson (pop. 43,000) is backed by green hills and lapped by azure seas. It has fine parks and gardens, a thriving arts scene, and a sunny disposition.

The New Zealand Company planned the city in 1839, buying land cheaply from the Maori and selling it at a profit to settlers, who began arriving in 1842. Nelson was declared New Zealand's second city in 1858, despite having only 3,000 inhabitants, and initially the colony struggled. The town has some fine Victorian villas, but workers' cottages from the same era attest to the struggling poor.

Today Nelson, along with adjoining Richmond, attracts a new wave of sun-seeking migrants, and the district's economy is driven by farming, forestry, fishing, and tourism.

Overlooking Trafalgar Street, the main drag, **Church Hill,** called

Pikimai ("climb up here") by the Maori, once housed a *pa* (fortified village), as well as the New Zealand Company settlement. The ramparts of Fort Arthur, built after the Wairau massacre in 1843 (see sidebar p. 176), can still be seen. From the top of the hill, **Christ Church Cathedral** (*tel 03/548-1008*) and its art deco tower lord it over the town. Guided tours run in the summer.

Nearby, **Nelson Provincial Museum** has a fine modern space with storyboards about the local Maori tribes and European settlers, but few artifacts. Rotating exhibits may hold more interest.

The **Suter Art Gallery** in historic Queens Gardens has a significant permanent collection of colonial artists such as John Gully (1819–1888), Gottfried

INSIDER TIP:

Feel like eating fish fresh from the ocean? Drop into one of Nelson's fantastic restaurants and savor deep-sea delights from Australasia's largest fish processing port.

—KERRY MARSHALL,
Mayor of Nelson

Lindauer, and Petrus Van der Velden, thanks to early collector Andrew Suter, Bishop of Nelson. Contemporary New Zealand art is also well represented, and the gallery has a good café.

The **World of WearableArt & Classic Cars Museum,** in the southwest suburbs, features weird and wonderful designs from the annual WOW fashion awards, even though they are now held

Crafts

New Zealand's artisans turn out a wide array of attractive crafts for domestic and tourist consumption. Areas such as Nelson and Waiheke Island are noted for arts and crafts, but studios and galleries stacked with pottery, glassware, and weavings can be found all over the country. Wood turners produce interesting work using native timbers such as kauri and rimu. Glassblowers in Nelson infuse glass with bits of local metal to create handmade beads that reflect both European and native aesthetics. Local tourist offices have brochures detailing regional artists and craft studios.

in Wellington. The exhibition, complete with mechanical catwalk, is very small but well done. The adjoining car museum has a fine selection of Detroit beasts from the days when oil was cheap and all-American.

Founders Heritage Park, 1 mile (1.6 km) northeast of the city center, is a collection of historic buildings and includes a windmill, the Nelson Port

Nelson Provincial Museum
- ✉ Hardy & Trafalgar Sts.
- ☎ 03/548-9588
- 💲 Donation

Suter Art Gallery
- ✉ 208 Bridge St.
- ☎ 03/548-4699
- 💲 $

World of WearableArt & Classic Cars Museum
- ✉ 95 Quarantine Rd., Annesbrook
- ☎ 03/547-4573
- 💲 $$–$$$

Founders Heritage Park
- ✉ 87 Atawhai Dr.
- ☎ 03/548-2649
- 💲 $

Wildlife Wonderland

Despite a lack of land mammals, New Zealand has an abundance of sea life and unique birds, which can be observed in their natural habitats at a number of locations. Many wildlife-spotting tours operate in the country. The Department of Conservation also oversees designated breeding areas for birds and other wildlife, often with blinds in which you can view animals without disturbing them.

Bottlenose dolphin and diver

Whales

The nutrient-rich waters around New Zealand attract 22 species of whales, the most commonly sighted being sperm, humpback, Bryde's, and southern right whales. Maori tradition has it that whales guided the first migrations to Aotearoa. Whalers also tracked the whales, hunting them relentlessly, though now the mammals are primarily sought by tourists. Whale-spotting is a major attraction, notably at Kaikoura on the South Island where sperm whales are often sighted.

Orcas, or killer whales, are also found in New Zealand waters, though strictly speaking these aquatic mammals belong to the dolphin family. The small population is most likely to be seen off the east coast of the North Island.

Dolphins

The most numerous of the ten dolphin species in New Zealand are the dusky and the common dolphin. The bottlenose dolphin is also found, while smaller Hector's and Maui dolphins are unique to the country.

Dolphins frolic all around the coasts and often accompany ferry or cruise boats. Swimming with the dolphins is a popular activity, particularly in the Bay of Islands and Kaikoura.

Modern New Zealand folklore has immortalized two dolphins: Opo, who frequented the seaside resort of Opononi and played in the shallows with children, and Pelorus Jack, a Risso's dolphin who supposedly accompanied ships across the Cook Strait, helping them to avoid dangerous rocks and currents.

Seals

After Captain Cook noted the profusion of seals in New Zealand, sealers promptly set up camps on the South Island and hunted the seals for fur to the brink of extinction.

Now protected, fur seals can be seen around the coast at a number of colonies, though again the South Island offers the best viewing opportunities, particularly at Kaikoura, the Otago Peninsula, the Catlins, and Cape Foulwind near Westport.

While fur seals are the most numerous species, other varieties include the much larger Hooker's sea lion and the rarer southern elephant seals and leopard seals. Hooker's sea lions can be seen coming ashore on the Otago Peninsula and in the Catlins.

Birds

Surrounded by ocean, New Zealand has a greater diversity of seabirds than any other

The rare yellow-eyed penguin breeds in New Zealand.

country. Species include penguins, albatrosses, petrels, shags, and terns, though the sooty shearwater is the most numerous.

Of the world's 16 species of penguin, 9 are found in New Zealand waters. The three main species are the little blue, yellow-eyed, and Fiordland crested penguin. Others inhabit New Zealand's Antarctic territories and sub-Antarctic islands. Penguins usually nest in sand dunes and are most easily spotted on the South Island.

The Otago Peninsula is also famous for its royal albatross colony, while huge gannet colonies can be seen at Muriwai Beach west of Auckland and Cape Kidnappers near Hastings.

Many native land birds are threatened, but unique species range from the brilliantly colored takahe to the national symbol, the flightless kiwi. The best place to get an overview of the country's bird species is at the Pukaha Mount Bruce National Wildlife Centre, near Masterton on the North Island. The shy, nocturnal kiwi is easily seen in kiwi houses around the country, but rarely spotted in the wild. ∎

EXPERIENCE: Whale Watch Kaikoura

With sightings of sperm whales all but guaranteed, Whale Watch Kaikoura has become the country's foremost wildlife experience, with 100,000 visitors a year taking the company's tours. The organization claims a 95 percent success rate; if you don't spot a whale, you get 80 percent of your money back. Along with sperm whales, dolphins are often sighted, and you may be lucky enough to see humpback whales, orcas, or blue whales.

Maori-owned and -operated, Whale Watch Kaikoura was established in 1987 by the Kati Kuri people, a subtribe of the Ngai Tahu, at a time when the town's fishing economy was in decline. From small tours on an inflatable craft, the business has grown to include a catamaran fleet directed to the whales by spotter planes.

EXPERIENCE:
Kayaking Abel Tasman National Park

The stunning coastline of Abel Tasman National Park can be explored on foot or by boat, but nothing compares to gliding through the beautiful coves to remote beaches in a kayak. You can rent a kayak and head off independently, or take a guided tour for a half day or up to as many as three days, staying in huts, campsites, or luxurious lodges along the way. You can also combine kayaking with a hike or water-taxi ride back.

Most operators are based in Marahau on the edge of the park; in Kaiteriteri, 6 miles (10 km) away; and in Motueka. Guided trips are popular, while independent rentals are generally only for groups of two or more with kayaking and outdoors experience. Camping gear and equipment are provided.

In Marahau, companies include **Abel Tasman Kayaks** (tel 03/527-8022, www .abeltasmankayaks.co.nz), **Kahu Kayaks** (tel 03/527-8300, www.kahukayaks.co.nz), and **Marahau Sea Kayaks** (tel 03/527-8551, msk .net.nz). In Kaiteriteri, try **Kaiteriteri Kayaks** (tel 03/527-8383, www.seakayak.co.nz).

exhibition, vintage vehicles, and a working train. On the same street, **Miyazu Japanese Garden** is a Japanese strolling garden.

Botanic Hill, above the gardens on the eastern edge of the city along Milton Street, has panoramic views and a marker proclaiming it as the geographical center of New Zealand.

Tasman Bay

Sunny Tasman Bay is dominated by the attractions of Nelson on one side and Abel Tasman National Park on the other, but in between lie a few points of interest. Nelson has a good city beach at Tahunanui, but for a long stretch of uncrowded sand, head to **Rabbit Island.** The island is accessed via a bridge open during the day—the turnoff is halfway between Richmond and the growing seaside town of Mapua.

As in Nelson city, the Tasman Bay region is riddled with artists' studios: potters, jewelers, painters, wood turners, and glassblowers. Pick up a brochure for a countryside art tour. Wineries are also flourishing, particularly in **Richmond** and **Upper Moutere,** once known as Sarau, where the German settlers who founded the town built an impressive Lutheran church.

Lower Moutere, near Motueka, is home to the **Riverside Community,** New Zealand's first commune, set up by pacifists during World War II. The community, which set the scene for the region's alternative lifestyles, can be visited and has a café.

The center of a fertile orchard region growing apples, pears, berries, hops, and kiwifruit, **Motueka** (pop. 7,000) is well supplied with amenities and is a popular base for visiting Abel Tasman National Park. The main town lies a little inland from its muddy port on Tasman Bay. The popular little resort of **Kaiteriteri,** 9 miles (14 km) north, has beautiful golden beaches and also makes a good base for the national park.

Abel Tasman National Park

New Zealand's smallest national park at 87 square miles (225 sq km), Abel Tasman is nevertheless one of its most famous. Coastal bays, lagoons, golden beaches, and calm, clear waters attract 180,000 visitors per year.

INSIDER TIP:

If you use the water taxis in Abel Tasman, you can craft your own one-way route through the park and explore more of the striking coastline.

—CHRISTY RIZZO,
Adventure Travel Expert

Most are day visitors, but longer stays can be justified by walking the Abel Tasman Coast Track or kayaking one of the finest coastlines in the country.

The park also contains marble gorges, granite and limestone hills, extensive beech forests, and a rain forest growing to the sea's edge. The park is named after Dutch explorer Abel Tasman, who anchored his ships near Wainui Bay in the north of the park on December 18, 1642. Four of his crew died after an altercation with the local Maori tribe, the Ngati Tumatakokiri.

The park's main entrance is the southern gateway of **Marahau,** 12 miles (20 km) from Motueka. Tiny Marahau is well equipped with services to explore the park,

including water transportation and kayak rentals. Accommodations are also available, but they are often fully booked in summer.

Reasonably priced cruises, water taxis, and scheduled launches run into the park from Marahau and farther south from Kaiteriteri. Boats can drop you anywhere along the coast up to Totaranui and pick you up later. A good

Sea kayaker and young seal in Abel Tasman National Park

day-trip option is to take a boat to Torrent Bay or Bark Bay, then walk back to Marahau along the **Abel Tasman Coastal Track.**

This track, one of New Zealand's Great Walks, between Marahau and Wainui Bay, is an

Tasman Bay

▲ Map p. 168

Visitor information

✉ Wallace St., Motueka

☎ 03/528-6543

easy, undulating 32-mile (51 km) trail that can be walked in three to five days. Huts must be booked well in advance in summer, when the trail can resemble a highway—or you can camp. More luxurious private lodgings are also available at Torrent Bay and Awaroa. The estuary at Awaroa and the stream at Onetahuti Beach can be crossed only when the tides are low, so tide charts must be consulted.

Another three-day trail loops back from Wainui Bay to Marahau, but this trail is a much more difficult walk through the interior of the park.

The alternative to walking is sea kayaking, a marvelous way to explore coves and remote beaches, while camping overnight or staying in huts or lodges. Kayak companies offer a range of options for both guided and independent rentals.

The northern gateway to the park is **Totaranui,** which has a Department of Conservation office and campground on a long bay with a beautiful beach. Many walkers start or finish the coastal track here and take a boat one-way to Marahau.

The road from Takaka in Golden Bay to Totaranui passes through the sleepy vacation town of **Pohara,** which has a safe beach. Just past Tarakohe harbor, with its cement shipping dock, **Ligar Bay** and **Tata Beach** have fine golden-sand beaches for swimming. The road then soon becomes unpaved but is very scenic. En route to the park, the 45-minute walk to **Wainui Falls** is well worth the effort.

The other entry into the park is a less-used back door. The unpaved Cannan Road leads off Takaka Hill to the interior of the park and its walking trails. This area is very different from the rest of the national park and is comprises marble gorges, limestone outcrops, sinkholes, and subterranean streams. Most visitors who come this way drive 7.5 miles (12 km) and then walk 45 minutes to **Harwood Hole,** a 577-foot (176 m) marble drop shaft straight down to the **Starlight Cave.** Great care should be taken around the hole, and the cave is suitable only for experienced cavers.

Caving

The karst landscape around Marlborough and Nelson is characterized by pockmarked cliffs and networks of caves. Once Maori burial sites, many of these caves are now filled with adventurers. The most famous, Harwood Hole, was discovered in 1957. Its 577-foot-deep (176 m) entry shaft was first explored by a harnessed schoolboy lowered down by local townspeople. But while the cave's celebrity brings adventurers from around the world, danger always exists. In 1960, a falling boulder killed the founder of the New Zealand Speleological Society as he explored the hole.

Golden Bay

Takaka Hill, the "marble mountain," shields Golden Bay. From Motueka the road west is a tortuous drive over the hill, but you are rewarded with fine views of the surrounding mountains and valley farmland. Just before the summit of Takaka Hill, New Zealand's only source of quarried

(Commercial St., tel 03/525-6268) has historical artifacts, but of most interest is its diorama of Abel Tasman's fateful meeting with Maori in 1642. Another institution worth sampling is the **Wholemeal Café** (60 Commercial St., tel 03/525-9426), a bustling hippie-style eatery with a variety of treats, including vegetarian specialties.

DOC Golden Bay Area Office

✉ 62 Commercial St., Takaka

☎ 03/525-8026

Vibrant kayaks line Kaiteriteri Beach in Nelson.

marble, are the **Ngarua Caves** (tel 03/528-8093, Sept.–June, $$–$$$), where guided tours leave on the hour from 10 a.m. to 4 p.m. Moa bones can be seen there. North of the Ngarua Caves is Harwood Hole (see sidebar, opposite).

Laid-back **Takaka,** the main town of Golden Bay, rests at the bottom of the hill and across the fertile Takaka Valley. The rural community is enlivened by murals, craft shops, dreadlocks, and bare feet. **Golden Bay Museum**

Just northwest of Takaka off SH60 is **Te Waikoropupu Springs** (better known as Pupu Springs), which have astonishingly clear waters with visibility measured to 207 feet (63 m). Water percolates into the springs from underground caves, and walking trails go through forest and past a water race used in old gold workings. The springs are 2.5 miles (4 km) north of town and then 2 miles (3 km) down the turnoff.

From Takaka, the scenic Abel Tasman Road runs to Totaranui

Takaka

🗺 Map p. 168

Visitor information

✉ Willow St.

☎ 03/525-9136

A waterfall pours over a ledge at Cupola Creek, Nelson Lakes National Park.

Nelson Lakes National Park

⚠ Map p. 168

Visitor Center

✉ View Rd., St. Arnaud

☎ 03/521-1806

(see p. 184) at the northern end of Abel Tasman National Park. Just off the road outside town is **Rawhiti Cave,** studded with stalactites. Guided tours are available.

The sleepy little town of Collingwood is the last settlement of any size in Golden Bay. It's a jumping-off point for Farewell Spit, **Kahurangi National Park,** and the **Heaphy Track** (see p. 219), which begins at the Aorere Valley, 17 miles (28 km) from Collingwood.

Farewell Spit is a 22-mile (35 km) arc of sand sheltering Golden Bay and finishing at the Cape Farewell lighthouse, the most

northerly tip of the South Island. Access to this important wading-bird habitat is restricted to tour groups, but the first few miles of walking tracks of this dune-strewn landscape are open to the public.

Nelson Lakes National Park

Sculpted by glaciers during the ice ages, Lakes Rotoiti and Rotoroa anchor the spectacular landscape of Nelson Lakes National Park. The two lakes reflect alpine peaks—the northern extreme of the Southern Alps—and are a mecca for aficionados of water sports and hiking.

St. Arnaud, the alpine village on the shores of Lake Rotoiti, is popular in summer for boating, trout fishing, and swimming, and in winter it services the nearby **Rainbow Ski Area.** Lying 54 miles (87 km) southwest of Nelson on SH63 between Blenheim and the West Coast, St. Arnaud is easily reached but bypassed by most visitors despite its scenic location on the doorstep of Nelson Lakes National Park.

Lake Rotoiti ("short lake"), serviced by St. Arnaud, attracts the most visitors, many of whom take a picture of the lake and pass on. The lakes and waterways teem with brown trout, particularly **Lake Rotoroa** ("long lake"), a 40-minute drive away. Beyond the lakes, beech-clad mountains harbor alpine valleys strewn with wildflowers and small tarns.

This hidden wonderland can only be reached on foot by

Sculpted by glaciers during the ice ages, Lakes Rotoiti and Rotoroa anchor the spectacular landscape of Nelson Lakes National Park. The two lakes are a mecca for aficionados of water sports and hiking.

walks such as the five-day **Travers-Sabine Circuit,** past towering mountains and remote lakes, or the three-day **Lake Angelus Track.**

The easiest way to sample the park's glory is on one of the short lake strolls, embracing water views, birdsong, and beech forest.

Murchison

The last town of note in the Nelson region, mountain-ringed Murchison is found on the dramatic Buller Gorge Heritage Highway (SH6), the gateway to the island's West Coast.

Born a rough-and-ready gold-mining town in the 1860s, Murchison was flattened in 1929 by a nearby earthquake that was powerful enough to shake the whole country. The **Murchison Museum** (60 Fairfax St., tel 03/523-9392) has some interesting photographs of the quake's devastation among the items in its rambling collection.

The **Buller River** provides

most of the town's attractions, including jet boating, white-water rafting, and kayaking. Nine miles (14 km) from Murchison on the way to Westport, the privately run **Buller Gorge Swingbridge** (tel 03/523-9809, $–$$) wavers high above the river for breathless views. A zipline, guided walks, and jet boating are also offered. ∎

EXPERIENCE: WWOOFing

In a country dominated by farming, the chance to live and work on a farm delivers unique insights into the New Zealand way of life. WWOOF (Willing Workers On Organic Farms) is a worldwide network offering volunteers (WWOOFers) the opportunity to do just that.

Originating in Britain, WWOOF spread to New Zealand in 1974. The work is unpaid, but farm hosts provide food and accommodations in exchange for help with gardening or other activities. These may include organic farming, weeding and mulching, making wine and cheese, or building straw-bale houses. While popular with students, volunteers of all ages participate.

To become a WWOOFer, you must register and pay a small fee to receive a list of some one thousand participating organic farms. You can join online, by mail, or by fax (WWOOF NZ, P.O. Box 1172, Nelson, NZ, tel & fax 03/544-9890, www .wwoof.co.nz).

Because food and lodging are provided, New Zealand immigration considers WWOOFing paid work, and a work or student visa is required. One-year working holiday visas are readily available for 18- to 30-year-olds from 26 countries, including Canada, the U.K., and the U.S.

From the oh-so-English city of Christchurch across sheep-strewn plains to the highest peaks of the Southern Alps

Christchurch & Canterbury

ChristChurch Cathedral and "Chalice" sculpture

Christchurch & Canterbury

First stop on the South Island for many visitors, Christchurch is the south's largest city and offers a glimpse of England in the Pacific. With Gothic churches, punting on the river, and fine gardens, this delightful city revels in its English heritage.

Unlike other, rowdier settlements, Christchurch was a planned Church of England venture designed to attract a better class of colonist. Imposing churches and elite schools instilled Old World values, and the city's stone architecture today forms the heart of Christchurch's vibrant cultural precinct.

NOT TO BE MISSED:

Christchurch has a number of worthwhile attractions and is the gateway to the surrounding Canterbury region, which includes the highest peaks of the Southern Alps. The city sprawls on the edge of the Canterbury Plains, but is bordered to the east by the scenic Banks Peninsula, a geological oddity rising steeply from the surrounding flatlands.

This large volcanic outcrop of pastoral hills and sheltered bays once housed a French colony, prompting the British to swiftly annex the South Island. The French settlers of Akaroa never lived to see Nouvelle Zéland proclaimed, but they left behind a picturesque town of Gallic influences, one of the highlights of this region.

The vast, rich farmland of the Canterbury Plains spreads inland until it hits the foothills of the alps. In the north you'll find pretty Hanmer Springs, the South Island's premier hot springs resort, while beyond lie the northern passes through the alps to the West Coast.

Arthur's Pass is the highest mountain pass and travels though the scenic national park of the same name. This alpine wonderland has a number of snowy peaks, fine hikes, and skiing in the park and at nearby ski slopes.

The most visited part of the alps lies farther south, where Aoraki/Mount Cook, the country's highest peak, towers over the landscape. The trip from Christchurch to Mount Cook via the Inland Scenic Route is one of the most popular and pretty journeys in New Zealand. Heading south across the Canterbury Plains, the route turns inland around Geraldine and travels through undulating farmland before it reaches semidesert plateau landscapes and stunning lakes, such as turquoise Tekapo. Looming behind, the glaciers and peaks of Mount Cook National Park have been the practice ground for many mountaineers, such as Everest conqueror Sir Edmund Hillary.

Aoraki/Mount Cook is the jewel of the alps, but the whole landscape is awe inspiring. For many, the highlight of a visit to the park is a drink in the lounge of the grand Hermitage Hotel, its floor-to-ceiling windows framing the "Cloud Piercer," as the mountain was known to the Maori. A short walk in the park is rewarded with wonderful vistas; scenic flights over the area offer even more stunning views.

From Aoraki/Mount Cook, the main tourist route presses on to Queenstown in Otago, the hub of the south for sightseers. The coastal route (SH1) takes you through the port of Timaru, halfway to Dunedin. ■

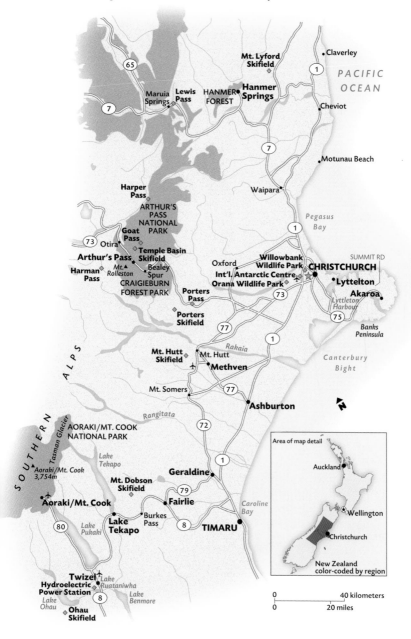

Christchurch

Clean, green, and very English, Christchurch is New Zealand's third most populous city and the gateway to the South Island. The city offers a host of attractions in a neat package, from Gothic architecture, museums, and manicured gardens to thriving restaurant, entertainment, and arts scenes. If boating on the Avon River is simply too English, you can take a tour to the former French town of Akaroa, ride a gondola to the top of the Port Hills, or balloon over the Canterbury Plains.

The Peacock Fountain at the Canterbury Museum

Christchurch

🗺 Map p. 191

Visitor information

✉ Old Chief
Post Office,
Cathedral Sq.

☎ 03/379-9629

**www.christchurchnz
.net**

History

The broad Canterbury Plains define the city's geography and history. Flat and grid-based, Christchurch sprawls inland from the Port Hills, which the first European settlers clambered over after arriving at Lyttelton port.

In 1848, the Canterbury Association, founded by Edward Gibbon Wakefield (1796–1862) and John Robert Godley (1814–1861),

set about luring potential landowners to the rich pastures of the plains. The association based its model firmly on England's class-conscious society, and the laborers and artisans who also arrived on the first four ships in 1850 were intended to serve, not become, the landed gentry.

A fabulously wealthy elite flourished on the sheep farms of the plains, and the scruffy early settlement soon took on a grander air. Wool barons built mansions in the fashionable suburb of Fendalton and helped fund grand private schools for their children. Fine parks of oak and elm and neoclassical stone buildings graced the city. The new aristocrats re-created England in the South Pacific, but the city also acquired a reputation for snobbishness and rigid social structures that long persisted.

A healthy economy and recent migration have broadened the city's overwhelmingly Anglo-Kiwi population base, but it remains very British, at least in appearance. Christchurch tourism overplays the English card, perhaps, but the legacy is the preservation of its delightful historic precinct.

Cathedral Square

The best place to start a tour of Christchurch is the heart of the city at Cathedral Square, dominated by **ChristChurch Cathedral** *(tel 03/366-0046)*. Building on this focus for the new Anglican colony began in 1864,

but the church did not open until 1881 and final completion had to wait until 1904.

This fine Gothic cathedral takes its name from Oxford University's Christ Church, but many of its decorations and artwork express local themes, including Antarctic exploration. Not to be missed, the antechamber to the left inside the main entrance details the church's history, and a panel door hides the narrow stone stairway to the tower. For a small fee, the winding, claustrophobic climb of 134 steps is

INSIDER TIP:

The world's best street performers descend on Christchurch in January for the World Buskers Festival. The cost is nothing more than the change in your pocket.

—DAVID LUNDQUIST,
National Geographic Field Scientist

Wizard of New Zealand

A treasured icon of Christchurch, the Wizard appears at Cathedral Square in summer to mock conventional wisdom and muse on everything from the joys of the English monarchy to globalization and the rise of the Chinese empire.

Dressed in the traditional black with a conical hat, the Wizard is a self-proclaimed "living work of art" who migrated to Christchurch in 1974. The city councilors at first tried to banish him, but he cast a spell on them and went on

to become one of New Zealand's great eccentrics. In 1990, he was proclaimed Wizard of New Zealand by then prime minister Mike Moore.

Born Ian Brackenbury Channell in England in 1932, the Wizard was a teaching fellow in sociology before embracing cosmology and unorthodoxy. Though age has wearied him, he still makes occasional appearances to muse on the world or cast spells of national importance. He even has a website: *www.wizard.gen.nz.*

Southern Encounter Aquarium & Kiwi House

- 🏛 Old Chief Post Office, Cathedral Square
- ☎ 03/359-7109
- 💲 $–$$$

www.southern encounter.co.nz

Christchurch Art Gallery

- 🅰 Map p. 197
- ✉ Worcester Blvd. & Montreal St.
- ☎ 03/941-7300

www.christchurch artgallery.org.nz

Arts Centre

- 🅰 Map p. 197
- ✉ 2 Worcester Blvd.
- ☎ 03/366-0989

www.artscentre .org.nz

rewarded by fine views of the city. Guided tours of the church also operate daily and the cathedral has a gift shop and café.

In the square facing the cathedral, the statue of John Robert Godley honors the city's founding

---

Christchurch By Night

Join the crowds at some of the hot spots in town.

Coyote (*126 Oxford Ter.*) Sante Fe décor in this Tex-Mex restaurant is the backdrop for tequila slamming to pulsing DJ sounds.

Christchurch Casino (*30 Victoria St.*) For something more sedate, bars in the casino have '80s cover bands and quiet conversation nooks.

Dux de Lux (*41 Hereford St.*) House brews, bands, and vegetarian food consistently attract enthusiastic crowds to this fashionable pub.

Sammy's Jazz Bar (*14 Bedford Row*) Off Manchester Street, just south of Cashel, this cool bar is worth hunting out for cocktails and good music.

---

father. This Anglican Tory decried the decline of the church's authority and growing egalitarianism in 19th-century England. He saw Christchurch as a chance to preserve British institutions in the Antipodes.

The square hums in summer with city workers, tourists, buskers, street stalls, and public speakers,

including the town crier and the Wizard (see sidebar p. 193).

In the old post office building, which also houses the very busy visitor information center, the small **Southern Encounter Aquarium & Kiwi House** features mostly local marine life and the inevitable kiwi house.

Other notable buildings on the Square include the **Press Building**, home to the city's leading newspaper since 1909. Built in Gothic style and topped by a corner tower, its windows are different on each of its four floors. On the opposite corner, the stoic **Old Government Buildings** date from 1911 and are now part of the Heritage Hotel.

Cultural Precinct

With much of the old city around Worcester Boulevard housing cultural attractions, the city has dubbed inner Christchurch the Cultural Precinct.

In the heart of the precinct, **Christchurch Art Gallery** is an impressive architectural landmark opened in 2003. It contains the definitive collection of Canterbury artists and a good selection of 18th- and 19th-century European paintings, favoring British artists. Don't miss the Maori portraits by Bohemian artist Gottfried Lindauer and "Cass" by Rita Angus, depicting a lonely Canterbury rail stop, voted New Zealand's most loved painting in a poll.

The **Arts Centre** is an arts-and-crafts hub and one of the city's most significant cultural attractions. It housed the University of Canterbury until 1974, but now the stately stone Gothic buildings

Springtime in Hagley Park, Christchurch

Canterbury Museum
Map p. 197
Rolleston Ave.
03/366-5000
www.canterbury museum.com

are home to craft shops, galleries, theaters, cinemas, bars, and cafés. Artists can be seen at work in their studios, and the weekend market specializes in crafts. Keep an eye out for advertised performances.

While modern museums have a tendency to overinteract and dumb down, **Canterbury Museum** is delightfully classical with a big collection of artifacts from New Zealand and the world. The moa diorama gives perspective to these giants, and the other bird exhibits cover almost all New Zealand species. The Antarctic exhibit is decidedly old-fashioned compared to the modern complex at the airport, but it gives a fascinating insight into the first explorers, and it's free.

City Gardens

Early settlers remarked on the drab vegetation of Christchurch's marshy plains and quickly set about transforming their surroundings. Sprawling **Hagley Park,** a green buffer right on the edge of the city center, is a fine city park covering 395 acres (160 ha). The park includes artificial lakes, sports grounds, a golf course, walking and cycling tracks, and the renowned Botanic Gardens.

The **Botanic Gardens** were founded in 1863 with the planting of an English oak to commemorate the marriage of Queen Victoria's eldest son to Princess Alexandra of Denmark. This delightful expanse of lawn and over 10,000 exotic and indigenous plants covers 74 acres (30 ha) on a lazy reach of the Avon River— don't miss the tropical conservatory. The gardens also have a café and visitor center.

Just west of Hagley Park, **Mona Vale** estate also straddles the Avon. It once belonged to the Deans, one of Christchurch's first settler families. Dating from 1899, the homestead is now a restaurant and function center for patrons only, but the gardens of European trees, rhododendrons, camellias, and annuals are free to visitors. The rose garden is a highlight.

Christchurch Walking Tour

Christchurch's British heritage is on ample display in this walking tour. Highlights include the old council chambers and the Canterbury Museum, but shops and cafés also abound. Flat and compact, it's an ideal city to explore on foot.

Punting on the Avon River

While this is an easy walk, the weary traveler can also catch the tram, with a day ticket allowing you to get on and off at will.

Starting at **Cathedral Square** ❶, walk behind the cathedral and head east on Worcester Street following the tram line: The **Christchurch Tramway** *(tel 03/366-7830, $–$$$)* takes visitors around a scenic city tourist loop. The tram turns at **New Regent Street** ❷ through Cathedral Junction tram station, a glass-roofed renovated strip of shops and cafés, and continues on past a fine row of Spanish mission–style shops built in 1931.

Turn left and follow the tramline down Armagh Street to **Victoria Square** ❸ on the corner of Colombo Street. Dissected diagonally by the Avon River, this block was once the commercial heart of the city, known as Market Square. Now a delightful park with statues

of Queen Victoria and Captain Cook, it has a pedestrian bridge that leads across the river to the floral clock and the modern town hall.

Back on Armagh Street, cross over the river to the **Provincial Council Buildings** ❹ (1858–1865), considered to be the crowning achievement of architect Benjamin Mountfort (1825–1898), who designed many of the city's Gothic Revival buildings. The old council chambers inside are a symphony in stone and wood, especially the magnificent arched ceiling trimmed in gold leaf.

Head back to the river and Oxford Terrace, passing the steps on the riverbank where punts *(tel 03/366-0337, $$–$$$$)* can be hired for a delightfully lazy tour at river level. On Oxford Terrace at the corner of Gloucester Street, **Our City O-Tautahi** ❺ *(tel 03/941-7460)* was once the home of the city council; it is now a small art gallery with changing exhibits.

Turn right onto Worcester Street. The architecturally innovative **Christchurch Art Gallery** ⑥ (see p. 194) and, in contrast on the next block, the Gothic **Arts Centre** (see p. 194) are Christchurch must-see attractions.

Worcester Street ends at the Canterbury Museum on Rolleston Avenue. Before entering the museum, detour to the right to exclusive **Christ's College** ⑦. Established as an Anglican boys' school in 1850, it is steeped in English tradition, right down to the students' blazers. Its fine buildings include the Big School, built, in 1863, now the library.

Next door to the college are two of the city's main attractions: the **Canterbury Museum** ⑧ (see p. 195) and next to it, the **Botanic Gardens** ⑨ (see p. 195). Farther along Rolleston Avenue is the **Curator's House** (tel 03/379-2252), a neo-Tudor cottage built in 1920 and now a restaurant.

Following Rolleston south to the river, the **Antigua Boatsheds** (2 Cambridge Ter., tel 03/366-5885) were built in 1882. Still popular

for boat rentals and afternoon tea in the café, in their heyday the boat sheds had a lady's waiting room and bands playing on Sunday.

From the boat sheds, follow Cambridge Terrace east and cross the river to Oxford Terrace where the strip of outdoor restaurants and bars facing the river is a popular evening venue. Walk down **Cashel Mall,** a pedestrian precinct with a diverse range of shops. A left turn at Colombo Street leads back to Cathedral Square. ∎

NOT TO BE MISSED:

Victoria Square • Provincial Council Buildings • Christchurch Art Gallery • Arts Centre

---

✚ See also area map p. 191

► Cathedral Square

⟷ 2 miles (3.2 km)

◷ 3 hours–full day

► Cathedral Square

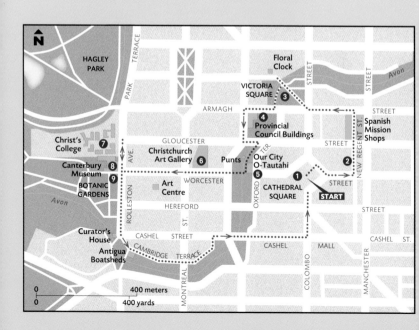

Christchurch Gondola

- ✉ 10 Bridle Path Rd.
- ☎ 03/384-0700
- 💲 $$–$$$$

www.gondola.co.nz

International Antarctic Centre

- 🄰 Map p. 191
- ✉ 38 Orchard Rd., Christchurch
- ☎ 03/353-7798
- 💲 $$$$–$$$$$

www.iceberg.co.nz

The *Nimrod* Expedition

On January 1, 1908, Ernest Shackleton and crew set sail aboard the *Nimrod* from Lyttelton en route to the South Pole. Once on Antarctica, they planned to use dogs, ponies, and an automobile to reach the Pole. Due to bad weather and car trouble, they gave up their quest after three months. The trip back to the coast took longer than expected, the party being overcome by hunger and dysentery, and when they arrived they found that their ship had already left for home. In a final effort, Shackleton set fire to their shelter in desperate hopes that the ship would see the smoke. Luckily, it did, and the party was rescued.

Christchurch Suburbs

In contrast to the flat Canterbury Plains, the volcanic **Port Hills** provide a dramatic amphitheater for the city. The hills are a favorite retreat of Christchurch residents, who walk, run, bicycle, paraglide, and climb the rugged rock outcrops and tussock-grass slopes. The first settlers crossed over on the Bridle Path, which was the main route between the city and Lyttelton until the rail tunnel was completed in 1867.

A farsighted member of parliament, Harry Ell (1862–1934), successfully lobbied for a network of scenic reserves in the hills along the **Summit Road,** which can be explored on a breathtaking drive. In 1918 Ell began building the **Sign of the Takahe** (www.signofthe takahe.co.nz), a rest house for travelers that resembles a medieval castle. Now a restaurant, this delightful foible is on Dyers Pass Road, halfway to the Summit Road.

The best way to appreciate the hills is from the top . The **Christchurch Gondola** provides spectacular views of the city, Lyttelton Harbour, and the Southern Alps on a clear day. From the parking lot on Tunnel Road near the Lyttelton tunnel entrance, the gondola shuttles up to the summit complex, restaurant, and museum every day until 9 p.m.

The best way to appreciate the hills is from the top. The Christchurch Gondola provides spectacular views of the city, Lyttelton Harbour, the plains, and the Southern Alps on a clear day.

Christchurch looks to England but also shares an affinity with the South Pole at the other end of the globe. The whiz bang **International Antarctic Centre** at the airport has a wealth of displays, interactive exhibits, and movies about the great icy continent. Highlights include the little blue penguins and the Antarctic chamber where you don arctic gear to experience a snowstorm, but non-Antarctic devotees may find this an expensive, frosty bore.

Northwest of the city, about 5 miles (8 km) behind the airport, **Orana Wildlife Park** *(tel 03/359-7109, $$–$$$$)* is a sprawling, struggling zoo with a collection of big animals (e.g., lions, tigers, giraffes), a few hard-to-see kiwis, and other native birds. Much smaller, but in a more attractive garden setting,

weathered, leaving behind a scenic landscape of steep hills and convoluted harbors and headlands.

Captain Cook named it after his botanist, Joseph Banks, but thought the peninsula was an island, an easy mistake given the dramatically different landscape jutting out into the sea from the flat plains. The Maori preferred the peninsula, with its forest and abundant sea life, to the plains, as

Villagers enjoy a café lunch on Main Street in Akaroa.

Willowbank Wildlife Park *(60 Hussey Rd., tel 03/359-6226, $$$–$$$$$)* houses a collection of small animals from around the world, a farm animal enclosure to delight small children, and a good kiwi enclosure, where the elusive birds are easy to see (and hear).

Banks Peninsula

On Christchurch's doorstep, the Banks Peninsula was formed by three gigantic volcanic eruptions that pushed the earth upward from the surrounding flatlands. Lava flows cooled and

did early settlers who sheltered in its harbors. Banks Peninsula was also home to the curious twist of history at Akaroa (see p. 200), where the French pushed to colonize the South Island.

With its sea aspect and charming cottages gripping the hillside, **Lyttelton** is a popular satellite of Christchurch, 7 miles (12 km) to the west. This historic town has old waterfront pubs and a growing number of trendy cafés, but it is also Christchurch's port and very much a working harbor with cranes and logs piled high.

Akaroa
🗺 Map p. 191
Visitor information
✉ 80 Rue Lavaud
☎ 03/304-8600
www.akaroa.com

Akaroa Museum
✉ 71 Rue Lavaud
☎ 03/304-1013
💲 $

The Giant's House
✉ 68 Rue Balguerie
☎ 03/304-7501
www.linton.co.nz

Easily reached from the city via a tunnel under the Port Hills, Lyttelton has a small museum, but of more interest is the **Timeball Station,** a curious Gothic structure on the hill with fine views of

Hector's Dolphins

By 2008 only 7,270 Hector's dolphins remained in the wild. These endangered mammals are found solely around the South Island and can be easily spotted by their round, black dorsal fins. Locals call them "Mickey Mouse ears." Because the dolphins live in shallow waters, they are frequently struck by boats or entangled in fishing nets, where they drown. New Zealand has taken protective measures to try to save the dolphins, but progress has been minimal. Populations grow slowly, as females give birth to one calf only every two to three years.

the harbor. Every day from 1876 to 1934, a huge ball was hoisted and dropped to signal Greenwich Time to ships in the harbor.

The delightful town of **Akaroa** is the jewel of the peninsula, 50 miles (80 km) from Christchurch. French whaling captain Jean Langlois founded Akaroa and in 1840 lured 60 settlers halfway across the world to start a French colony. Langlois had grand visions and urged France to annex the South Island, but by the time the settlers

arrived, the Treaty of Waitangi had been signed and the colonists were greeted by the Union Jack flying in Akaroa Harbour.

English and German settlers followed, but those first French families stamped the town with its lingering flavor. French names grace the streets and pretty cottages provide a French provincial air. Surrounded by scenic hills on a stunning harbor, Akaroa makes a wonderful day or overnight trip.

Much of the French influence has been re-created in the name of tourism. Local cafés serve French food and buildings sprout French shutters. Streets such as Lavaud and Cross were renamed Rue Lavaud and Rue Croix in 1968, prompting local wags to erect signs such as Rue Matics, Rue Barb, and Rue de Remarks.

But there's no denying the colonial charm of the town, and its history can be explored at the **Langlois-Eteveneaux House,** one of the original cottages, now part of the **Akaroa Museum,** which also includes the old **Court House** and **Customs House.**

The best thing to do in town is simply to wander the waterfront and the streets lined with cottages and old churches, such as St. Peter's (1863) on Rue Balguerie. **The Giant's House,** the funky gardens/workshop of local artist Josie Martin, makes a colorful stop.

You can book activities ranging from kayaking to swimming with dolphins through the information center. Harbor cruises, billed as wildlife tours, are popular, for Hector's dolphins and penguins can often be seen in these waters. ∎

EXPERIENCE: Surfing Lessons

With all that coastline, New Zealand has an abundance of surf and quality waves. Surfing is a popular pastime for Kiwis and visitors alike, but plenty of uncrowded waves can be found off the beaten track and outside the main summer holiday season.

For beginners, surfing lessons are offered at locations all around the country, and unlike in some surfing classes in places like Hawaii or Australia, class numbers are generally low.

Surf schools provide boards and wet suits, a must in the often chilly waters of New Zealand. A spring suit will suffice up north in summer, but a full wet suit is needed farther south.

The 1966 surfing movie classic *Endless Summer* put the North Island's Raglan on the world surfing map, and it remains the country's most famous break. The Raglan Surfing School has popular 3.5-hour lessons.

The big city, Auckland, has the biggest concentration of surfers and surf schools, with good breaks nearby, particularly on the west coast beaches such as Muriwai. The east coast of the North Island also has good surf and surf schools, notably at Gisborne and Mount Maunganui.

Most South Island surf schools are along the east coast at Kaikoura, Christchurch, and Dunedin, which has good surfing at city beaches.

A surfer rips at popular Wainui Beach, near Gisborne on the North Island.

Surfing New Zealand
(www.surfing.co.nz) lists operators, including the following. Check also with local tourist offices.

Aotearoa Surf
Auckland, tel 09/431-5760, www.aotearoasurf.co.nz

Liquid Gold Surf Tours
2 Rutene Rd., Kaiti, Gisborne, tel 06/863-7273, www.liquidgoldsurf.co.nz

Muriwai Surf School
Behind Sand Dunz Café, Muriwai Beach, tel 021/478-764, www.muriwaisurfschool.co.nz

New Zealand Surf School
Tay St., Marine Parade, Mount Maunganui, tel 07/574-1666, www.nzsurfschools.co.nz

NZ Surf Tours
P.O. Box 17509, Greenlane, Auckland, tel 09/828-0426, www.newzealandsurftours.com

Raglan Surfing School
5 Whaanga Rd., Whale Bay, Raglan, tel 07/825-7873, www.raglansurfingschool.co.nz

Southcoast Surf Clinic
17a East Ave., Dunedin, tel 03/455-6007, www.surfcoachnz.com ∎

North Canterbury

North Canterbury is often just a pass-through zone for visitors heading north to Marlborough or to the West Coast over the passes of the Southern Alps. However, Hanmer Springs has the finest hot-springs resort in the South Island, and Arthur's Pass National Park is noted for its superb alpine scenery with notable ski slopes nearby.

Soaking in hot pools at Hanmer Springs

Lewis Pass

Map p. 191

Visitor information

42 Amuri Ave., Hanmer Springs

03/315-7128

Christchurch to Lewis Pass

Lewis Pass is one of three main routes through the Southern Alps to the West Coast. Take SH1 north out of Christchurch and turn off onto SH7 at Waipara. The highway northwest though the alps is a lonely one through farmland and forest, but it passes the hot-springs resort of Hanmer Springs.

Few destinations on SH1 demand a stop before Hanmer Springs or Kaikoura (see pp. 176–177). Wine buffs will find **Waipara** an exception. This budding wine-growing district, one hour north of Christchurch near the Hanmer Springs turnoff, is a relative newcomer in New Zealand, but has quickly established a reputation for fine wine.

Pegasus Bay *(tel 03/314-6869)* consistently rates as one of the country's top boutique wineries, particularly for its Riesling, Chardonnay, and Pinot Noir. The restaurant serves dishes prepared from fresh local produce, and the tasting room has good platters. **The Mud House Winery** *(tel 03/314-6900)* has grown to become one of the region's largest producers, offering a wide variety of wines. Its restaurant offers fine dining. **Waipara Springs** *(tel 03/314-6777)* is also on the main highway and has a rustic wine bar and café serving reasonably priced fare.

Nestled in a high-country basin 50 miles (81 km) north of Waipara, **Hanmer Springs** has long drawn visitors in search of its curative waters. Flanked by a phalanx of shade trees, this pretty town has a fine hot-springs complex right on the main street, with a series of rock pools filled with waters from the springs at around 95°F (35°C). Complete with swimming pools, water slide, café / restaurant, and gift shop, this is the South Island's best-maintained and most extensive springs resort.

The town has a host of good accommodations and a wide range of other activities when soaking in the pools begins to pall. The **Hanmer Forest** has pleasant walks starting from the town. Adventure activities abound, and in winter Hanmer Springs is a ski town, with two small ski areas in the surrounding mountains. The swift Waiau River nearby has jet boating, white-water rafting, and bungee jumping at the scenic bridge outside town.

Once a Maori greenstone trading route, **Lewis Pass** is the northernmost of the three main passes through the Southern Alps. At 2,835 feet (864 m), it is lower and easier to negotiate than Arthur's Pass (see pp. 204–205) but more lightly traveled, avoiding the camper-van trains that block roads all over the South Island in summer.

North of the Pass

Just northwest of Lewis Pass, **Maruia Springs** *(tel 03/523-8840, www.maruiasprings.co.nz)* is a small hot-springs resort nestled in the valley next to the highway, surrounded by thickly wooded mountains. The springs were well known to the Maori and a favorite place to camp on the journey through Lewis Pass. European settlers were also attracted to the thermal waters

Japanese Baths

Based more on socializing than scrubbing, the Japanese bath (*onsen*) is gaining international popularity. The bather washes thoroughly before stepping into the communal bath, which is deeper and hotter than its western counterpart—like a zen hot tub. Traditionally, the onsens were coed, but that is less common now.

and built bathing huts for modesty, followed by a hotel.

Now, Japanese owners have brought Japanese bathing traditions to this remote part of the South Island, with segregated communal bathhouses and individual spas. The outdoor

---

Hanmer Springs
🗺 Map p. 191

Hanmer Springs Thermal Pools & Spa
✉ Amuri Ave.
☎ 03/315-7511
💲 $–$$$
www.hanmersprings.co.nz

EXPERIENCE: Climb Every Mountain

The Southern Alps offer demanding, ice-strewn climbing and have long been practice slopes for the world's mountaineers. Sir Edmund Hillary, who conquered Mount Everest with Tenzing Norgay in 1953, cut his climbing teeth in the alps, which includes 19 peaks over 10,000 feet (3,000 m), the highest of which is Aoraki/Mount Cook at 12,316 feet (3,754 m).

For budding mountaineers, alpine hikers, or those looking for a one-shot taste of peak bagging, trained guides offer world-class climbing and mountaineering courses. Three of the best-known organizations are **Alpine Guides** (*Mount Cook Village, tel 03/435-1834, www.alpineguides.co.nz*) based in Aoraki/Mount Cook National Park, **Aspiring Guides** (*Level 1, 99 Ardmore St., Lake Wanaka, tel 03/443-9422, www.aspiringguides.com*), and **Adventure Consultants**

(*58 McDougall St., P.O. Box 739, Lake Wanaka, tel 03/443-8711, www.adventureconsultants.co.nz*), which operate mostly in Mount Aspiring National Park.

Courses range from basic mountain skills for hikers and climbers to ice climbing and technical mountaineering. Alpine hikes and climbing expeditions are also arranged. For serious mountaineers, the **New Zealand Alpine Club** (*www.alpineclub.org.nz*) is an excellent resource and runs most of the alpine huts. The courses don't require experience, though a good level of fitness is essential and basic rock-climbing and rope skills are preferred.

Plenty of places offer rock-climbing experience in New Zealand (*www.climb.co.nz* is a good resource), from indoor venues to cliff faces at noted rock-climbing locations, particularly in Canterbury, Wanaka, Taranaki, and Wellington.

rock pools are at their best on a snowy winter's day, when snow flakes drift down to refresh steaming bathers.

Arthur's Pass

The most direct way to the West Coast from Christchurch is via Arthur's Pass on SH73. At 3,018 feet (920 m) it is the highest of the main passes over the Southern Alps. For many years it was also the most treacherous, subject to landslides and avalanches, as well as the most tortuous, with a procession of switchback turns outside Otira. Recent work, especially the impressive Otira Viaduct, have improved this route immensely.

Flanked by glittering peaks, the road is spectacular. Even better is

the rail link between Greymouth and Christchurch, New Zealand's most scenic train journey. The TranzAlpine runs daily in both directions and passes through the 5-mile-long (8 km) **Otira Tunnel,** one of the longest tunnels in the world when it opened in 1923. The tunnel's length meant this stretch of the line had to be electrified because the buildup of fumes would otherwise be hazardous to passengers.

The tunnel starts at **Arthur's Pass Village,** the main settlement of the area, 3 miles (5 km) south of the pass itself. This tiny alpine hamlet has a population of just 50, but gets over a quarter of a million visitors a year. It has a busy restaurant where kea (mountain parrots; see sidebar p. 216) roam, and accommodations cater to the hikers, mountaineers, and skiers who flock to the surrounding **Arthur's Pass National Park.**

The 282,935-acre (114,500 ha) national park straddles the Southern Alps and has 16 peaks over 6,500 feet (2,000 m). Its flora ranges from beech forest in the east to rain forest on the western slopes. The park also has superb hiking, from good short walks to the popular two-day **Goat Pass Track,** the five-day **Harper Pass,** and the tougher **Harman Pass** route. Even on short walks, be well equipped and prepared for changeable weather. The park gets 177 inches (450 cm) of rain annually, and it can snow at any time.

For a taste of the park's beauty, the **Devil's Punchbowl Waterfall** is a one-hour round-trip walk from the parking lot on Punchbowl Road, just north of the village. The waterfall can be seen from the highway, but the walk takes in beautiful beech forest. From the same parking lot, another 1.5-hour trail leads to the **Bridal Veil Falls.**

The **Dobson Nature Walk** leads from the top of the pass and is an excellent 30-minute loop through alpine terrain, with wildflowers blooming in summer. The longer 3.5-hour **Bealey Valley Walk** to the foot of Mount Rolleston is well worth the effort. The scenic trail starts 1.2 miles (2 km) north of the village and goes through beech forest and tussock clearings before crossing the Bealey River at The Chasm.

The more demanding hike to **Temple Basin,** the nearby club

ski area, starts at the pass and takes three hours round-trip. It is rewarded with panoramic mountain views and alpine meadow wildflowers in summer.

Ski Areas: Before Arthur's Pass, the road from Christchurch crosses **Porters Pass,** which is actually the highest point on SH73 at 3,103 feet (946 m). Nearby in the Craigieburn Range, Porters

INSIDER TIP:

If you're a keen foodie, take a cooking class at Seagars in Oxford, or just grab a coffee and a muffin at their café.

—ROY FERGUSON,
*New Zealand Ambassador to the
United States*

ski field is the closest commercial skiing area to Christchurch, just 55 miles (89 km) away. Other ski slopes in the ranges, such as Craigieburn, Broken River, and Mount Cheeseman, are also popular with day-trippers.

Nearby **Mount Hutt,** the most developed ski area near Christchurch, has a long season (*June–Oct.*) and is regarded as one of the best skiing destinations in the country. Nearby **Methven,** a pleasant sleepy town in summer, has accommodations, and in winter it thrives on après-ski. Methven offers a host of other attractions to lure visitors year-round, including fishing, golf, jet boating, hiking, and mountain biking. ∎

Arthur's Pass National Park

⬛ Map p. 191

Visitor information

✉ SH73, Arthur's Pass Village

☎ 03/318-9211

Oxford

⬛ Map p. 191

Seagars at Oxford

✉ 78 Main St., Oxford

☎ 03/312-1435

www.seagarsat oxford.com

Tourists and Kiwis alike flock to southern slopes like Mount Hutt in Canterbury.

Ski New Zealand

New Zealand has some of the best skiing in the Southern Hemisphere, with a ski season lasting from June to October. Major ski fields include those on the slopes of the Ruapehu volcano in the North Island, but most skiing takes place in the South Island, particularly near Queenstown and Wanaka, as well as outside Christchurch.

Unlike ski resorts in other countries, New Zealand's tend to have a nature-first policy, with limited development on the mountains and accommodations in surrounding towns. In addition to the main resorts, a host of smaller club areas with limited facilities are scattered around the country.

Mount Ruapehu

Mount Ruapehu offers a unique opportunity to ski down the slopes of a volcano. Though normally quiet, Ruapehu is the most active of three volcanoes in Tongariro National Park and has a steaming crater lake.

Two areas on the mountain offer the North Island's best skiing. Popular **Whakapapa** (see p. 132) on the northern slopes has panoramic views, 14 lifts, and 30 groomed trails. Smaller **Turoa** (see p. 133) on the southern slopes has the country's longest vertical drop at 2,369 feet (722 m), nine lifts, and over 20 groomed trails. From the top lift, it is a one-hour walk to the crater lake.

You can stay in Whakapapa Village, 4 miles (6 km) from the ski area, but most accommodations are to be found in the towns of National Park and Ohakune (see p. 133), which also has the best après-ski scene.

Canterbury

Arguably the best ski area in New Zealand, **Mount Hutt** (see p. 205) is the highest commercial field, with the longest season. Wide slopes offer first-class powder skiing, boarding, and cross-country skiing. A two-hour drive from Christchurch, the area is serviced by the ski village of Methven.

A number of club ski areas are found in the nearby Arthur's Pass/Craigieburn Range. **Porters Ski Area** is the main commercial field and the closest to Christchurch, 55 miles (89 km) away.

In North Canterbury, the hot-springs resort of Hanmer Springs (see p. 203) services two nearby areas: the small club slopes of Hanmer Springs, and family-friendly Mount Lyford, with a nearby alpine village offering accommodations.

Mackenzie Country

In the shadow of Aoraki/Mount Cook, more remote Mackenzie Country has uncrowded ski areas with great views of New Zealand's highest mountain.

Near Lake Tekapo, **Roundhill** has undulating slopes and good snow cover for beginning and intermediate skiing. **Mount Dobson** has the country's largest beginner/intermediate slope and soft powder. And near Twizel, remote **Ohau** (see p. 213) has excellent snow, varied terrain, and uncrowded slopes for intermediate and advanced skiers.

Wanaka

On a fine lake, the scenic alpine town of Wanaka, an hour northeast of Queenstown on the South Island, is a popular base for skiing in the surrounding mountains.

With a vertical drop of 2,313 feet (705 m) spread over three basins, **Treble Cone** has exhilarating skiing with a panoramic backdrop of the peaks above Lake Wanaka below. Advanced and intermediate skiers rate it the best for downhill runs, off-piste powder skiing, and consistently good snow, while recent work has delivered wide groomed slopes for all levels.

High-altitude **Cardrona** (see pp. 251 & 253), on the back road to Queenstown, is a

family resort with good child-care facilities and gentle rolling slopes suitable for beginners, while more demanding runs cater to all levels.

Across the valley from Cardrona, **Waiorau Snow Farm** is a cross-country terrain park with 16 miles (25 km) of groomed trails and expanses of open country for ski touring, with traditional skiing and snowboarding also available.

EXPERIENCE:
Get into the Action

Some operators and resorts for stellar South Island skiing:

Queenstown Snow Centre
Camp & Shotover Sts.,
Queenstown
03/442-4640

Mount Hutt Snow Centre
94 Main St., Methven
03/302-8811
www.nzski.com/mthutt

Lake Wanaka
Four ski resorts
www.skilakewanaka.com

Queenstown

In a superb setting on Lake Wakatipu, Queenstown is the South Island's number-one alpine resort, known for its party action.

Less than half an hour from Queenstown, **Coronet Peak** has top-class on-mountain facilities and stunning views of the surrounding ranges and Lake Wakatipu. A wide range of terrain caters to all levels in the South Island's birthplace of skiing.

A spectacular range that defines Queenstown views, **The Remarkables** hosts a popular ski area with three basins that cater to boarders and skiers from beginner to advanced. ∎

South Canterbury

Heading south across the flat-as-a-board farmland of the Canterbury Plains, the main highway (SH1) south to Dunedin reaches the city of Timaru. Most visitors turn off before Canterbury's second city to travel the spectacular inland road to the Southern Alps and mighty Aoraki/Mount Cook.

Sheep in a paddock overlooked by the Arrowsmith mountains

Timaru

⬛ Map p. 191

Visitor information

✉ 2 George St. (opposite railway station)

☎ 03/688-6163

Timaru

The largest city in southern Canterbury, Timaru (pop. 27,000) was a whaling station from 1838, but European settlement began in earnest in 1859 when 120 British immigrants disembarked from the *Strathallan*. The city's name is said to derive from Te Maru, or a "place of shelter," where Maori canoes found a haven along the rugged coast, but shipwrecks littered the treacherous bay until construction began

on an artificial harbor in 1877.

Halfway between Christchurch and Dunedin, Timaru is a logical overnight stop on SH1, but tends to lose out to more touristed Oamaru to the south. Mindful of Oamaru's regeneration of its historic precinct, Timaru has also undergone a pleasing facelift in an attempt to shake off its struggling provincial air.

Many fine buildings and whole streetscapes survive from the city's heyday, particularly along Beswick,

Cains, and Barnard Streets. Among the interesting commercial buildings, the delightfully old-fashioned **Royal Arcade** off Stafford Street has cast-iron columns and ornate Victorian shop fronts. **St. Mary's Anglican Church** (*24 Church St.*), built in 1880, is pure English Gothic, and the tower can be climbed for views of the city. Built in 1911, **Sacred Heart Basilica** (*Craigie Ave.*), south of town on the main road, has a large copper dome and is the town's most imposing structure.

The **Terrace,** a renovated street of café-bars and restaurants, is well worth a visit and has striking views over the terraced piazza above Caroline Bay. This popular, if dated, local beach resort comes alive with fairground attractions over Christmas to New Year.

The **South Canterbury Museum** (*tel 03/687-7212, closed Mon.*) on Perth Street houses the usual historical suspects—Maori and settler exhibits—and a replica of the airplane flown in 1902 by locally born Richard Pearse (1877–1953). The quiet, dreamy Pearse constructed his monoplane from bamboo, steel, wire, and canvas. Contrary to world opinion, Kiwis will tell you that Pearse was the first man to fly, a year before the Wright Brothers took off in the *Flyer*.

Housed in a 1908 homestead, the **Aigantighe Art Gallery** (*49 Wai-iti Rd., tel 03/688-4424, closed Mon.*) has an extensive collection of New Zealand, Pacific, Asian, and European art, particularly British Victorian paintings, and a delightful sculpture garden.

Don't miss the **Goldie Room** with its famous Maori portraits by C. F. Goldie.

Christchurch to Aoraki/ Mount Cook

The most direct route southwest from Christchurch to Queenstown goes via Aoraki/ Mount Cook. The inland road has spectacular scenery with rural landscapes giving way to glacial lakes and the drama of the Southern Alps. This is as

---

EXPERIENCE: Ballooning

The flat Canterbury Plains are ideal for hot-air ballooning. The spreading patchwork of plains farmland stretching to the snow-capped Southern Alps makes for a spectacular panorama. Departure is at dawn for pristine views; the four-hour flights include a champagne breakfast.

Aoraki Balloon Safaris (tel *03/302-8172, www.nzballooning.co.nz*) operates out of Methven, 58 miles (94 km) southwest of Christchurch at the foot of the alps, providing dramatic views of Aoraki/ Mount Cook and other peaks. **Balloon Adventures Up Up and Away** (*tel 03/381-4600, www.ballooning.co.nz*) departs from Christchurch for close-up views of the city and the panorama beyond.

---

stunning a drive as any in a country filled with scenic roads.

About an hour's drive south of Christchurch on SH1, the rural town of **Ashburton** makes a convenient first stop, but the town motto "Whatever It Takes" sums it up—Ashburton tries hard to attract tourists but lacks attractions.

**Aoraki/
Mount Cook
National Park**

🅰 Map p. 191

Visitor information

✉ 1 Larch Grove,
Aoraki/Mount
Cook Village

☎ 03/435-1186

Just over the Rangitata River, 22 miles (36 km) south of Ashburton, turn off the main highway onto SH79 and note the delightfully pretty town of **Geraldine**, at the junction of pasture and foothills. Grab a coffee or stretch your legs on streets lined with

---

Sir Edmund Hillary

Born in Auckland, the world's most famous mountain climber was first a professional beekeeper. On his days off, however, he got a taste for mountaineering on New Zealand's Southern Alps. After serving in the Royal New Zealand Air Force during World War II, Hillary became intent on scaling Mount Everest. In 1953 he reached the top alongside Sherpa Tenzing Norgay. After spending 15 minutes at the summit resting and eating cake, he descended, quipping, "Well, we knocked the bastard off." In 1958, he led the first vehicle party to reach the South Pole.

---

shade trees and historic buildings. The visitor information center (tel 03/693-1006) has details on the thriving local craft scene and a number of nearby excursions.

Farther on past Fairlie, the road (SH8) climbs to Burkes Pass and **Mackenzie Country,** named after a sheep rustler turned folk hero caught herding a stolen flock into the then unexplored Canterbury highlands. The landscape changes dramatically in the shadow of the alps, revealing a harsh but beautiful highland basin of tussock grass and stunning lakes.

The first of the lakes is **Lake Tekapo,** a breathtaking turquoise stretch of water framed by the snowy Southern Alps. The small hamlet of the same name is tour bus heaven, a required stop on the way to Queenstown. Souvenir shops line the main street and tour groups fill the cafés during the day, but few stay on, though the town has a good selection of accommodations. The big new thing in Tekapo is the **Alpine Springs and Spa,** with hot pools and an ice rink to cater to the ski-season crowds heading to nearby **Mount Dobson.**

Lake Pukaki, 25 miles (40 km) farther on, is even more stunning with views straight up the lake to towering Aoraki/Mount Cook. Also turquoise, the lake's color is a product of fine powdered rock ground by the glaciers upstream and carried by the meltwater into the lake. Past the dam on Sh80 is the turnoff to Aoraki/Mount Cook; the main highway continues on to Twizel (see p. 213). There is a visitor center (SH8, tel 03/435-3280) at the lake.

Aoraki/Mount Cook National Park

With 19 peaks over 10,000 feet (3,000 m), Aoraki/Mount Cook National Park is the crowning glory of the Southern Alps, which stretch the length of the island. The park is a forbidding landscape of ice and rock, 40

A bronze statue of Sir Edmund Hillary at home among the Southern Alps

INSIDER TIP:

Aoraki/Mount Cook, our highest and most sacred peak, lords over the tussock-covered Mackenzie Plains and is as impressive as anything in the Himalaya.

—COLIN MONTEATH,
National Geographic Photographer

percent of it covered by glaciers, but access to the park is via a surprisingly easy drive along the shore of Lake Pukaki up to the Aoraki Mount Cook Village.

The village is dominated by **The Hermitage** (see p. 303), a grand dame among New Zealand hotels since 1884. Most day visitors don't get beyond The Hermitage and its fantastic views of the park, but at the very least, take one of the short walks to

better appreciate the grandeur of the area. The tiny village also has other accommodations for an overnight stay.

Standing tallest among the cluster of peaks is Aoraki, the "Cloud Piercer." Until recently plain old Mount Cook, it was officially renamed **Aoraki/Mount Cook** in 1998 as part of the government's treaty settlement with the Ngai Tahu people. At 12,316 feet (3,754 m), it is the tallest peak in New Zealand, though it lost 33 feet (10 m) when a large section of rock sheared off in 1991.

The mountain is a magnificent sight, but often shrouded in cloud. It appears that even Captain Cook, after whom the mountain was named, missed it as he sailed along the west coast, for there is no mention of it in his journals.

Mount Cook has long attracted climbers and is a training ground for New Zealand mountaineers, including Sir Edmund Hillary, conqueror of Mount Everest (see sidebar p. 210). Though not high by world standards, the climb starts low and the ascent is tough. Since the peak was first scaled on Christmas Day 1894, more than 200 people have died on or around it.

This is not a one-peak park, however, and other great mountains such as Tasman, Sefton, Eli Mueller, Godley, and Murchison. The **Tasman Glacier,** visible from the main highway at the entrance to the park, is the largest glacier in New Zealand at 18 miles (29 km) long and up to 2 miles (3 km) wide.

Though increasingly rock-covered in the lower reaches as the glacier retreats, the ice is up to 2,000 feet (600 m) deep in parts.

Lupins blossom on the shores of Lake Tekapo.

de Beaumont, Haast, Dampier, and the Minarets compete for climbers' and sightseers' attention. Peaks can also be climbed from the West Coast, for Aoraki/ Mount Cook borders Westland Tai Poutini National Park (see pp. 226–229), but for nonmountaineers the two parks are separated by a two-day drive.

Glaciers: The park also has dozens of glaciers, the five major ones being the Tasman, Hooker, The Tasman Glacier can be skied in winter, when helicopters drop skiers on the upper reaches, and ski planes also land in summer for up-close viewing. Other sightseeing flights and mountain guides offer a variety of ways to explore the glaciers and the park.

Walks: The easiest way to get out into the park is on one of the many short walks from the village. **Governors Bush Walk,** a one-hour loop up behind the village, goes through stands of silver beech and offers good views of the mountains. The **Kea Point Walk,** two hours round-trip, starts from The Hermitage and leads up to the Mueller Glacier moraine wall through subalpine grasslands. The walk ends at a viewing deck with stunning panoramas of the mountains, Hooker Valley, and the Mueller Glacier.

The **Hooker Valley Track** is a little more demanding, but is highly recommended for its superb views of mountains, glaciers, and lakes. The trail crosses two suspension bridges and passes Mueller Lake before reaching Hooker Lake. The hike takes three hours round-trip from the parking lot at the end of the Hooker Valley Road; add an extra hour if starting from the village. Get up-to-date trail and weather information before heading off at the Department of Conservation visitor center.

Twizel

The closest town to the national park, **Twizel** was built in 1968 as a temporary construction village for 6,000 workers employed on the Upper Waitaki hydroelectric power plant. The hydro project was the largest undertaken in New Zealand, and when it was completed 18 years later, the town was due for demolition. The residents successfully fought to retain the town, which lives in large part on tourism, with Aoraki/Mount Cook only 40 miles (65 km) away and a number of scenic lakes with good trout fishing nearby.

Though Twizel lacks old-fashioned charm, the well-stocked

A Humbling Rockslide

Around midnight on December 14, 1991, a rockslide started at the peak of Aoraki/Mount Cook. What began as a dull rumble quickly escalated into a rock avalanche that registered 3.9 on the Richter scale. Nearby climbers watched as the mountain seemed to collapse upon itself. By the next morning, the mountain had shrunk from a triumphant 12,349 feet (3,764 m) to a slightly less triumphant 12,316 feet (3,754 m). The mountain is still New Zealand's tallest.

town of 1,200 makes a good base and has reasonably priced accommodations. The visitor information center *(Market Pl., tel 03/435-3124)* has full details.

Plenty of activities are offered around Twizel, but the main attraction is the chance to see the kaki, or black stilt, one of the world's rarest wading birds. The **Ahuriri Conservation Park** south of town operates a breeding program and offers tours *(book at visitor information center).*

Lake Ruataniwha on the southern edge of town is popular for boating, as is **Lake Benmore,** the site of the hydro dam to the east. **Lake Ohau,** 19 miles (30 km) west of Twizel, is popular for boating, swimming, and fishing and as a base for the **Ohau ski field** west of the lake. ∎

Stunning scenery, glaciers, old mining towns, and wilderness sandwiched between the Southern Alps and a rugged coastline

West Coast

An adventurer climbs an ice face in a Fox Glacier crevasse, Westland Tai Poutini National Park.

West Coast

Cut off from the rest of the South Island by the Southern Alps and lashed by drenching rains from the Tasman Sea, the West Coast is a rugged landscape of snow and ice, dense forest, lakes, and wild beaches.

The Coast, as it is known for short, stretches 373 miles (600 km) north to south but is seldom more than 19 miles (30 km) wide. It is a frontier land, inhospitable but beautiful, where miners flocked to the goldfields and hacked settlements out of the thick bush.

Wild West Coast towns peopled by hard-living, hardworking pioneers sprang up almost overnight in the 1860s when Westland, as the Coast is also known, was briefly the fastest growing region and biggest exporter in New Zealand. As gold waned, boomtowns became ghost towns, but a new breed of miners followed to hack away at coal seams. Coasters are proud of their working-class roots and still see themselves as rugged and self-reliant. Today the Coast is one of the most lightly populated areas of New Zealand, and the main towns of Greymouth, Westport, and Hokitika struggle to keep their youths. Coal mines still operate, but tourism is now the biggest industry.

The dramatic scenery lures hundreds of thousands of visitors every year, most on a beeline for the Fox and Franz Josef Glaciers in Westland National Park. Near the coast with no need to drive through snow to reach them, these great valleys of ice 1,000 feet (300 m) thick are among the most accessible glaciers in the world. Even more astonishing, they emerge in temperate rain forest.

The West Coast is both densely forested and desolate. When Captain Cook passed in 1770, he remarked, "No country upon earth can appear more rugged and barren." Thomas Brunner (1821–1874), the first European to travel the length of the Coast in the 1840s, battled the wilderness on the ground but found it just as intimidating, saying: "For what reason the natives choose to live here I cannot imagine."

Few Maori lived on the West Coast, but it did have one great treasure: *pounamu* (greenstone or New Zealand jade). For 300 years from around 1400, the Ngati Wairangi controlled the trade of this precious hard stone, prized throughout the North Island. The Ngai Tahu then invaded and took over the resource, lugging the stone high over passes through the Southern Alps.

Those passes today provide spectacular gateways to the West Coast. The northern routes via Arthur's Pass and Lewis Pass were the only way to the Coast until the Haast Pass road

Kea

The inquisitive and mischievous kea (*Nestor notabilis*) is an alpine parrot native to the Southern Alps. Unpredictable, noisy, fearless, and easily accustomed to humans, keas can sometimes be found at picnic grounds or outside cafés, such as at Arthur's Pass Village. These scavengers eat insects, berries, and other plants and will dine on carrion such as dead sheep. This habit earned keas an exaggerated reputation as sheep killers, resulting in their widespread shooting by farmers until they gained protection in 1986. They have adapted to eating scraps thrown by visitors who are delighted at the antics of these cheeky green parrots, which let out a loud *keeeaaa* call. But keas also have a destructive bent, with a penchant for the rubber around windshields, although tents, bags, or anything they can get beaks into may also suffer. Keas can also be aggressive, so take care.

NOT TO BE MISSED:

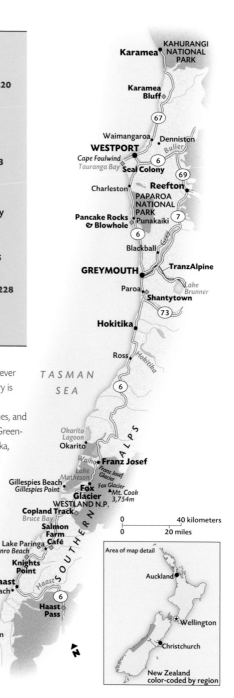

in the south was opened in 1965. Whichever road you take, stunning mountain scenery is guaranteed.

On the Coast, historic towns, old mines, and deserted beaches can also be explored. Greenstone is still a precious resource in Hokitika, where renowned workshops carve stone as well as bone, shell, and wood. Stock up on fine crafts and souvenirs here. The main town of Greymouth is the gateway to old mining settlements, and farther north, a stunning coastal drive takes in the strange "pancake" rocks of Punakaiki, another West Coast must-see.

The very far north around Karamea leads to Kahurangi National Park, a wilderness as remote as any in New Zealand. Here you'll find the Heaphy Track, one of New Zealand's Great Walks. ■

Westport & Beyond

The coal-mining town of Westport is the gateway to western reaches of the diverse Kahurangi National Park, lying at the very north of the West Coast. To the south, the rugged coastline is home to seals and the famed "pancake" rocks of Punakaiki in Paparoa National Park.

Two hikers pass through pampas grass along the Heaphy Track.

Westport
- ⛰ Map p. 217

Visitor information
- ✉ 1 Brougham St.
- ☎ 03/789-6658

www.westport
.org.nz

**Coaltown
Museum**
- ✉ Queen St.
- ☎ 03/789-8204
- 💲 $–$$

Westport

Where the Buller River meets the sea, Westport is the West Coast's main port and owes its existence to coal. Gold miners first settled Westport in 1861, but the pickings were lean and the coal mines north of the town soon drove development. They still produce most of New Zealand's coal.

Westport is a dour town, but the area has a number of points of interest, most notably Punakaiki to the south and Kahurangi National Park to the north. In the town, **Coaltown Museum** celebrates Westport's main industry with a re-created mine, interesting displays, and a huge brake drum from the Denniston Incline.

Westport is a crossroads to the north and east of the South Island. Heading toward Nelson in the north, SH6 follows the Buller River through the stunning Buller Gorge. About 12 miles (20 km) from Westport, the twisting road is cut into the mountain and be-comes an amazing one-lane drive under a rock roof. SH6 continues up the river to Murchison (see p. 187). Alternatively, turn off SH6 near the small town of Inangahua, 28 miles (45 km) from Westport, to Reefton and the main highway to the east coast via Lewis Pass.

North of Westport

Heading north of Westport, SH67 goes through lightly populated country and ends just past Karamea at start of the Heaphy Track, the area's main lure.

On the way, turn off at Waimangaroa for **Denniston,** 6 miles (9 km) off the highway, high on the Rochfort Plateau. Once a thriving coal-mining center, Denniston is now almost a ghost town, but its good walks include the very steep **Denniston Walkway.** This forested bridle trail leads to the Denniston Incline,

....

Kahurangi National Park is a large wilderness, most of it inaccessible, but hiking trails explore rushing rivers, alpine fields, and coastal forest.

....

an impressive cabling feat that transported coal trucks up and down the mountain.

The road north then travels through old coal towns, shadows of their former selves, before climbing inland around the scenic, forested **Karamea Bluff** and descending back to the coast and

the isolated town of **Karamea,** gateway to **Kahurangi National Park.** The park is a large wilderness, most of it inaccessible, but hiking trails explore rushing rivers, alpine fields, and coastal forest. The park's rich vegetation varies markedly from the West Coast's thick podocarp forest and superb tropical-looking nikau palms to

The Denniston Incline

Dubbed the "eighth wonder of the world" by locals, the Denniston Incline was constructed in 1879 to carry coal from the top of the Denniston plateau. Sending wagons filled with 12 tons of coal down the exceptionally steep tracks was a difficult venture and called for a sturdy braking system—which sometimes failed. Many unfortunate souls met their demise at the bottom of the incline after mishaps caused tons of coal to rain down on them.

beech forests in the east.

The **Heaphy Track** is the most famous of the park's walks, a 40-mile (82 km), five-day hike from the Aorere Valley, near Collingwood in Nelson, to Kohaihai, 10 miles (15 km) north of Karamea. This Great Walk (see p. 19) overnights in huts and must be booked through the Department of Conservation.

You can walk just part of the Heaphy for a quick taste, or try

Kahurangi National Park

⛰ Map p. 217

Visitor information

✉ Millers Acre/ Taha o te Awa, 79 Trafalgar St., Nelson

☎ 03/546-9339

**Paparoa
National Park**

🗺 Map p. 217

Visitor information

✉ Main Rd.,
Punakaiki

☎ 03/731-1895

Blowholes

**Blowholes are formed as
a by-product of erosion.
Waves beating against the
coast will slowly cause the
softer rock to crumble,
eventually producing
underwater caves. In time,
bits of the top of the cave
wear away, creating small
holes—the blowholes.
When a wave pours into
the mouth of the cave, it
is funneled out through
these holes. The pressure
from the pounding waves
results in highly impressive
eruptions.**

the **Oparara Basin** for short forest hikes to spectacular limestone outcrops. On the road to the Heaphy Track, turn off at McCallums Mill Road and travel 10 miles (16 km) on well-maintained gravel road. There you'll find the start of the easy, 20-minute walk to the impressive limestone **Oparara Arch** over the river. The **Moria Arch** *(1 hour round-trip)* is similar, while the **Crazy Paving** and **Box Canyon Caves** (bring a flashlight) are close to the road.

South of Westport

Seven miles (11 km) from Westport, a fine 1.5-hour round-trip walk goes from **Cape Foulwind** along the coast to a populous seal colony. You can also drive to **Tauranga Bay** for a five-minute walk to the seals.

The once-booming town of **Charleston** on the Nile River, 17 miles (27 km) south of Westport, hasn't done much since the gold ran out, but Norwest Adventures *(182 Queen St., Westport; tel 03/788-8168, www.cave rafting.com, $$$$$, no children under 10)* runs popular cave-rafting trips and glowworm cave tours *($$$$$)* up the Nile River from its base here.

Far and away the highlight of this part of the West Coast, **Punakaiki** *(www.punakaiki.co.nz),* about 37 miles (60 km) south of Westport on SH6, is famed for its pancake-stack rock formations, the product of weathered limestone lifted from the seabed by seismic action. The **Pancake Rocks and Blowholes walk** is an easy 20-minute loop from the village and takes in the most spectacular outcrops along this

> Far and away the highlight of this part of the West Coast, Punakaiki is famed for its pancake-stack rock formations.

stunning stretch of coast, part of **Paparoa National Park.**

Punakaiki has a small selection of accommodations, a tavern, and a café at the national park visitor center, which has good displays on the park and information on walks. These include the 2.5-hour round-trip **Pororari River Track,** which follows a spectacular limestone gorge. ■

Pioneers

European New Zealanders celebrate their pioneering past and often attribute aspects of the national character to the first settlers and their resourcefulness, strength of will, and propensity for hard work.

In the late 18th century, New Zealand was seen as one of the world's last outposts, a remote and hostile land. Though nearby Australia was settled in 1788, few Europeans had ventured farther east.

Sealers established the first settlement in 1792, a rough camp in remote Dusky Sound where they braved the torrential rains. Others followed, attracted by high prices for seal fur and oil. A few took Maori wives and stayed on. One settler, 16-year-old James Caddell, was the only survivor of a Maori attack in 1810 and later married a chief's daughter. He bore facial tattoos and could barely speak English when discovered by Europeans 13 years later.

In the north, whalers had the most significant contact with the Maori from 1792. Mostly English and American, the whalers roamed the South Pacific hunting sperm whales for oil and ambergris, taking shelter in the Bay of Islands. The village of Kororareka traded with the ships and soon acquired a reputation for debauchery. Beginning in 1809, traders settled the port, followed by missionaries in 1814.

Statue to the settlers of 1842, Wakefield Quay, Nelson

British Colonization

Few settlers ventured beyond the Bay of Islands, and by the time Britain annexed New Zealand in 1840, the European population was still only a few hundred. But the New Zealand Company had acquired Maori land and was selling it off to settlers from England and Scotland, many of them first-time farmers. They cleared, plowed, and planted grass to graze sheep. Many lived harsh, isolated lives, but early North Island settlements also ran into problems with local Maori due to suspect land deals.

Mass settlement had to wait for the discovery of gold in Otago in the 1860s. Miners then flocked from the Australian and Californian fields. Towns sprang up overnight as thousands flooded Otago, then the West Coast, then the Coromandel in the North Island. Mostly young and overwhelmingly male, these settlers were mainly English, but Irish, German, and Chinese miners also worked the fields. Their families followed, along with traders, domestics, and others. When the gold ran out, other mines provided some work, and on the West Coast the coal mines attracted many Welsh miners.

In the north of the North Island, the mighty kauri forests attracted settlers in the 1870s. The wealth of this fine timber provided one of New Zealand's main exports, and the rugged workers who felled the logs lived in remote camps. In addition, up to 20,000 gum diggers fossicked in the swamps for kauri gum, the fossilized sap of the trees used in varnish and linoleum. ∎

Greymouth & Hokitika

Most Coasters make their home in the central West Coast, particularly in the main town of Greymouth and nearby Hokitika. Greymouth celebrates its heritage at Shantytown and provides interesting side trips to old mining towns, while Hokitika is the greenstone capital of New Zealand—a great place to stock up on crafts.

A gathering of the Black Powder Musket Club, a shooting group from the Greymouth region.

Greymouth

🅰 Map p. 217

Visitor information

✉ Herbert & Mackay Sts.

☎ 03/768-5101

www.greydistrict .co.nz

Greymouth

The largest town and unofficial capital of the Coast, Greymouth was home to the large Maori settlement of Mawhera when the first European, Thomas Brunner, arrived in 1846. The township was laid out in 1865 at the time of the great gold rush, but in later years coal, forestry, and fishing assumed greater importance.

At the mouth of the Grey River, this utilitarian town has just enough interest for an overnight stay and is the western terminus for the famous TranzAlpine, the country's most stunning rail journey over the Southern Alps from Christchurch.

The **History House Museum** has pioneer displays focusing on mining as well as a large collection of historical photos. Family-run **Monteith's Brewing** was proudly the Coast's own until bought by the large DB Breweries, which tried to close the flagship Greymouth plant. A public outcry forced its reopening, and now brewery tours run every day.

In the mornings, keep an eye out for the eerie rolling clouds of The Barber, the icy wind as sharp as a barber's razor that blows in from the Grey Valley.

The big attraction around Greymouth is **Shantytown,** 7 miles (11 km) south of town off SH6. This replica of an 1880s gold town with its Wild West streetscapes and stores does a good job of re-creating the era. Steam-train rides, gold panning, and forest walks are part of the experience.

To the east of Greymouth, **Lake Brunner** is the West Coast's largest and prettiest lake and is reached by turning off SH7, which runs northeast through the Grey Valley. In the valley about 16 miles (25 km) from Greymouth, **Blackball** is an old coal- and gold-mining town, famous for the miners' strike of 1908 that helped form the country's union movement. Wander around the old town or have a beer in the historic **Formerly the Blackball Hilton** *(26 Hart St.),* which had to amend

its name after a run-in with the hotel chain. It is the sole pub left in a town that once had dozens.

Farther north at pretty **Reefton,** the highway heads inland to Christchurch via Lewis Pass. Named for its gold-bearing quartz reefs, this historic hamlet has a **museum** on the highway east of town crammed with goldfield relics. Reefton's visitor informa-

Greenstone

New Zealand greenstone is a dark green nephrite jade, different from the lighter and rarer jadeite prized in China. Greenstone rocks are usually found in rivers, particularly the Arahura and Taramakau Rivers near Hokitika, but also on West Coast beaches. The hard stone was the major source of trade between the North and South Island Maori, used for adzes, clubs, and ornament. The Maori name for the South Island is Te Wai Pounamu or "the greenstone water," and under the Treaty of Waitangi the Ngai Tahu tribe was given controlling rights to West Coast pounamu in 1997.

tion center *(tel 03/732-8391)* has details on good short walks to old gold and coal mines.

Hokitika

The town of Hokitika, 25 miles (40 km) south of Greymouth, boomed in the gold rush of

History House Museum
Visitor information
- ✉ Gresson St.
- ☎ 03/768-4028
- 🕐 Closed Sat.–Sun. in winter
- 💲 $
www.history-house.co.nz

Monteith's Brewing
- ✉ Turamaha & Herbert Sts.
- ☎ 03/768-4149
- 💲 $$$ (tours)
www.monteiths.co.nz

Shantytown
- 🗺 Map p. 217
- ✉ Rutherglen Rd., Paroa
- ☎ 03/762-6634
- 💲 $$–$$$$
www.shantytown.co.nz

Hokitika
- 🗺 Map p. 217
Visitor information
- ✉ Tancred St.
- ☎ 03/755-6166
www.hokitika.org

**West Coast
Historical
Museum**

Tancred St.

☎ 03/755-6898

An artisan carves greenstone in Hokitika.

1864. Thousands flocked from the Australian goldfields and dozens of ships ran aground as they entered the treacherous harbor at the mouth of the Hokitika River. By late 1866, Hokitika was one of the biggest towns in New Zealand, and in 1873 it became the capital of New Zealand's short-lived Westland Province.

Hokitika fell into decline in the 20th century, leaving wide streets lined with grand buildings, detailed in the "Hokitika Heritage Walk" brochure. For a good walk, head south of the visitor information center to the **Gibson Quay** heritage area on the river, along to the **Sunset Point Lookout** at the river mouth, then on to the wild beach.

The town's many fine souvenir, art, and craft stores are the main attraction, featuring everything from glassblowing to *paua* (abalone shell) jewelry, but Hokitika is noted for its greenstone-carving workshops. This is one of the best places in New Zealand to stock

up on all kinds of souvenirs.

The **West Coast Historical Museum** in the neoclassical Carnegie Building once housed the town library, funded by American philanthropist Andrew Carnegie.

Hokitika is noted for its greenstone-carving workshops. This is one of the best places in New Zealand to stock up on all kinds of souvenirs.

It now has good displays on greenstone, gold, and the pioneering past. Visitors can pan for gold at the miner's hut in the museum's courtyard.

Thousands flock to Hokitika's **Wild Foods Festival** (*www.wild foods.co.nz, tickets required*) in March for bush food and West Coast specialties, ranging from

Bush Food

Perhaps eating fried wasp larvae isn't your thing, but what about earthworm truffles? If so, you should head to the Wild Foods Festival, where these tasty items can be had, right alongside sautéed lamb's tails. You can also sample bunny burgers, fish eyes, wasp-larva-flavored ice cream, an entire catalogue of testicles, deep fried dolphin, and possum paté. You'll have to line up for these delicacies. Held in March, the festival brings about 20,000 people to the town of 3,000.

violence and mysticism in the lives of the Maori. The Okarito Lagoon is a major wading-bird sanctuary, home to the rare white heron, or *kotuku*. Nearby rain forests also host the Okarito brown kiwi. **Okarito Nature Tours** (*tel 03/753-4014, $$$–$$$$*) has popular eco-kayaking tours and kayak rentals.

For a fine two-hour round-trip walk, head south along the beach until you come to the footbridge and then back via the inland trail, which climbs to **The Trig** for spectacular views of Aoraki/Mount Cook on a clear day. ■

Maori carving in Hokitika

wild boar to whitebait patties, deep-fried grasshoppers, and *huhu* grubs (a Maori delicacy of roasted larvae).

South of Hokitika, the gold town of **Ross** (*03/755-4077, www.ross.org.nz*) produced the Honourable Roddy nugget, the largest gold nugget found in New Zealand at 6.19 pounds (2.81 kg). It was presented to King George V for his 1911 coronation, only to be subsequently melted down to make a royal tea set. Ross's renovated **Miner's Cottage Museum** (1885) has gold and pioneering exhibits.

About 22 miles (35 km) south of Ross, turn off SH6 to **Okarito** on the coast. This isolated settlement on a wild beach was the setting for Keri Hulme's Booker Prize–winning novel *The Bone People,* about the legacy of

Glaciers & South

Franz Josef and Fox Glaciers are far and away the West Coast's main attractions. Lying in the rugged Westland National Park, these are among the world's most accessible glaciers. The road then follows the coast south to lonely Jackson Bay, passing Haast and the turnoff for the road to Wanaka and Queenstown.

Sunset over Lake Matheson and Mount Tasman

Westland Tai Poutini National Park

🏔 Map p. 217

Visitor information

✉ Main Rd., Franz Josef

☎ 03/752-0796

Westland Tai Poutini National Park

The West Coast's biggest attraction, Westland Tai Poutini National Park extends from the highest mountains of the Southern Alps to the beaches of the West Coast, encompassing skyscraping peaks, forests, lakes, and rivers. Above all it is famous for its glaciers—Franz Josef and Fox—which are easily accessible just off the main road and surprisingly close to the sea.

Lying on the western flank of the Southern Alps, the park is split by the Alpine Fault, which pushes up a chain of peaks over 10,000 feet (3,000 m), including Aoraki/Mount Cook. The West Coast's prolific rainfall dumps huge volumes of snow on the mountains, feeding 140 glaciers in the park, but Franz Josef and Fox Glaciers are by far the biggest and contain two-thirds of the park's glacial ice.

These two colossal brutes of blue-tinged ice push down

through rain forest at the lower reaches, but the glaciers are receding. Over the last one hundred years they have retreated more than 1.5 miles (2.5 km), despite modest advances in the 1990s.

The park centers on the two small villages of Franz Josef and Fox, on the highway close to their respective glaciers. Both have a range of accommodations but can be overrun in peak times, when it pays to book ahead. Walking trails lead close to the glaciers for viewing, but to get onto the ice, you must take a guided walk or, even better, a helicopter to land on the glaciers' upper reaches. A host of flight-seeing planes buzz overhead on busy days.

Franz Josef Glacier

This 7.5-mile-long (12 km) glacier was named after the Austro-Hungarian emperor by German geologist Julius von Haast (1822–1887), who explored the area in 1865. The terminal face of this steep, 7,000-year-old glacier lies 12 miles (19 km) from the sea, but originated from an older glacier that did reach the sea.

Glacial melt feeds the Waiho River, and a 45-minute walk along the river from the parking lot leads to within a few hundred feet of the glacier. The area close to the glacier is roped off, with good reason. Tons of ice can crash down from the melting terminal face without warning. To get up close to the glacier, take one of the guided walks,

which can be booked in the village and which equip you with ice-climbing gear to venture onto the glacier.

Franz Josef village is 3 miles (5 km) from the glacier parking lot. The **National Park Visitor Centre** has informative displays on the park and a full rundown on the area's attractions and services.

Fox Glacier

Fox Glacier doesn't get the same volume of visitors as Franz Joseph, even though the walk is easier and the views no less

EXPERIENCE:
Heli-skiing

One of the most amazing ways to experience the majesty of the Southern Alps is to ski the remote upper snowfields. If you are an intermediate or advanced skier, a chopper will take you to the top of some amazing slopes, pick you up at the bottom, and then take you to the next pristine slope.

Companies offering this ultimate skiing experience include **Harris Mountains Heli-Ski** (Shotover & Camp Sts., Queenstown, tel 03/442-6722, & 99 Ardmore St., Wanaka, winter only, tel 03/443-7930, www.heliski .co.nz) and **Wilderness Heliskiing** (Alpine Guides, Mount Cook Village, tel 03/435-1834, www.heliskiing.co.nz).

awesome. This 8-mile-long (13 km) glacier drops 8,500 feet (2,600 m) on its journey down the Southern Alps and was named after William Fox (1812–1893), a former prime minister of New Zealand.

From the parking lot, a 30-minute walk leads along the

valley to the end of the track and the terminal face of the glacier, just 130 feet (40 m) away. Guided walks onto the river of ice can be booked in Fox Glacier village, 5 miles (8 km) from the glacier parking lot.

The lake is 4 miles (6 km) from Fox Glacier, just off the road to **Gillespies Beach,** which presents another side to the national park with its black-sand and quartz-pebble beach. A seal colony is a 1.5-hour walk along the coast.

The rustic Café Nevé at the foot of Fox Glacier

The **Fox Glacier Informa-tion Centre** (39 Sullivans Rd., tel 03/751-0044) in town provides visitor information. Fox Glacier is smaller than Franz Josef, but has a quiet alpine village feel and a selection of places to stay.

West of the village, **Lake Matheson** reflects Aoraki/Mount Cook and Mount Tasman in its mirror waters for a classic postcard shot on a clear day. A lakeside boardwalk leads though forest and takes about an hour for the circuit. A good café at the parking lot serves breakfast and lunch.

South to Haast

From Fox Glacier, the highway south goes past the **Copland Valley,** where the well-known **Copland Track** heads over an alpine pass through the Southern Alps to Mount Cook Village. This hazardous crossing is only for experienced mountaineers, but hikers can go as far as the **Welcome Flat Hut** and its hot pools, a seven-hour walk.

The road hits the coast again at **Bruce Bay,** where a good fish-and-chips caravan sets up in summer. Farther south on the

Paringa River, the **Salmon Farm Café** (tel 03/751-0837) serves fresh salmon overlooking the fish ponds. Anglers can catch their own quinnat salmon or trout in **Lake Paringa** a few miles on.

After traveling inland, the road heads back to the sea at **Knights Point,** with a fine view from the lookout, and then follows the coast most of the way to Haast.

Haast, 74 miles (118 km) from Fox Glacier, is the southern entry/ exit point for the West Coast. Though no destination in itself, Haast has cheaper accommodations than the often full glacier towns. Haast's multiple personality comprises three towns: Haast Junction, where SH6 meets the

INSIDER TIP:

When traveling between Fox Glacier and Haast, a 40-minute walk through lowland forest just past Lake Moeraki brings you to Munro Beach, one of New Zealand's most perfect small beaches.

—BRENT OPELL,
National Geographic Field Scientist

road to Jackson Bay, Haast Beach along that road, and the main Haast Township, 1 mile (2 km) along the SH6 to Wanaka. The excellent **Haast Visitor Centre** (*SH6 & Jackson Bay, tel 03/750-0809*) at the junction has the lowdown on the West Coast if this is the start

of your explorations.

The last lonely stretch of the Coast lies along the 31-mile (50 km) dead-end road to **Jackson Bay.** Originally a whaling station, Jackson Bay had plans in 1875 to attract settlers and

EXPERIENCE:
How to Visit the Glaciers

An organized tour of the glaciers is a must if you're in the area.

Franz Josef Glacier Guides offers glacier walks, ice climbing, and heli-hikes.
  SH6, Main Rd.
  Franz Josef Glacier
  Tel 03/752-0763
  www.franzjosefglacier.com
  $$$$

Fox Glacier Guiding has many tour choices. In addition to hikes on the glacier, it has a heli-trek up to Chancellor Dome.
  SH6
  Fox Glacier
  Tel 03/751-0825
  www.foxguides.co.nz
  $$$$

develop as a port to rival Hokitika, but these hopes eventually buckled under the town's isolation and perpetual downpours. Today, Jackson Bay is a sleepy fishing village noted for lobsters and whitebait.

From Haast, SH6 heads inland up the Haast River and over the **Haast Pass** to Wanaka and Queenstown. This spectacular route has a number of short walks and scenic stops as it makes the journey through Mount Aspiring Park (see p. 254). ∎

Glaciers

Like most glaciers around the world, the Fox and Franz Josef Glaciers are retreating, though, strictly speaking, some part of a glacier is always on the move downhill, borne on meltwater. High snowfalls on the Southern Alps in the 1980s actually saw the terminal face of these glaciers advance for a decade, but it was a movement against the long-term trend.

Glaciers are formed by snow that accumulates in a basin, repeatedly freezes and thaws and becomes compacted—now called névé. As more snow and ice are dumped at the head of the glacier, névé compacts further under pressure, until it becomes blue-tinged glacial ice.

Fox and Franz Josef are temperate glaciers, sitting on ground that is warmer than in most other glacial regions. This results in meltwater at the base of the glacier, which lubricates it and helps it slide down the mountain. Friction further increases melting and basal sliding, and the West Coast glaciers move very rapidly compared to other glaciers—up to 13 feet (4 m) per day.

Composed of layers of ice, glaciers also move internally, some layers moving faster

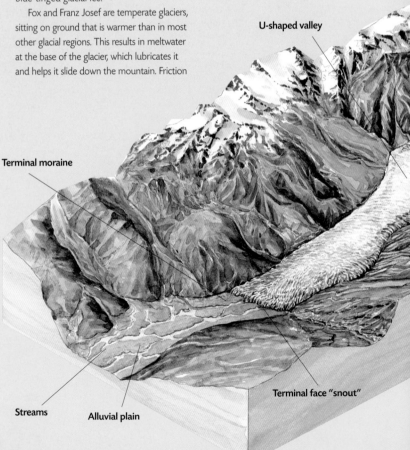

U-shaped valley

Terminal moraine

Terminal face "snout"

Streams

Alluvial plain

than others, helping the glacier flow slowly like a viscous fluid. The top layer of about 65 feet (20 m) at Fox and Franz Josef moves faster, but is also more brittle and prone to cracking, resulting in deep crevasses or *bergschrunds*. This makes glaciers dangerous to travel over, for heavy snowfall can cover the crevasses, creating snow bridges that collapse under a climber's weight.

Glaciers gouge out the rock beneath as they travel, collecting large amounts of debris, from huge boulders to fine powder ground out by the constant abrasion. Called "rock flour," this powder is responsible for the milky gray color of glacial rivers. The debris carried by glaciers is deposited at their sides as mounds of rock and gravel called moraines.

Glaciers grind out deep U-shaped valleys over time, as opposed to V-shaped river valleys. Many of the great lakes in the South Island are the product of ancient glaciers that have long since melted. ■

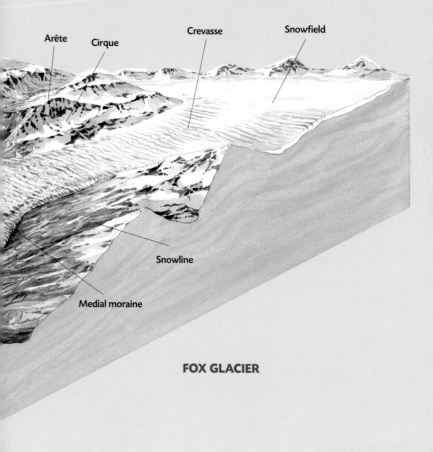

Arête Cirque   Crevasse   Snowfield

Snowline

Medial moraine

FOX GLACIER

From lakes, majestic mountains, and stunning desert landscapes in Otago to stately Victorian cities along the coast and fascinating wildlife nearby

Otago

Autumn reaches Arrowtown in Central Otago.

Otago

Otago encompasses extremes, from historic Dunedin on a fertile coast teeming with sea life, to the interior's surreal, desertlike landscapes stretching out in the shadow of the Southern Alps.

The jewel in Otago's crown is Queenstown, the country's number-one resort, located on a stunning glacial lake backed by the majestic alps. In summer, this impossibly pretty alpine town teems with tourists and activities, from the adventurous to the pedestrian, but the international party continues in winter when skiers flock to the surrounding mountains.

Queenstown makes a great base for exploring Central Otago, but for those who like their resorts a little less frenetic, Wanaka also has a glorious lake and snow-tipped-peak views.

Most of the Southern Alps in Otago are encompassed by Mount Aspiring National Park, a gorgeous wilderness area with the country's best alpine hiking trails, notably the Routeburn Track. The northern part of the park contains the Haast Pass, the gateway through the mountains to the West Coast via a stunning highway drive.

From Queenstown, you can venture into the heart of Central Otago, to the plateau desert with its craggy schist landscapes, a favorite backdrop for some iconic Kiwi paintings. Farther from the sea than any other region of the country, it is the hottest in summer, the driest and the coldest in winter. The harsh but beautiful landscapes were not immediately amenable to settlement, but old goldfield towns attest to a 19th-century boom.

It was gold that first brought large numbers of Europeans to New Zealand, and the richest fields were those in Central Otago, discovered in 1860–1861. Miners flocked from all over the world, towns sprang up overnight, and though the rush lasted little more than a decade, in that time New Zealand's population doubled.

Much of the wealth flowed through Dunedin, which became the country's largest and grandest city. Banks, offices, hotels, and im-

A woodworker shapes a piece in Oamaru, home to many artisans.

posing churches of stone quickly replaced the dwellings of the early settlers, pious Presbyterians who fled religious persecution in Scotland to build a new world based on farming.

Dunedin still clings to its Scottish roots, and much of its early legacy remains. The most southerly of New Zealand's main population centers, it is a gracious city strung out on hills around a fine harbor. It makes an interesting stop, though it lies off the Christchurch–Queenstown–Milford tour-bus route—which is part of its appeal.

The biggest attraction for many lies outside the city on the Otago Peninsula. Combining pastoral views with glorious seascapes, the peninsula is also home to an accessible array of wildlife—giant albatrosses, seals, penguins, and sea lions can be viewed in their natural habitat.

Those journeying along the coastal route can also visit Oamaru, a sleepy town that once had grander dreams and, like Dunedin, boomed during the gold rush. A delightful historic precinct preserves grand Victorian buildings carved of white stone, and penguins also call Oamaru home. ∎

NOT TO BE MISSED:

Dunedin & Otago Peninsula

The 1860s gold rush made Dunedin the largest and grandest city in New Zealand, and though long since surpassed, it remains an elegant city with fine Victorian architecture. On the city's doorstep, the Otago Peninsula is one of the best places in the country to see marine wildlife.

Statue of poet Robert Burns in The Octagon, Dunedin

Dunedin

🗺 Map p. 234

Visitor information

✉ 48 The Octagon Central

☎ 03/474-3300

www.cityofdunedin.com

Dunedin

Sprawled across steep hills at the end of a long harbor, Dunedin is the South Island's second city, with a population of 118,000. A gracious mix of stately buildings, museums, and art galleries, Dunedin is easy to negotiate but large enough to hum with urban life, much of it provided by the University of Otago and its 20,000 students.

Maori settled the coastal areas of Otago from around 1100, fishing the rich local waters and hunt-ing moa. The first whalers and sealers arrived in the 1820s, but the colony really took off when settlers from the Free Church of Scotland landed in 1848.

Led by Capt. William Cargill (1784–1860) and the Reverend Thomas Burns (1796–1871), they first called the settlement New Edinburgh, but then opted for Dunedin, an old Scots name for Edinburgh. These pious folk set about creating a new vision of their homeland, but were soon engulfed by the gold rush in 1861.

Fortunes were made overnight from the Central Otago goldfields, and the riches flowed through Dunedin. By the 1880s, Dunedin was New Zealand's showpiece. Imposing banks, churches, hotels, and company buildings sprang up in the central city and cable cars plied the hilly streets.

Though the gold eventually ran out and Dunedin was supplanted by upstart northern cities, wealth from farming fed the city right through to the mid-20th century. However, Dunedin is enjoying something of a revival, thanks largely to the university, which has tripled in size since the 1980s and stimulates the city's artistic and nightlife scenes. Tourism is also a growing industry, with visitors attracted by the city's charms and easy access to wildlife on the nearby Otago Peninsula.

The **Otago Museum** is a great place to spend a rainy day. This

INSIDER TIP:

The First Church and its associated museum on Moray Place often put on classical music concerts at midday on Fridays, usually for free.

—MARCUS TURNER,
National Geographic Contributor

fine museum has one of the country's largest collections, spread over three floors. The Tangata Whenua Gallery has impressive Maori artifacts, dominated by an

World's Steepest Street

It may not be Mount Everest, nor even Aoraki/Mount Cook, but the climb to the lofty heights of Baldwin Street is one of Dunedin's must-do attractions.

Baldwin Street is the steepest street in the world, according to the *Guinness Book of Records*, with a gradient of 1 in 2.86 (or 19 degrees), which means that for every 2.86 feet (0.87 m) traveled horizontally, it goes up 1 foot (0.3 m). The title is disputed, however, by Canton Avenue in Pittsburgh, among other contenders.

Regardless, this is one mighty steep street, and the climb to the top will get the lungs working overtime, even though it is only a short thoroughfare off North Road. Every summer up to a thousand competitors run up and down it in the Baldwin Street Gutbuster race.

Otago Museum
✉ 419 Great King St.
☎ 03/474-7474
www.otagomuseum.govt.nz

enormous war canoe and superbly carved meetinghouse panels. Other Polynesian and Melanesian cultures are well represented, European settlement and maritime history are covered, and natural history exhibits detail South Island geology and bird life, including the giant moa, penguins, and the nearly extinct takahe.

Just a few blocks away, housed in an impressive modern building,

Dunedin Walking Tour

A stroll through Dunedin's inner-city streets reveals grand churches, banks, and office buildings from the 19th-century days when this was the country's biggest city and its financial hub.

Thanks to the fabulous wealth of the 1860s gold rush, Dunedin boasts the largest concentration of Victorian architecture in New Zealand. The heart of the city is the leafy **Octagon ❶**, lined with historic buildings and restaurants spilling onto the sidewalk. Start your walk at the tourist office *(48 The Octagon Central, tel 08/474-3300),* housed in the imposing Italianate **Municipal Chambers** (1880), and then continue next door to the neo-Gothic **St. Paul's Cathedral ❷**, the city's Anglican cathedral, completed in 1919.

At the front of the church, the **statue of Robert Burns,** dedicated to Scotland's favorite son, is an icon for a city that clings to its

Scottish roots. The poet was the uncle of the Reverend Thomas Burns, founding father and religious leader of the early settlement.

From The Octagon, head south past the public art gallery along Princes Street for one block, then turn left on Moray Place. On the next corner at Burlington Street, the sky-piercing **First Church ❸** was built by the first settlers from the Free Church of Scotland. Completed in 1873, it was designed by Robert Lawson, the architect responsible for much of Dunedin's majestic neo-Gothic architecture.

From the church, head down Burlington Street and turn right onto Dowling Street with its fine Victorian streetscape. Buildings include the wedge-shaped **Commerce Building** and the **Imperial Building** (1906) on opposite corners, **Garrison Hall** (1877) displaying a bulging royal coat of arms carved in stone, and imposing **Milford House ❹** (1883), once the New Zealand Clothing Factory, now an art gallery.

At the top of the street, turn left onto Princes Street, the main thoroughfare and commercial district of the old city. Solid financial houses here include the **National Bank of New Zealand** (rebuilt 1912) and the old headquarters of the **Bank of New Zealand** (1883). Across Rattray Street, the

Dunedin's First Church

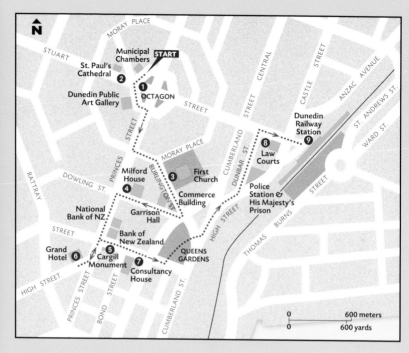

North

STUART
MORAY PLACE
Municipal Chambers **START**
St. Paul's Cathedral ❷
Dunedin Public Art Gallery
❶ OCTAGON
STREET
CENTRAL STREET
CASTLE STREET
ANZAC AVENUE
ST. ANDREWS ST.
Dunedin Railway Station
PRINCES STREET
MORAY PLACE
CUMBERLAND STREET
DUNBAR ST.
❽ Law Courts
❾
WARD ST.
RATTRAY
DOWLING ST.
Milford House ❹
BURLINGTON ST.
❸ First Church
Commerce Building
Police Station & His Majesty's Prison
HIGH STREET
STREET
National Bank of NZ.
Garrison Hall
STREET
Bank of New Zealand
THOMAS BURNS
Grand Hotel ❻
Cargill Monument
QUEENS GARDENS
HIGH STREET
PRINCES STREET
BOND STREET
STREET
❼ Consultancy House
CUMBERLAND ST.

0 _____ 600 meters
0 _____ 600 yards

Cargill Monument ❺ (1863) is dedicated to Dunedin's founder, Capt. William Cargill, and opposite on Princes Street is the **Grand Hotel** ❻, the city's finest when built in 1883 and still functioning as a hotel and casino.

Walk east along Rattray Street, past historic buildings such as **Consultancy House** ❼ (1908) on Bond Street, built in the American style of the time and hailed as a skyscraper, despite being only seven stories high. The area lies on reclaimed land, much of the fill provided by the 30 feet (9 m) lopped off the top of Bell Hill, on which First Church stands.

Turn left through Queens Gardens and then veer right onto High Street. On the corner of Dunbar Street, the old **Police Station** (1896) and **His Majesty's Prison** (1896) next door carried out colonial justice dispatched by the impressive **Law Courts** ❽ (1899) around the corner on Castle Street.

Past the Law Courts, the magnificent **Dunedin Railway Station** ❾ is the city's most photographed building. Built in Flemish Renais-

✚ See area map p. 234
► The Octagon
⟷ 1.5 miles (2 km)
⏱ 2 hours
► Railway Station

NOT TO BE MISSED:

The Octagon • First Church • Law Courts • Dunedin Railway Station

sance style in 1904, its ornate facade of stone and concrete earned New Zealand Railways architect George Troup the nickname "Gingerbread George." Be sure to see the impressive tile-lined booking hall inside. Upstairs in the station, the **New Zealand Sports Hall of Fame** (tel 03/477-7775, www.nzhalloffame.co.nz, $) has well-presented memorabilia devoted to Kiwi sporting heroes. ∎

Dunedin Public Art Gallery

🅰 Map p. 239

✉ 30 The Octagon

☎ 03/477-4000

www.dunedin.art .museum

Otago Settlers Museum

✉ 31 Queens Gardens

☎ 03/477-5052

💲 $

www.otago.settlers .museum

Olveston

✉ 42 Royal Ter.

☎ 03/477-3320

💲 $$–$$$

www.olveston.co.nz

Yellow-Eyed Penguins

The yellow-eyed penguin is the largest temperate-climate penguin and is unique to New Zealand. Named for the yellow stripe extending back from the eye, the bird has the Maori name *hoihoi* (noise shouter). The penguins nest from the Banks Peninsula near Christchurch to Stewart Island. The best chances of seeing them are on the Otago Peninsula and the Catlins in Southland.

Among the rarest penguins, they seek secluded nests in coastal forest, but habitat destruction and introduced animals, such as dogs, threaten their survival. They can live up to 20 years, but after hatching around November, the chicks head north in February or early March for winter feeding, traveling up to 300 miles (500 km) in a dangerous journey that sees only 15 percent survive.

the cornerstone of the **Dunedin Public Art Gallery** is its European art collection, one of the best in New Zealand, featuring many of the great masters. While the paintings may not be major works, they span from the Renaissance to impressionism. The collection also includes extensive early and contemporary New Zealand art. Exhibits rotate and only a fraction of the collection is displayed at any one time.

Not art but history is the focus of the **Otago Settlers Museum,** dedicated to Dunedin's founding fathers. Divided into two sections—transportation and settlers—it has vintage cars, penny farthings, an early Dunedin cable car, and Josephine the steam engine. The photographs and exhibits from early Dunedin hold the most interest. The Otago goldfields, maritime history, and city development are covered. One gallery is lined to the ceiling with portraits of the early Scottish settlers: a grim parade in black and white and sepia.

Also of historic interest is **Olveston,** a grand mansion built between 1904 and 1906 for merchant David Theomin in Jacobean style and inhabited by the Theomin family until donated to the city in 1966. Lavishly furnished with a fine art collection, it is a fascinating record of Edwardian privilege and luxury. One-hour guided tours of the house must be booked in advance, or you can walk through the formal gardens.

More Places to Visit in Dunedin

Dunedin lays claim to the world's steepest street, according to the *Guinness Book of Records* (see sidebar p. 237). Baldwin Street was once serviced by a cable car, but the only way up now is to walk. It's about 2 miles (3 km) northeast of the Octagon off North Road.

Tours of the **Cadbury chocolate factory** *(280 Cumberland St.,* tel 03/467-7967, www.cadbury.co.nz /cadburyworld/visit.htm, $$–$$$) have long attracted chocolate fans to Dunedin. The visits include a movie and a look at the factory, culminating at the chocolate waterfall. Of course, there's a retail outlet and a visitor center. Reservations are advisable for the 75-minute tours. Shorter, cheaper tours go on Sundays and holidays,

Graduates stand outside of the University of Otago, New Zealand's oldest (1869).

but the factory is closed then.

Speights Brewery *(200 Rattray St., 03/477-7697, $$–$$$)* also has tours. These 90-minute visits include a sampling of beers from one of the country's oldest breweries. Locals fill up containers from the tap outside on Rattray Street, not with beer but with pure spring water piped from

beneath the brewery and used in the brewing process.

The **University of Otago** on Cumberland Street near the Otago Museum comes alive at the end of February during Orientation Week when "scarfies," as students are called because of the scarves they once wore, flood the city. The **Registry Building** (1879) with its distinctive clock tower is one of the city's architectural gems and lies on the banks of the quaintly named Water of Leith.

St. Kilda Beach, 2.5 miles (4 km) south of The Octagon, is as fine a stretch of white-sand surf beach, backed by dunes, as you will find in any city, though a wetsuit will come in handy. Adjoining **St. Clair** is one of the city's most popular beaches and has saltwater pools with a café. The Hydro pub right on the shore is also a popular place for a drink.

Tunnel Beach Walkway, 5 miles (8 km) southwest of the city, is a fine 40-minute round-trip walk along clifftop farmland down to the beach, accessed by a hand-hewn tunnel.

The Dunedin Railway Station is the starting point for the **Taieri Gorge Railway** *(tel 03/477-4449, www.taieri.co.nz, $$$$$),* a spectacular journey along the Taieri River Gorge through the rugged mountains of Central Otago. A diesel engine pulls 1920s carriages daily to Pukerangi *(4 hours round-trip)* and to Middlemarch *(6 hours round-trip)* on Fridays and Sundays in summer. Middlemarch is at the start of the 95-mile (150 km) **Central Otago Rail Trail** *(www.centralotagorailtrail.co.nz)* to

Clyde, the most popular bicycling route in the country. Touring bicycles can be rented in Dunedin, Middlemarch, and other towns in Central Otago.

Otago Peninsula

This once volcanic peninsula on Dunedin's doorstep is a crooked claw of inlets and bays, steep sheep-covered hills, and a castle, no less. It has become Dunedin's prime attraction, offering easy access to seaborne wildlife, such as albatrosses, penguins, seals, and sea lions.

Tour operators have the wildlife franchise and, apart from seals, wildlife is elusive unless you take tours. Even on your own, the peninsula makes a wonderful day trip with fine scenery.

The trip begins on the outskirts of Dunedin on the Portobello Road, which wends around the eastern edge of Otago Harbour just a few feet from the water. The first stop of interest, **Glenfalloch Woodland Gardens** *(430 Portobello Rd., tel 03/476-1775)*, has lovely gardens surrounding an 1871 homestead. Walks lead through grounds planted with exotic trees, rhododendrons, azaleas, magnolias, and fuchsias.

About halfway along Portobello Road, the tiny township of **Portobello** has a few accommodation and dining options. Just outside town, the **Marine Studies Centre** *(Hatchery Rd., tel 03/479-5826, www.marine.ac.nz, $–$$)*, part of the University of Otago research center, has educational displays on the peninsula's rich marine life and a small aquarium for viewing local species.

At the entrance to Otago Harbour, Taiaroa Head is home to the **Royal Albatross Centre** *(tel 03/478 0499, www.albatross.org.nz, tours $$$–$$$$$)*, one of the biggest attractions on the peninsula. The

Children enjoy an interactive exhibit at the Royal Albatross Centre.

world's only mainland breeding colony of the huge royal northern albatross can be visited on walking tours, the best way to see these magnificent birds. The optimal viewing season, December to February, is also the main tourist season, when reservations are advisable. Tours are also the only way to take in the Taiaroa Head fort.

Pilots Beach, just before the center, is a favorite spot for seals to fish and sun themselves on the rocks. After sunset, little blue penguins make their way up the beach here to their nests.

Along the road to Taiaroa Head, tour operators offer more eco-viewing experiences. **Monarch Wildlife Cruises** (tel 03/477-4276, www.wildlife.co.nz, $$$$$), has popular one-hour boat tours from a dock at Wellers Rock to see albatrosses, seals, and other species. They also offer half- and full-day cruises from the Dunedin harbor, returning by bus.

Penguin Place (Harrington Point Rd., tel 03/478-0286, $$–$$$$$) just off Portobello Road, is a private reserve that protects the endangered yellow-eyed penguin (see sidebar p. 240). Tours must be reserved. Penguin breeding grounds can be viewed at close range via a series of camouflaged tunnels and blinds on farmland leading to the beach.

Seals, penguins, and sea lions also visit ocean beaches such as **Allans Beach** and **Victory Beach** on the peninsula's east coast, but access is difficult unless you go on a tour.

Heading back to Dunedin from Portobello, take the inland Highcliff Road for fine views of the peninsula. Turn off onto Sandymount Road for an excellent short walk (20 mins. one-way) to **The Chasm,** high above the windswept vertical cliffs with views across the peninsula.

Another popular walk (40 mins. one-way) goes from the end of Seal Point Road to pretty

INSIDER TIP:

It's possible to see the royal albatrosses for free if you head toward Taiaroa Head in the early evening, when the adults are returning to their nests.

—MARCUS TURNER,
National Geographic Contributor

Sandfly Bay, where yellow-eyed penguins nest and can be viewed from blinds. Sea lions also visit.

Farther along Highcliff Road is the turnoff to **Larnach Castle** (Camp Rd., tel 03/476-1616, www.larnachcastle.co.nz, $–$$$$$), once the residence of William Larnach (1833–1898). Typical of the era's entrepreneurs, Larnach amassed a fortune through land deals, farming, and timber and flaunted it at his Gothic "castle."

A visit to this impressive mansion is on every itinerary. The grounds have a café, and you can take a self-guided tour of the castle. For overnight stays, the stables have been converted into well-appointed, themed rooms with breathtaking views. ■

North Otago

On the main highway between Dunedin and Christchurch, Oamaru is the prime attraction, with nesting penguins and a delightful historic precinct crammed with grand buildings. On the way, don't miss the bizarre Moeraki Boulders, half-buried in the beach.

The Corinthian columns that support the Bank of New South Wales are made from local limestone.

Oamaru
⬛ Map p. 234
Visitor information
✉ 1 Thames St.
☎ 03/434-1656
**www.visitoamaru
.co.nz**

Oamaru

Oamaru, 71 miles (114 km) north of Dunedin, boomed with the gold rush and then the frozen-meat trade, resulting in a legacy of grand buildings carved from local limestone. Imposing banks, churches, warehouses, and even an opera house are relics of embarrassing wealth that has long since left this sleepy town of 13,000.

Roughly halfway between Dunedin and Christchurch on SH1, the town's historic charms, and its waddling penguins, have transformed this rural center into a growing tourist destination.

The heart of the historic town lies around the old waterfront at the southern end of Thames Street, the main street. The Port of Oamaru closed in the 1970s, leaving intact Victorian streetscapes that have been revived as the **Oamaru Historic Precinct** around Tyne and Harbour Streets. Cafés, craft and antique stores, markets, and artisans' studios cater to a steady stream of visitors.

INSIDER TIP:

Oamaru is a hidden gem and well worth a stop. The refurbishment of the historic quarter is fostering a wonderful revival of traditional crafts.

—COLIN MONTEATH,
National Geographic Photographer

Brochures from the tourist office outline the many fine buildings in the historic precinct and along Thames Street. Neoclassical designs and Corinthian columns predominate, and the town's easily worked, creamy white limestone helped create some superbly ornate architecture.

The story of Oamaru stone is told at the **North Otago Museum,** itself housed in a grand stone building that was once a library, the Oamaru Athenaeum. Photographs and artifacts elucidate colonial times and a display on Janet Frame, one of New Zealand's best loved writers, highlights her 14 years in Oamaru, the setting for her early novels.

Housed in a spectacular former bank building, the **Forrester Gallery** has rotating exhibits and a permanent collection of local artists' work.

Oamaru's little blue penguins prove that tourism can drive conservation. The birds used to nest under houses and were once considered a pest. Those pre-ecotourism days have long since passed, and the little blues are now a town icon. They can be seen waddling ashore every evening at the old quarry, now the **Oamaru Blue Penguin Colony,** where a viewing platform, visitor center, and daytime nest-viewing facility have been erected.

Rare yellow-eyed penguins (see sidebar p. 240) also nest at Bushy Beach, on the southern outskirts of town. The Department of Conservation has built blinds for viewing the shy penguins, which are easily spooked, so stay out of sight or take a tour arranged through the tourist office. ∎

North Otago Museum
- ✉ 60 Thames St.
- ☎ 03/434-1652
- wwwnorthotago museum.co.nz

Forrester Gallery
- ✉ 9 Thames St.
- ☎ 03/434-1653
- www.forrestergallery .com

Oamaru Blue Penguin Colony
- 🅰 Map p. 234
- ✉ Waterfront Rd.
- ☎ 03/433-1195
- 💲 $$–$$$
- www.penguins.co.nz

Moeraki Boulders

One of the more curious geological sights in New Zealand, the Moeraki Boulders are 49 miles (78 km) from Dunedin, just off the highway from Oamaru. Almost perfect spheres of gray rock up to 10 feet (3 m) across lie scattered along the beach, half buried in the sand.

Southern Maori tradition has it that the boulders are food baskets washed overboard from the ancestral canoe, *Te Araiteuru,* which brought Maori to New Zealand from the homeland, Hawaiki. Geologists say they are concretions, a product of the crystallizing process of mudstone. They usually form before the surrounding sedimentary rock, making them harder and less subject to weathering. You can see boulders still emerging from the cliff as it erodes.

A café above the beach caters to the throngs, and around the bay along the fine beach lies the pretty village of Moeraki, once a whaling station.

Central Otago

In the shadow of the Southern Alps, the schist plateau of Central Otago is a harsh, eerie landscape of craggy mountains, arid grasslands, and lakes, one of the finest scenes on the glorious New Zealand canvas. At the foot of the alps on a superb lake, Queenstown is the country's number-one alpine resort, Wanaka is a smaller version, and other old gold towns and wineries wait to be explored.

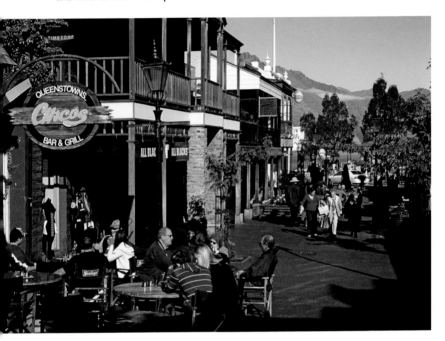

Cafés and souvenir shops in popular Queenstown

Cromwell to Alexandra

Most of Central Otago is sparsely populated, but it was not always so, for in the 1860s thousands flocked to the Central Otago goldfields, the richest in the country and the driving force for the early settlement of New Zealand.

The richest fields were around Cromwell, and a number of points of interest lie around Cromwell and Alexandra. Old gold mines and ghost towns dot the hills, lakes nestle in dammed valleys, and wineries now flourish where tent cities once housed miners.

Cromwell is a town with a split personality. Its modern town center is a car-free pedestrian precinct. On its outskirts are the Wild West streetscapes of Old Cromwell Town, a collection of a dozen historic buildings relocated after the town was flooded by the Clyde Dam in 1993. Tourist shops, art galleries, and a café make this a pleasant stop.

Cromwell also has plenty of accommodations when other towns are booked in summer. The **Cromwell information center** *(47 The Mall, tel 03/445-0212)* has a wealth of information on wineries and old mining settlements to explore in the surrounding district.

A five-minute drive south of Cromwell, the struggling hamlet of **Bannockburn,** self-dubbed the "heart of the desert," has a clutch of old buildings from its gold-mining past. Just north of town, a road leads past the Mt Difficulty Winery to the old sluices where miners dug in what was Otago's richest alluvial goldfield. A signposted walking trail provides a glimpse of goldfield history.

Seventeen miles (27 km) north of Cromwell off SH8, a steep gravel road leads to the ghost town of **Bendigo** and beyond to the old gold diggings. Bendigo is now nothing more than a couple of old stone cottages, part of the nearby winery, but there is an interesting walk through the old goldfields, 1.8 miles (3 km) farther up a steep road. The desert countryside with its schist rock outcroppings is dramatic.

Just past the Clyde Dam as you head toward Alexandra, the pretty village of **Clyde** is an oasis of greenery in the desert, with European trees and well-watered lawns. Historic stone buildings line the main street, with cafés for a lunchtime stop and a selection of accommodations. A fine walking trail follows the town's emerald green river; you can also bike along the **Central Otago Rail Trail,** which terminates here.

Alexandra is an attractive, well-stocked town and a good base from which to explore the

---

EXPERIENCE:
Central Otago Rail Trail

Bicycling is a surprisingly popular way to tour New Zealand, given all those mountains, but for the hill shy, the mostly flat Central Otago Rail Trail is an excellent way to explore the goldfield and desert country of Central Otago.

The rail line from Dunedin to Clyde opened up the region, but the trains stopped running in 1963. The track from Middlemarch to Clyde was ripped up in the 1980s, but eventually it became the 95-mile (150 km) Central Otago Rail Trail in 2000.

A tourist steam train *(tel 03/477-4449, www.taieri.co.nz, see p. 241)* still runs from Dunedin to Middlemarch, a scenic way to reach the eastern end of this popular bicycling route. Touring bicycles can be hired in Clyde, Alexandra, Middlemarch, and Dunedin, or tour operators run all-inclusive tours. For a comprehensive rundown on the trail and operators, see the excellent website *www.centralotagorailtrail.co.nz.*

---

surrounding area. Wineries and orchards abound, the town has good craft stores, and the interesting museum at the **information center** *(22 Centennial Ave., tel 03/448-9515)* highlights the gold rush and screens wonderful archival footage on Otago.

A pleasant walk along the river leads to historic **Shaky Bridge,** where there's a winery café just below the **Alexandra clock,** a

Queenstown

▣ Map p. 234

Visitor information

✉ Shotover &
    Camp Sts.
☎ 03/442-4100

www.queenstown-vacation.com

Queenstown Regional Visitor Centre

✉ 38 Shotover St.
☎ 03/442-7935

Skyline Gondola

✉ Brecon St.
☎ 03/441-0101
$ $$$$

www.skyline.co.nz

town icon set into the rugged hills as you come into town from the north. You can walk to the clock for fine views or drive to the **Tucker Hill Lookout** for the best views of the whole valley.

....

The best place to start a tour of Queenstown is on the Skyline Gondola. Offering the most remarkable view of The Remarkables and the town, the scenery is breathtaking year-round.

....

Queenstown

On the shores of serene Lake Wakatipu, set against jagged mountains aptly named The Remarkables, Queenstown is the South Island's most famous tourist destination in one of its most stunning settings.

Those who knew it when it was a quaint village groan, and the local press forever bemoans inappropriate development, but visitors flock to this well-endowed alpine resort.

Walk down to the lake through The Mall past just a handful of the town's many restaurants and bars and you'll hear a dozen languages spoken. In summer, tour operators offer every activity and tour imaginable, the restaurants buzz, and the bars go bang till the wee hours. With well over a million visitors a year, Queenstown Lakes is the fastest-growing region in New Zealand. This is a resort for all seasons

and tastes, from luxury indulgences to backpackers' bars, from summer hiking to winter skiing, from superb scenery to adventure pursuits.

The best place to start a tour of Queenstown is on the **Skyline Gondola,** which shuttles up Bob's Peak through a gash in the pine trees to a viewing terminal with a buffet restaurant and café. Offering the most remarkable views of The Remarkables and the town, the scenery is breathtaking year-round. The adventurous can tandem paraglide back down, the foolhardy can bungee jump, the fun-loving can take a second chairlift at the top

Gold Fever

Queenstown attracted Maori greenstone hunters before William Gilbert Rees established the area's first farm in 1860. But sheep farming was soon forgotten when shearers discovered gold in the Shotover River in 1862. Even Rees' homestead was designated a goldfield, but he did well from the rush, selling meat to miners and shipping supplies and gold across the lake.

Named after Queen Victoria, Queenstown and neighboring Arrowtown were deluged with fortune seekers, but the area declined as the gold petered out. By 1900, Queenstown's population had dwindled to 200, and it would have to wait until the 1970s for a new gold rush—tourism.

and luge back, and the energetic can walk the trails.

The national bird, the kiwi, can be viewed at the small **Kiwi & Bird life Park** next to the gondola terminal on Brecon Street. The rare and not-so-rare birds here include the kea, weka, kakariki parrots, and the endangered black stilt. Headsets explain the birds and natural features. Maori

The Remarkables. A skating rink is open to the public outside of ice-hockey practice times.

Not much is left of Queenstown's historic buildings, but **William's Cottage,** on the corner of Marine Parade and Earl Street, is Queenstown's oldest building, dating from 1864. Restored to its original condition, it is now a shop.

Underwater World (tel

**Kiwi &
Birdlife Park**

✉ Brecon St.
☎ 03/442-8059
💲 $$$$$
www.kiwibird
.co.nz

TSS Earnslaw

✉ Real Journeys
   Steamer Wharf,
   Beach St.
☎ 03/249-7416
💲 $$$–$$$$
www.realjourneys
.co.nz

Paragliding high above Queenstown and Lake Wakatipu

displays and conservation shows round out the tourist experience.

Another impressive way to view Queenstown is aboard the **TSS Earnslaw,** the coal-fired Lady of the Lake, departing from the refurbished steamer wharf on Beach Street. Check out the engine rooms and historic displays. Some cruises also take in the **Walter Peak Farm,** a homestead and farm in a scenic lakeshore setting.

A short walk from the city center, **Queenstown Gardens** provide a pleasant stroll around flower plantings and pine stands, with fine views of the lake and

03/442-8538, $), part of the Kawerau jet boat complex on the jetty at the end of The Mall, is a submerged observatory where you can see giant trout through cloudy glass.

For many visitors, Queenstown is all about the many activities that can be booked at the busy visitor information center or at one of the other booking offices on Shotover Street.

Looking for something to do? How about bungee jumping, jet boating, white-water rafting, river surfing, canyoning, skydiving, hang gliding, parasailing, kayaking, or horseback riding? Or else take a fishing, walking, winery, 4WD, or mountain-bike tour, to name but a few.

Scenic flights buzz the heavens for the best views of the South Island's mountains, lakes, and fjords, and in winter heliskiing is offered. Queenstown is also a good place in which to arrange tours to other parts of the South Island if you are short of time, particularly to Milford Sound by bus or air.

EXPERIENCE:
Routeburn Track

Many rate this Department of Conservation (DOC)-designated Great Walk as the best in the country, but with numbers of hikers rivaling the Milford Track, it must be booked ahead from October to April, preferably online (www.doc.govt.nz, search for Routeburn) before you come to New Zealand. The track offers a wide variety of terrain and the country's best alpine scenery through Mount Aspiring and Fiordland National Parks. It is normally a three-day walk from Glenorchy, near Queenstown, to The Divide in Fiordland, traversing beech forest and alpine terrain. Transportation to the start can be arranged in Queenstown, as well as from The Divide at the other end. Off-season, the four DOC huts on the trail cannot be reserved, but there are two campsites.

For information on walks around town, and some of the world's finest hiking nearby in the Southern Alps including the Routeburn, Greenstone, and Rees-Dart tracks (see opposite), head to the informative Department of Conservation (DOC) office on Shotover Street.

Around Queenstown

While development drives Queenstown, delightful **Arrowtown,** 13 miles (21 km) northeast, clings to its goldfield heritage. In a valley backed by rugged mountains, shade trees line peaceful streets, and many original buildings from the gold rush survive. The picturesque main drag, Buckingham Street, is lined with eateries and tourist stores, for Arrowtown is a popular day trip out of Queenstown. A selection of lodgings offer an alternative retreat.

Gold discovered in the Arrow River in 1862 built the town, which had a population of 7,000 at its peak. The **Lakes District Museum & Information Centre** (49 Buckingham St., tel 03/442-1824) fields visitor queries, has displays on the town's gold-mining history, and rents out gold pans so you can try your luck in the river.

Off the top end of Buckingham Street, the old gold diggings are worth a look. Here you'll find the **Chinese settlement,** with its original stone buildings and displays on the hardships faced by Chinese miners. Good walking trails lead through the hills around town, and a 4WD track heads all the way up into the mountains to remote **Macetown,** with ghost town relics in a scenic gorge.

The quickest route from Queenstown to Arrowtown is the main highway SH6, but take Gorge Road out of Queenstown for the scenic back route with its glorious blend of pastoral and alpine views. It passes Arthur's Point, 3 miles (5 km) north of Queenstown, where jet boats hurtle along the Shotover River for a thrilling ride.

Another detour off the back road leads to **Coronet Peak** ski area, where lifts operate in summer for sightseers and mountain bikers. Nearby is **Skippers Canyon,** an old gold-mining area and adventure playground for bungee jumping and white-water rafting. Note that most rental car companies forbid travel on the scenic but hair-raising Skippers Road. Also on the back road, the **Millbrook Resort** (Malaghans Rd., tel 03/441 7000) has a world-class golf course, resort facilities, and expensive accommodations.

Queenstown's and the world's first bungee-jumping site was at the old **Kawarau Bridge,** 14 miles (23 km) northeast of town on SH6. **A. J. Hackett Bungy** (see sidebar p. 252; tel 03/442-4007, $$$$$) offers the complete bungee experience with a variety of jumps and a bungee museum in a modern complex. This is the place to jump, and you'll have plenty of onlookers, including clapping tour groups who delight in the bravery, or foolishness, of others.

Two miles (3 km) east on SH6, **Gibbston Valley Winery** (tel 03/442-6910) is the best-known of the area's many vineyards and one of the pioneers of Central Otago's renowned Pinot Noir. Informative half-hour vineyard and wine cellar tours ($$) with tastings are held throughout the day. Pick up a copy of the Central Otago Wine Map to put together a winery tour in the region.

A scenic road heads 25 miles (40 km) west of Queenstown

Ski Wonderland

Queenstown is New Zealand's premier ski resort in winter, with four main ski areas nearby. Coronet Peak is the closest to Queenstown, 11 miles (18 km) away with runs suitable for all abilities and weekend night skiing. Noted for its views, The Remarkables field is 50 minutes away by car or bus and is good for beginner to intermediate skiers. Cardrona, on the way to Wanaka, is a high-altitude field noted for dry snow and wide slopes, while Treble Cone, close to Wanaka, is the largest and particularly good for advanced skiers and boarders.

to **Glenorchy,** hugging Lake Wakatipu all the way. In a glorious setting, this tiny outpost is a hive of adventure activity with jet boating, kayaking, and skydiving.

Glenorchy is also the place to arrange a ride to the trailheads of some of New Zealand's finest hikes, including the famed **Routeburn Track** (see sidebar opposite), a three-day hike through the alps to Fiordland.

Many walkers choose to return via the **Greenstone** or **Caples Tracks,** or these two can be combined as a four- to five-day loop walk through forested valleys, ending at Lake Wakatipu. Alternatively the more demanding **Rees-Dart**

Adrenaline Rush

Though extreme activities and sport are now found around the globe, New Zealand popularized adventure tourism and still proudly calls itself the "adrenaline capital of the world."

Jet boating on the Shotover River, Queenstown

Bungee jumping, based on Vanuatu land divers who jump off a wooden tower with vines tied to their ankles, originated in New Zealand with A. J. Hackett, a Kiwi daredevil who grabbed headlines by plunging off the Eiffel Tower in 1987. A year later, Hackett founded the world's first commercial bungee operation at the Kawarau Bridge just outside Queenstown (see p. 251). The Kawarau site is still the most popular place to jump, but you can also throw yourself off the Queenstown gondola (see p. 248), 335-foot-deep (102 m) Skippers Canyon (see p. 251), or a host of other places.

Watersports

Jet boating, though relatively sedate by comparison, is another New Zealand invention. Self-taught engineer Bill Hamilton developed a boat that would negotiate the swift, shallow rivers of the South Island. Using a hydro-jet engine, which shoots out water through a steerable nozzle, the jet boat scoots along the water with most of the hull above the surface, reducing drag and allowing for ferocious speeds with high maneuverability. The design has plenty of commercial applications, but in New Zealand the jet boat is best known as a thrill-seeking craft, hurtling passengers along rivers all over the country. Queenstown is known as the home of the jet boat, with rides offered on the Shotover and Kawarau Rivers.

With so many swift-flowing rivers, New Zealand has taken to white-water rafting like a duck to, well, white water. The Shotover and Kawerau Rivers are popular sites, as are the Rangitata and Buller Rivers, also in the South Island. The North Island has plenty of rafting as well, the most exciting being the Kaituna River near Rotorua, which goes over 10-foot (3 m) Okere Falls.

Riding the rapids gave rise to black-water rafting, an inner-tube ride through a cave at Waitomo on the North Island (see p. 112). Operators have since dreamed up a number of other caving adventures, including underground rock climbing and rappelling.

Zorbing & More

Jumping off mountains and out of planes is another New Zealand specialty, usually while strapped to someone who knows what he or she is doing. Parasailing off Bob's Peak in Queenstown (see p. 248) is a spectacular way to see the town, while Wanaka and Taupo are noted tandem skydiving centers.

Variations on a theme include bungee swinging, rap jumping, and river sledging. Inventive New Zealanders have also come up with Zorbing (rolling downhill in a giant plastic ball outside Rotorua; see p. 126) and Fly by Wire (Queenstown again) where you pilot a flying machine strung on a wire between two hills.

Track takes in valley and alpine pass terrain.

Those not walking or flying to Fiordland and Milford Sound will have to take the SH6 south from Queenstown through dramatic desert landscapes before heading over the Southern Alps. At the bottom of Lake Wakatipu on SH6, **Kingston** was once the railhead and port for the steamers that plied the lake to Queenstown. Past glories can be relived on the **Kingston Flyer** *(tel 03/248-8848, Oct.–April, $$$$–$$$$$)* a restored steam train than runs twice a day through the scenic gorge to Fairlight, 9 miles (14 km) south, with bus connections to Queenstown.

Wanaka

Lying on a superb lake backed by snow-topped mountains, with skiing in winter and a host of activities year-round, Wanaka is inevitably described as a mini-Queenstown. With plenty of accommodations and restaurants but without Queenstown's crowds, Wanaka's setting seems even more spectacular, if only because development doesn't compete so volubly with nature.

Nevertheless Wanaka (pop. 5,000) is a rapidly growing town, attracting residents as well as visitors to the shores of **Lake Wanaka,** popular for boating, fishing, waterskiing, and swimming from the beach in the town center.

Wanaka is also the gateway to the hiking trails and snowy peaks of Mount Aspiring National Park and to the **Treble Cone** and **Cardrona** ski fields, 12 miles (20 km) and 21 miles (34 km)

away, respectively. Cardrona is near the tiny township of the same name, along the high-altitude 73-mile (117 km) Cardrona Road between Wanaka and Queenstown, a scenic alternative to SH6.

Wanaka has myriad activities, from lake cruises and jet boating to white-water rafting, kayaking, and canyoning (which involves rappelling down waterfalls, among other thrills). Aerial activities include flight-seeing, skydiving, and paragliding operating out of Wanaka's

Cinema Paradiso

For a unique dinner and movie experience, try Wanaka's **Cinema Paradiso** *(Ardmore St., 03/443-1505).* It has a full menu that can be enjoyed before the film, during intermission, or afterward. Paradiso offers a variety of unique seating, including vintage couches, an upholstered car, and seats from a Chinese airplane.

busy little airport. There you'll also find the **New Zealand Fighter Pilots Museum** *(tel 03/443-7010, www.nzfpm.co.nz, $–$$).* Based around its fine collection of World War II fighter planes, the museum provides a fascinating insight into the history of aviation. Its collection features in the **Warbirds over Wanaka** air show, held every second year.

On the way to the airport toward Cromwell, **Puzzling World** *(tel 03/443-7489, www.puzzlingworld .com, $)* on SH6 is a quirky attraction

Wanaka
⬛ Map p. 234
Visitor information
✉ Lakefront, Ardmore St.
☎ 03/443-1233
www.lakewanaka .co.nz

featuring skewed buildings, optical illusions, and a maze for family fun.

Mount Aspiring National Park

Straddling the Southern Alps, Mount Aspiring National Park's mix of remote wilderness, alpine meadows, and forested river valleys makes it heaven for hikers and mountaineers.

Part of the Te Wahipounamu South West New Zealand World Heritage site, the park is centered around the jagged peak of Mount Aspiring near Wanaka. To the west and south, the park extends into

INSIDER TIP:

The huts in New Zealand's national parks are comfortable and clean and make multi-day hikes an absolute must for outdoor enthusiasts.

—CHRISTY RIZZO,
Adventure Travel Expert

the dense forest of Fiordland, while its north includes Haast Pass, the gateway to the West Coast.

The southern reaches closer to Queenstown are the best-known to hikers. Here you'll find the famous **Routeburn Track** (see sidebar p. 250) and other popular trails. However, the most visited part of the park is the northern end, where SH6 cuts through from Wanaka to the West Coast.

Glacier-carved valleys punctuate rugged peaks, and **Mount Aspiring,** known as New Zealand's Mat-

terhorn because of its steep faces, is the only peak over 10,000 feet (3,000 m) outside Aoraki/Mount Cook National Park. Rugged high-altitude terrain, snow, and ice make much of the park accessible only to experienced mountaineers, but alpine guides in Wanaka offer mountaineering courses for beginners, as well as guided hikes.

Hikes in the Matukituki Valley near Wanaka provide easy access to the central reaches of the park. A one-hour drive from Wanaka, the **West Matukituki Track** goes from the parking lot to the Aspiring Hut (two hours) for great views of the valley; experienced hikers can climb to the top of the valley (3.5 hours more).

The more popular **Rob Roy Track** branches off the West Matukituki Track, 15 minutes from the parking lot, and is an easy three- to four-hour walk that crosses the river before climbing through a gorge into beech forest, then into an alpine valley with views of the Rob Roy Glacier.

For information on the park, contact DOC offices in Wanaka and Queenstown, the Haast Visitor Centre (*SH6 & Jackson Bay Rd., tel 03/750-0809*) at Haast township on the West Coast, or the Makaroa Visitor Centre (*tel 03/443-8374*), in the park on SH6 between Wanaka and Haast.

Haast Highway

The road from Wanaka to the West Coast is one of the most spectacular drives in the country, with a number of scenic stops on the way. It crosses the Haast Pass, the most southerly of the

Rippon Vineyard overlooking Lake Wanaka

three main passes through the Southern Alps.

The main highway, SH6, heads north of Wanaka to **Lake Hawea** and its tiny resort town, then along the lake shore and across The Neck, a narrow strip of land separating Lake Hawea from the northern end of Lake Wanaka. The lake and mountain scenery on this stretch is superb, but the real jaw-dropper begins when the road enters the wilderness of Mount Aspiring National Park.

The road leaves Lake Wanaka and follows the Makaroa River upstream to the **Makaroa Visitor Centre,** where interesting displays highlight the natural and human history of the area. Park staff can fill you in on points of interest and walks just off the highway.

Six miles (10 km) from the visitor center, an easy 30-minute round-trip walk leads over a river swing bridge and through beech forest to the scenic **Blue Pools,** where trout feed at the mouth

of Blue River. A little farther along, at **Cameron Creek,** a 15-minute round-trip walk to a viewing platform is rewarded with views of the valley and surrounding mountains.

For the best views, the **Haast Pass** at 1,847 feet (563 m) marks the highest point on the road. A trail leads up above the timberline to a viewpoint with stunning vistas. This more demanding walk takes just over an hour.

Over the pass, the highway follows the Haast River to the coast and passes a number of waterfalls, including the high **Thunder Creeks Falls,** an easy five-minute walk from the road through forest. A couple of miles farther, **Pleasant Flat** is indeed a pleasant picnic/camping area next to a mountain stream.

The road continues its descent to the coast, and halfway between Haast Pass and Haast township, the **Roaring Billy Waterfall** can be reached by a fine 25-minute round-trip walk through lush forest and tree ferns. ■

Stunning fjords, peaks, and lakes give way to rich farmland ringed by scenic coastline and anchored by Stewart Island.

Fiordland & Southland

A hiker on the Milford Track takes in MacKay Falls.

Fiordland & Southland

Below Dunedin and the 45th parallel, the deep south is about as close as most people get to Antarctica, to which New Zealand was once attached. Fjords, lakes, hiking trails, and the surprising beauty of remote Stewart Island make it worth the trip.

Mount Tutoko, Fiordland's highest peak

Ancient glaciers carved the primordial landscape of Fiordland, leaving behind the famous fjords of the southwest coast, which shelter from the sea behind alpine peaks and dense forest. To the east, on the leeward side of the mountains, the wilderness yields to glacial lakes and the spreading grasslands of Southland sheep farms.

The region's main lure, Milford Sound, draws a road train of tour buses daily from Queenstown, and with good reason. A boat trip through the fjord and its cathedral of peaks is stunning, but getting there is half the reward. The road to Milford travels through the most accessible reach of New Zealand's most imposing wilderness: Fiordland National Park, the largest in New Zealand and part of Te Wahipounamu (the South West New Zealand World Heritage site). Thousands of visitors flock to the park each year, most staying overnight in the small resort of Te Anau on the scenic lake of the same name, the last town before Milford Sound.

Much smaller Manapouri township on another fine, eponymous lake is the departure point for Doubtful Sound, the only other fjord to have regular tours. Apart from these two fjords, the rest of the park remains virtually untouched. It has, however, some of the greatest hiking trails in the country, among them the Milford Track and the Kepler Track.

NOT TO BE MISSED:

A cruise across Lake Te Anau to see the glowworms of Te Anau Caves 262

Stunning viewpoints and walks along the Milford Road 262–263

Awe-inspiring Milford Sound, by water or air 266–267

Milford Track, the "finest walk in the world" 264–265

Less visited but no less beautiful Doubtful Sound 267

Natural splendor of the scenic Catlins Drive 272–273

Kiwi spotting on Stewart Island 274–275

Rakiura Track, a superb hike around Stewart Island 275

While Fiordland is wilderness untamed, neighboring Southland has been formed by the human hand. Scottish settlers labored in a harsh domain to create rich sheep farms, and their heritage lives on. The names of towns and rivers mimic Scotland, and the Scottish "burr" lingers on in the voices of Southland.

Southland's prime attraction is the coastal route through the Catlins between Invercargill and Dunedin. Scenery ranges from rugged coastline and sweeping beaches to inland forest and waterfalls. This remote southeast corner of the South Island also teems with sealife, notably seals, sea lions, dolphins, and penguins, including the rare yellow-eyed penguin.

Lying below the South Island, a remote last stop before Antarctica, is one last delightful surprise. Stewart Island, just across the Foveaux Strait, is washed by remarkably warm currents. It has sheltered coves, white-sand bays, and forests with giant ferns: the last jewel in New Zealand's abundant crown. ∎

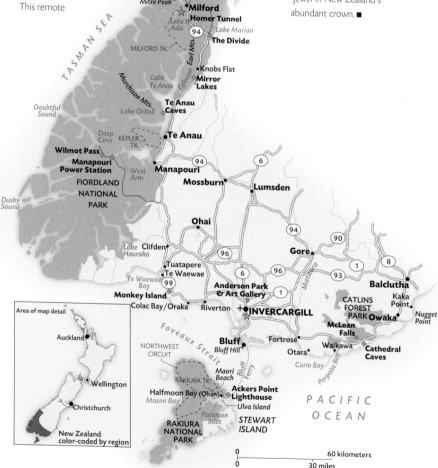

Fiordland

The scenery doesn't get any more spectacular than in remote, brooding Fiordland, with its rugged mountains and stunning fjords. Fiordland National Park encompasses almost the whole region, including famed Milford Sound, one of the country's main tourist attractions, and Doubtful Sound. On the edge of the park, the resort towns of Te Anau and Manapouri accommodate visitors.

A mother-and-daughter team kayaks Doubtful Sound, Fiordland National Park.

Fiordland National Park

◭ Map p. 259

Visitor information

✉ Lakefront Dr., Te Anau

☎ 03/249-7924

Fiordland National Park

The wildest, wettest, and most remote part of New Zealand is also its most breathtaking. Drenched by the roaring forties, the winds that blow unimpeded across the Southern Ocean, the park's towering mountains are rent by water—sea, lakes, and rivers.

Most visitors to the park seek the famed beauty of Milford Sound, accessed by road from Te Anau along one of the world's most scenic routes. The other main destination is Doubtful Sound, a quieter introduction to the fjords.

Formed by tectonic folds and faults in the earth's crust dating back 500 million years, the park is composed mostly of gneiss, schist, and granite rock. Glaciers have gouged the landscape over the last two million years to create deep U-shaped valleys, many of which have filled with water to become fjords and inland lakes.

Forest clings to steep rock faces, growing in only a thin layer of soil, and tree avalanches are common. Beech forest dominates and is often moss draped. Above 3,300 feet (1,000 m), tussock grass and alpine flowers grow.

The park is home to threatened birds, including the colorful, flightless takahe, once thought extinct until discovered in the Murchison Mountains, above Te Anau Caves, in 1948. The last few remaining kakapo, another flightless Fiordland parrot, have been transferred to offshore islands away from predators. Yellow-crowned parakeets, robins, kaka, and long- and short-tailed bats thrive in the Eglinton Valley. Many other species exist throughout the park, including the brown kiwi.

Marine life here is unique. High rainfall creates a layer of fresh water on the sounds. Stained by tannins washed down from the forest, this layer gives the calm waters a black, glassy surface that restricts light to all but the top 130 feet (40 m) of the sounds. Subtropical, cool-water, and deep-water fish all thrive closer to the surface among the sponges and rare black coral trees.

Mountains and water dominate Fiordland. Milford Sound averages 255 inches (650 cm) and more than 180 days of rain a year. Sunshine is a rarity, but the fecund weather is dramatic

when rain pours down and dozens of waterfalls ribbon along sheer mountain sides.

Te Anau & Manapouri

Lying next to Lake Te Anau, the South Island's largest lake, the township of Te Anau is the jumping-off point for Milford Sound in Fiordland National Park. This prosperous, pretty resort is a mini-Queenstown, well supplied with hotels and restaurants, as well as lake and mountain views.

**Fiordland/
Te Anau**

🗺 Map p. 259

Visitor information

✉ Lakefront Dr.

☎ 03/249-8900

EXPERIENCE:
Hiking Fiordland

Fiordland National Park contains three of the country's nine Great Walks (see p. 19) and a number of merely grand ones. The Great Walks are Department of Conservation (DOC)–controlled trails encompassing the best hiking in the country. In summer, they must be booked at DOC offices or, better, online well in advance at www.doc.govt.nz.

The Milford Track is best known (see pp. 264–265) but the Routeburn Track (see p. 250) competes as one of the finest walks in New Zealand. It is normally walked from Glenorchy, near Queenstown, to The Divide in the park, but it can also be done in reverse. The other Great Walk is the Kepler Track, a three- or four-day strenuous loop walk from Lake Te Anau to Mount Luxmore and Lake Manapouri.

Though a pleasant base, Te Anau has few attractions in itself, but the **Te Anau Wildlife Centre** (tel 03/249-7924) on the Manapouri Road, a ten-minute walk

Te Anau Caves

 Map p. 259

✉ Real Journeys,
    Visitor Centre,
    Lakefront Dr., Te
    Anau

☎ 03/249-7416

$ $$$–$$$$$

**www.realjourneys
.co.nz**

from the Department of Conservation visitor center, displays a wide range of native birds, including the rare takahe, and provides an informative introduction to the species found in the national park.

The town's top diversion lies across the lake. The stunning **Te Anau Caves** are reached by a lake cruise, then a walking tour

13 miles (21 km) south in an even more stunning location on Lake Manapouri. This resort serves mostly to take the visitor overflow from Te Anau and is the departure point for trips to Doubtful Sound (see p. 267).

Te Anau to Milford

If the Milford Track is the finest

Hermit of Milford

One of the highlights of the Milford Track is the high Sutherland Falls, named after Donald Sutherland (1843–1919), the hermit of Milford Sound. An adventurer, the young Scotsman was in turn a fisherman, soldier under Garibaldi in Italy, and merchant seaman before jumping ship in New Zealand. He fought in the Maori wars, was a sealer and gold prospector before setting sail in a small boat from Dunedin with his dog in 1877. He

landed in Milford Sound and made it his home for 40 years. Living a hermit's life for many years, he prospected and explored the region, but ended his isolation in 1890 when he married Elizabeth Samuels in Dunedin. They built the Chalet at Milford, catering to summer visitors after the opening of the Milford Track. A taciturn host, Sutherland was a self-proclaimed authority on the region, which he regarded as his own realm.

---

that follows the pounding water of an underground stream. The stream originates in Lake Orbell high above in the Murchison Mountains before disgorging into Lake Te Anau. Named Te Anau-au or "cave of swirling waters" by early Maori visitors, the caves were not rediscovered until 1948.

Cave tours end with a boat ride through a darkened grotto illuminated by hundreds of twinkling glowworms (see sidebar p. 112). Outside the North Island, this is the best chance to see these luminescent, web-spinning worms.

Te Anau's sister town is the small hamlet of Manapouri, just

walk in the world, then the 74-mile (119 km) road from Te Anau to Milford Sound must be the world's finest drive. As the road approaches the park's great hulking mountains, you'll find yourself craning your neck from your vehicle to take them all in.

A number of short walks and viewpoints along the road allow you to fully appreciate the splendor of the terrain. An excellent first stop out of Te Anau, tranquil **Mirror Lakes** at the 36-mile (58 km) mark is easily reached via a boardwalk next to the road. The small lakes reflect the towering

Earl Mountains for a postcard photo opportunity.

The Eglinton Valley broadens out at the tiny settlement of **Knobs Flat** (39-mile/63 km mark) and the stretch of road known as the **Avenue of the**

Disappearing Mountains, so called because of the optical illusion that seems to make the string of mountains on either side disappear. Farther on, the **Lake Gunn Nature Walk** leads through red beech forest for a pleasant 45-minute round-trip walk.

The Divide (52-mile/85 km mark) is the lowest pass through the Southern Alps at 1,740 feet (531 m) and is a trailhead for one of New Zealand's greatest walks, the **Routeburn Track** (see p. 250). For a taste of the splendor of the Routeburn, you can walk just part of it to **Key Summit** (*2–3 hours round-trip*) for stunning views.

Just past The Divide is the turnoff to **Hollyford Valley** along a gravel road. One mile (1.6 km) in is the trail to **Lake Marion Falls.** A

lovely 20-minute walk leads from a suspension bridge to the gantry overlooking the falls; another steep one-hour walk leads to alpine **Lake Marion. Gunns Camp,** 11 miles (17 km) from the main road, has a store and small museum crammed with local detritus.

The main road continues to climb to **Homer Tunnel** (63-mile/101 km mark). After nearly 20 years of construction, the 4,170-foot (1,270 m) tunnel opened in 1954 and made Milford Sound accessible to the world.

The road then descends sharply through the Cleddau Valley to the last stop before Milford, **The**

Mitre Peak mirrored in Milford Sound at sunset

Walk: Milford Track

Billed in New Zealand as the "finest walk in the world," the Milford Track from Lake Te Anau to Milford Sound takes in all the diverse glory of Fiordland—lakes, alpine meadows, mountains, glaciers, and fjords.

From late October to late April, this popular walk can be done only in one direction as a four-day, three-night hike. Just 40 independent hikers are allowed on the track each day, so reserve months ahead *(starting July 1, www.doc.govt.nz).*

Bookings are not required in winter, but snow and avalanches make it suitable only for experienced alpine hikers. Be well equipped for all weather (expect plenty of rain) and carry all your own food. You overnight in basic huts, which have cooking facilities, toilets, and bunks with mattresses. The track can also be done as a pricey guided walk *(www.ultimatehikes.co.nz)* with food and transportation, staying at more luxurious huts with hot showers.

Start with a cruise on Lake Te Anau from Te Anau Downs to **Glade Wharf ❶**. The track crosses a swing bridge over the Clinton River,

Hikers cross a wire bridge at Giant Gate Falls on the Milford Track.

then follows the river through beech forest for an hour to **Clinton Hut ❷**, the first overnight stop and the end of a short Day One.

The walk begins in earnest on Day Two *(10 miles/16 km, 6 hours)* with a gradual climb following the river to **Clinton Forks** at a confluence with the river's North Branch. The trail follows the West Branch through mostly beech forest for about 40 minutes to a lake. A short side trail leads to **Hirere Falls.**

Back on the track, you walk through a narrowing valley between granite walls before you comes to grassy flats with glorious views north to Mackinnon Pass. The trail climbs through changing higher altitude flora before reaching **Mintaro Hut ❸** at the end of the second day.

Day Three *(8.7 miles/14 km, 6 hours)* resumes the climb to Mackinnon Pass for two hours to the fine views around **Mackinnon Memorial ❹**, dedicated to Quintin Mackinnon, who explored the area in 1888. It is then 20 minutes to the highest point of the track at the **Pass Day Shelter** (3,507 feet/1,069 m).

The walk then drops 3,180 feet (970 m) over 5 miles (8 km) past the Roaring Burn stream, a spectacular stretch of waterfalls and cascades. From the private Quintin Hut, a side trip *(1.5 hours round-trip)* leads to the impressive **Sutherland Falls ❺**, the highest falls in New Zealand, dropping 1,904 feet (580 m) over three leaps. Back at Quintin Hut, it is a one-hour walk to **Dumpling Hut ❻** for a well-earned rest on the third night.

Day Four *(11 miles/18 km, 6 hours)* descends gradually from the hut to the Arthur River and down to the historic **Boatshed,** where a swing bridge crosses the river. It is then 20 minutes to **MacKay Falls ❼** and Bell

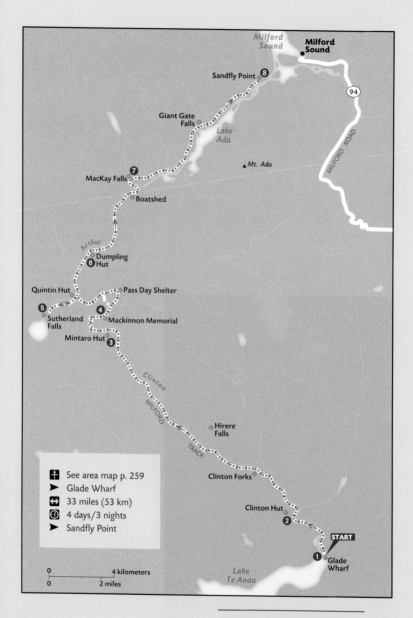

Milford
Sound

**Milford
Sound**

94

Sandfly Point ◆ ❽

Giant Gate
Falls ◆

*Lake
Ada*

MILFORD ROAD

▲ *Mt. Ada*

MacKay Falls ◆ ❼

◆ Boatshed

Arthur

◆ Dumpling
❻ Hut

Quintin Hut ◆   ◆ Pass Day Shelter

❺   ❹

◆ Sutherland
Falls   ◆ Mackinnon Memorial

Mintaro Hut ◆ ❸

Clinton

MILFORD

◆ Hirere
   Falls

TRACK

Clinton Forks ◆

Clinton Hut ◆
❷

START

❶
◆ Glade
   Wharf

*Lake
Te Anau*

✚ See area map p. 259
▶ Glade Wharf
↔ 33 miles (53 km)
🕐 4 days/3 nights
▶ Sandfly Point

0 _____ 4 kilometers
0 _____ 2 miles

Rock. The track presses on to Lake Ada and **Gi-ant Gate Falls,** where a shelter makes an ideal lunch stop. About an hour past the lake you reach the flat end of the valley and **Sandfly Point ❽**, where boats take you on the short last leg to Milford Sound. ∎

NOT TO BE MISSED:

Mackinnon Memorial • Suther-land Falls • MacKay Falls • Giant Gate Falls

Milford Sound Boat Tours

Real Journeys

☎ 03/249-7416

🕐 2.5 hrs. & overnight

💲 $$$$$

www.realjourneys .co.nz

Red Boats

☎ 03/441-1137

🕐 2.25 hrs.

💲 $$$$$

www.redboats.co.nz

Chasm. An excellent 15-minute round-trip walk leads through glorious moss-draped forest to a waterfall and deep gorge carved out by the river.

Milford Sound

Milford Sound is Fiordland's, if not New Zealand's, most famous attraction. Though not the largest of the fjords, its peaks make it the most spectacular. **Mitre Peak,** named for its resemblance to a bishop's hat, is the standout, rising 5,551 feet (1,692 m) almost vertically from the sea.

The road from Te Anau ends at the small settlement of Milford, clinging to the end of Milford Sound. Dominated by a large cruise center resembling an international airport, the hamlet has the Milford Hotel, a lodge,

INSIDER TIP:

There's a reason it's so green and beautiful in the fjords: It rains. A lot. It may seem basic, but remember to bring a raincoat.

—JANE SUNDERLAND, *National Geographic Editor*

and a small airport, but not much else. Most visitors stay in Te Anau, though Milford is serene when tour groups have departed.

Fjord cruises depart throughout the day, but try to avoid the insane peak time around 1 p.m. when the tour buses roll in. The many tour operators offer similar services on large boats, which explore the 10-mile (16 km) length of the sound with stops to see plunging waterfalls and wildlife on the rocks.

Cruises turn around at the fjord's concealed entrance to the Tasman Sea, where Captain Cook sailed by thinking Milford was a cove. It took until 1810 for Europeans to discover the majesty that lay behind the bend. Cruises return via **Stirling Falls** and **Harrison Cove** with

A mossy beech forest along the Milford Track

Mount Pembroke (6,608 feet/2,014 m) and its glacier looming behind. The **underwater observatory** at Harrison Cove can be visited to view black coral and sealife four stories below the surface (see sidebar).

From the airport, small sightseeing planes buzz Milford Sound throughout the day and provide a close-up view of the mountains, though the grandeur of the peaks mirrored in the glassy water is best appreciated at sea level.

Doubtful Sound

Doubtful Sound is less visited than Milford Sound but no less beautiful. Though its peaks are not as immediately impressive, the second largest of the sounds is much more peaceful and more of a wilderness experience. Eight-hour cruises double as nature tours, and the fjord is home to seals, penguins, and bottlenose dolphins, a rarity this far south.

Captain Cook gave the fjord its name in 1770: Doubting that the winds in the sound would carry him back to sea, he sailed on by. A few hardy explorers and sealers visited, but it remained largely isolated until construction began on the Manapouri Power Station in the 1960s.

Trips to Doubtful Sound are very much an all-day experience, starting in Manapouri with a boat tour across **Lake Manapouri** to **West Arm,** where you board buses to spiral underground for 1.3 miles (2 km) to the **Manapouri Power Station.** This hydroelectric station, completed in 1972, has massive turbines driven by lakewater surging down through a 6-mile (10 km) tunnel to Doubtful Sound at sea level.

A spectacular road built to service the power plant then runs from West Arm to **Deep Cove** on Doubtful Sound, where cruises depart. The road goes through temperate rain forest, past moss gardens and the towering **Cleve Garth Falls,** and then over the 2,200-foot (670 m) **Wilmot Pass.**

From the wharf at Deep Cove, cruises take in the length of the sound, similar in many ways to the Milford cruises, but without the distraction of hordes of visitors and the buzzing of overhead flights. ∎

EXPERIENCE:
Beneath the Surface

Milford Sound's unique chemistry limits the amount of sunlight that penetrates the depths of the water. The darkness allows deepwater wildlife to live within 130 feet (40 m) of the surface. The result is a unique, life-filled environment that Jacques Cousteau said was one of his top-ten favorite dives. Creatures include red and black coral, 11-legged sea stars, tube worms, and scarlet wrasses. The Milford Deep Underwater Observatory (Harrison Cove, tel 03/441-1137, www.milforddeep.co.nz) allows you to experience the sound from a viewing chamber 34 feet (10 m) down. **Fiordland Expeditions** (43 Luxmore Dr., Te Anau, tel 03/249-9005, www.fiordlandexpeditions.co.nz) also offers scuba diving for direct views underwater.

Mitre Peak Cruises
- ☎ 03/249 -8110
- 🕐 2 hrs.
- 💲 $$$$$

www.mitrepeak.com

Cruising Milford Sound
- ☎ 03/249-7735
- 🕐 1.5 hrs.
- 💲 $$$$$

www.cruisingms.co.nz

Doubtful Sound Boat Tours

Real Journeys
- ✉ Real Journeys, Pearl Harbour, Manapouri
- ☎ 03/249-6602
- 🕐 8 hrs. & overnight
- 💲 $$$$$

Southland

The sheep-farming plains of Southland spread out from Invercargill, one of the world's most southerly cities. Southland is primarily a transit zone to Stewart Island or Fiordland, but the Catlins drive takes in wonderful coastal and forest scenery with wildlife-viewing opportunities. The Southern Scenic Route from Invercargill to Fiordland is similarly picturesque.

Schoolchildren touch a tuatara at the Southland Museum in Invercargill.

Invercargill

🅼 Map p. 259

Visitor information

✉ Visitor Centre, Southland Museum & Art Gallery, Queens Park

☎ 03/214-6243

Southland Museum & Art Gallery

✉ Queens Park, 108 Gala St.

☎ 03/219-9069

Invercargill

Southland's commercial center and New Zealand's southern-most city, Invercargill (pop. 50,300) was founded in 1856 by Scottish settlers who laid out a well-planned town on a level site. Farming, then lumber and coal, resulted in rapid growth and some fine Victorian buildings in the 19th century. The wool boom of the 1950s also brought great wealth to the city, but Invercargill has struggled in recent decades and the tourism

boom has largely passed it by.

Invercargill is a city of wide streets dotted with historic buildings and fine gardens, but it is mostly just an overnight stop along the Southern Scenic Route or on the way to Stewart Island.

The city's main focus is **Queens Park,** a 200-acre (81 ha) green lung with botanical gardens, aviary, animal enclosure, golf course, and more. At the park's main entrance, the **Southland Museum & Art Gallery** has Maori and colonial exhibits, but of most interest are the "Beyond the Roaring 40s" gallery about the sub-Antarctic islands and the prehistoric tuatara reptiles, survivors of the dinosaur age.

Anderson Park & Art Gallery on the city's northern outskirts is a fine neo-Georgian house set in 60 acres (24 ha) of landscaped gardens and featuring a good collection of New Zealand art.

Bluff

Drab Bluff, Invercargill's port 17 miles (28 km) to the south, is the end of the road. Or at least the end of SH1, which runs the length of the country from Cape Reinga in the north to Stirling Point on the south side of town, where a much photographed signpost points to more exotic worlds.

Southland's main location for exporting frozen meat, fertilizer, and aluminum is primarily a place to catch the ferry to Stewart Island. Points of interest include Bluff Hill for views of the island and the surrounding plains. The **Bluff Maritime Museum** *(241 Foreshore Rd., tel 03/212-7534)* traces the history of the port and local industry, including oyster dredging. Bluff is a mecca for oyster buffs, who eagerly await the opening of the season in March, when New Zealand's plumpest oysters go on sale and are shipped to restaurants all over the country.

Around Invercargill

The diligent Scottish settlers of Southland transformed tussock-covered swampy plains into rich farmland that once produced over 20 percent of the country's exports. In the days when the country "rode on the sheep's back," Southland sat tall. Those glory days have receded but sheep farming and dairying are still major industries.

Tuataras

The Southland Museum in Invercargill has long been famous for its tuataras, relics from the age of the dinosaurs. The tuatara is the only surviving member of the Sphenodontidae family, lizardlike reptiles that thrived 220 million years ago. Extinct on the mainland and classified as endangered since 1895, the tuatara is found only on offshore islands and in captivity. Southland Museum ran the first successful breeding program and exhibits the reptiles in its tuatarium. The star of the show and largest specimen is Henry, reputed to be 130 years old, and grumpy by all accounts, with a habit of biting off his girlfriends' tails.

Gore, 41 miles (66 km) north of Invercargill on SH1, is the main inland service town for Southland and also the country-music capital of New Zealand. Every May the town comes alive for the ten-day **New Zealand Gold Guitar Awards.** The rest of the year it's a sleepy place straddling the

Anderson Park & Art Gallery

🗺 Map p. 259

✉ 91 McIver Rd.

☎ 03/215-7432

A signpost at Invercargill's Bluff points to distant destinations.

Mataura River, with trout fishing the major tourist lure. The Gore visitor center *(Hokonui Dr. & Norfolk St., tel 03/203-9288)* has the full lowdown on the town.

Most visitors bypass Gore and the plains in favor of the less direct but more scenic Catlins road (see pp. 272–273) along the east coast or the western Southern Scenic Route to Te Anau.

Southern Scenic Route

The back road from Invercargill to Te Anau is a leisurely drive following SH99 west along the coast before turning inland. First stop of note is **Riverton,** 24 miles (39 km) from Invercargill. This pleasant but chilly seaside resort brashly bills itself as the Riviera of the South, and it does have good sheltered beaches. Farther west, **Colac Bay/Oraka** is a popular surfing spot immortalized by a statue of a surfer riding a wave.

At Te Waewae Bay, a short detour can be made to **Monkey Island,** a whale lookout for local Maori who called it Te Puka O Takatimu ("anchor stone of the Takatimu canoe"). Walk across to the island at low tide and up to the viewing platform for great coastal and Fiordland views.

Tiny **Tuatapere,** about halfway along the scenic route, is the only town of any note before Manapouri. It has a visitor information office *(tel 03/226-6739)* with details on local attractions. Next door, the **Bushman's Museum** *(31 Orawia Rd., tel 03/226-6399)* has displays on the region's sawmilling history.

Clifden, 8 miles (13 km) from Tuatapere, has an old suspension bridge as well as caves just north of the town, but they are not developed and care should be taken. Clifden is also the turnoff to scenic **Lake Hauroko,** New Zealand's deepest, 19 miles (30 km) away on a mostly unpaved road. Walks at the lake range from 30 minutes to 3 hours long. ■

EXPERIENCE: Kiwi Spotting

Few Kiwis (as New Zealanders call themselves) have seen a kiwi (the nocturnal bird and national symbol) in the wild. Though kiwi houses all over the country offer glimpses of these long-beaked, flightless birds, it requires great planning or luck to see them in their natural habitat. Some tour operators can give you a head start with kiwi guides.

A North Island brown kiwi forages for food.

One of the biggest concentrations of kiwis can be found on **Stewart Island** at the very bottom of the country. Populations of the Stewart Island brown kiwi, or tokoeka, number around 20,000. At **Mason Bay,** on the island's remote side, kiwis can even be seen foraging on the beach during the day. Mason Bay can only be reached by an overnight hike or chartered flight.

Alternatively, from the main settlement of Oban, boat tours go to a small offshore island where kiwis nest. **Phillip Smith's Bravo Adventure Cruises** (tel 03/219-1144) has evening tours, depending on weather and numbers, with a high success rate. If you keep still, the vision-impaired birds often come pecking at your feet searching for food. Tours can be heavily booked; allow two or three days on Stewart Island in case of cancellation.

At **Okarito,** near the glaciers on the West Coast of the South Island, **Okarito Kiwi Tours** (The Strand, Okarito, tel 03/753-4330, www.okaritokiwi tours.co.nz) claims a 90 percent success rate in finding a rare local subspecies of kiwi.

A long-running kiwi tour is in the **Trounson Kauri Park** on the Kauri Coast in Northland, where a Department of Conservation program has helped the North Island brown kiwi population increase to over 200. Though you will usually hear kiwis, sightings are not guaranteed. The **Kauri Coast Top 10 Holiday Park** (Trounson Park Rd., Kaihu, Dargaville, tel 09/439-0621, www.kauricoast-top10.co.nz) runs nightly kiwi tours, weather permitting.

Other good hunting grounds in which to spot the North Island brown kiwi include Aroha Island, Waitangi Forest, and Puketi State Forest. Kapiti Island near Wellington is the best place to sight the little spotted kiwi, but overnight stays require a permit (see p. 164). ∎

Drive through the Catlins

The winding coastal route from Invercargill to Dunedin runs through the region known as the Catlins. This fine drive takes in forest and rugged coastline and has a number of points of interest lying off the road, from beach strolls and waterfalls to excellent wildlife spotting.

The lighthouse at Waipapa Point warns ships of a rocky shore.

The scenic stretch from Invercargill to Balclutha can be driven straight through in two hours (add another 1.5 hours to Dunedin on SH1), but allow the better part of a day to take some side trips and sample the route's delights.

From **Invercargill** drive 31 miles (50 km) to Fortrose and turn off to Otara and the coastal road to **Waipapa Point ❶**. Take in its golden beach and lighthouse, built after the *Tararua*

Big-Wave Surfing

Unprotected against the swells of the Southern Ocean, the Catlins are home to some of the biggest waves in the world. Big-wave surfers come from all over to ride Papas, a wave that reaches 33 feet (10 m). This is tow-in surfing: participants rely on jet boats to get to the waves. Not for amateurs, this type of surfing is a thrilling and dangerous sport.

---

wrecked off the coast here in 1881, killing 131 people. Continue east to **Slope Point ❷**, the southernmost point on the South Island. It's a 20-minute walk across private farmland *(access allowed but closed in lambing season, Sept.–Oct.)* to a sign pointing to the South Pole.

Next along is **Curio Bay ❸**, where low tide exposes a 180-million-year-old fossilized forest with imprints of ferns visible in the rocks. Yellow-eyed penguins nest here, while at adjoining Porpoise Bay, Hector's dolphins can be seen in summer.

The road then passes through Waikawa, which has a small museum and the good Niagara Falls Café for a mealtime pit stop. Back on the main road, it is 12 miles (20 km) to the turnoff to pretty **McLean Falls ❹**, a 45-minute round-trip walk through forest.

Just past the falls road, a turnoff leads to **Cathedral Caves ❺** *($)*, an impressive 100-foot-high (30 m) cliff cavern carved out by the sea. Located on Maori land, the caves

are reached by a one-hour round-trip walk
through forest and along the beach,
but they are accessible only at low tide.

Matai Falls 6 are the
easiest falls in the Catlins
to reach, lying just
off the main
road. A

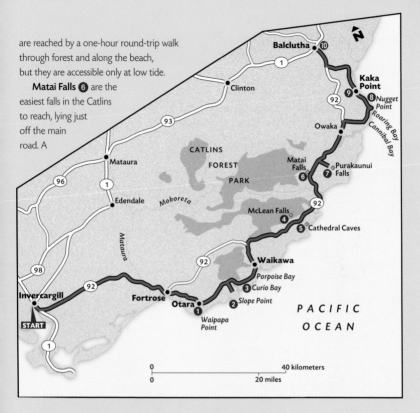

20-minute round-trip walk leads to the
waterfall and the **Horseshoe Falls** just above
for a pretty two-falls-in-one deal. Not far away,
Purakaunui Falls 7 are even more scenic and
involve a similar walk but a more lengthy drive
on gravel roads.

Just past Owaka township, take the turnoff
to **Cannibal Bay**, where Hooker's sea lions
can often be seen. These huge beasts lumber
ashore after a feeding foray to roll in the
sand and sleep in the sun. Keep your distance—
they can charge with remarkable speed.

From Cannibal Bay, gravel roads continue
on to **Nugget Point 8** lighthouse, perched
on top of a cliff and reached by a spectacular
track with drop-offs on either side. Seals play
on the rocks below, and sea lions and little
blue and yellow-eyed penguins also inhabit this
nature wonderland. Just before the lighthouse
at **Roaring Bay**, yellow-eyed penguins can

✚ See area map p. 259
▶ Invercargill
↔ 99 miles (158 km)
◔ 4–5 hours
▶ Balclutha

NOT TO BE MISSED:

**Waipapa Point • Curio Bay
• Cathedral Caves • Matai Falls
• Nugget Point**

---

be viewed from a blind (*best before 7 a.m. or
after 4 p.m.*).

Kaka Point 9, 6 miles (10 km) away, is
small summer resort with a gentle beach. It
is the last town of note before **Balclutha 10**,
where the Catlins drive ends. ∎

Stewart Island

Last but not least of New Zealand's main islands, Stewart Island belies its extreme southerly location. It is rich with forests and wildlife, its white-sand beaches washed by surprisingly warm currents. This remote natural paradise has fine hiking and abundant birdlife, including the kiwi, more easily seen here than anywhere else in New Zealand.

Sunset over Mason Bay, Rakiura National Park, Stewart Island

Stewart Island

⛰ Map p. 259

Visitor Information

✉ 12 Elgin Ter. (near ferry terminal), Oban

☎ 03/219-1400

Rakiura National Park

⛰ Map p. 259

Visitor Information

✉ Main Rd., Stewart Island

☎ 03/219-0009

Oban & Around

The Maori call the island Raki-ura, or "glowing skies," possibly in a reference to aurora australis, the southern lights. About 85 percent of the island, approximately 388,000 acres (157,000 ha), is encompassed by New Zealand's newest national park, **Rakiura National Park.**

For walkers it is paradise, with hikes traversing beach and forest, lasting from half an hour to two weeks. Tour operators offer less strenuous glimpses of the island's

beauty by boat, bus, or helicopter.

The island is also a refuge for native species isolated from the ravages farther north, including the elusive kiwi, the flightless, half-blind, nocturnal bird so rarely seen in the wild. Those on a pilgrimage to meet the national symbol have the best chance here.

Oban, also referred to as Halfmoon Bay, is the island's charming small settlement. It is well supplied with accommodations, a pub, restaurants, and services such as tours, water taxis,

Tui

The tui is one of New Zealand's better-known birds and also one of its loudest. With two voice boxes, this large, iridescent honeyeater is capable of singing two different songs at once. As well as producing its song, which is a mixture of melody and atonal coughing, the tui frequently mimics sounds, such as the songs of other birds, human voices, and even the ring of a cell phone. Residents across the country have complained of sleep loss.

rental cars, and scooters. The small **Rakiura Museum** (*Ayr St., Mon.–Sat. 10 a.m.–12, Sun. 12–2 p.m.*) is worth a look and has Maori artifacts, photos, and objects from European settlement. Other amusements around town include a small aquarium and a glass-bottom-boat ride that allows you to view the island's marine life and kelp forests.

Offshore **Ulva Island** is a prime attraction, easily reached by water taxi from Golden Bay. Free of predators, the island's regenerating forest teems with birdlife, including weka, kaka, tui, Stewart Island robin, and the rare saddleback, a member of New Zealand's ancient wattlebird family. Walking trails traverse the island, and informative guided walks can also be arranged.

Nature and walking are what Stewart Island is all about. The

Rakiura Track is one of New Zealand's Great Walks, a three-day hike from Lee Bay east of Oban. Hikers will see wonderful coastal scenery before heading inland through forest to Paterson Inlet and looping back to Oban. For a day-walk taste of the trail, Lee Bay to Maori Beach is three hours round-trip (six from Oban) through wonderful coastal and forest terrain.

Another good walk from the town is to **Ackers Point lighthouse** (*3 hours round-trip*), a hike that passes historic **Ackers**

....

Nature and walking are what Stewart Island is all about. The Rakiura Track is one of New Zealand's Great Walks, a three-day hike from Lee Bay east of Oban.

....

Cottage and affords fine coastal views. Muttonbirds teem in summer at dusk, when little blue penguins can also be seen.

Longer hikes include the classic 9- to 11-day **Northwest Circuit** for experienced hikers. The walk takes in **Mason Bay,** backed by impressive sand dunes and noted for kiwis that can often be seen, unusually, during the day. Charter flights also go to Mason Bay, though the best way to see kiwis is on a night tour from Oban, which gives you an excellent chance of seeing the elusive birds up close at a nearby inlet (see p. 271). ∎

Ferry to Bluff

- ✉ Stewart Island Experience, Visitor Terminal, Oban
- ☎ 03/219-0034
- 🕐 3 times daily Oct.–April, once daily May–Sept.
- 💲 $$$$–$$$$$

Stewart Island Flights

- ✉ Invercargill airport
- ☎ 03/218-9129
- 🕐 3 flights daily

Stewart Island Helicopter Adventures

- ✉ 250 Ocean Rd., Bluff
- ☎ 03/212-7770

TRAVELWISE

Planning Your Trip 276–278 • Getting Around 278–280 • Practical Advice 280–282 • Emergencies 282 • Health 283 • Hotels & Restaurants 284–309 • Shopping 310 • Entertainment 311 • Activities 312–313

Horse trekking on Lake Tekapo, South Island

PLANNING YOUR TRIP
When to Go

Summer (Dec.–Feb.) is the best season to visit New Zealand. The main tourist season runs from October through May. Outside these months, some attractions, tours, and accommodations close shop, particularly in beach areas. Travel is possible year-round, though, even in midwinter (July/August).

The international tourist season peaks in February/March, when the main tourist towns are overrun and roads are clogged with motor homes. Finding accommodations and rental vehicles can be difficult, especially on the South Island, so book in advance. December is a little quieter, but New Zealanders flock to resorts for summer break from around Christmas to the end of January. October/November and April/ May are much less crowded, cooler, and cheaper, although you miss the summer's charm.

New Zealand has a temperate climate, with regional variations. The Far North of the North Island is subtropical in summer and mild in winter, while the far south of the South Island is mild in summer and cold in winter. Snow tends to be confined to the mountains and rarely falls elsewhere.

Average maximum/minimum temperatures for Auckland range from 75/60°F (24/16°C) in January (midsummer) to 59/46°F (15/8°C) in July. In the south, Dunedin ranges from 66/52°F (19/11°C) in January to 50/38°F (10/3°C) in July.

The roaring forties, west winds that blow across the Southern Ocean between latitudes 40°S and 50°S, bring most of the weather. This makes the west coast wetter than the east, particularly on the South Island, where the Southern Alps trap drenching rains. If you hit Milford Sound on a clear day, consider yourself blessed.

Being surrounded by sea, the country's rainfall is fairly high, with winter slightly wetter than summer. Winds are very changeable, like the weather. It can go from sunshine to showers, from gentle breezes to blustering winds, all in an afternoon.

What to Bring

Given the changeable weather conditions, even summer visitors should bring warmer clothes such as a sweater, windbreaker, and light rain jacket. Kiwis dress fairly casually, and outdoor fashion is very suited to conditions and activities in New Zealand.

Shorts and T-shirts are fine for beach areas in summer, but bring nicer clothes for restaurants and nightclubs. In winter, bring sturdy warm clothes.

Good walking shoes are essential. Sport shoes are fine for around cities and short walks, but hiking shoes are recommended for many walks, allowing you to get closer to nature. Serious hikers should be well prepared for all conditions, including freezing temperatures in the mountains, even in summer.

Most anything you forget can easily be bought in New Zealand, but film is expensive. Accessories for cameras and electronics can be a hassle to find outside main cities, so make sure you bring all cables, chargers, batteries, etc.

Though seldom really hot, New Zealand is noted for fierce sunshine with high UV levels, so good sunglasses and sunscreen are essential. Binoculars are great for wildlife spotting.

Insurance

Travel insurance is a wise investment. Make sure your big-ticket items—cameras, laptops, etc.—are adequately covered. Travel insurance might save you more than it costs if renting a motor vehicle. Insurance offered by car rental companies comes with large deductibles, but your travel insurance policy may cover the deductible at much more reasonable rates.

Entry Formalities

Visas: Visitors from over 50 countries— including the U.S., Canada, Mexico, Japan, South Africa, and countries of the European Union—do not need a visa for stays of up to three months. British citizens can visit for up to six months without a visa. Australian citizens and permanent residents do not need visas at all.

Those not on the visa-free list must apply for a visitor visa before entering the country. Check at www.immigration.govt.nz.

Working-holiday visas valid for 12 months are available for 18- to 30-year-olds from 26 countries, including Canada, France, Germany, Japan, the U.K., and the U.S. This visa is for those who intend to supplement their travels with short-term work, primarily agricultural work, and is not valid for permanent work.

Customs: You are allowed to bring in 4.75 quarts (4.5 l) of wine or beer and one 1.18-quart (1.125 l) bottle of spirits, plus 200 cigarettes or 8.2 ounces (250 g) of tobacco or 50 cigars (or a mixture of all three weighing no more than 8.2 ounces/250 g).

Customs officials strictly enforce laws designed to protect agricultural industries from imported pests and diseases. Any food and plant items must be declared or you risk fines.

Anyone entering or leaving New Zealand with more than NZ$10,000 must declare it to customs.

How to Get to New Zealand

Most international flights go into Auckland, with Air New Zealand (www.airnz.com) being the major carrier.

From North America, Air New Zealand has direct flights between Auckland and Los Angeles, San Francisco, and Vancouver, with partner airline connections to other U.S. and Canadian cities. Qantas also flies Los Angeles–Auckland direct, while United Airlines code-shares on Air New Zealand flights.

Pacific stopovers are possible on North American flights. Auckland is a major Pacific hub with flights to and from Hawaii, Tahiti, Fiji, and a number of other Pacific islands. Smaller airlines such as Air Tahiti Nui, Air Pacific, Air Vanuatu, and Polynesian Blue also service the Pacific from Auckland, some with connections to the U.S. From South America Aerolineas Argentinas and LAN Chile fly to Auckland.

More flights go the other direction around the world. Numerous daily flights go to and from Australian cities, particularly Sydney, Brisbane, and Melbourne, with connections to Asia, Europe, and North America. Though Air New Zealand and Qantas are the main operators, Emirates, Virgin/Pacific Blue, and others fly to and from Australia and beyond.

Some of the cheapest flights from Europe go via Asia. Air New Zealand and Cathay Pacific fly London–Auckland via Hong Kong, while Malaysian Airlines, Singapore Airlines, Thai Airways, and other Asian carriers offer direct flights between their home bases and Auckland with connections to Europe.

New Zealand's other main international airport is Christchurch, but flights are more limited. Most go to Australia's east coast cities, but direct flights also go to and from Singapore, Tokyo, Osaka, Seoul, Fiji, and Rarotonga.

You can also fly direct into Wellington and Queenstown from Australia with Air New Zealand and Qantas, while Hamilton and Dunedin have flights to and from Brisbane and the Gold Coast, Australia, with Air New Zealand.

The great majority of visitors arrive at Auckland airport *(www.auckland-airport.co.nz)*, 13 miles (21 km) south of the city, reached by bus, taxi, or numerous airport shuttle services. For connecting domestic flights, a free bus operates between the international and domestic terminals, which are about a half-mile (1 km) apart.

A NZ$25 departure tax is not included in ticket prices and must be paid at the airport when leaving.

GETTING AROUND
By Air
Air New Zealand *(tel 0800 737 000, www.airnz.co.nz)* operates an extensive domestic air network, with daily jet service to Auckland, Hamilton, Wellington, Christchurch, Queenstown, and Dunedin. Air New Zealand

Link covers another 20 regional cities with smaller aircraft, from Kaitaia in the north to Invercargill in the south.

Australian airline Qantas *(tel 0800/808-767, www.qantas.co.nz)* services main cities and tourist centers only–Auckland, Rotorua, Wellington, Christchurch, and Queenstown. Virgin's Pacific Blue *(tel 0800/670-000, www.flypacificblue.com)* flies to and from Auckland, Wellington, and Christchurch.

For cheaper flights, purchase discounted tickets through airline websites or travel agents, book well in advance, or travel in off-peak times.

Apart from the three majors, a few small airlines cover regional routes. These include Soundsair *(tel 0800/505-005, www.soundsair.co.nz)*, with scenic flights across the Cook Strait from Wellington to Picton, Nelson, Blenheim, and Kaikoura; and Stewart Island Flights *(tel 03/218-9129, www.stewartislandflights.com)* between Invercargill and Stewart Island.

By Car
The most popular way to get around New Zealand is to rent a car or motor home. Public transport travels to all main destinations but is not always frequent. Often, remote gems can be reached only with your own vehicle. Most New Zealand roads are stunning scenic drives.

Driving is on the left side of the road. Apart from Auckland rush hour, driving is not too fraught, but travel times can be slow. Roads twist, climb, and dip, straight stretches and freeways are rare, and roads are narrow and can suddenly converge on one-lane bridges.

Major international companies and homegrown operators rent cars. Some New Zealand companies do a pretty good job, but enough operators offer worn-out vehicles, iniquitous fine print, and prohibitive cancellation fees to make major companies the best bet.

Hertz *(tel 0800/654-321, www.hertz.co.nz)*, Thrifty *(tel 0800/737-070, 03/359-2720, www.thrifty.co.nz)*, Budget *(tel 0800/283-438, 09/529-7784, www.budget.co.nz)*, and Avis *(tel 0800/284-722, 09/526-3256, www.avis.co.nz)* have offices all over the country and at airports. Book well in advance in the peak February/March season, when all rental vehicles are on the road.

Insurance deductibles are high (your travel insurance may cover you; see Insurance p. 277) and rates are seasonal—overpriced in summer, dirt cheap in winter.

If traveling between the North and South Islands, some rental companies insist you leave rental cars at the ferry terminal and pick up another across the strait (check when you rent).

Any valid driver's license allows you to drive in New Zealand. Members of AAA and other automobile associations should bring membership proof to receive reciprocal rights with AA New Zealand *(tel 0800/500-444, www.aa.co.nz),* including 24-hour roadside assistance and free maps and touring publications.

By Motor Home

The popular motor home or camper van combines vehicle with accommodation in one neat package. This can be a boon in main tourist centers in summer, when No Vacancy signs go up, but high-season rates for motor homes can be higher than a car and motel combined. Shoulder and low-season rates are much more reasonable. Smaller vans are easier for driving on New Zealand's narrow, twisting roads.

New Zealand has an excellent network of campgrounds and motor camps. Many cater to families and have good facilities and stunning settings next to a beach, lake, or forest.

Major rental agencies include Kea *(tel 0800/520-052, 09/441-7833, www.keacampers .com),* Apollo *(tel 0800/113-131, 09/255-5532, www.apollocamper.co.nz),* Maui *(tel 0800/651-080, 09/275-3013, www.maui.co.nz),* and Britz *(tel 0800/831-900, 09/275-9090 www.britz.co.nz).*

Depots are often outside the airport (sometimes a long way), cancellations attract big penalties, and large deposits are required. Insurance premiums are also high.

By Train

The once grand national rail service is now a

shadow of its former self since privatization. TranzScenic *(tel 04/495-0775, www.tranzscenic. co.nz)* operates only three routes, but guarantees comfortable travel with superb scenery.

Among the world's most scenic rail journeys, the TranzAlpine train between Christchurch and Greymouth runs from one side of the South Island to the other through grandeur of the Southern Alps.

The TranzCoastal from Christchurch to Picton via Kaikoura is another fine journey, hugging spectacular coast much of the way.

The Overlander runs from Auckland to Wellington via Hamilton and skirts the volcanoes of Tongariro National Park.

Rail passes are available and include the Wellington–Picton ferry but don't offer great value. Urban rail services are limited to Auckland and Wellington and are not very extensive.

By Bus

New Zealand has an extensive bus network, allowing you to see all main tourist sights by public transport, if you have time.

Intercity *(tel 09/623-1503, www.intercity .co.nz),* the main operator servicing major cities and towns, offers bus passes valid for a year and covering one-way travel with unlimited stops along North and South Island routes. Its Flexi-Pass allows unrestricted travel and is purchased in five-hour blocks of travel time. The Travelpass *(www.travelpass.co.nz)* includes ferry and train options. Passes also include travel on Newmans Coach Lines *(tel 09/623-1504, www.newmanscoach.co.nz),* which has sightseeing tours to main tourist attractions such as Milford Sound and the Bay of Islands.

A number of smaller bus companies run regional routes. One of the most useful, Atomic Shuttles *(tel 03/349-0697, www.atomictravel .co.nz)* has services all over South Island. Tourist offices have a full rundown on local bus and coach tour operators, which cover attractions off main bus routes. These include transport to and from trailheads of the most popular walks.

A number of tour buses for backpackers run set routes, picking up and dropping off at hostels. They include Kiwi Experience (tel 09/366-9830, www.kiwiexperience.co.nz) and Magic Travellers Network (tel 09/358-5600, www.magicbus.co.nz), which offer passes that allow you to get on and off at will.

By Ferry

Two companies service the Cook Strait, crossing between Wellington on the North Island and Picton on the South Island: Interislander (tel 0800/802-802, 04/498-3302, www.interislander.co.nz) and Bluebridge (tel 0800/844-844, 04/471-6188, www.bluebridge.co.nz).

Well-equipped vehicle/passenger ferries cross in a little over three hours, with up to nine daily departures. In Wellington, the Bluebridge terminal is opposite the main railway station. The Interislander terminal is 1.5 miles (2.4 km) north, and a free shuttle runs to and from the train station. In Picton, the ferry terminal is near town center.

From the ferry terminal in downtown Auckland, Fullers (tel 09/367-9111, www.fullers.co.nz) has ferries to Auckland suburbs such as Devonport and to the Hauraki Gulf islands of Rangitoto, Waiheke, and Great Barrier. Sealink (tel 0800/732-546, 09/300-5900, www.sealink.co.nz) also has ferries to Waiheke and Great Barrier Island.

Other ferries operate in the Bay of Islands and Rawene in Northland, Wellington, and the Marlborough Sounds and between Bluff and Stewart Island (see p. 232).

By Bicycle

Cyclists from all over the world flock to New Zealand in summer. Many bring their own bicycles, but bikes are easily purchased or rented. One of the easiest places to rent touring bikes is in the towns of Central Otago, along the 95 miles (150 km) of the Central Otago Rail Trail (www.centralotago railtrail.co.nz), the country's most popular cycling route.

PRACTICAL ADVICE
Communications

Post Offices: New Zealand Post offers efficient service, with delivery times of four to ten days to most parts of the world. Post offices are open weekdays from around 8.30 a.m. to 5 p.m. and until 1 p.m. on Saturdays. Other retail outlets such as convenience stores also sell stamps and offer basic postal services.

Telephone: New Zealand has good telephone services and an extensive network of public telephones, which use coins, credit cards, or prepaid phone cards. Most hotels and motels have in-room phones but add a surcharge to rates, while even budget hostels will have a phone for guest use.

The cheapest way to call overseas is on a landline using an international phone card available from many convenience stores. Typically, stores offer discounted Internet telephone service; you dial a toll-free New Zealand number, enter your PIN, then enter the overseas number. Country rates vary between card companies—retailers will have details.

Telecom New Zealand (www.telecom.co.nz) and Vodafone (www.vodafone.co.nz) provide mobile telephone services. A Vodafone SIM card for NZ$35 is a worthwhile investment for calling locally for accommodation bookings, activities, etc., from your mobile phone. National calls cost NZ$0.89 per minute, as do international calls to Australia, Canada, Ireland, the U.K., and the U.S., or NZ$1.39 to the rest of the world. The card includes NZ$5 worth of calls (NZ$10 extra when you register) and can be bought from mobile phone shops and electronic stores such as the Dick Smith chain. Recharges are sold at convenience stores and drugstores. Telecom has slightly better coverage in rural areas, but you have to buy a complete handset.

The emergency number is 111. The internal access code to dial out of the country is 00 (followed by country code, area code, number). The country code is 64. Area codes in New Zealand are: 09 Auckland and Northland; 07 Coromandel, Bay of Plenty, and Waikato; 06 Hawke's Bay, Gisborne, Palmerston North, and Wairarapa; 04 Wellington; 03 South Island.

Internet: Internet cafés proliferate, and many

tourist information offices have coin-operated pay terminals. Many accommodations offer Internet access, usually in the lobby. Some offer intranet access in rooms, though wireless services, usually at high rates, are more common if you have your own laptop. Cafés often have free wireless access.

Conversions

New Zealand uses the metric system, so road signs are in kilometers, gas is sold in liters, and stores sell in grams and kilos.

1 kilometer = .62 miles
1 meter = 3.28 feet or 39.37 inches
1 liter = 0.264 U.S. gallons
1 kilogram = 2.20 pounds

Women's clothing sizes

U.S.	6	8	10	12	14	16
NZ	36	38	40	42	44	46

Men's clothing sizes

U.S.	36	38	40	42	44	46
NZ	46	48	50	52	54	56

Women's shoes sizes

U.S.	6	6.5	7	7.5	8	8.5
NZ	38	38	39	39	40	41

Men's shoes sizes

U.S.	8	8.5	9.5	10.5	11.5	12
NZ	41	42	43	44	45	46

Electricity

The New Zealand electricity supply is 230V AC, 50 Hz. Plugs have three flat pins (one vertical, two angled), as used in Australia. Many hotel and motel bathrooms have two-prong, 110-volt sockets for electric razors, but it's a good idea to bring an adapter and dual voltage appliances.

Holidays

January 1 (New Year's Day)
January 2 (Day after New Year's Day)
February 6 (Waitangi Day)
March/April (Good Friday, Easter Monday)
April 25 (Anzac Day)
1st Monday in June (Queen's Birthday)
4th Monday in October (Labor Day)
December 25 (Christmas Day)
December 26 (Boxing Day)

Liquor Laws

The minimum drinking age is 18 in licensed premises. Children are allowed in pubs with their parents.

Media

Most New Zealand cities have a daily newspaper covering local and international news. The two main newspapers are Auckland's *New Zealand Herald* and Wellington's *Dominion Post.*

Popular local magazines include the *New Zealand Listener* for entertainment and current affairs, *North & South* for current affairs, the Auckland lifestyle magazine *Metro,* and *Cuisine* for all things food and wine.

The publicly owned national broadcaster TVNZ runs the TV1 and TV2 television channels. Local productions include the soaps *Shortland Street* and *Outrageous Fortune* and the irreverent *bro'Town,* a Polynesian *South Park.* Other free-to-air channels include C4, a music and infomercial station, and Maori TV, with the most New Zealand content.

Radio New Zealand, the national broadcaster, is supplemented by a host of regional AM and FM stations throughout the country.

Money Matters

The unit of currency is the New Zealand dollar, comprising 100 cents. Notes come in $5, $10, $20, $50, and $100 denominations, while copper 10c, silver 20c and 50c, and gold-colored $1 and $2 coins are in circulation.

Traveler's checks are readily exchanged at banks and money changers, but rates are lower than cash, and a cashing fee of at least 1 percent usually applies. Exchanging cash attracts similar fees.

Depending on fees charged by your home bank, using credit cards—or better, debit cards—for purchases and cash withdrawals through ATMs might be cheaper and is certainly more convenient. However, fewer fees usually apply when withdrawing cash from a savings account via ATMs and EFTPOS retail outlets connected to international banking networks such as Cirrus, Maestro, and Plus. They are found everywhere in New Zealand. Check fees and overseas access with your bank before you leave.

Visa and MasterCard are the most widely accepted credit cards. American Express and Diners Club, in that order of acceptance, tend to be limited.

A 12.5 percent goods-and-services tax applies to all purchases but is almost always included in quoted prices (be wary of businesses that do not include it). It is not refundable for overseas visitors when leaving.

Opening Times

Most shops and businesses are open Monday to Friday from 9 a.m. to 5 p.m., and for late-night shopping until 9 p.m. one or two nights per week (Thurs. and/or Fri.). Large supermarkets usually stay open until 8 or 9 p.m., some until midnight or later in cities, where convenience stores and gas stations are open 24 hours.

Saturday shopping is from around 10 a.m. to 5 p.m., though some shops close at 2 p.m. Most shops close on Sundays, but shopping malls are open from 10 a.m. to 4 p.m. Souvenir shops in main tourist centers are open late most nights.

Time Differences

New Zealand lies near the International Date Line and is one of the first countries in the world to see the new day. New Zealand is +12 hours GMT, 2 hours ahead of Sydney, and 17 hours ahead of New York standard time. New Zealand daylight saving time is from the last Sunday in September to the first Sunday in April.

Tipping See p. 10

Travelers with Disabilities

Accommodations and most public facilities are required to provide wheelchair access and disabled bathrooms. Even many short walking trails are wheelchair friendly.

Taxis and tour operators with wheelchair access vehicles can be found in major centers. Many car rental companies will fit hand controls to vehicles if contracted well in advance, and motor homes with wheelchair hoists can be rented.

An excellent website for disability services is *www.weka.net.nz,* with good transport and travel sections.

Visitor Information

New Zealand's main visitor information network is coordinated under the i-SITE brand by the national tourism body Tourism New Zealand *(www.newzealand.com).* Over 80 offices book accommodations, tours, and transport and offer information and brochures, primarily advertising literature.

In general, these offices provide good service but can be overrun in peak summer season. Also, i-SITE offices are commercial enterprises, representing local operators and taking a cut on all bookings, so they avoid making recommendations that differentiate between operators.

Smaller regional tourist offices are found in almost every town. They may be run by volunteers and may not take bookings, but they do have lots of information.

For information on national parks and walks, the Department of Conservation (DOC) has a network of offices in parks and towns. Offices often list local tourist services, accommodations, etc., but in general don't make bookings. Their website *(www.doc.govt. nz)* has an excellent rundown on New Zealand parks and recreation.

EMERGENCIES
Crime & Police

New Zealand is generally a safe country with low crime rates. Theft from parked cars is a recurrent problem, particularly in remote tourist parking lots such as at trailheads. Avoid leaving valuables in your car or, if you must, lock them out of view in the trunk.

Some local police stations have become community police offices tucked away in shopping areas, but they are there if you need to report a crime or obtain a crime report for travel insurance.

Embassies & Consulates

U.S. Embassy, 29 Fitzherbert Terrace, Wellington, tel 04/462-6000, fax 04/472-3478, www.newzealand.usembassy.gov

U.S. Consulate-General, Level 3, Citigroup Center, 23 Custom Street East, Auckland, tel 09/303-2724, fax 09/366-0870

Canadian High Commission,125 The Terrace, Wellington, tel 04/473-9577, fax 04/471-2082, www.geo.international.gc.ca/asia/newzealand

Canadian Consulate, 9th Fl., 48 Emily Pl., Auckland, tel 09/309-3690, fax 09/307-3111

British High Commission, 44 Hill St., Wellington, tel 04/924-2888, fax 04/473-4982 www.britishhighcommission.gov.uk/newzealand

British Consulate-General, Level 17, 151 Queen St., Auckland, tel 09/303-2973, fax 09/303-1836

British Consulate, 1st Fl., Harley Chambers, 137 Cambridge Terr., Christchurch, tel 03/374-3367, fax 03/374-3368

Emergency Phone Numbers

The emergency number for police, ambulance, and fire is 111.

What to Do in a Car Accident

In the event of an accident, check all vehicles to see if anyone is injured. Contact emergency services and seek help from bystanders to assist the injured. Failure to stop, check, or assist is a serious offense.

If someone is injured, report the accident to police as soon as possible. If another vehicle or property is damaged, you must notify the owner or report the accident to police within 48 hours.

Write down the name, address, registration number, and insurance company of the other driver(s) involved, and the details of witnesses and any police officers in attendance. Give your details, but it is best not to admit liability for any accident.

Report accidents to your rental car or insurance company as soon as possible. If you will be claiming the deductible on your travel insurance, make sure you have a copy of the rental agreement, insurance coverage, repair quotes, police report, and all receipts.

HEALTH

New Zealand has high-quality medical treatment and world-class hospitals. Visitors requiring emergency treatment for a motor vehicle, sport, or recreational accident are covered by New Zealand's accident compensation scheme (ACC). Otherwise, you'll have to pay for medical treatment, and while health care is significantly cheaper than in the U.S. or the U.K., travel insurance is highly recommended.

Healthline is a toll-free, 24-hour telephone medical advice service: tel 0800/611-116.

Tap water is safe to drink in New Zealand, but streams and lakes may contain bugs such as giardia, so their water should be boiled or treated before drinking. Amoebic meningitis is very rare but can occur in geothermal waters, such as hot pools in Rotorua. Keep your head above the water to deter infection.

New Zealand has no snakes or dangerous wild animals, though the rare, red-striped katipo spider, found only in coastal sand dunes, is poisonous. The greatest danger in the wild is exposure in alpine areas for ill-equipped hikers and rips and currents at surf beaches.

Hotels & Restaurants

Exclusive country lodges, international chain hotels, delightful B&Bs, roadside motels, and well-equipped backpacker or campground cabins—New Zealand has a big range of accommodations to suit all budgets.

On arrival, pick up a free accommodation guide at the airport or tourist office. Motels, hotels, B&Bs, and backpacker chains all produce their own guides with member listings. The most useful free guides are the comprehensive *Jasons Motels, Apartments & Motor Lodges* (also online at *www.jasons.com*) and the guides from the Automobile Association *(www.aatravel.co.nz)*, all covering sightseeing and/or accommodations.

If you are on a tight schedule and know your itinerary, book all your accommodations before you arrive, especially in the peak summer season when tourist towns fill up. Beware, though, that accommodations in New Zealand often will not refund cancellations. Trying to find same-day accommodation in the high season can be frustrating and time-consuming, though it is less problematic outside tourist areas.

Hotels & Motels

Hotels range from five-star luxury to humble pubs. Big international chains (Hilton, Hyatt, Sheraton, etc.) have hotels in the main cities, but individual hotels and small chains such as Scenic Circle *(www.scenic-circle.co.nz)* and Millennium *(www.millenniumhotels.co.nz)* are more common in tourist towns.

Travel agents or online booking services such as www.wotif.com or www.ezibed.com offer discount deals that are often cheaper than booking direct. The latter specialize in discounted hotel bookings up to 28 days ahead.

Hotel rates vary considerably with the season. Four-star hotels start at around NZ$140 per room, though more often are around NZ$200 or more.

At the very top end, a range of boutique hotels, luxury lodges, and elite resorts—such as the Huka Lodge near Taupo or the Millbrook Resort near Queenstown—offer opulence at extravagant prices.

Mid-range hotels cost from NZ$90 up to NZ$180. These may be pubs but are more likely to be private hotels, with just rooms and maybe a café if you are lucky. They compete with motels, or motor lodges as they are called in New Zealand. Many motels in New Zealand have seen better days, but are usually clean, have kitchens, and offer comfort at reasonable prices. Newer motels are usually much better appointed, with rates starting from at least NZ$120.

At the bottom end, pubs in cities and towns often have rooms upstairs, usually basic but sometimes well-appointed motel-style rooms. They start at around NZ$50 for a double without bathroom, but can be noisy if your room is near the bar.

B&Bs

Bed-and-breakfast accommodations are booming, with more homeowners converting rooms or erecting specially designed accommodations. Some are in magnificent heritage buildings, and top-end B&Bs offer some of the finest accommodations in New Zealand. At the bottom end, more basic guesthouse-style places offer budget rooms with shared facilities.

Depending on the room rate, breakfast might be light continental-style or a grand affair. Most B&Bs are convivial places, allowing you to meet Kiwis and fellow travelers in a home atmosphere, or to be completely independent if you choose. Most cost around NZ$120 to NZ$180.

The *New Zealand Bed & Breakfast Book,* available in bookshops, has extensive listings online *(www.bnb.co.nz)*. The *B&B Directory of New Zealand (www.bed-and-breakfast.co.nz)* is similar.

Budget Accommodations

Campgrounds, known as holiday parks, offer a wide choice of budget accommodations in addition to campsites and powered sites for motor homes. Rooms range from cheap spartan cabins and backpacker rooms to motel units and apartments. Campgrounds are usually well equipped with communal kitchens, laundries, entertainment areas, playgrounds, and sometimes a pool or even hot-spring baths. Many are on the beach or a lake.

New Zealand is well set up for backpackers, with hostels ranging from big-city hotels to remote farm homesteads. Most independent backpacker hostels belong to one of three hostel networks: Budget Backpacker Hostels *(www.bbh.co.nz)*, YHA *(www.stayyha.com)*, and VIP Backpackers *(www.vip.co.nz)*. Many hostels are well appointed with good-value double rooms that appeal to older couples on a budget. Along with communal cooking facilities and well-appointed common areas, many offer bicycles, tours, free pickup, and a host of extras.

Other

Apartment hotels are springing up everywhere in cities and resorts. Some offer luxury, but most are minimalist new buildings with modern rooms and fully equipped kitchens. If you don't want all the services of a big hotel, these can offer excellent value.

Holiday homes, or baches as they are called, can also be rented, usually only for longer stays, though sometimes short term *(www.bookabach .co.nz, www.holidayhouses.co.nz)*. Real estate agents often handle them, though some tourist offices list them.

Tourist offices also handle farm stays and homestays, which can sometimes offer great value. They may just be a room in a family home but are often self-contained units or converted bungalows.

Restaurants

Fine-dining restaurants and more casual cafés are readily available, particularly in big cities, which are also home to numerous Indian, Chinese, Southeast Asian, Middle Eastern, and other restaurants, reflecting New Zealand's broadening immigrant mix and offering some of the best dining value.

Wonderful dining experiences can be found, but a lot of restaurants offer similar variations of lamb/beef/venison/fish on a tower of mashed kumara (sweet potato) at high prices, regardless of quality. Top chefs are limited in resort towns, where chefs come and go. Add inexperienced waitstaff and hordes of diners in the tourist season, and you could be waiting an eon for a very ordinary meal.

That said, New Zealand has wonderful fresh foods—seafood, meat, fruits, and vegetables— and plenty of restaurants and cafés in which to try it. Most eateries are licensed to serve alcohol or you can BYO (Bring Your Own wine or beer bought elsewhere). Smoking is not allowed in New Zealand restaurants, cafés, and bars but may be allowed in some outdoor areas.

Closing hours vary for public holidays, when some restaurants add a surcharge of around 15 percent. Many cafés offering light meals are only open for breakfast and/or lunch. Most restaurants are open for lunch and dinner. Closures are shown in the following listings below using the abbreviations below:

L = Lunch

D = Dinner

Listings: Hotels and restaurants for each destination are listed by price, then in alphabetical order. Prices are in New Zealand dollars.

Credit Cards: Abbreviations used are: AE: American Express; DC: Diners Club; MC: MasterCard; V: Visa.

■ AUCKLAND

⊞ HILTON AUCKLAND
$$$$$
PRINCES WHARF, 147 QUAY ST.
TEL 09/978-2000   FAX 09/978-2001
www.hilton.co.nz
At the end of Princes Wharf, Hilton Auckland's generous use of glass and open space brings the harbor in. Rooms employ local

timber, and ceiling-to-floor windows and balconies in the front apartments deliver wow factor plus.

🛈 166 🅿 🛗 🚫 🛎 🏊 📺
🏧 All major cards

🏨 **SKYCITY GRAND HOTEL**
$$$$$
90 FEDERAL ST.
TEL 09/363-6000   FAX 09/363-6383
www.skycityauckland.co.nz
You won't get lost if staying underneath the Sky Tower spire, visible all over the city. Superior facilities and service make this five-star hotel popular with business travelers as well as tourists. It is part of the huge SkyCity casino, entertainment, and dining complex, which also includes its sister hotel, the four-star SkyCity Hotel.

🛈 316 🅿 🛗 🚫 🛎 🏊 🍴 📺
🏧 All major cards

🏨 **WESTIN AUCKLAND LIGHTER QUAY**
$$$$$
21 VIADUCT HARBOUR AVE.
TEL 09/909-9000   FAX 09/909-9001
The bright new face on Auckland's hotel scene overlooks Viaduct Harbour, a short stroll from the city's swankest dining/nightlife precinct. Superior service, sleek decor, spa center, and the excellent location put it ahead of most. Expansive windows deliver superb waterfront views in deluxe rooms, though most superior rooms face rows of new apartment blocks.

🛈 172 🅿 🛗 🚫 🛎 🏊 📺
🏧 All major cards

🏨 **PEACE & PLENTY INN**
$$$$–$$$$$
6 FLAGSTAFF TER., DEVONPORT
TEL 09/445-2925   FAX 09/445-2901
www.peaceandplenty.co.nz
In genteel Devonport, just around the corner from the main street cafés, this delightful B&B makes a wonderful retreat from downtown Auckland, only a ten-minute ferry ride away. Spacious rooms in a meticulously restored Victorian villa are complemented by warm hospitality and sumptuous breakfasts. Homesick pet lovers can take Stanley the Labrador for a stroll around Devonport's streets.

PRICES

HOTELS
The cost of a double room in the high season is indicated by **$** signs (NZ dollars).

$$$$$	Over $240
$$$$	$160–240
$$$	$110–160
$$	$70–110
$	Under $70

RESTAURANTS
The cost of a three-course meal without drinks is indicated by **$** signs (NZ dollars).

$$$$$	Over $65
$$$$	$50–65
$$$	$30–50
$$	$20–30
$	Under $20

Winter rates are more reasonable.
🛈 7 🅿 🚫 🛎 🏧 MC, V

🏨 **HERITAGE HOTEL**
$$$–$$$$$
35 HOBSON ST.; TOWER WING, 22–24 NELSON ST.
TEL 09/379-8553   FAX 09/379-8554
www.heritagehotels.co.nz
This luxury hotel in a classic art deco building offers regularly discounted rooms, suites, and apartments, many with kitchens. Rooms in the main building have high ceilings, timber floors, and 1920s élan, while the modern Tower Wing has contemporary decor. The hotel has a heated rooftop swimming pool, indoor pool, sauna, spa, two gymnasiums, and tennis court, right in the city center with harbor views from many rooms.

🛈 325 🅿 🛗 🚫 🛎 🏊 📺
🏧 All major cards

🏨 **COPTHORNE HOTEL AUCKLAND HARBOUR CITY**
$$$
196–200 QUAY ST.
TEL 09/377-0349   FAX 09/307-8159
www.millenniumhotels.co.nz/copthorneharbourcity

This 1970s high-rise hotel has seen better days, but its location is superb, downtown on the waterfront near Viaduct Quay. All rooms have wonderful harbor views. Although there's no pool or a surfeit of bars, the hotel is surrounded by nightlife and restaurants. The reasonable rates make it worth a look.

① 186 P 🔄 🚫 🚭 🍸
🔳 All major cards

🏨 THE QUADRANT
$$–$$$
10 WATERLOO QUADRANT
TEL 09/984-6000   FAX 09/984-6001
www.thequadrant.com
This funky apartment hotel near the university on the edge of downtown lacks the extras and service of a big hotel but offers good value. Compact studio, one-, and two-bedroom apartments have fully equipped kitchens and modern furnishings. Extras include Wi-Fi, DVD library, and gaming consoles, but the lack of air-conditioning can be a drawback on hot days.

① 250 P 🔄 🚫 🍸 🔳 All major cards

🏨 OAKS SMARTSTAY ON HOBSON
$$
188 HOBSON ST.
TEL 09/337-5800   FAX 09/337-5900
www.theoaksgroup.co.nz
Well-appointed modern apartments with kitchenettes and laundry facilities offer a good deal for couples wanting a small studio. Two-bedroom apartments are exceptional value for families. Though centrally located near the casino, a nearby homeless mission mars the good location, but the area is quite safe and rooms are a cut above most apartment hotels.

① 117 P 🔄 🚫 🚭 🔳 MC, V

🏨 PARNELL INN
$–$$
320 PARNELL RD.
TEL 09/358-0642   FAX 09/367-1032
www.parnellinn.co.nz
In the fashionable suburb of Parnell, this welcoming motel/guesthouse makes a good budget choice. The city is a short bus ride or 25-minute walk away, and the Auckland Museum is nearby. Attractive, well-kept rooms have nice touches, and a small café is on the premises.

① 16 P 🚫 🔳 MC, V

🏨 SHAKESPEARE TAVERN
$–$$
61 ALBERT ST. (AT WYNDHAM ST.)
TEL 09/373-5396   FAX 09/373-5397
www.shakespearehotel.co.nz
This classic old pub is in the city center near the casino. The struggling but architecturally impressive facade belies good refurbished rooms with private bathrooms, some with balcony, for a budget value with character. The downstairs restaurant and boutique brewery bar are a bonus.

① 10 🚫 🔳 MC, V

SOMETHING SPECIAL

🍴 DINE BY PETER GORDON
$$$$$
LEVEL 3, SKYCITY GRAND HOTEL, 90 FEDERAL ST.
TEL 09/363-7030
www.skycitygrand.co.nz
Chef Peter Gordon, the man who put the f in fusion in these parts, lends his name to this fine-dining restaurant. The towering space with stunning finishes and an urbane bar is a prelude to intricately constructed dishes employing a global lexicon of tastes and textures. Though a little fussy, a tad pretentious, and a wallet denter, this is one of New Zealand's finest and most innovative restaurants. Leave room for amazing desserts.

🍴 70 P 🕐 L Sat., Sun. 🚫 🚭
🔳 All major cards

🍴 EURO RESTAURANT & BAR
$$$$$
SHED 22, PRINCES WHARF
TEL 09/309-9866   FAX 09/308-9189
www.eurobar.co.nz
On Princes Wharf overlooking the harbor, Chef Simon Gault runs one of the city's top restaurants, beloved of the glitterati for dinner, late-night barhopping, and expense-account lunches. Dine inside or out on the verandah overlooking luxury yachts. The seasonal menu has a seafood emphasis in summer, but features a wide variety of produce and styles.

🍴 120 🚫 🚭 🔳 All major cards

🚫 No smoking   🚭 Air Conditioning   🏊 Indoor Pool   🏊 Outdoor Pool   🍸 Health Club   🔳 Credit Cards

¶ HARBOURSIDE
$$$$
IST FL., FERRY BLDG., 99 QUAY ST.
TEL 09/307-0486   FAX 09/307-0523
www.harboursiderestaurant.co.nz
One of Auckland's finest seafood restaurants,
Harbourside's emphasis is on fresh fish, such
as char-grilled yellowfin tuna with port wine
jus. The menu also features beef and lamb,
but entrées often offer the most interesting
seafood creations. The upstairs deck overlooks
the ferry docks below.
🔲 340 🚫 🚫 All major cards

¶ IGUAÇU RESTAURANT & BAR
$$$$
269 PARNELL RD., PARNELL
TEL 09/358-4804   FAX 09/358-0587
www.iguacu.co.nz
Parnell is home to one of Auckland's most
popular dining strips, and this trendy brasserie
with large windows, terra-cotta tiles, and
atrium mezzanine is in the middle. The in
place in Parnell for a decade, Iguaçu features
Mediterranean and Asian influences, steaks,
pan-fired lamb, and seafood. Lunch offers
value dining.
🔲 120 🚫 🚫 🚫 All major cards

¶ SOUL BAR & BISTRO
$$$$
VIADUCT HARBOUR
TEL 09/356-7249
www.soulbar.co.nz
This buzzing favorite in the city's liveliest
dining precinct packs in a designer casual clientele daily for lunch and dinner, kicks on at
the bar until late, then returns for breakfast
egg creations to soak up the booze from the
night before. The varied fusion menu leans
toward seafood and fish, such as pan-fried
hapuku with fennel, lime, and sumac crumbs
on goat-cheese mashed potatoes. The deck
overlooking the water is the place to be.
🔲 200 🅿 🚫 🚫 🚫 All major cards

¶ GPK
$$$–$$$$
262 PONSONBY RD.
TEL 09/360-1113   FAX 09/376-6832
www.gpk.co.nz
A couple miles west of downtown, fashion-
able Ponsonby Road is one of the city's

favorite café strips, and GPK was one of
Auckland's first gourmet pizza joints. This
ever popular café combines unusual pizza
fusions with a broader menu of oysters,
salmon, steaks, etc. Open for breakfast, lunch,
and dinner.
🔲 120 🚫 🚫 All major cards

¶ KHAO THAI CUISINE
$$$
CHANCERY ST. & O'CONNELL ST.
TEL 09/377-5088   FAX 09/377-5077
www.khao.co.nz
Chic decor, dimmed lights, and fine dining in
a heritage building alert you to the fact this
is not your usual Thai restaurant. This fusion
restaurant showcases classic dishes such as
red curry and pad Thai noodles, along with
creations like sizzling hot plate of beef fillet on
roast vegetables with chili sauce.
🔲 120 🕐 L Sat. & Sun. 🚫
🚫 All major cards

¶ MECCA CHANCERY
$$$
SHOP C, 103 CHANCERY LN.
TEL 09/356-7028   FAX 09/356-7028
www.meccacafe.com
Just off the High Street shopping precinct in a
wonderful piazza location, Mecca is a top spot
for breakfast, lunch, or dinner. One in a chain
of restaurants, the reasonably priced menu is
as much Mediterranean as Middle Eastern.
The meze, seafood, and tapas platters stand
out for a light meal.
🔲 120 🚫 All major cards

¶ THE CATCH SEAFOOD CAFÉ
$$–$$$
AUCKLAND FISH MARKET, 22 JELLICOE ST.
TEL 09/377-5249
West of Viaduct Harbour, the Auckland Fish
Market is home to all things seafood, includ-
ing this wonderful café for lunch. Reasonably
priced, superfresh seafood ranges from
humble fish and chips to popular seafood
platters with a half or full crayfish. Dining
is mostly outside under the awning—magic
on fine days. The market has other dining
options from fish-and-chips stalls to upscale
Hong Kong–style seafood.
🔲 60 🕐 D Sun.–Thurs. 🚫
🚫 AE, MC, V

MANUKA
$$–$$$
49 VICTORIA RD., DEVONPORT
TEL 09/445-7732 FAX 09/445-7891
www.manukarestaurant.co.nz
A short ferry ride from central Auckland, the seaside village of Devonport makes a pleasant day trip. This airy corner café is popular for its wood-fired pizzas. It has other reasonably priced fare, from seafood entrées to steaks, and makes good platters, including one for vegetarians. Open for breakfast, lunch, and dinner. Dining is casual.

🔲 50 ⬛ ⬛ ⬛ All major cards

CAFÉ MIDNIGHT EXPRESS
$$
59 VICTORIA ST. W.
TEL 09/303-0312 FAX 09/303-0514
www.cafemidnightexpress.co.nz
With a tent-style roof and Turkish artifacts, this cheerful restaurant near the Sky Tower has been serving reasonably priced food for nearly 20 years. Tasty Turkish dishes such as döner kebab and karni yarik (stuffed eggplant) are accompanied by rice and salad. Servings are huge.

🔲 50 ⬛ L Sun. ⬛ ⬛ AE, MC, V

SATYA SOUTH INDIAN CAFÉ
$$
271 KARANGAHAPE RD.
TEL 09/377-0007
Queen Street heads up the hill to Karanga-hape Road, a slightly seedy, always interesting area with a selection of budget Asian restaurants. Satya packs them in thanks to consistently good curries and thali plate meals appealing to meat eaters as well as vegetarians. The waitstaff struggles on a Saturday night—go during the week.

🔲 70 ⬛ ⬛ ⬛ MC, V

TANUKI'S SUSHI & SAKE BAR
$$
319 QUEEN ST.
TEL 09/379-5353 FAX 09/379-5151
www.sakebars.co.nz
This urban secret has long been out. At the top end of Queen Street, where cheap Japanese and Korean restaurants abound, Tanuki's has rustic Japanese decor, a big range of sake, and the usual Japanese specialties and dinner

boxes at reasonable prices. Downstairs, the Tanuki Cave is a funky bar for a drink with yakitori or kushiage snacks on skewers.

🔲 106 ⬛ L ⬛ ⬛ All major cards

◼ NORTHLAND

WHANGAREI

🏠 LODGE BORDEAUX
$$$$
361 WESTERN HILLS DR.
TEL 09/438-0404 FAX 09/438-0405
www.lodgebordeaux.co.nz
West of city center on the main highway, this lodge has luxurious studio, one-, and two-bedroom kitchen suites, all with double spa baths. Rated five-star with lots of extras and fine hospitality, this small, family-run boutique lodge is the top option in town.

🏠 15 ⬛ ⬛ ⬛ ⬛
⬛ All major cards

GYBE
$$$$
QUAYSIDE, TOWN BASIN MARINA
TEL 09/430-0406 FAX 09/430-7341
www.gybe.co.nz
Though it doesn't quite have the best waterfront location of the Town Basin eateries, this stylish restaurant does have the best food and service, in a fine two-story villa overlooking the river. A wide menu shows innovation and old favorites, such as steaks and seafood—the seafood chowder and seafood platters are particularly superb.

🔲 150 ⬛ ⬛ All major cards

KILLER PRAWN
$$$–$$$$
26–28 BANK ST.
TEL 09/430-3333 FAX 09/430-3131
www.killerprawn.co.nz
In downtown Whangarei, this cheerful restaurant's signature dish is prawns in a spicy tomato broth with chunky bread for dunking, while other seafood dishes dominate the menu, including paella, tempura fish, and green-lipped mussels with the sauce of your choice. Upstairs, pizzas are offered at reasonable prices.

🔲 140 ⬛ Sun. ⬛
⬛ All major cards

BAY OF ISLANDS

Paihia

🏨 **EDGEWATER PALMS APARTMENTS**
$$$$$
8–10 MARSDEN RD.
TEL 09/402-0090   FAX 09/402-5910
www.edgewaterapartments.co.nz
This new breed of apartment hotels offers one- and two-bedroom apartments overlooking the water and one of New Zealand's most scenic views. An easy walk into town, the apartments are on the main road.
ⓘ 34 🅿 🔄 🅢 🔄 🏊 🅢 All major cards

🏨 **PAIHIA BEACH RESORT & SPA**
$$$$$
116 MARSDEN RD.
TEL 09/402-0111   FAX 09/402-6026
www.paihiabeach.co.nz
Around the headland from the main shopping stretch, this is Paihia's top apartment complex. Opposite the beach with great views, studio, one-, and two-bedroom apartments are suitably luxurious for the price. The day spa, sauna, and fine restaurant top off the indulgence.
ⓘ 22 🅿 🔄 🅢 🔄 🏊 🅢 All major cards

🏨 **BAY VIEW MOTEL**
$$$–$$$$
MARSDEN RD. & BAYVIEW RD.
TEL 09/402-7338   FAX 09/402-7279
www.bayviewmotelbayofislands.co.nz
Numerous motels provide cheap accommodations. Many are dowdy, but for a few dollars more, the Bay View is a cut above most, with well-kept one-bedroom units, many with sea views, and a great location in the center of Paihia.
ⓘ 11 🅿 🅢 🅢 All major cards

🏨 **COPTHORNE HOTEL & RESORT**
🍴 **$$$–$$$$**
TAU HENARE DR.
TEL 09/402-7411   FAX 09/402-8200
www.milleniumhotels.co.nz/
copthornebayofislands
Right in the Waitangi Treaty Grounds and only a mile (1.6 km) from the center of Paihia, this four-star hotel is a serene retreat with ocean views, gardens, and a golf course. The hotel has seen better days, but discounts through travel agents and last-minute Web bookings can make it a good deal. The water-view rooms with balconies are worth the extra cost. ⓘ 145 🅿 🅢 🔄 🏊 🅢 All major cards

🍴 **35° SOUTH RESTAURANT & BAR**
$$$–$$$$
69 MARSDEN RD.
TEL 09/402-6281   FAX 09/402-6220
www.35south.co.nz
This aquarium restaurant has pole position perched over the water in an octagonal building next to the wharf. The menu strongly features seafood but also offers steaks, duck, and a good prix fixe. The deck is a sublime spot for a drink on a sunny day. Open for breakfast, lunch, and dinner.
🍴 90 🅿 🅢 🅢 All major cards

🍴 **ONLY SEAFOOD**
$$$–$$$$
40 MARSDEN RD.
TEL 09/402-6066   FAX 09/402-7083
Set off the main road upstairs in a two-story villa overlooking the sea, Only Seafood is a Paihia institution. Only seafood gets the nod with dishes such as seafood filo parcels, game fish with roasted cashews, smoked salmon with brie, and seafood platters with a sashimi bent.
🍴 95 🅿 🕐 L 🅢 🅢 All major cards

🍴 **WAIKOKOPU CAFÉ**
$$–$$$
TREATY GROUNDS, TAU HENARE DR.
TEL 09/402-6275   FAX 09/402-6276
In the Waitangi Treaty Grounds, this good-value café is a great spot for breakfast or lunch surrounded by greenery on an outdoor deck. The corn and coriander fritters, Cajun chicken salad, and ribs are specialties, and the beef, lamb, and seafood dishes are done with style.
🍴 150 🅿 🕐 D 🅢 🅢 MC, V

Russell

🏨 **DUKE OF MARLBOROUGH HOTEL**
🍴 **$$$–$$$$$**
35 THE STRAND
TEL 09/403-7829   FAX 09/403-7828
www.theduke.co.nz
On the waterfront near the Paihia ferry

dock, this is one of the country's oldest inns. Renovations have maintained the history while enhancing the charm. Though a little short on luxury for the price, the waterfront rooms and suites are a delight (don't bother with the back rooms). The popular restaurant has two dining sections serving good pub fare and fancier meals.

ⓘ 26 🅿 Ⓢ 🗝 All major cards

🏠 HANANUI LODGE & APARTMENTS
$$$–$$$$$
4 YORK ST.
TEL 09/403-7875   FAX 09/403-8003
www.hananui.co.nz
In the town center, this complex is divided into two sections: luxurious waterfront apartments and cheaper units in the lodge behind. Modern, well-appointed apartments range from studio to two-bedroom, while the lodge has older motel-style units with kitchens.

ⓘ 16 🅿 Ⓢ 🗝 All major cards

SOMETHING SPECIAL

🍽 KAMAKURA
$$$$
29 THE STRAND
TEL 09/403-7771   FAX 09/403-7733
www.kamakura.co.nz
Kamakura offers some of the finest dining north of Auckland. The innovative menu features dishes like venison medallions, Dijon rack of lamb, market fish with mango prawn salsa, date- and feta-stuffed peppers, and seafood laksa. The bifold doors open out in summer and tables spill onto the grassy banks to make the most of the waterfront location.

🔲 75 🅿 Ⓢ 🗝 All major cards

MANGONUI

🍽 MANGONUI FISH SHOP
$
BEACH RD.
TEL/FAX 09/406-0478
Billing itself as "world famous" may be stretching it, but this renowned fish shop on stilts over the harbor is a de rigueur lunch (or dinner) stop for fish and chips. Oysters, lobster, and other seafood are also offered;

with fishing boats moored alongside, it doesn't get much fresher. Eat at picnic tables on the deck outside.

🔲 40 🗝 MC, V

HOKIANGA

🏠 COPTHORNE HOTEL & RESORT HOKIANGA
$$$
SH12, OMAPERE
TEL 09/405-8737   FAX 09/405-8801
www.millenniumhotels.co.nz/
copthornehokianga
If traveling the Kauri Coast loop, this is the best hotel on Northland's west coast, in the sleepy coastal resort of Opononi/Omapere. Though some rooms are a little worn, the water setting is serene and rates are reasonable for the offered facilities.

ⓘ 34 🅿 Ⓢ 🏊 🗝 All major cards

◼ CENTRAL NORTH ISLAND

WAITOMO

🏠 WAITOMO CAVES HOTEL
$–$$$
HOTEL ACCESS RD.
TEL 07/878-8204   FAX 07/878-8205
www.waitomocaveshotel.co.nz
Only a five-minute walk to Glowworm Caves, this grand resort hotel built in 1908 is a Waitomo institution, albeit a neglected one. The hotel is slowly being refurbished, but until completed, romantics will have to overlook the shabbiness and musty odor. Most rooms are hostel-like but cheap; large suites are grander.

ⓘ 33 🅿 Ⓢ 🗝 All major cards

COROMANDEL PENINSULA

Whitianga

🏠 WATERFRONT MOTEL
$$$$–$$$$$
2 BUFFALO BEACH RD.
TEL 07/866-4498   FAX 07/866-1201
Stylish motel units, studios, and two-bedroom apartments offer good standards in a great position opposite the main beach and around

the corner from shops. Inflated summer prices drop dramatically in winter.

ⓘ 16 🅿 🛇 🅰 All major cards

🏨 OCEANSIDE MOTEL
🍽 $$$–$$$$
32 BUFFALO BEACH RD.
TEL 07/866-5766   FAX 07/866-4803
www.oceansidemotel.co.nz
Less than a mile from town on the best stretch of beach, this well-kept motel with apartments has a great position and slightly more reasonable summer rates in expensive Whitianga.

ⓘ 12 🅿 🛇 🅰 All major cards

🍽 THE FIRE PLACE
$$$$
9 THE ESPLANADE
TEL 07/866-4828   FAX 07/866-0102
www.thefireplace-restaurant.com
This restaurant offers consistently good dining in a lovely setting, with a huge fireplace at the front. Dine inside or out on the large verandah overlooking greenery-draped ponds. Wood-fired pizzas, seafood, curries, and entrées with a Mediterranean influence dominate the menu.

🪑 200 🕐 L in winter 🅰 All major cards

🍽 SALT
$$$$
1 BLACKSMITH LN.
TEL 07/866-5818
www.whitiangahotel.co.nz
At the front of the Whitianga Hotel, Salt has a great position with a large deck overlooking yachts in the river. Seafood features prominently on a varied menu that includes steak and sometimes Thai dishes.

🪑 130 🅰 All major cards

BAY OF PLENTY

Mount Maunganui/Tauranga

🏨 OCEANSIDE TWIN TOWERS
$$$–$$$$$
1 MAUNGANUI RD.,
MOUNT MAUNGANUI
TEL 07/575-5371   FAX 07/575-0486
www.twintowers.co.nz
Near town center and the beach, these tower

blocks offer some of the best accommodations in town, including suites and apartments. The facilities include restaurants, small pool, sauna, and gym.

ⓘ 70 🅿 ➡ 🛇 🏊 🛗 🅰 All major cards

🏨 THE PAVILIONS
$$$–$$$$$
4 MARINE PARADE., MOUNT MAUNGANUI
TEL 07/572-0001   FAX 07/574-6666
www.pavilion.net.nz
Opposite the beach and near the Mount, the location is unbeatable. Well-appointed luxury apartments of one to three bedrooms have sea views and balconies in this new, low-rise development.

ⓘ 13 🅿 ➡ 🛇 🅰 All major cards

🏨 BAY PALM MOTEL
$$–$$$
84 GIRVEN RD., MOUNT MAUNGANUI
TEL 07/574-5971   FAX 07/574-5972
www.baypalmmotel.co.nz
This better class of motel has studios and one- and two-bedroom units with kitchens, spa baths, and a heated swimming pool. Out of Mount Maunganui near the golf course, it is a short walk to Ocean Beach and the Bayfair Mall.

ⓘ 16 🅿 🛇 🏊 🅰 All major cards

🏨 Hotel 🍽 Restaurants ⓘ No. of Bedrooms 🪑 No. of Seats 🅿 Parking 🚇 Metro 🕐 Closed ➡ Elevator

🍴 ASTROLABE

$$$

82 MAUNGANUI RD., MOUNT
MAUNGANUI
TEL 07/574-8155   FAX 07/547-8156
www.astrolabe.co.nz
The hippest place in Mount Maunganui has
stylish decor and mostly Mediterranean-
influenced dishes. Expect truffle oil, aioli, and
some surprises on an innovative menu.

🔲 50 🔲 🔲 🔲 All major cards

🍴 WHARF STREET RESTAURANT

$$$

8 WHARF ST., TAURANGA
TEL 07/578-8322   FAX 07/577-6603
www.wharfstreet.co.nz
Unprepossessing from the outside, Wharf
Street offers classic decor and wonderful
views over the harbor. The food is consistently
good without overmixed flavors. Seafood is
widely featured, but lamb, steaks, and contemporary influences are also on the menu.

🔲 50 🔲 Mon. 🔲 🔲 All major cards

🍴 AMPHORA CAFÉ-BAR

$$–$$$

43 THE STRAND, TAURANGA
TEL 07/578-1616   FAX 07/576-9846
www.amphoraonthestrand.co.nz
This popular Italian restaurant offers a large
varied menu, from pasta and pizza to plenty
of seafood. Servings are large and prices moderate. Dine in the Victorian-style restaurant or
outside on the main waterfront street.

🔲 90 🔲 🔲 All major cards

Whakatane

🏨 TUSCANY VILLAS MOTOR INN

$$$

57 THE STRAND
TEL 07/308-2244   FAX 07/308-2255
www.tuscanyvillas.co.nz
Despite the kitsch architectural homage to
Tuscany, this is Whakatane's most luxurious
spot to stay, right in the town center. Well-
appointed studio and one-bedroom suites
have kitchenettes, king beds, and spa baths.

🛈 28 🅿 🔲 🔲 All major cards

🏨 WHITE ISLAND RENDEZVOUS

$$–$$$

15 THE STRAND E.
TEL 07/308-9588   FAX 07/308-0303
www.whiteisland.co.nz
Good motel rooms overlook the waterfront,
a short stroll from town. It's run by an island
tour operator, with package deals available.

🛈 25 🅿 🔲 🔲 🔲 All major cards

🍴 ROQUETTE RESTAURANT & BAR

$$$

23–29 QUAY ST.
TEL 07/307-0722
www.roquette-restaurant.co.nz
Along the river from the tourist office,
Roquette offers surprisingly fine dining in the
provinces. The modern menu features dishes
such as a good seafood risotto and venison
T-bone on rosti with port wine jus.

🔲 40 🔲 🔲 All major cards

🍴 WHARF SHED

$$$

2 THE STRAND, MAIN WHARF
TEL 07/308-5698
www.wharfshed.com
Right on the river with casual all-wood decor,
Wharf Shed's breezy verandah tables are
highly sought on balmy evenings. Seafood
features prominently, but beef, lamb, poultry,
and vegetarian dishes are also on the straight-
forward but well-presented menu.

🔲 86 🅿 🔲 🔲 All major cards

ROTORUA

SOMETHING SPECIAL

🏨 PEPPERS ON THE POINT

$$$$$

214 KAWAHA POINT RD.
TEL 07/348-4868   FAX 07/348-1868
www.peppers.co.nz
This recent addition to Rotorua's luxury lodge
scene is a converted 1930s mansion on a
peaceful point on Lake Rotorua, 2 miles
(3 km) north of town. Set on seven acres
(3 ha) of gardens with a private beach and
jetty, the lodge has huge luxury suites and
cottages decorated with antiques; the four-
bedroom villa offers rock-star indulgence.

🛈 9 🅿 🔲 🔲 🔲 🔲 All major cards

MILLENNIUM HOTEL ROTORUA
$$$–$$$$$
ERUERA ST. & HINEMARU ST.
TEL 07/347-1234   FAX 07/348-1234
www.millenniumhotels.co.nz
A short stroll to the town center, this large four-star hotel encapsulates the Rotorua experience with a day spa, thermally heated swimming pool, gymnasium, saunas, and spa pools. Try to get a lake-view room.
① 227 P ⊖ ⓢ ⓒ ⓩ ⓨ
⓪ All major cards

NGONGOTAHA LAKESIDE LODGE
$$$–$$$$
41 OPERIANA ST., NGONGOTAHA
TEL/FAX 07/357-4020
www.rotorualakesidelodge.co.nz
This small intimate B&B, 6 miles (9 km) north of downtown Rotorua, offers fine hospitality and rooms right on the lake. Great views and serenity are guaranteed, and trout fishing is on your doorstep.
① 3 P ⓢ ⓪ MC, V

PRINCES GATE HOTEL
$$$–$$$$
1057 ARAWA ST.
TEL 07/348-1179   FAX 07/348-6215
www.princesgate.co.nz
Built in 1897, this gorgeous double-story wooden hotel lies just outside the entrance to the Government Gardens, right in the middle of town. Beautifully restored, the boutique hotel's well-equipped rooms offer good value.
① 52 P ⓢ ⓩ ⓪ All major cards

REGAL PALMS
$$$–$$$$
350 FENTON ST.
TEL 07/350-3232   FAX 07/350-3233
www.regalpalms.co.nz
This high-quality motel/resort has a heated swimming pool, children's playground, mini-golf, gym, sauna, and tennis court. Big modern rooms have spa baths. Although more expensive than most, the facilities and service are excellent in this spacious, well-kept complex.
① 44 P ⓢ ⓒ ⓩ ⓨ ⓪ All major cards

HEYWOODS MOTOR LODGE
$$–$$$
249 FENTON ST.
TEL/FAX 07/348-5586
www.heywoodsmotel.co.nz
Rotorua is overrun with cheap motels, many of them strung out along Fenton Street. This is one of the better appointed motels, and like many, has hot spa baths, including some in the units, and a heated swimming pool.
① 23 P ⓢ ⓩ ⓪ All major cards

SUDIMA HOTEL
$$–$$$
1000 ERUERA ST.
TEL 07/348-1174   FAX 07/346-0238
www.sudimahotels.com
In a fabulous position on the lakefront next to the Polynesian Spa, this large hotel is a favorite with tour groups. Facilities include restaurants, bar, day spa, individual hot pools, and heated swimming pool. Rooms are dated and need an upgrade, but online discounts make it a bargain for the facilities offered.
① 248 P ⊖ ⓢ ⓩ ⓪ All major cards

LAKEHOUSE HOTEL
$
41–45 LAKE RD.
TEL 07/348-5585
Near the lake just north of town center, this rambling backpacker hotel built in 1870 has lots of old-fashioned style and lake views from the upper balconies. Well-kept single, double, and dorm rooms with shared bathrooms are basic but don't come much cheaper.
① 48 P ⓢ ⓪ MC, V

BISTRO 1284
$$$$
1284 ERUERA ST.
TEL/FAX 07/346-1284
www.bistro1284.co.nz
In a small cottage in central Rotorua, fine dining and good service are assured in what is widely regarded as the city's best restaurant. Noted for beef and lamb dishes, the small dinner-only menu is distinguished by fresh produce and exquisite attention to detail.
⊞ 35 ⓒ L; D Sun. ⓢ ⓪ All major cards

YOU AND ME
$$$
1119 PUKUATUA ST.

⊞ Hotel ⓘⓘ Restaurants ① No. of Bedrooms ⊞ No. of Seats P Parking 🚇 Metro ⓒ Closed ⊖ Elevator

TEL 07/347-6178

Iron Chef comes to Geyser City in this interesting fusion restaurant hidden away upstairs on Pukuatua Street. Japanese chef Hiroyuki Teraoke worked for 30 years in Europe before opening this intimate restaurant. Seafood features strongly, as do lamb and venison, on a heavily French-influenced menu with delicate Japanese touches.

🍴 44 🕐 L; D Sun., Mon. 🚭
🅰 All major cards

🍴 ZANELLI'S
$$$
1243 AMOHIA ST.
TEL 07/348-4908
www.zanellis.net.nz

For over 20 years, Zanelli's has dished up quality Italian food. The limited menu concentrates on doing good seafood, veal, pasta, and risotto dishes, but no pizza. Delicious desserts include homemade gelato, tiramisu, and weekly specials.

🍴 56 🕐 L; D Sun., Mon. 🚭
🅰 All major cards

🍴 FAT DOG CAFÉ & BAR
$$–$$$
1161 ARAWA ST.
TEL 07/347-7586
www.fatdogcafe.co.nz

Fat dog mosaics, sea horses, and paintings brighten the funky interior of this popular Rotorua institution. Light meals, snacks, and more substantial Kiwi favorites are well prepared and presented.

🍴 100 🚭 🅰 All major cards

🍴 CAPERS EPICUREAN
$–$$
1181 ERUERA ST.
TEL 07/348-8818   FAX 07/348-1388
www.capers.co.nz

This busy central deli has a good selection from the counter or light meals prepared in the kitchen. Very popular for breakfast and lunch, or coffee and cake anytime, it's also open for dinner five nights a week, when it is less crowded.

🍴 90 🕐 D Sun., Mon. 🚭
🅰 All major cards

TAUPO

SOMETHING SPECIAL

🏨 HUKA LODGE
$$$$$
HUKA FALLS RD.
TEL 07/378-5791   FAX 07/378-0427
www.hukalodge.com

The granddaddy of New Zealand's luxury lodges, Huka Lodge has been making the world's great hotel lists for over a decade. Once a modest fishing lodge, this retreat offers sumptuous rooms and fine dining in the classic main lodge. The exclusive Owner's Cottage can also be rented.

ℹ 24 🅿 🚭 🅰 All major cards

🏨 🍴 MILLENNIUM MANUELS TAUPO
$$$$
243 LAKE TERRACE
TEL 07/378-5110   FAX 07/378-5341
www.millenniumhotels.co.nz

Stroll across the grass from one of the few hotels right on New Zealand's largest lake, or take in the view from the rooms, the good bistro, or the restaurant. Renovated rooms and good service put it ahead of many hotels in this chain.

ℹ 51 🅿 🔌 🚭 ❄ 🏊 🏋 🅰 All major cards

🏨 ABOVE THE LAKE AT WINDSOR CHARTERS
$$$–$$$$
46 ROKINO RD.
TEL 07/378-8738   FAX 07/378-8748
www.troutfishingtaupo.com

Taupo's trout fishing attracts anglers from around the world, and this welcoming B&B is an ideal spot for anglers and others seeking home-style hospitality. The owners run fishing charters, and rooms are spacious and comfortable (upstairs has lake views).

ℹ 3 🅿 🚭 🅰 MC, V

🏨 SAILS MOTOR LODGE
$$$–$$$$
138 LAKE TERRACE
TEL 07/377-0655   FAX 07/378-0488
www.sailstaupo.co.nz

At one of the fancier motels strung along the lake, sail-topped balconies finish off modern architectural styling. Lake views and the excellent location within walking distance of downtown make this a standout.

🛈 16 🅿 🚫 🛇 All major cards

🏨 LAKEFRONT MOTOR LODGE
$$–$$$
2 TAHAREPA RD.
TEL 07/378-9020   FAX 07/378-9021
www.lakefrontmotorlodge.co.nz
South of town center, this well-equipped motel gets points for its lake views from some units, hot mineral spa baths in many units, and reasonable rates. Seniors and weekday discounts apply.

🛈 17 🅿 🚫 🏊 🛇 AE, MC, V

🍴 THE BACH
$$$$
2 PATAKA RD.
TEL 07/378-7856
www.thebach.co.nz
On the lakefront with views of the volcanoes of Tongariro National Park, this converted former bach (holiday house) offers Taupo's finest dining. Good service and an excellent wine list complement innovative well-balanced dishes, such as its signature dish: confit of duck with braised red cabbage and honey truffle jus.

🍴 40 🕐 L 🚫 🛇 All major cards

🍴 WATERSIDE RESTAURANT & BAR
$$$
3 TONGARIRO ST.
TEL 07/378-6894
In the town center overlooking the lake, this delightful restaurant has fires in winter and outdoor tables for balmy summer nights. Seafood features prominently among well-presented modern New Zealand dishes with moderate prices.

🍴 150 🚫 🛇 All major cards

🍴 SILK THAI
$$–$$$
2 ROBERTS ST.
TEL 07/378-1139
www.silkthai.co.nz
Next to the Waterside Restaurant, Silk Thai also has stunning lake views. The good Thai food is free of the blandification typical of many New Zealand Thai restaurants. That said, homage is paid to the Kiwi rack of lamb,

their signature dish marinated in Thai spices and served on a sizzling platter.

🍴 64 🚫 🛇 All major cards

TONGARIRO NATIONAL PARK

SOMETHING SPECIAL

🏨 CHATEAU TONGARIRO
$$$–$$$$$
SH48, MOUNT RUAPEHU
TEL 07/892-3809   FAX 07/892-3704
www.chateau.co.nz
At the base of Mount Ruapehu volcano, this imposing old-money hotel from the 1930s is a New Zealand icon in a stunning setting. A variety of rooms in old and new wings range from tired to superb. It pays to pay extra for a room with a view.

🛈 106 🅿 🚻 🚫 🍷 🛇 All major cards

NAPIER

🏨 SCENIC CIRCLE TE PANIA HOTEL
$$$–$$$$
45 MARINE PARADE
TEL 06/833-7733   FAX 06/833-7732
www.scenic-circle.co.nz
This four-star, six-story, horseshoe-shaped hotel is downtown, opposite the beach and the Ocean Spa. All rooms face out to sea with ceiling-to-floor windows. Discounts through online booking agencies make this a best buy.

🛈 109 🅿 🚻 🚫 🍴 🍷 🛇 All major cards

🏨 SEA BREEZE
$$
281 MARINE PARADE
TEL 06/835-8067   FAX 06/835-0512
Napier has many delightful B&Bs strung along the lakeshore and on Bluff Hill. This downtown Victorian villa survived the earthquake and has an English seaside boardinghouse charm, themed rooms, and reasonable prices.

🛈 3 🅿 🚫 🛇 MC, V

🍴 CHAMBER RESTAURANT
$$$$
12 BROWNING ST.
TEL 06/835-7800
www.countyhotel.co.nz
In the posh County Hotel, one of the few substantial buildings to survive the 1931

earthquake, Chamber's menu combines the classics with innovation. Starters include smoked salmon on gourmet potato salad with caper vinaigrette, and entrées range from lobster-based seafood platters to herb-crusted lamb rack. A good selection of fine local wines accompanies.

🍴 65 🕐 L 🚭 🏧 All major cards

🍴 PACIFICA KAIMOANA
$$$$
209 MARINE PARADE
TEL 06/833-6335
www.pacificarestaurant.com
This is an excellent restaurant to try New Zealand's fresh seafood. Fish is the specialty, crusted with herbs and grilled, or perhaps in coconut taro cream, while oysters and scallops are featured in season. Meat lovers are also not denied in this fine restaurant in a breezy casual location opposite the sea.

🍴 40 🕐 Mon. 🚭 🏧 All major cards

■ WELLINGTON

🏨 BOLTON HOTEL
$$$$–$$$$$
BOLTON ST. & MOWBRAY ST.
TEL 04/472-9966   FAX 04/472-9955
www.boltonhotel.co.nz
A favorite with business travelers, this relatively new five-star hotel ranks as the city's best. Chic neutral rooms offer superior facilities and extra touches. Discounts for weekend stays and off-season times can be very attractive.

🛏 144 🅿 🛗 🚭 🔆 🏊 🐝
🏧 All major cards

🏨 🍴 COPTHORNE HOTEL WELLINGTON ORIENTAL BAY
$$$–$$$$$
100 ORIENTAL PARADE
TEL 04/385-0279   FAX 04/384-5324
www.millenniumhotels.co.nz
A short stroll from Te Papa Museum, this four-star hotel in chic Oriental Bay is on the edge of downtown but near the beach. Recent renovations have restored this nine-story hotel to high standards, and sleek contemporary rooms have balconies, many with wonderful harbor views.

🛏 117 🅿 🛗 🚭 🔆 🏊
🏧 All major cards

🏨 MUSEUM HOTEL
$$$–$$$$
90 CABLE ST.
TEL 04/802-8900   FAX 04/802-8909
www.museumhotel.co.nz
Opposite Te Papa Museum and the waterfront, the location doesn't get any better than this for sightseers. This comfortable tourist hotel has good rooms but is barely four stars, so look for discounts through online booking sites. Parking costs extra.

🛏 160 🅿 🛗 🚭 🔆 🏊 🐝
🏧 All major cards

🏨 AITKEN ON MULGRAVE
$$
7 AITKEN ST., THORNDON
TEL 04/473-1870   FAX 04/473-4014
www.wellingtoncityhotel.co.nz
Behind the railway station, but within walking distance of Wellington's attractions, these serviced apartments don't have the full service of a hotel but offer exceptional value. Well-kept studio suites have kitchenettes with dishwasher and washing machine, DVD player, TV, stereo, and free wireless broadband.

🛏 48 🛗 🚭 🏧 All major cards

🏨 🍴 HOTEL IBIS WELLINGTON
$$
153 FEATHERSTON ST.
TEL 04/496-1880   FAX 04/496-1881
www.ibishotel.com
This downtown three-star hotel is very central. Rooms are simple but comfortable with broadband, and the hotel has a bistro and bar. This well-presented budget hotel offers good value.

🛏 200 🅿 🛗 🚭 🔆 🐝 🏧
All major cards

🍴 SHED 5
$$$$–$$$$$
QUEENS WHARF
TEL 04/499-9069
www.shed5.co.nz
Housed in an 1888 wool store overlooking the water on central Queens Wharf, this is one of Wellington's finest seafood restaurants. From simple fish and chips with a Chinese twist to whole-roasted fish topped with steamed cockles in a spicy

---

🚭 No smoking 🔆 Air Conditioning 🏊 Indoor Pool 🏊 Outdoor Pool 🐝 Health Club 🏧 Credit Cards

tomato salsa, the dishes show flair, and the desserts are superb.

🔳 180 🔇 🖂 All major cards

🍴 CAFÉ BASTILLE
$$$–$$$$
16 MAJORIBANKS ST., MOUNT VICTORIA
TEL 04/382-9559
www.bastille.co.nz

In a restaurant world dominated by fusion, innovation, and competing flavors, this French restaurant relies simply on fine cooking tradition. From Provençal fish soup and homemade pork sausages to duck breast with kumara soufflé in red wine sauce, the dishes are superbly cooked and presented, and Bastille consistently rates among the city's best restaurants.

🔳 70 🕐 L, D Sun. 🔇 🖂 All major cards

SOMETHING SPECIAL

🍴 KAI IN THE CITY
$$$–$$$$
21 MAJORIBANKS ST., MounT VICTORIA
TEL 04/801-5006
www.kaicity.co.nz

On the eastern edge of downtown, this rare Maori restaurant is a chance to sample fine local cuisine. Try the hangi (traditional oven) specialties or the Tangaroa seafood platter featuring oysters, mussels, tuna, salmon, kina (sea egg) fritters, kaanga wai (fermented corn), and paraoa (Maori bread). This welcoming restaurant offers a unique indigenous experience.

🔳 30 🕐 L 🔇 🖂 AE, MC, V

🍴 ONE RED DOG
$$–$$$
9–11 BLAIR ST.
TEL 04/384-9777
www.onereddog.co.nz

Off Courtenay Place, One Red Dog was one of the town's first gourmet pizza restaurants. This very popular bar-restaurant remains a favorite for pasta, salads, pizzas, and calzones washed down with a pint on tap.

🔳 120 🔇 🖂 All major cards

🍴 CAFFE L'AFFARE
$–$$
27 COLLEGE ST.
TEL 04/385-9748   FAX 04/385-9261
www.laffare.co.nz

PRICES

HOTELS
The cost of a double room in the high season is indicated by $ signs (NZ dollars).

$$$$$	Over $240
$$$$	$160–240
$$$	$110–160
$$	$70–110
$	Under $70

RESTAURANTS
The cost of a three-course meal without drinks is indicated by $ signs (NZ dollars).

$$$$$	Over $65
$$$$	$50–65
$$$	$30–50
$$	$20–30
$	Under $20

This popular café made espresso the drink of choice in 1990s Wellington and continues to serve excellent coffee. This is the place for a big breakfast, light lunch, or coffee and cake. With an open kitchen and tables spilling onto the pavement, this spot is popular with inner-city clientele.

🔳 80 🕐 D, L Sun. 🔇 🖂 All major cards

MARTINBOROUGH

🏨 PEPPERS MARTINBOROUGH HOTEL
🍴 $$$–$$$$
THE SQUARE
TEL 06/306-9350   FAX 06/306-9345
www.martinboroughhotel.co.nz

In the town center, this hotel with its superb restaurant is the jewel of the Wairarapa wine district. The imposing Victorian hotel has refurbished rooms with French doors opening onto wide verandahs upstairs, and equally delightful rooms open to the garden. The restaurant is hailed far and wide for fine dining, combining French and Italian influences to match the area's superb wines.

🚪 16 🅿 🔇 🖂 All major cards

▨ MARLBOROUGH & NELSON

PICTON/MARLBOROUGH SOUNDS

SOMETHING SPECIAL

🏠 **BAY OF MANY COVES RESORT**
$$$$$
QUEEN CHARLOTTE SOUND, PICTON
TEL 03/579-9771   FAX 03/579-9777
www.bayofmanycovesresort.co.nz
Perfect for a honeymoon or romantic get-away, plush apartments with balconies over-look the water and are nestled into hillside greenery. Fine dining and attentive service round out this special experience. This luxury resort can be reached only by a 30-minute water-taxi ride from Picton or by helicopter.
🛈 11 Ⓢ ⚏ ⊗ All major cards

🏠 **PORTAGE RESORT**
🍴 $$$–$$$$$
KENEPURU SOUND
TEL 03/573-4309   FAX 03/573-4362
www.portage.co.nz
At the end of serene Kenepuru Sound, this three-star resort has a swimming pool, spa, and Te Weka Restaurant or the more informal Snapper Café for meals. Most rooms and suites have sea views and are the place to get away from it all. Only 15 minutes by water taxi from Picton, or 1.5 hours by car.
🛈 35 Ⓟ Ⓢ ⚏ ⊗ All major cards

🏠 **PERANO APARTMENTS**
$$$–$$$$
20 LONDON QUAY, PICTON
TEL/FAX 03/573-9280
www.perano.co.nz
On the waterfront in the town center, fully equipped one-, two-, and three-bedroom apartments have wonderful harbor views. Though the architecture is not simpatico with old Picton, these luxury apartments are good value.
🛈 12 Ⓟ Ⓢ Ⓕ ⊗ MC, V

🍴 **LE CAFÉ**
$$$
12–14 LONDON QUAY, PICTON
TEL 03/573-5588
www.lecafepicton.co.nz
The waterfront and outside tables attract crowds from breakfast through dinner. Steaks, rack of lamb, and seafood feature on a well-presented, straightforward menu.
🍴 100 Ⓢ ⊗ All major cards

NELSON

🏠 **GRAMPIAN VILLA & GRAMPIAN COTTAGE**
$$$–$$$$$
209 COLLINGWOOD ST.
TEL 03/545-8209   FAX 03/548-7888
www.grampianvilla.co.nz
In a leafy Victorian suburb, a five-minute walk from downtown, Grampian Villa is a glorious two-story B&B offering four-star-plus standards. Four delightful, spacious suites are furnished with antiques, and three have French doors and verandahs overlooking the city. Its nearby cottage has cheaper rooms. Book through hotel booking websites for the best rates.
🛈 8 Ⓟ Ⓢ ⊗ All major cards

🏠 **RUTHERFORD HOTEL NELSON**
🍴 $$$–$$$$
TRAFALGAR SQUARE
TEL 03/548-2299   FAX 03/546-3003
www.rutherfordhotel.co.nz
Refurbished rooms offer good value in this older four-star hotel in an excellent down-town locale. Try to get a top-floor room for great views. The facilities include a pool, gym, and excellent Japanese restaurant.
🛈 112 Ⓟ Ⓒ Ⓢ Ⓕ ⚏ 🍸
⊗ All major cards

🏠 **CEDAR GROVE MOTOR LODGE**
$$$
TRAFALGAR ST.& GROVE ST.
TEL 03/545-1133   FAX 03/545-1134
www.cedargrove.co.nz
Units, suites, and apartments, some with air-conditioning and spa bath, are offered in this well-kept motel. Superior rooms, good service, and a central position over the river from downtown make it very popular.
🛈 23 Ⓟ Ⓢ Ⓕ ⊗ All major cards

Ⓢ No smoking Ⓒ Air Conditioning ⚏ Indoor Pool ⚏ Outdoor Pool 🍸 Health Club ⊗ Credit Cards

🏨 ORANGE APARTMENTS

$$–$$$$

79–85 NILE ST.

TEL 03/548-7000

Cheaply built but modern, well-appointed apartments, from studio to four-bedroom, offer great value in a downtown location just east of the cathedral. All apartments have fully equipped kitchens and broadband.

🛈 42 🅿 ⊗ ⊗ All major cards

🍴 BOAT SHED CAFÉ

$$$$

351 WAKEFIELD QUAY

TEL 03/546-9783

www.boatshedcafe.co.nz

This Nelson institution is perched over the water on increasingly popular Wakefield Quay. The location couldn't get any better for a mainly seafood restaurant, nor the seafood fresher. From hearty breakfasts to lighter lunches and the substantial dinner menu, the food is well presented.

🔢 60 ⊗ All major cards

🍴 HOPGOODS RESTAURANT & BAR

$$$$

284 TRAFALGAR ST.

TEL 03/545-7191

The top end of Trafalgar Street, overlooked by the cathedral, is a fashionable place for a meal or drink, and Hopgoods serves consistently good contemporary fare. Lamb and seafood dishes are prominent on a sophisticated menu from an experienced chef/owner, who provides stability in a city where chefs come and go.

🔢 50 🕐 Sun., L Mon. ⊗ ⊗ All major cards

🍴 CAFE AFFAIR

$$$

295 TRAFALGAR ST.

TEL 03/548-8295

www.cafeaffair.co.nz

Opposite Hopgoods, this attractive restaurant serves breakfast, lunch, and dinner. Tables on the pavement outside are ideal for an alfresco coffee or meal. The straightforward menu is reasonably priced and features pasta, pizza, seafood, and stone-grilled steaks, their specialty.

🔢 80 ⊗ ⊗ All major cards

🍴 MORRISON STREET CAFÉ

$$

244 HARDY ST.

TEL 03/548-8110

www.morrisonstreetcafe.co.nz

In this fashionable café with dining outdoors as well as in, good breakfast and lunch fare is served with a twist. Mediterranean and Asian influences, such as mussel laksa and chorizo/mushroom pilaf, define an interesting menu.

🔢 70 🕐 D ⊗ All major cards

BLENHEIM

🏨 CHATEAU MARLBOROUGH HOTEL

$$$$

HIGH ST. & HENRY ST.

TEL 03/578-0064   FAX 03/578-2661

www.marlboroughnz.co.nz

Good service, stylish rooms, heavenly beds, and reasonable prices make this modern hotel with medieval flourishes a top choice. A stroll from town center, it makes a great base for exploring the vineyards.

🛈 30 🅿 ⊟ ⊗ 🅲 ≋ ⊗ All major cards

KAIKOURA

🏨 KAIKOURA GATEWAY MOTOR LODGE

$$$–$$$$

16–18 CHURCHILL ST.

TEL 03/319-6070   FAX 03/319-7080

www.kaikouragateway.co.nz

On the highway with a pool and sauna, this motel is one of the town's newer breed. Comfortable units, including one- and two-bed units, offer high standards at a reasonable price.

🛈 20 🅿 ⊗ ≋ ⊗ All major cards

🏨 WHITE MORPH MOTOR INN

$$$–$$$$

92–94 THE ESPLANADE

TEL 03/319-5014   FAX 03/319-5015

www.whitemorph.co.nz

On the waterfront in town, well-appointed studio units have small kitchens and offer some of the best accommodations in town. Units range from unexciting standard studios to excellent spa studios with ocean views and a two-bedroom family suite.

🛈 20 🅿 ⊗   ⊗ All major cards

🏨 Hotel 🍴 Restaurants 🛈 No. of Bedrooms 🔢 No. of Seats 🅿 Parking 🚇 Metro 🕐 Closed ⊟ Elevator

🍴 42.25 SOUTH RESTAURANT & BAR
$$$–$$$$
146 THE ESPLANADE
TEL 03/319-7145   FAX 03/319-5359
On the Esplanade, looking across the ocean to the mountains, this restaurant's fine position is complemented by well-cooked food, including steaks and seafood. Kaikoura means "meal of crayfish," and this is the best place in town to sample it in season.

🍴 40 🍴 L 🚭 💳 MC, V

■ CHRISTCHURCH & CANTERBURY

SOMETHING SPECIAL

🏨 THE GEORGE CHRISTCHURCH
🍴 $$$$–$$$$$
50 Park TerRACE
TEL 03/379-4560   FAX 03/366-6747
www.thegeorge.com
One of New Zealand's finest boutique hotels, the George boasts luxury in peaceful greenery on the edge of downtown. Generous rooms have indulgent extras and decor from neochintz to modern cool in the suites. Two fine-dining restaurants and superior service, including a butler if required, round out the hotel's credentials.

ⓘ 55 🅿 🚭 🚭 🏊 💪 💳 All major cards

🏨 HERITAGE CHRISTCHURCH
$$$–$$$$$
28–30 CATHEDRAL SQ.
TEL 03/377-9722   FAX 03/377-9881
www.heritagehotels.co.nz
On Cathedral Square in the heart of the city, rooms are available in the modern tower or the Old Government Building, where large apartments have towering ceilings. Both offer luxury, but the latter have heritage wow factor.

ⓘ 174 🅿 🚭 🚭 🏊 🏊 💪
💳 All major cards

🏨 QUEST APARTMENTS
$$$–$$$$$
113 WORCESTER ST.
TEL 03/964-6200   FAX 03/964-6204
www.questchristchurch.co.nz
Quality studio, one-, two-, and three-bed-

room apartments are fully equipped, including dishwasher and washer/drier, at excellent rates. Right above the tramline near Cathedral Square, the location is excellent, though first floor apartments can be noisy.

ⓘ 78 🅿 🚭 🚭 💳 All major cards

🏨 MILLENNIUM
$$$–$$$$
14 CATHEDRAL SQ.
TEL 03/365-1111   FAX 03/365-7676
www.millenniumhotels.co.nz
In a great location on the square, the Millennium's recent renovations have put it back up with Christchurch's best hotels. Rated 4.5 stars, rooms are attractive and spacious, especially executive rooms.

ⓘ 179 🅿 🚭 🚭 🏊 💪 💳 All major cards

🏨 CHATEAU ON THE PARK
🍴 $$–$$$$
189 DEANS AVE.
TEL 03/348-8999   FAX 03/348-8990
www.chateau-park.co.nz
Across the expanse of Hagley Park from downtown, this resort-style hotel is nestled away from the city bustle in 5 acres (2 ha) of gardens. It has the feel of grand English manor, 1970s style, with large rooms, restaurants, bars, and a pool. Look for discounts at this good four-star hotel.

ⓘ 193 🅿 🚭 🚭 🏊 🏊 💳 All major cards

🏨 CHATEAU BLANC SUITES APARTMENT HOTEL
$$–$$$
CRANMER SQ., MONTREAL ST.
& KILMORE ST.
TEL 03/365-1600   FAX 03/353-0974
www.chateaublanc.co.nz
Near the casino and an easy walk to town center, spacious suites with balconies, separate sitting rooms, and kitchens are very comfortable. Some suites look a little tired, but regularly discounted rates are exceptional value for the standards and location.

ⓘ 38 🅿 🚭 🚭 💪 💳 All major cards

🏨 TUSCANA MOTOR LODGE
$$
74 BEALEY AVE.
TEL/FAX 03/377-4485
www.tuscana.co.nz

🚭 No smoking 🚭 Air Conditioning 🏊 Indoor Pool 🏊 Outdoor Pool 💪 Health Club 💳 Credit Cards

Bealey Avenue, the wide boulevard running along the northern edge of the city center, has a number of motels. This is one of the best, offering fine hospitality and good rooms, a 15-minute walk from the center.

[i] 12 [P] [S] [A] All major cards

[H] LIVING SPACE
$–$$
96 LICHFIELD ST.
TEL 03/964-5212   FAX 03/964-5245
www.livingspace.net

A Victorian warehouse converted into funky student-style apartments provides excellent rooms at cheap prices in a great location. Compact modern studios have kitchenettes and broadband but no air-conditioning. Good communal lounges and outdoor areas sport postmodern colors.

[i] 80 [⊟] [S] [A] All major cards

[H] SAGGIO DI VINO
$$$$$
185 VICTORIA ST.
TEL 03/379-4006
www.saggiodivino.co.nz

With the country's best wine cellar and a wide range of New Zealand vintages by the glass, *vino* comes to the fore, but this fine restaurant is also *saggio* (wise) when it comes to food. The interior is rustic Mediterranean, the menu European, and the produce fresh local, from New Zealand truffles to venison loin served with bread gnocchi, mushroom, spinach, and thyme jus.

[⊞] 50 [⊕] L [S] [A] All major cards

[H] MINX DINING ROOM & BAR
$$$$
96 LICHFIELD ST.
TEL 03/374-9944
www.minxbar.co.nz

Urban cool decor meets fine-dining formal at this handsome restaurant. From slow-cooked, melt-in-the-mouth lamb to seared scallops, the menu offers well-cooked food with innovation but without the mélange of competing flavors typical of many peers.

[⊞] 50 [⊕] L [S] [A] All major cards

[H] INDOCHINE
$$$
209 CAMBRIDGE TERRACE

TEL 03/365-7323
www.indochine.co.nz

This stylish restaurant and cocktail bar offers a fusion experience, in dining and decor. The eclectic menu starts with dim sum, but entrées such as seared tuna steak with scallion relish and chili, or glazed pork belly with prawn and crab pastries, show as much European as Asian influence.

[⊞] 60 [⊕] L, D Sun. [S] [A] All major cards

[H] DUX DE LUX
$$–$$$
41 HEREFORD ST.
TEL 03/366-6919
www.thedux.co.nz

This ever popular pub does good vegetarian and seafood pub fare with a pinch of style. The food-ordering lines are the longest in the Southern Hemisphere, matched by the wait for your meal, but prices are reasonable, the pizzas first-rate, and the outside tables are a pleasant spot to sip house brews.

[⊞] 140 [S] [A] All major cards

[H] MYTHAI RESTAURANT & MONKEY BAR
$$–$$$
84 HEREFORD ST.
TEL 03/365-1295

Something of a Christchurch institution, Mythai has a legion of loyal followers who come for the reasonably priced Thai food and funky bar. Good service and a central position are winners, as are the curries and other Thai classics, though Thai food in New Zealand does tend to be chili free.

[⊞] 50 [S] [A] All major cards

[H] TWO FAT INDIANS
$$–$$$
112 MANCHESTER ST.
TEL 03/371-7273
www.twofatindians.co.nz

A modern café ambience, big selection of beers, and long menu of Indian favorites make this Christchurch's most popular Indian restaurant. Tandoori dishes, kormas, biryanis, and vegetarian dishes are all prominent, and the light fluffy breads are perfect for curry dipping. Banquets (minimum four) are a great value.

[⊞] 150 [P] [⊕] L [S] [A] All major cards

MOUNT COOK

SOMETHING SPECIAL

🏨 **HERMITAGE HOTEL**
🍴 **$$$–$$$$$**
TERRACE RD.
TEL 03/435-1809   FAX 03/435-1879
www.hermitage.co.nz
What a setting, what a view. This grande dame of New Zealand hotels (1884) has comfortable rooms in different wings, many with stunning views of the mountain, as well as motel rooms and chalets. Hunt around for online discounts to avoid paying the stratospheric rack rates. The fine restaurants and bars look straight up to the "Cloud Piercer."
🛈 214 🅿 ⬍ 🚭 🅢 🅢 All major cards

◼ WEST COAST

FRANZ JOSEF

🏨 **SCENIC CIRCLE FRANZ JOSEF GLACIER COUNTRY HOTEL**
$$$$–$$$$$
SH6
TEL 03/752-0729   FAX 03/752-0709
www.scenic-circle.co.nz
In the center of the township, this older resort hotel has big but dated rooms. It is comfortable and large, with plenty of rooms, a definite plus in a town where every hotel can be full.
🛈 177 🅿 ⬍ 🚭 🅢 All major cards

🏨 **ALPINE GLACIER MOTEL**
$$$–$$$$
CRON ST. & CONDON ST.
TEL 03/752-0226   FAX 03/752-0221
www.alpineglaciermotel.com
This friendly motel in the town center has mountain views. Spotless rooms with kitchen facilities are well appointed and a good value in an expensive part of New Zealand. The hot tub is welcome after a day on the glacier.
🛈 24 🅿 🚭 🅢 All major cards

FOX GLACIER

🏨 **TE WEHEKA**
$$$$$
MAIN RD.
TEL 03/751-0730
www.teweheka.co.nz
This luxury B&B hotel offers large well-appointed rooms, along with a comfortable lounge and library.
🛈 20 🅿 🚭 🅢 MC, V

🏨 **FOX GLACIER LODGE**
$$$$
SULLIVAN RD.
TEL 03/751-0888   FAX 03/751-0026
www.foxglacierlodge.co.nz
This cheery alpine lodge, pine lined with a peaked roof, has a cozy feel. It is just behind the main street shops.
🛈 8 🅿 🚭 🅢 All major cards

🏨 **MISTY PEAKS**
$$$$
130 COOK FLAT RD.
TEL 03/751-0849
www.mistypeaks.co.nz
This modern homestead B&B offers some of the best accommodations at the glaciers. Just outside Fox township, Misty Peaks has stunning mountain views and generous hospitality.
🛈 5 🅿 🚭 🅢 All major cards

◼ OTAGO

DUNEDIN

SOMETHING SPECIAL

🏨 **CORSTORPHINE HOUSE**
🍴 **$$$$$**
MILBURN ST.
TEL 03/487-1000   FAX 03/487-6672
www.corstorphine.co.nz
Surrounded by 12 acres (5 ha) of lawn and garden, this grand mansion dating from 1863 re-creates an age of privilege. Sumptuously furnished with antiques, theme rooms range from Moroccan to Scottish, and the Conservatory Restaurant next to the house offers fine dining.
🛈 8 🅿 ⬍ 🚭 🅢 All major cards

🏨 **THE BROTHERS HOTEL**
$$$–$$$$
295 RATTRAY ST.

TEL 03/477-0043 FAX 03/477-0070
www.brothershotel.co.nz
The 1920s stately residence of the Christian Brothers has been converted into a boutique hotel, retaining much of its charm. Perched on a hill, the hotel offers stunning views from the balcony and is only a ten-minute walk from The Octagon.

ⓘ 15 🅿 🄢 🄰 All major cards

🏨 LARNACH LODGE & STABLES
$$$–$$$$
CAMP RD., OTAGO PENINSULA
TEL 03/476-1616 FAX 03/476-1574
www.larnachcastle.co.nz
Unfortunately the accommodations at Larnach, 10 miles (16 km) from Dunedin, aren't in the castle building, but the well-appointed themed rooms in the purpose-built lodge have amazing views right across the Otago Peninsula. The corner Sea Room has the best panorama of all. The original stables next door have more basic attic rooms.

ⓘ 21 🅿 🄢 🄰 All major cards

🏨 SCENIC CIRCLE
DUNEDIN CITY HOTEL
$$$–$$$$
PRINCES ST. & DOWLING ST.
TEL 03/470-1470 FAX 03/470-1477
www.scenic-circle.co.nz
Big, well-maintained rooms and a great location two blocks from The Octagon make this four-star hotel a good choice. Though not brimming with character, it is well run, and online discounts can make it an exceptional value. Try to get a harbor-view room.

ⓘ 110 🅿 ⊜ 🄢 🈴 🄰 All major cards

🏨 LIVING SPACE
$$
192 CASTLE ST.
TEL 03/951-5000 FAX 03/951-5001
www.livingspace.net
Like its sister hotel in Christchurch (see p. 302), Living Space's funky student-style apartments in a restored heritage building offer great value in the city center. The modern compact studio apartments have kitchenettes and broadband.

ⓘ 128 🅿 ⊜ 🄢 🄰 All major cards

🏨 ARDEN STREET B&B
$–$$
36 ARDEN ST., NORTH EAST VALLEY
TEL 03/473-8860 FAX 03/473-8861
www.ardenstreethouse.co.nz
A charming 1930s house built by a Scottish sea captain has nautical touches and views from the top of one Dunedin's steepest streets near the Botanic Gardens. Older, quirky rooms, with and without bathrooms, are good value, and the hostess offers warm Kiwi hospitality.

ⓘ 5 🅿 🄢 🄰 MC, V

🍴 BELL PEPPER BLUES
$$$$
474 PRINCES ST.
TEL 03/474-0973
www.bellpepperblues.co.nz
Chef Michael Coughlin runs this Dunedin institution, which sets the benchmark for fine dining in Dunedin. The menu reflects Mediterranean, Asian, and other influences, such as beef rib eye grilled with Szechuan pepper, mushroom strudel, cumin parsnip, and beef jus. The Denver leg venison is a signature dish, and the desserts are divine.

🪑 50 🄲 L, D Sun. 🄢 🄰 All major cards

🍴 HIGH TIDE

$$$

29 KITCHENER ST.

TEL 03/477-9784

www.hightide.co.nz

Hidden away in the desolate dock area, this highly regarded restaurant perched on the water's edge looks across the sea to twinkling lights of the hillside villas. Despite the name, this is not a seafood restaurant, and an innovative menu highlights the best of New Zealand produce, such as venison and hapuka fish steaks.

🍴 65 🕐 L, D Mon. 🚭 🞈 All major cards

🍴 THE REEF

$$$

329–333 GEORGE ST.

TEL 03/471-7185

Three blocks north of The Octagon in the city's busiest restaurant strip, the Reef is always popular and serves excellent seafood at moderate prices. Eat the finger-licking good Singapore-style chili crab with your hands. The seafood platter provides a varied smorgasbord of mostly local seafood.

🍴 32 🕐 L 🚭 🞈 All major cards

🍴 GREAT TASTE

$–$$

12 ST. ANDREW ST.

TEL 03/479-2088

www.greattaste.co.nz

When in a student town, eat as the students do, though this restaurant is packed with locals from all walks of life. The à la carte menu features seafood and steaks with a salad bar, but the incredibly cheap Asian-style buffet is most popular and is even cheaper at lunchtime.

🍴 130 🚭 🞈 All major cards

QUEENSTOWN

SOMETHING SPECIAL

🏨 EICHARDT'S PRIVATE HOTEL

$$$$$

MARINE PARADE

TEL 03/441-0450   FAX 03/441-0440

www.eichardtshotel.co.nz

This delightful boutique hotel, a Queenstown original, combines rock-star prices with old-

money gentility. In an unbeatable position near the lakefront in the restaurant district, rooms have gigantic beds, fireplaces, dressing rooms, and heated mirrors and floors.

ℹ️ 5 🅿️ 🞈 🚭 🞈 All major cards

🏨 SOFITEL QUEENSTOWN
HOTEL & SPA

$$$$$

8 DUKE ST.

TEL 03/450-0045   FAX 03/450-0046

www.sofitelqueenstown.com

Elegantly appointed rooms have balconies with mountain or lake views. Extras include an LCD television in the bathroom and espresso machines. This luxury hotel heavily promotes its day spa, and all rooms have Jacuzzis.

ℹ️ 82 🅿️ 🞈 🚭 🞈 🞈 🞈 All major cards

🏨 MILLBROOK

$$$$–$$$$$

MALAGHANS RD.

TEL 03/441-7000   FAX 03/441-7007

www.millbrook.co.nz

Nestled in a valley ringed by peaks on the back road to Arrowtown, this resort boasts extensive recreational facilities, including a championship golf course, day spa, tennis courts, gym, and indoor lap pool. Villas and cottages scattered throughout the expansive grounds range from studio units to four-bedroom homes.

ℹ️ 243 🅿️ 🚭 🞈 🞈 🞈 🞈
🞈 All major cards

🏨 NOVOTEL GARDENS QUEENSTOWN

$$$–$$$$

EARL ST. & MARINE PARADE

TEL 03/442-7750   FAX 03/442-7578

www.accorhotels.com.au

In a winning location near the town center on a quiet stretch of lakefront, the reasonably priced Novotel has good four-star rooms with a balcony upstairs or opening on to the garden downstairs.

ℹ️ 204 🅿️ 🞈 🚭 🞈 🞈 All major cards

🏨 MERCURE RESORT QUEENSTOWN

$$$

SAINSBURY RD.

TEL 03/442-6600   FAX 03/442-7354

www.mercure.com

Four-star chain hotels in Queenstown often offer great deals, and the older Mercure usually has the best rates. Though about 1.5 miles (2.4 km) from town, it has wonderful views of the lake and The Remarkables, and extensive resort facilities.

ⓘ 148 🅿 ➰ 🚫 ⛱ 🛇 🚫 All major cards

🏨 TURNER HEIGHTS APARTMENTS
$$$
TURNER ST.
TEL 03/442-8383   FAX 03/442-9494
www.turnerheights.co.nz
On the hill at the end of central Shotover Street, these alpine-style one- and two-bedroom apartments are cute, quiet, and a great value. Fully equipped and well furnished, some have spa baths and expansive lake views.

ⓘ 12 🅿 🚫 🚫 All major cards

🏨 BELLA VISTA MOTEL
$$–$$$
36 ROBINS RD.
TEL 03/442-4468   FAX 03/442-4491
www.bellavistamotels.co.nz
This chain motel a little north of town center has modern, clean, well-equipped rooms. Friendly management and reasonable rates in expensive Queenstown make it one of the better motel buys.

ⓘ 24 🅿 🚫 🚫 All major cards

🏨 SHERWOOD MANOR HOTEL
$$–$$$
GOLDFIELD HEIGHTS, FRANKTON RD.
TEL 03/442-8032   FAX 03/442-7915
www.sherwoodmanorhotel.co.nz
Opposite the lake, this smaller apartment-style hotel/motel has wonderful lake and mountain views. Well-appointed studio, one-, and two-bedroom apartments all have kitchen facilities. It is out of town toward Frankton, where prices are more reasonable

ⓘ 78 🅿 🚫 ⛱ 🚫 All major cards

🍴 WAI WATERFRONT RESTAURANT
$$$$$
STEAMER WHARF, BEACH ST.
TEL 03/442-5969
www.wai.net.nz
One of Queenstown's finest restaurants, Wai is in a superb setting with tables outside on the waterfront. It serves innovative approaches to

tuna, pork, beef, lamb, etc., with an excellent selection of wines, many from Central Otago. For a first-class dining feast, the degustation menu features seven courses, with wine suggestions.

🔳 50 🕐 L 🚫 🚫 All major cards

🍴 BATHHOUSE CAFÉ
$$$–$$$$$
28 MARINE PARADE.
TEL 03/442-5625
www.bathhouse.co.nz
In the restored Coronation bathing shed right on the lake, the Bathhouse bustles with diners basking in the sun over breakfast or a bistro lunch. In the evening, prices skyrocket for the dinner menu that does some fine-dining pirouettes with duck, venison, rack of lamb, rabbit, and salmon.

🔳 32 🚫 All major cards

🍴 AMISFIELD BISTRO
$$$
10 LAKE HAYES RD.
TEL 03/442-0556
www.amisfield.co.nz
This superb winery/restaurant between Queenstown and Arrowtown is in a lovely setting with views of Lake Hayes. Well worth the 15-minute drive, the varied menu has mostly Mediterranean-inspired dishes. The "trust the chef" set includes a number of taste treats, such as marinated olives, chorizo, pork belly, roasted pumpkin with feta—whatever is available that day. Open for lunch or an early dinner (closes at 8 p.m.).

🔳 70 🅿 🕐 Mon. 🚫 🚫 AE, MC, V

🍴 FISHBONE BAR & GRILL
$$$
7 BEACH ST.
TEL 03/442-6768
www.fishbonequeenstown.co.nz
This fun restaurant with fish-filled decor and affable service covers the seafood spectrum from "fush and chups to lobster," as its signboard says. The menu features oysters, mussels, paua, and char-grilled salmon steaks, and the seafood platter groans with fruits of the sea. Very popular and moderately priced; it pays to make a reservation.

🔳 65 🕐 L 🚫 🚫 All major cards

🏨 Hotel 🍴 Restaurants ⓘ No. of Bedrooms 🔳 No. of Seats 🅿 Parking 🚇 Metro 🕐 Closed 🚪 Elevator

🍴 WINNIES GOURMET PIZZA BAR
$$$
7 THE MALL
TEL 03/442-8635
www.winnies.co.nz
Upstairs with balcony dining in summer or inside with a roaring log fire in winter, ever-popular Winnies has steak, fish, and pasta on the menu, but most popular are the gourmet pizzas such as the Pescara seafood pizza and the Montonara, with chicken, brie, sun-dried tomatoes, and sweet chili sauce. Winnies also has pool tables and is open until 2 a.m.

�'t 90 🚭 🏦 All major cards

🍴 SPEIGHT'S ALE HOUSE
$$–$$$
STANLEY ST. & BALLARAT ST.
TEL 03/441-3065
www.speights-alehouse.co.nz
In a restored heritage building, this always popular pub does great food at reasonable prices. Huge servings focus on traditional fare, such as pies, lamb shanks, and fish and chips, with a Speight's beer recommended for each dish. Boisterous when a rugby match plays on the big screen, this is value Kiwi dining at its best.

�'t 80 🚭 🏦 All major cards

WANAKA

🏨 EDGEWATER RESORT
🍴 $$$$
SARGOOD DR.
TEL 03/443-8311   FAX 03/443-8323
www.edgewater.co.nz
Right on Lake Wanaka just outside town, this is the place for a great recreational vacation, with tennis courts and bicycle and kayak rentals. Studio rooms are well appointed, but the expansive one-bedroom suites, many opening to the lawns and lake, offer kitchens and greater comfort. The resort has two excellent restaurants.

🛏 104 🅿 🚭 🏦 All major cards

🏨 WANAKA LUXURY APARTMENTS
$$$$
8 STONEBROOK DR.
TEL 03/443-4943   FAX 03/443-6036
www.wla.co.nz
In a suburban estate on the town's edge,

semi-detached apartments are spacious and wonderfully appointed, with some of the best room standards in Wanaka. One- and two-bedroom apartments have kitchenettes but are not really set up for cooking, and there is a Jacuzzi and small heated swimming pool.

🛏 16 🅿 🚭 🌊 🏦 All major cards

🏨 THE MOORINGS
$$$–$$$$
17 LAKESIDE RD.
TEL 03/443-8479   FAX 03/443-8489
www.themoorings.co.nz
These new motel units and apartments in a stylish complex lie just around the corner from the main street. The beautifully appointed motel units have great views of the lake, while the two- and three-bedroom apartments are fully equipped and have decks, many with water views.

🛏 22 🅿 🚭 🏦 All major cards

🏨 LAKEVIEW MOTEL
$$
64–68 LISMORE ST.
TEL 03/443-6955   FAX 03/443-7029
One street back from the lake, this motel is one of the better buys in Wanaka, with great views of the water and town. A short walk to town center, its comfortable studio units have kitchens and cable TV.

🛏 6 🅿 🚭 🏦 MC, V

🍴 SARGOODS
$$$–$$$$
SARGOOD DR.
TEL 03/443-8311
www.edgewater.co.nz
At the Edgewater Resort, Sargoods offers some of the town's best dining. Innovative fare shows a variety of influences, from French to Japanese, and might include scallops seared with lemongrass, veal in truffle oil, or Satan's kiss—strawberry panna cotta with cayenne ice cream and chocolate cake. Tables outside on the terrace are the place to dine.

�'t 100 🅿 🕐 L 🚭 🏦 All major cards

🍴 THE REEF
$$$
145 ARDMORE ST.
TEL 03/443-1188
Upstairs overlooking the lake, the Reef has

superb views of snowcapped peaks and serves good seafood at moderate prices. The calamari and groaning seafood platters are particularly recommended at this casual, family-friendly restaurant.

🍴 50 🚫 ⚠ AE, MC, V

🍴 CAFÉ LAGO
$$–$$$
151–153 ARDMORE ST.
TEL 03/443-2040
In the new complex in town, opposite the bustling Trout Bar, this small restaurant has glimpses of Mount Aspiring from outside tables, and a small but interesting menu. Lunch and dinner dishes are prepared with care, prices are moderate, and the platters are highly recommended.

🍴 28 🕐 D Sun.–Wed. 🚫 ⚠ All major cards

■ FIORDLAND & SOUTHLAND

TE ANAU

SOMETHING SPECIAL

🏨 FIORDLAND LODGE
$$$$$
472 TE ANAU MILFORD HWY.
TEL 03/249-7832   FAX 03/249-7449
www.fiordlandlodge.co.nz
Luxury seekers will have to head 3 miles (5 km) north of town to this delightful lodge above Lake Te Anau. The lodge was built of stone and rough-hewn logs, and the lobby has towering ceilings, a huge log fire, and expansive windows. Lodge rooms have wonderful lake and mountain views, and families can rent one of two log cabins. Fine dining and matching wines are offered.

ⓘ 12 🅿 🚫 🚫 ⚠ All major cards

🏨 CAMPBELL AUTOLODGE
$$$
42 LAKEFRONT DR.
TEL 03/249-7546   FAX 03/249-7814
www.cal.co.nz
The quality chalet-style one-bedroom apartments on the waterfront are a perennial favorite but are often full, so book well ahead. Well-kept grounds, good service, and fully

equipped rooms make this motel a better buy than some large hotels that fill up with tour groups.

ⓘ 10 🅿 🚫 ⚠ All major cards

🏨 KINGSGATE HOTEL TE ANAU
$$$
20 LAKEFRONT DR.
TEL 03/249-7421   FAX 03/249-8037
www.millenniumhotels.co.nz
One of the largest hotels in town, the Kingsgate gets lots of tour groups but offers good rooms at regularly discounted rates. Across the road from the lake and a pleasant stroll from town, the location is good, and it is better maintained and cheaper than Te Anau's other large hotels.

ⓘ 105 🅿 🚫 ⚠ All major cards

🏨 RADFORDS LAKEVIEW MOTEL
$$$
56 LAKEFRONT DR.
TEL 03/249-9186   FAX 03/249-9187
www.radfordslakeviewmotel.co.nz
This well-kept lakeside motel has studio, one-, and two-bedroom units. All units have lake views (best in upstairs rooms), and some have spa baths. Welcoming managers, a central location, and high standards make it very popular.

ⓘ 14 🅿 🚫 ⚠ All major cards

🏨 TE ANAU LAKEVIEW HOLIDAY PARK
$–$$
1 TE ANAU-MANAPOURI RD.
TEL 03/249-7457   FAX 03/249-7536
www.teanau.info
Te Anau accommodations tend to be expensive and full in peak season, so head to this holiday park near the lake for budget options. A huge variety of rooms range from spartan but modern singles in the well-equipped lodge to A-frame cabins, comfortable tourist apartments, and motel units, all at attractive rates.

ⓘ 200 🅿 🚫 ⚠ AE, MC, V

🍴 LA TOSCANA
$$$
108 MILFORD RD.
TEL 03/249-7756
In a town not renowned for fine dining, you'll

get straightforward pasta and pizzas at moderate prices at this ever-popular restaurant. It stays open later than most and gets a big thumbs-up from locals.

🍴 42 🕐 L 🚭 🅰 MC, V

🍴 REDCLIFFE CAFÉ & BAR
$$$
12 MOKONUI ST.
TEL 03/249-7431
In the town center, this charming, relocated wooden cottage is decorated with items on the history of the building and rave reviews from the cast of Lord of the Rings. One of Te Anau's most consistent restaurants, Redcliffe's flavors are fusion and the produce fresh local. The venison and pork belly come highly recommended.

🍴 50 🕐 L 🚭 🅰 MC, V

INVERCARGILL

🏨 ASCOT PARK HOTEL
🍴 $$
TAY ST. & RACECOURSE RD.
TEL 03/217-6195   FAX 03/217-7002
www.ascotparkhotel.co.nz
It's hard to figure why small Invercargill needs this huge hotel/motel complex spread around acres of garden on the eastern outskirts. Often nearly empty, it has quality hotel rooms and motel units at bargain rates. The good facilities include an indoor heated pool, sauna, gym, bar, and restaurant.

🛏 96 🅿 🚭 🏊 🏋 🅰 All major cards

🏨 KELVIN HOTEL
🍴 $$
KELVIN ST. & ESK ST.
TEL 03/218-2829   FAX 03/218-2287
www.ilt.co.nz
This large three-star hotel in the heart of the city has very well-appointed rooms with cable TV and all the trimmings at cheap rates, as is the case all over Invercargill. The hotel also has a popular bar and good restaurant.

🛏 60 🅿 🚭 🅰 All major cards

🍴 ZOOKEEPERS CAFÉ
$$
50 TAY ST.
TEL 03/218-3373
This fun, funky café—easy to spot by the cor-

rugated iron animals atop the verandah—is an Invercargill institution. Open 10 a.m. until late, the café offers big breakfast and soups, fish, and steaks done well and at moderate prices.

🍴 120 🚭 🅰 All major cards

STEWART ISLAND

🏨 RAKIURA LODGE
$$–$$$
8 MIRO CRESCENT, OBAN
TEL/FAX 03/219-1003
www.rakiuralodge.co.nz
This small, friendly, high-quality lodge has immaculate modern rooms off a well-equipped central sitting/dining/kitchen area, and an outside deck for lounging. It is only a five-minute walk to town.

🛏 4 🅿 🚭 🅰 MC, V

🏨 SOUTH SEA HOTEL
🍴 $–$$$
THE WATERFRONT, OBAN
TEL 03/219-1059   FAX 03/219-1120
www.stewart-island.co.nz
This hotel has lots of character. Rooms are fairly basic but, being on the waterfront, some have sea views. The cottage motel units behind have kitchens. The glassed-in restaurant overlooking the harbor serves good food, and the bar is sometimes lively. What better place to hang out and meet locals than the local pub.

🛏 17 🅿 🅰 AE, MC, V

🍴 CHURCH HILL CAFÉ BAR
$$$
36 KAMAHI RD., OBAN
TEL 03/219-1323
On the hill above the ferry dock, this excellent restaurant is a surprise find in the island's tiny main settlement. Intimate dining inside, or at tables on the lawn, is accompanied by wonderful harbor views. Seafood dominates the menu, but stone-grilled steaks and other fare are offered, including muttonbird (a somewhat oily local delicacy).

🍴 40 🅿 🚭 🅰 All major cards

Shopping

New Zealand has some distinctive shopping opportunities. A host of art-and-crafts items make interesting gifts, such as Maori greenstone carving, *paua* (abalone) shell jewelry, bone and wood carvings, woolen items, and wines.

Galleries and souvenir shops abound in the main cities and tourist towns, and arts and crafts are found around the countryside and in backcountry studios.

For one-stop shopping, the best destination in the country is **Hokitika** on the South Island's West Coast. Famed as the center for Maori greenstone carving, a host of galleries and studios sell a variety of crafts and jewelry.

For last-minute shopping, Auckland and Christchurch are well supplied with souvenir shops, though prices are often higher than in the countryside.

In **Auckland**, wander Queen Street or check out Westfield Downtown Mall *(11–19 Customs St.)* for cheaper souvenirs. The Old Customs House *(Customs St. & Albert St.)* has more expensive and duty-free souvenirs. Victoria Park and Aotea Square markets are good craft haunts. High Street in downtown Auckland has chic New Zealand fashion outlets, as does the suburb of Newmarket. The city has some interesting craft galleries, such as Pauanesia *(35 High St., tel 09/366-7282)*, with handcrafted gifts from the Pacific. The suburb of Parnell has more upscale gift shops, including Elephant House Crafts *(237 Parnell Rd., tel 09/309-8740)*, crammed with New Zealand handicrafts.

In **Christchurch**, souvenir shops congregate around Cathedral Square, particularly the northern end and along Colombo Street. The Arts Centre is also a place to find arts and crafts.

Maori Arts: *Pounamu* (greenstone or New Zealand jade) has been highly prized for centuries. Found only on the South Island's West Coast, greenstone was the main trade item between South and North Island tribes. The West Coast is still the center for greenstone crafts, but carved jade jewelry and ornaments are sold everywhere.

The most famous greenstone art form is the Maori *tiki* (more correctly *hei-tiki*), small pendants worn around the neck. The small humanoid figures with tilted head and protruding tongue are popular with Maori and non-Maori.

Bone carving is another traditional craft with practical and ornamental uses. Bone jewelry, particularly stylized fishhook pendants, is very popular and uses traditional and modern motifs.

Maori wood carvers produced some of the finest work in Polynesia, and the art form has enjoyed a recent revival. *Mere* (short paddle-like war clubs) are popular traditional items, though the finest examples used to be made of greenstone. Many pieces in souvenir shops are crude examples, but individual wood carvers and centers such as Te Puia in Rotorua produce fine works.

Abalone (paua) shell was used as inlay in Maori carvings and today is popular in jewelry and inexpensive ornaments in souvenir shops.

Maori women weavers once made magnificent cloaks of rolled flax fibers fastened with bird feathers. Almost a lost art, cloaks are again being produced, but are very expensive and use imported feathers or rabbit or possum fur. More common are *kete*, woven flax baskets fashioned as handbags.

Clothing: New Zealand has a thriving fashion industry, with young and established designers well represented in major city boutiques. The World of WearableArt Festival, held annually in Wellington and displayed at the WOW Museum in Nelson, showcases avant-garde fashion.

Outdoor-loving New Zealanders also produce high-quality outdoor fashion, from hiking gear to rugged, checked Swanndri shirts and jackets beloved by Kiwi farmers. Rugby fashion has also gravitated to the mainstream with the Canterbury line of rugby jerseys.

Entertainment

New Zealand has a small, thriving arts scene, from theater, ballet, and symphony orchestras to Maori cultural performances, Pacific rap artists, and rock bands.

The Tourism New Zealand website (www.newzealand.com) lists up-to-date arts, culture, music, sports, and food and wine events.

Of all performing arts festivals, the New Zealand International Arts Festival (www.nzfestival.co.nz) is the country's largest, held every other year in Wellington.

Combining the film festivals of the major cities, the New Zealand International Film Festival (www.nzff.co.nz) tours the country with a wide selection of non-mainstream films.

Theater: In Auckland, the main professional theater company is Auckland Theatre Company (www.atc.co.nz), which performs annually at various venues, including the Maidment Theatre, Aotea Centre, Town Hall, and Skycity Theatre.

Theater is particularly strong in Wellington, represented by the long-running Circa (www.circa.co.nz), Downstage (www.downstage.co.nz), and Bats (www.bats.co.nz) theater companies.

Christchurch has the professional Court Theatre (www.courttheatre.org.nz), while Dunedin has Fortune Theatre (www.fortunetheatre.co.nz).

Classical Music, Ballet, & Opera:
The cultural center of New Zealand, Wellington is home to New Zealand Symphony Orchestra (www.nzso.co.nz), which performs around the country.

The Royal New Zealand Ballet (www.nzballet.org.nz) is also based in Wellington and tours regularly, while New Zealand Opera (www.nzopera.com) calls Auckland home.

Maori Performing Arts: Traditional Maori music and dance are a big part of the tourist experience, most often organized through tour operators in Rotorua. Two of the most accessible and professional troupes

perform at Te Puia in Rotorua and at the Auckland Museum.

To see Maori arts at their best, the Te Matatini Maori Performing Arts Festival (www.tematatini.org.nz) is held every second year.

Nightlife: Country pubs can be great places to meet locals or hear bands, but the buzzing nightlife is in the main cities, where bars and clubs party late, particularly Friday and Saturday nights.

AUCKLAND (See also p. 60.)
The most popular nightlife precinct is by the waterfront on **Viaduct Basin** spilling over to nearby **Princes Wharf.** At night, waterfront restaurants become bars, many featuring DJs and live music. Another good area for bars and clubs is around **Vulcan Lane/High Street** in the city's heart. Victoria Street has **SkyCity Casino** and some sophisticated bars.

At the top end of Queen Street, **Karangahape Road** has several music venues, from hip-hop clubs to Irish pubs. The inner suburban strips of **Parnell Road** and particularly **Ponsonby Road** have plenty of chic bars that go off on weekends.

WELLINGTON (See also p. 159)
Cuba Street/Courtenay Place and side streets form the heart of Wellington's ebullient nightlife scene. An evening stroll will turn up a host of bars, clubs, and pubs. The waterfront, particularly **Queens Wharf,** also has some good restaurant/bars.

CHRISTCHURCH (See also p. 194)
The most popular nightlife strip is **Oxford Terrace,** by the riverside near the corner of Hereford Street. After menus are put away, a string of restaurant/bars pump out music and beers until dawn on weekends. Plenty of other venues are scattered around the city.

Activities

Blessed with glorious landscapes, New Zealand's activities focus on getting up close and personal with nature. Every tourist town has a host of activities and tour operators; local tourist offices will connect you with them.

Adrenaline Activities: New Zealand was one of the first countries to popularize adrenaline activities like bungee jumping, white-water rafting, tandem skydiving, etc., and operators all over the country offer a myriad of ways to scare yourself witless. For an overview, see p. 252.

Canoeing & Kayaking: Canoeing the Whanganui River through the wilderness of Whanganui National Park is so popular that it has been designated as a Great Walk and must be booked through the DOC. The three- to five-day journey can be arranged with operators in Taumarunui, Pipiriki, Ohakune, and Wanganui, who provide all gear, pickup, and drop-off.

The most popular sea-kayaking trip, along the coast of Abel Tasman National Park, can be arranged with operators as a guided trip or by experienced kayakers independently. The DOC website has full details on both these journeys.

Sea kayaking is also popular in the Marlborough Sounds and especially Fiordland, where operators in Te Anau, Manapouri, and Milford offer spectacular trips on Milford and Doubtful Sounds.

Fishing: Fish are found in abundance. Rainbow and brown trout and quinnat salmon thrive in New Zealand lakes and rivers. Lake Taupo and the rivers that flow into it (especially the Tongariro) are famous for trout fishing. Rotorua and South Island destinations such as Lake Brunner are also good for trout. Salmon thrive in the east coast rivers of the South Island. A fishing permit from the DOC (www.doc.govt.nz) is required; the season runs from October to May.

The Bay of Islands and Tutukaka in Northland are the main centers for game fishing, for prizes such as marlin, and deep-sea angling for plenty of tasty fish, including snapper, hapuku, tarakihi, mullet, and blue cod. Kiwis love to fish anywhere, from piers to surf casting from beaches. A license is not required.

Golfing: New Zealand has more than 400 golf courses, reputedly the highest per capita in the world. Top courses include Kauri Cliffs in the Bay of Islands, Cape Kidnappers in Hawkes Bay, and Millbrook near Queenstown. While green fees are high at these exclusive resort courses, fees at local links start as low as NZ$10, averaging around NZ$30. The New Zealand Golf Guide (www.golfguide.co.nz) provides details.

Horseback Riding: Horseback riding is a popular pastime all over the country. Commercial operators offer riding across farms, forests, and beaches, from one hour to many days, and usually have horses for all abilities.

The South Island has high-country riding and backcountry expeditions, particularly in Otago and Canterbury. Riding centers can be found on the West Coast, Kaikoura, Tekapo, Queenstown, and Dunedin. On the North Island, Pakiri Beach and South Kaipara near Auckland have noted riding centers, and horses can also be rented at Waitomo, Taupo, and other destinations.

Visitor information centers have details on riding operators, or search www.truenz.co.nz /horsetrekking for trekking centers.

Mountaineering & Rock Climbing:

The Southern Alps have been a training ground for many world-class mountaineers, including Sir Edmund Hillary. Mount Cook and Mount Aspiring National Park are major climbing destinations and the preserve of experienced mountaineers, but Alpine Guides (tel 03/435-1834, www.alpineguides.

co.nz) at Mount Cook, Aspiring Guides *(tel 03/443-9422, www.aspiringguides.com),* and Adventure Consultants *(tel 03/443-8711, www.adventureconsultants.co.nz)* in Wanaka have introductory mountaineering courses.

Top rock-climbing destinations in New Zealand include Port Hills and Castle Hill near Christchurch, Wharepapa near Te Awamutu, and Whanganui Bay near Taupo. The Climb New Zealand website *(www.climb.co.nz)* has information on many more sites.

Skiing: Though snowfields are not as extensive as many in Europe and North America, New Zealand offers spectacular backcountry skiing and the best skiing in the Southern Hemisphere when summer hits El Norte. For a rundown on the main snowfields, see pp. 206–207.

Walking & Hiking: Walking trails are everywhere and provide a delightful way to appreciate the countryside. Many are easy strolls, suitable for families, though serious and not-so-serious hikes can also be found.

National parks have wonderful hiking, known as tramping in New Zealand, from five-day coastal walks to alpine crossings. The most famous and popular trails are designated as Great Walks, and limits are placed on the number of walkers to protect the environment. Overnighting is assigned to designated campsites or huts, which must be booked in peak summer season, along with the walks.

Longer hikes usually require some experience, and hikers should be self-sufficient in food and water and fully equipped for extreme weather conditions.

The two most famous walks are the four-day Milford Track (see pp. 264–265) through stunning Fiordland National Park, and the one-day Tongariro Crossing (see pp. 134–135) between the volcanoes of Tongariro National Park.

Other Great Walks include the Abel Tasman Coastal Walk (3–5 days, Abel Tasman National Park), Heaphy Track (4–6 days, Kahurangi National Park), Kepler Track (4 days, Fiordland National Park), Lake Waikaremoana Track (3–4 days, Te Urewera National Park), Rakiura Track (3 days, Stewart Island), Routeburn Track (3 days, Mount Aspiring and Fiordland National Parks), and the Tongariro Northern Circuit (3–4 days, Tongariro National Park).

The Department of Conservation (DOC) has offices in national parks and towns for information on hundreds of walks. The DOC website *(www.doc.govt.nz)* takes bookings for most Great Walks and provides a host of essential information on tramping.

Water Sports: With such a long coastline, New Zealanders have a variety of ways to enjoy the sea. Sailing is something of a national obsession, especially after New Zealand won the America's Cup yachting race. Auckland, the City of Sails, is a good place to arrange a sailing adventure. Sailing operators in the Bay of Islands and Nelson will also take you on the water.

Scuba diving is at its best in the upper half of the North Island, with diving at many sites along the east coast, from the White Island volcano to Goat Island near Leigh, and the Poor Knights Island Marine Reserve near Tutukaka, which has good visibility, rich marine life, and the country's best diving. Good diving can also be found farther north around the Bay of Islands, particularly Three Kings Islands.

The South Island also has unique diving, most notably in the sounds of Fiordland, where a freshwater layer atop seawater attracts subtropical, deep-, and shallow-water species to the surface. Milford Sound has the world's biggest population of black coral. Two informative diving websites are *www.divenewzealand.com* and *www.nzunderwater.org.nz.*

Raglan on the west coast of the North Island is the country's most renowned surfing destination, but there are plenty of others, including Piha and Muriwai near Auckland, Whangamata on the Coromandel Peninsula, and Gisborne. For surf reports and information on the most popular breaks, check *www.surf.co.nz.*

INDEX

National Geographic

TRAVELER
New Zealand

Published by the National Geographic Society

John M. Fahey, Jr., *President and Chief Executive Officer*
Gilbert M. Grosvenor, *Chairman of the Board*
Tim T. Kelly, *President, Global Media Group*
John Q. Griffin, *President, Publishing*
Nina D. Hoffman, *Executive Vice President; President, Book Publishing Group*

Prepared by the Book Division

Kevin Mulroy, *Senior Vice President and Publisher*
Leah Bendavid-Val, *Director of Photography Publishing and Illustrations*
Marianne R. Koszorus, *Director of Design*
Barbara Brownell Grogan, *Executive Editor*
Elizabeth Newhouse, *Director of Travel Publishing*
Carl Mehler, *Director of Maps*
Barbara A. Noe, *Series Editor*
Cinda Rose, *Series Art Director*

Staff for This Book

Lawrence M. Porges, *Project Editor*
Kay Kobor Hankins, *Designer & Illustrations Editor*
Patricia Daniels, *Text Editor*
Heather McElwain, *Travelwise Editor*
Lise Sajewski, *Copyeditor*
Al Morrow, *Design Assistant*
Jan Mucciarone, *Indexer*
Hedgehog House New Zealand, *Research*
Michael McNey & Mapping Specialists, *Map Production*
Hunter Braithwaite, Jack Brostrom, Bridget A. English, *Contributors*
Richard Wain, *Production Project Manager*
Meredith Wilcox, *Illustrations Specialist*

Jennifer A. Thornton, *Managing Editor*
R. Gary Colbert, *Production Director*

Manufacturing and Quality Management

Christopher A. Liedel, *Chief Financial Officer*
Phillip L. Schlosser, *Vice President*
Chris Brown, *Technical Director*
Nicole Elliott, *Manager*
Monika D. Lynde, *Manager*
Rachel Faulise, *Manager*

Founded in 1888, the National Geographic Society is one of the largest nonprofit scientific and educational organizations in the world. It reaches more than 285 million people worldwide each month through its official journal, *National Geographic,* and its four other magazines; the National Geographic Channel; television documentaries; radio programs; films; books; videos and DVDs; maps; and interactive media. National Geographic has funded more than 8,000 scientific research projects and supports an education program combating geographic illiteracy.

For more information, please call 1-800-NGS LINE (647-5463) or write to the following address:

National Geographic Society
1145 17th Street N.W.
Washington, D.C. 20036-4688 U.S.A.

Visit us online at www.nationalgeographic.com/books

For information about special discounts for bulk purchases, please contact National Geographic Books Special Sales: ngspecsales@ngs.org

For rights or permissions inquiries, please contact National Geographic Books Subsidiary Rights: ngbookrights@ngs.org

National Geographic Traveler: New Zealand
ISBN: 978-1-4262-0233-9

- **Alaska** (2nd Edition)
- **Amsterdam**
- **Arizona** (3rd Edition)
- **Australia** (3rd Edition)
- **Barcelona** (3rd Edition)
- **Beijing**
- **Berlin**
- **Boston & environs**
- **California** (3rd Edition)
- **Canada** (2nd Edition)
- **The Caaribbean** (2nd Edition)
- **China** (2nd Edition)
- **Costa Rica** (3rd Edition)
- **Cuba** (2nd Edition)
- **Dominican Republic**
- **Egypt** (2nd Edition)
- **Florence & Tuscany** (2nd Edition)
- **Florida**
- **France** (2nd Edition)
- **Germany** (2nd Edition)
- **Great Britain** (2nd Edition)
- **Greece** (3rd Edition)
- **Hawaii** (3rd Edition)
- **Hong Kong** (3rd Edition)
- **India** (2nd Edition)
- **Ireland** (2nd Edition)
- **Italy** (3rd Edition)
- **Japan** (3rd Edition)
- **London** (2nd Edition)

- **Los Angeles**
- **Madrid**
- **Mexico** (2nd Edition)
- **Miami & the Keys** (3rd Edition)
- **Naples a& Southern Italy**
- **New York** (2nd Edition)
- **New Zealand**
- **Panama**
- **Paris** (2nd Edition)
- **Peru**
- **Piedmont & Northwest Italy**
- **Portugal**
- **Prague & the Czech Republic**
- **Provence & the Côte d'Azur** (2nd Edition)
- **Romania**
- **Rome** (3rd Edition)
- **St. Petersburg**
- **San Diego** (2nd Edition)
- **San Francisco** (3rd Edition)
- **Shanghai**
- **Sicily** (2nd Edition)
- **South Africa**
- **Spain** (3rd Edition)
- **Sydney**
- **Taiwan** (2nd Edition)
- **Thailand** (3rd Edition)
- **Venice**
- **Vietnam**
- **Washington, D.C.** (3rd Edition)

AVAILABLE WHEREVER BOOKS ARE SOLD